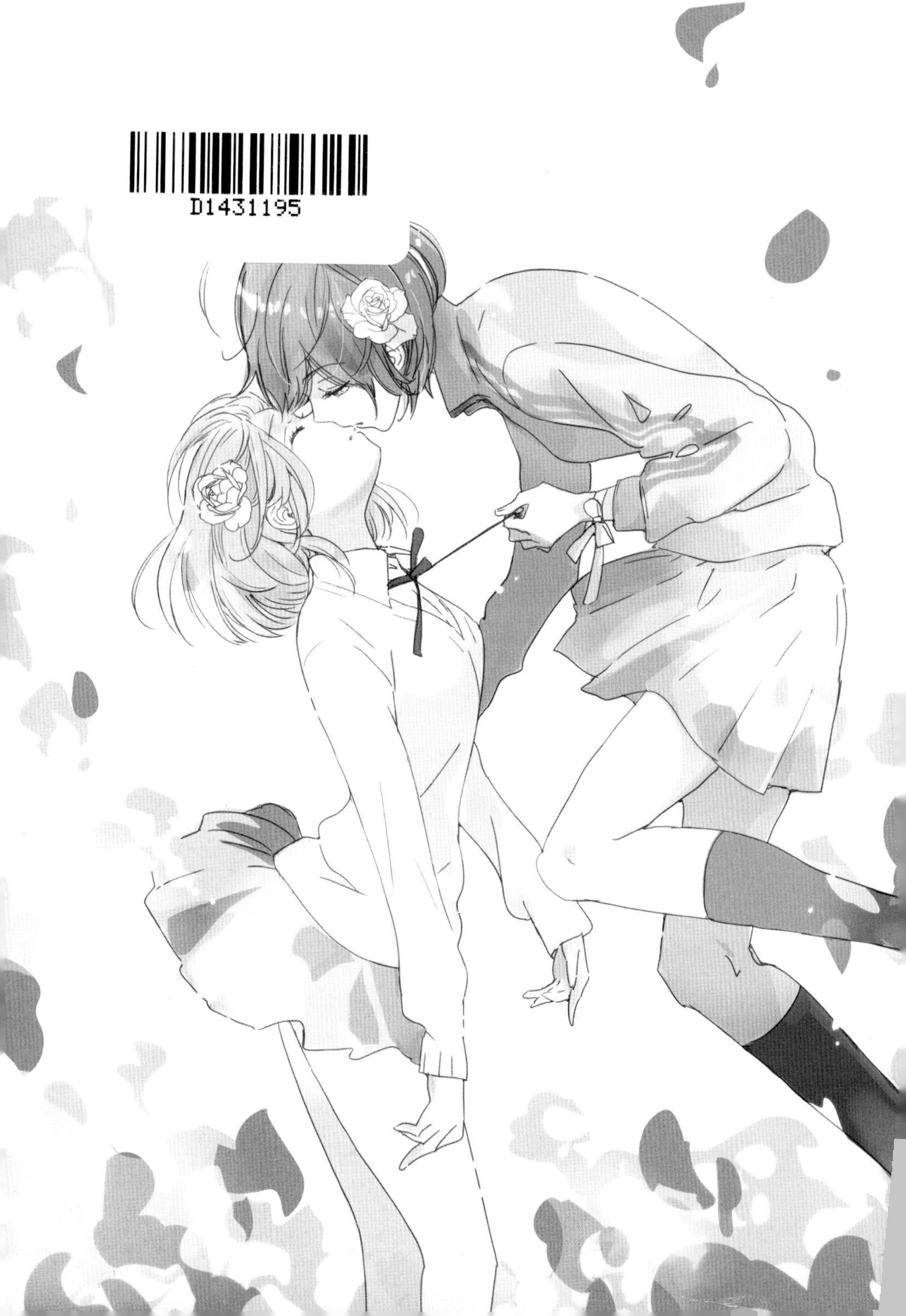

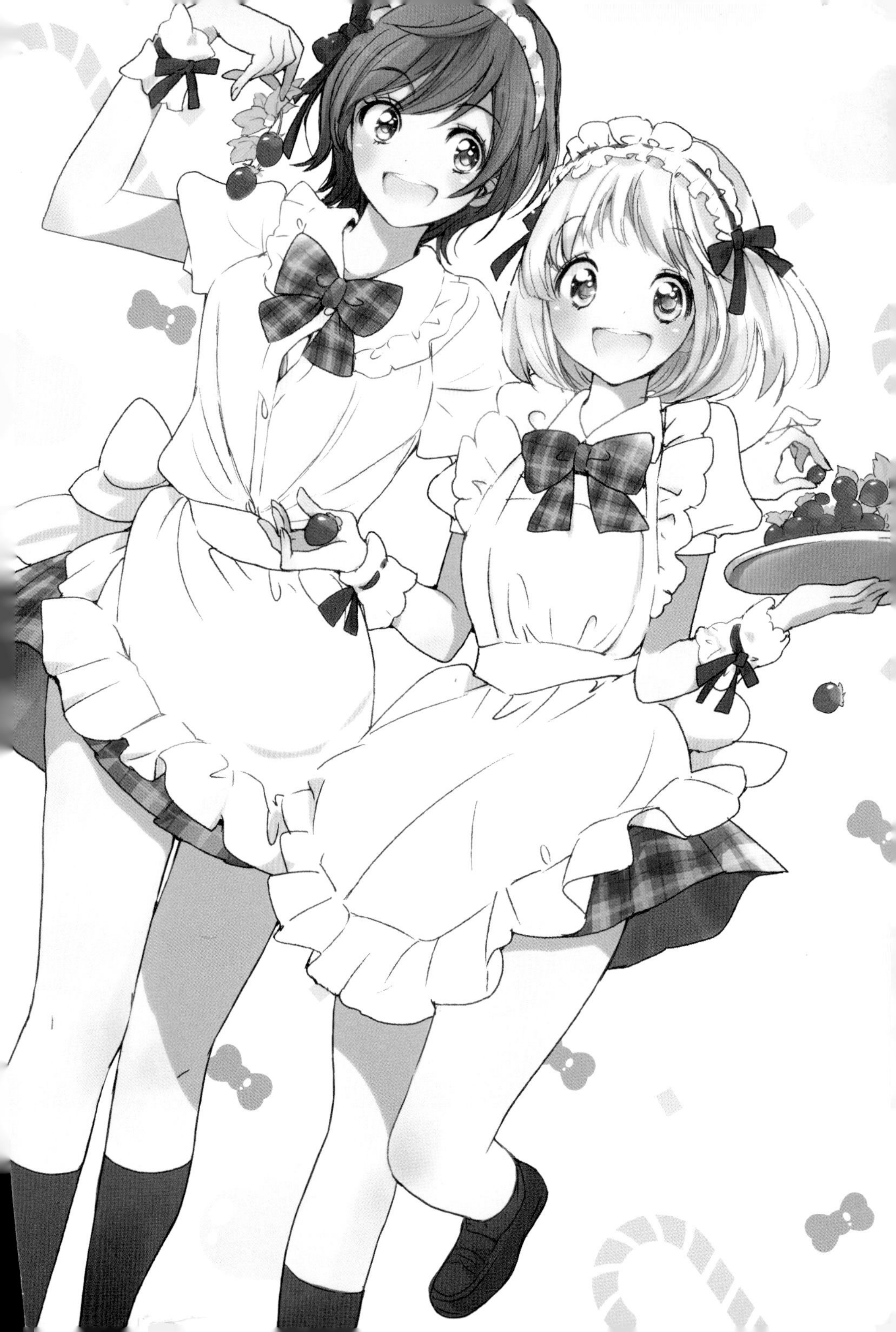

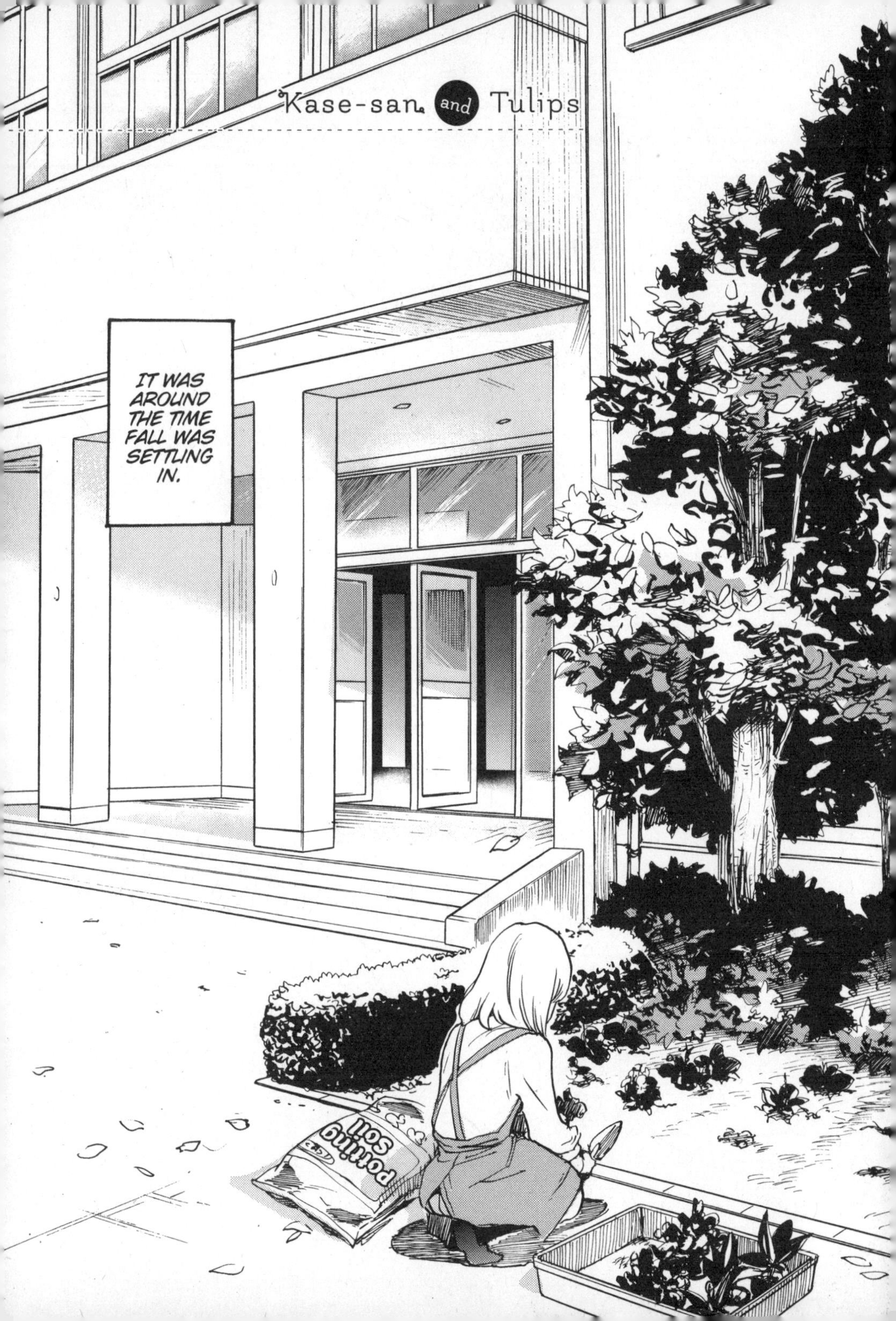

Kase-san and Tulips
IT WAS AROUND THE TIME FALL WAS SETTLING IN.
Potting Soil

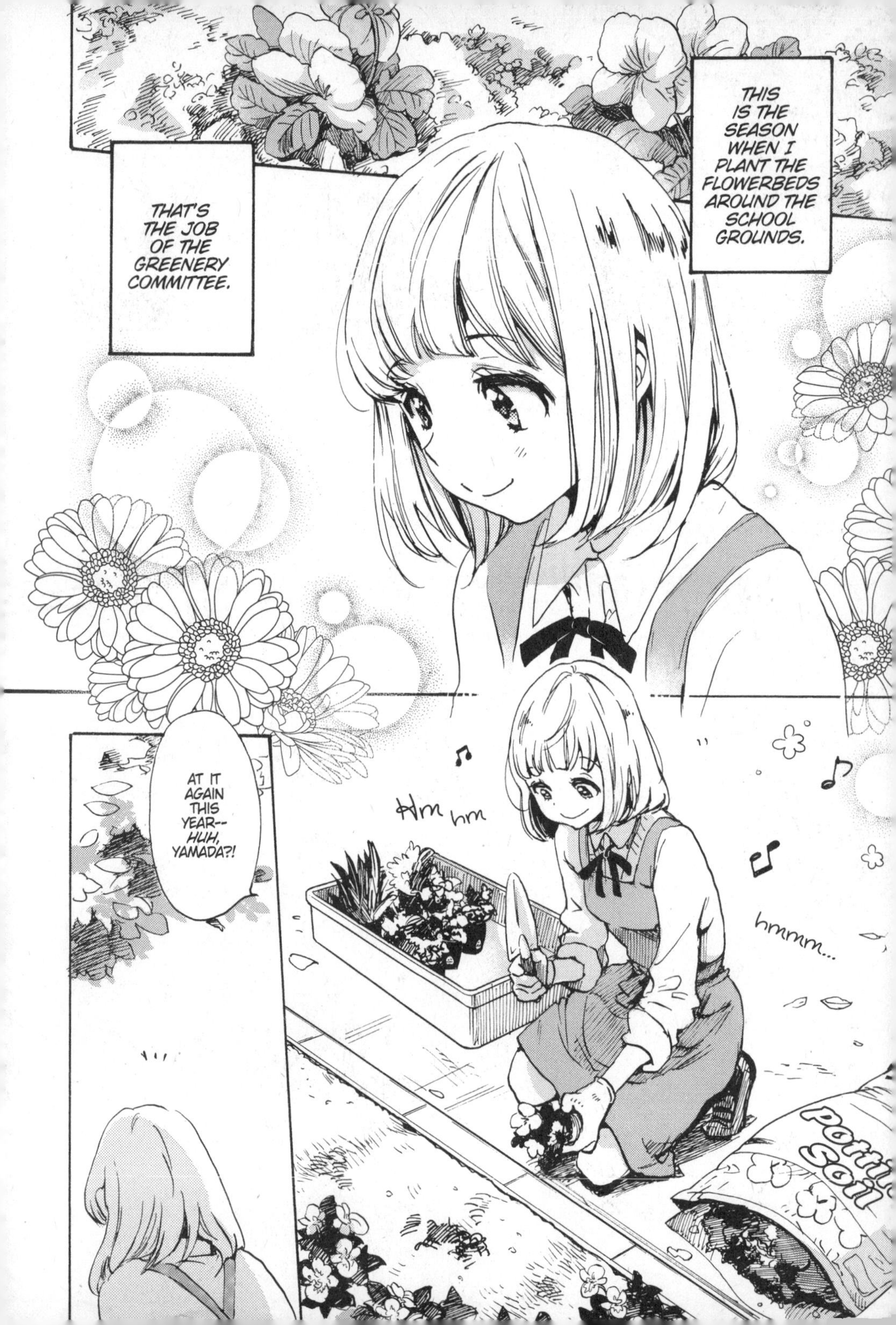
THIS IS THE SEASON WHEN I PLANT THE FLOWERBEDS AROUND THE SCHOOL GROUNDS.
THAT'S THE JOB OF THE GREENERY COMMITTEE.
Hm hm
hmmm...
AT IT AGAIN THIS YEAR-- HUH, YAMADA?!

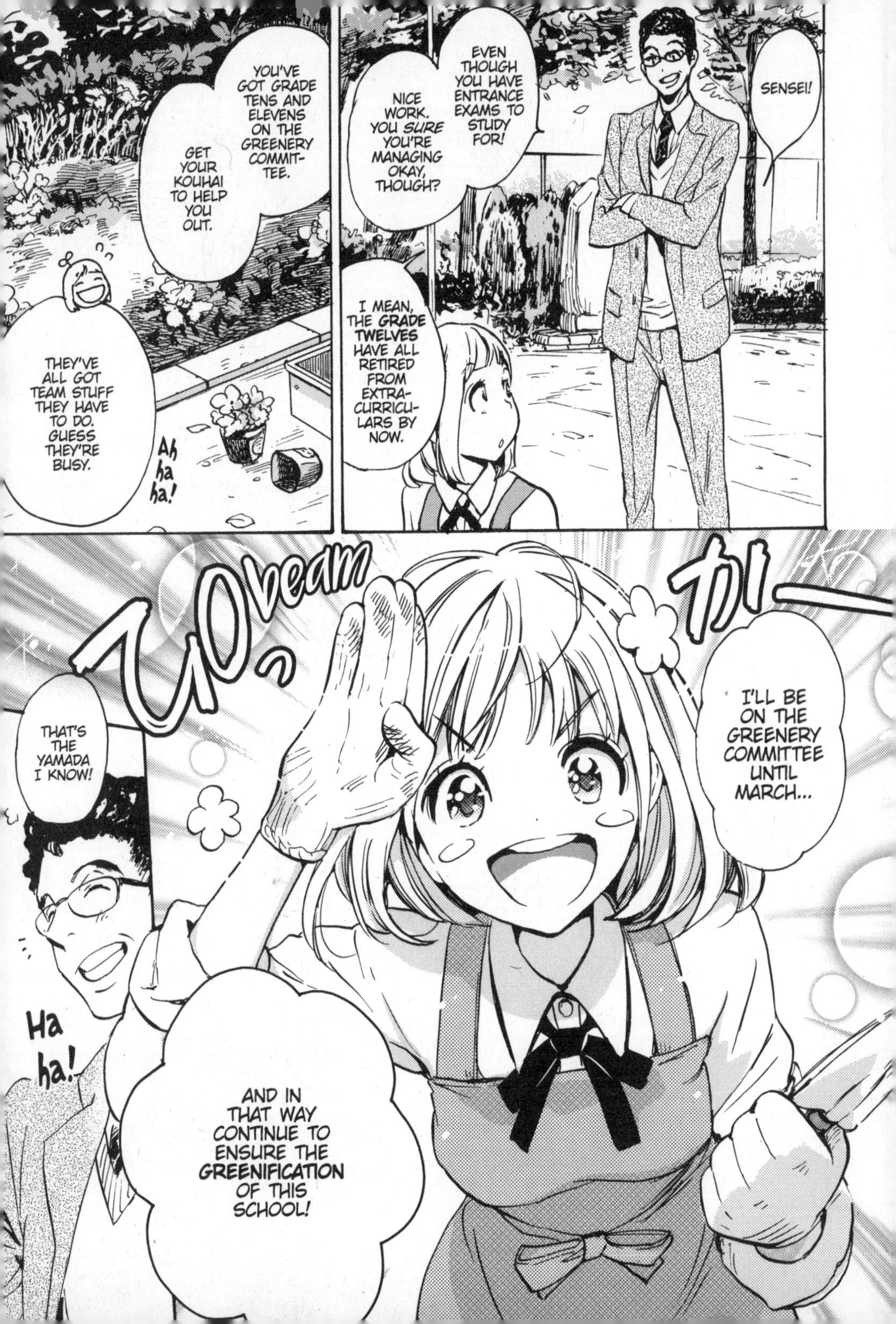
SENSEI!
EVEN THOUGH YOU HAVE ENTRANCE EXAMS TO STUDY FOR!
NICE WORK. YOU *SURE* YOU'RE MANAGING OKAY, THOUGH?
I MEAN, THE **GRADE TWELVES** HAVE ALL RETIRED FROM EXTRA-CURRICULARS BY NOW.
YOU'VE GOT GRADE TENS AND ELEVENS ON THE GREENERY COMMIT-TEE.
GET YOUR KOUHAI TO HELP YOU OUT.
THEY'VE ALL GOT TEAM STUFF THEY HAVE TO DO. GUESS THEY'RE BUSY.
Ah ha ha!
カー
I'LL BE ON THE GREENERY COMMITTEE UNTIL MARCH...
beam
AND IN THAT WAY CONTINUE TO ENSURE THE **GREENIFICATION** OF THIS SCHOOL!
THAT'S THE YAMADA I KNOW!
Ha ha!

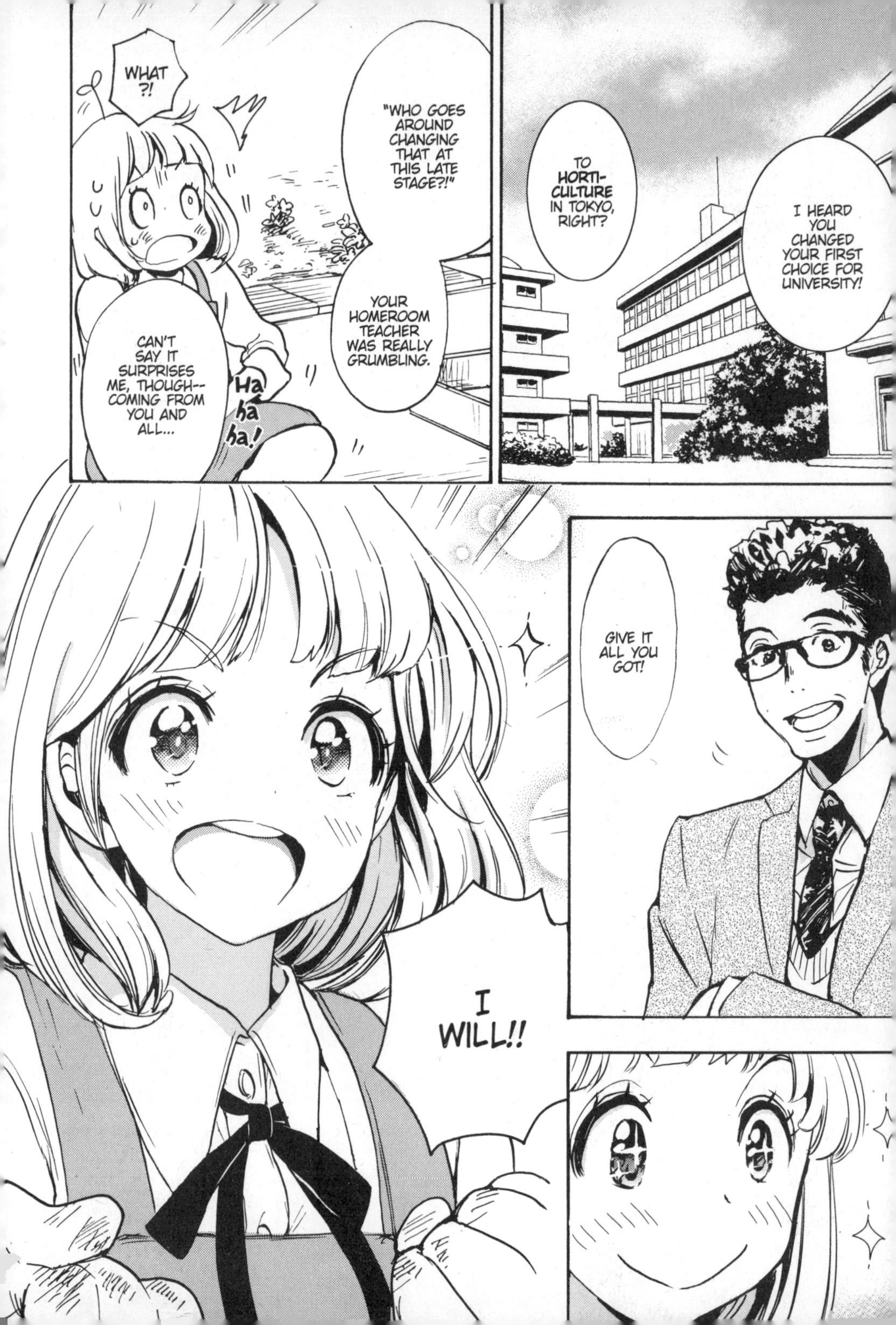
I HEARD YOU CHANGED YOUR FIRST CHOICE FOR UNIVERSITY!
TO HORTICULTURE IN TOKYO, RIGHT?
"WHO GOES AROUND CHANGING THAT AT THIS LATE STAGE?!"
YOUR HOMEROOM TEACHER WAS REALLY GRUMBLING.
WHAT ?!
CAN'T SAY IT SURPRISES ME, THOUGH-- COMING FROM YOU AND ALL...
Ha ha ha!
GIVE IT ALL YOU GOT!
I WILL!!

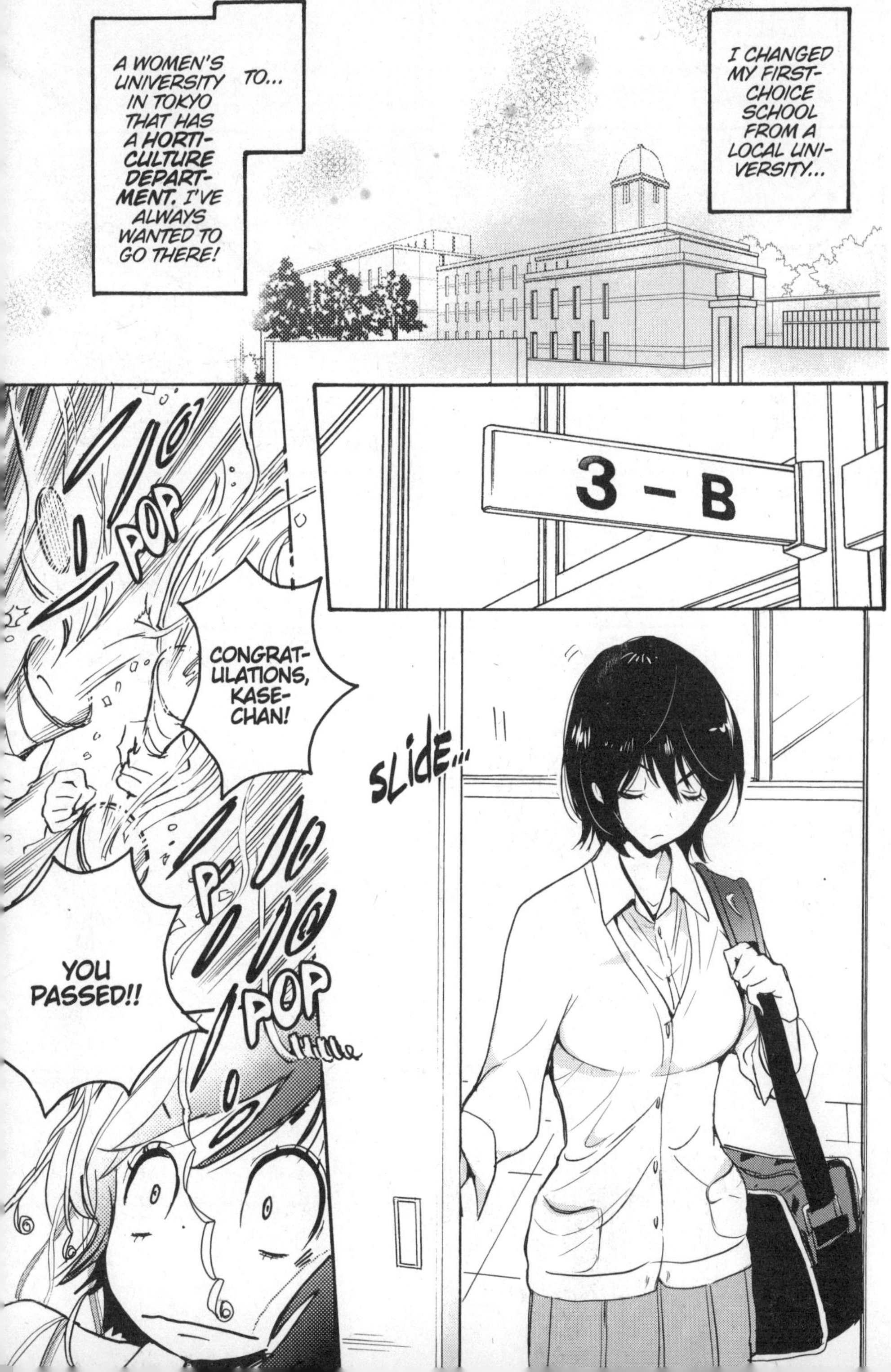

I CHANGED MY FIRST-CHOICE SCHOOL FROM A LOCAL UNIVERSITY...
TO...
A WOMEN'S UNIVERSITY IN TOKYO THAT HAS A HORTICULTURE DEPARTMENT. I'VE ALWAYS WANTED TO GO THERE!
3 – B
SLIDE...
POP
CONGRATULATIONS, KASE-CHAN!
YOU PASSED!!
POP

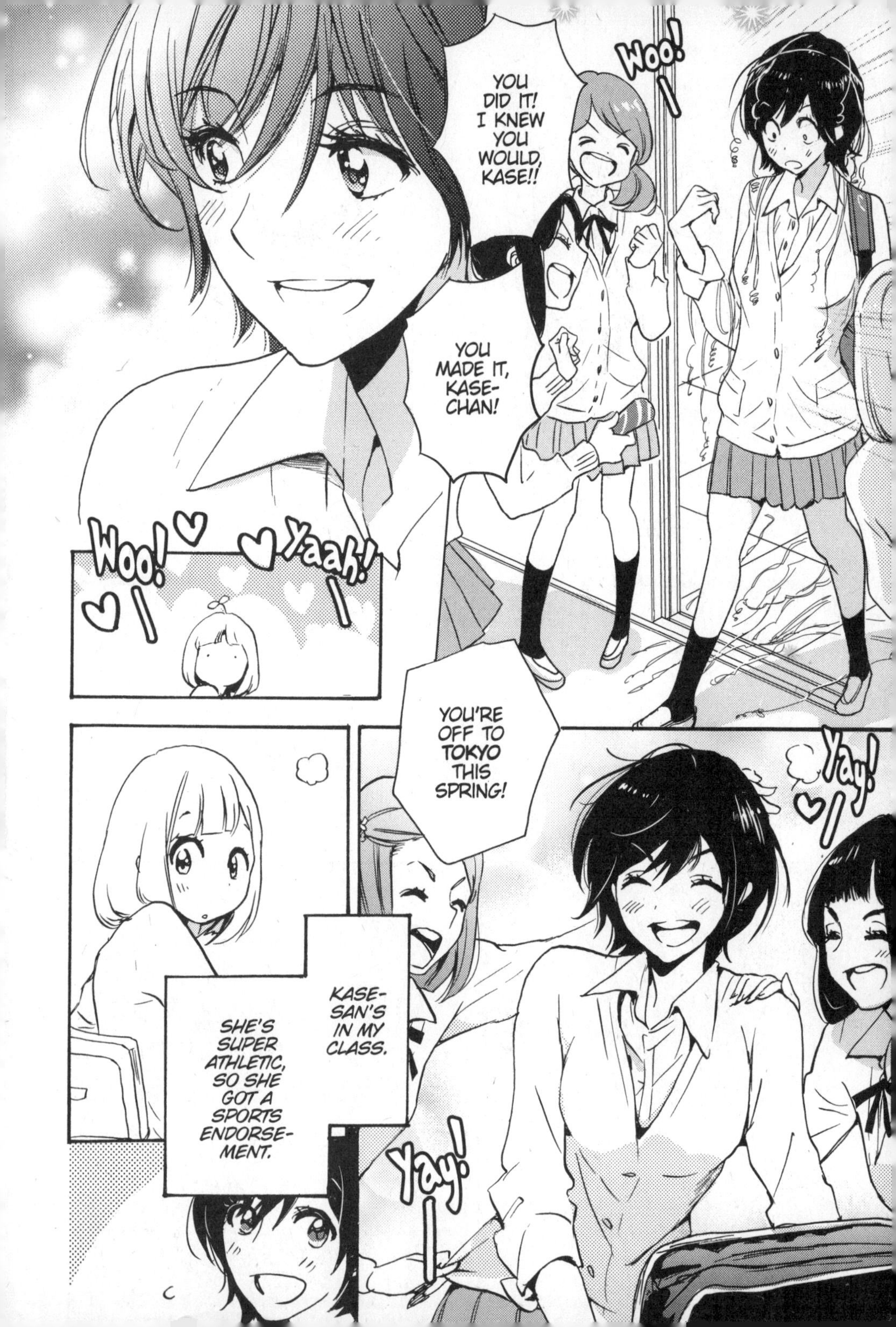

Woo!
YOU DID IT! I KNEW YOU WOULD, KASE!!
YOU MADE IT, KASE-CHAN!
Yaah!
Woo!
YOU'RE OFF TO TOKYO THIS SPRING!
Yay!
Yay!
KASE-SAN'S IN MY CLASS.
SHE'S SUPER ATHLETIC, SO SHE GOT A SPORTS ENDORSEMENT.

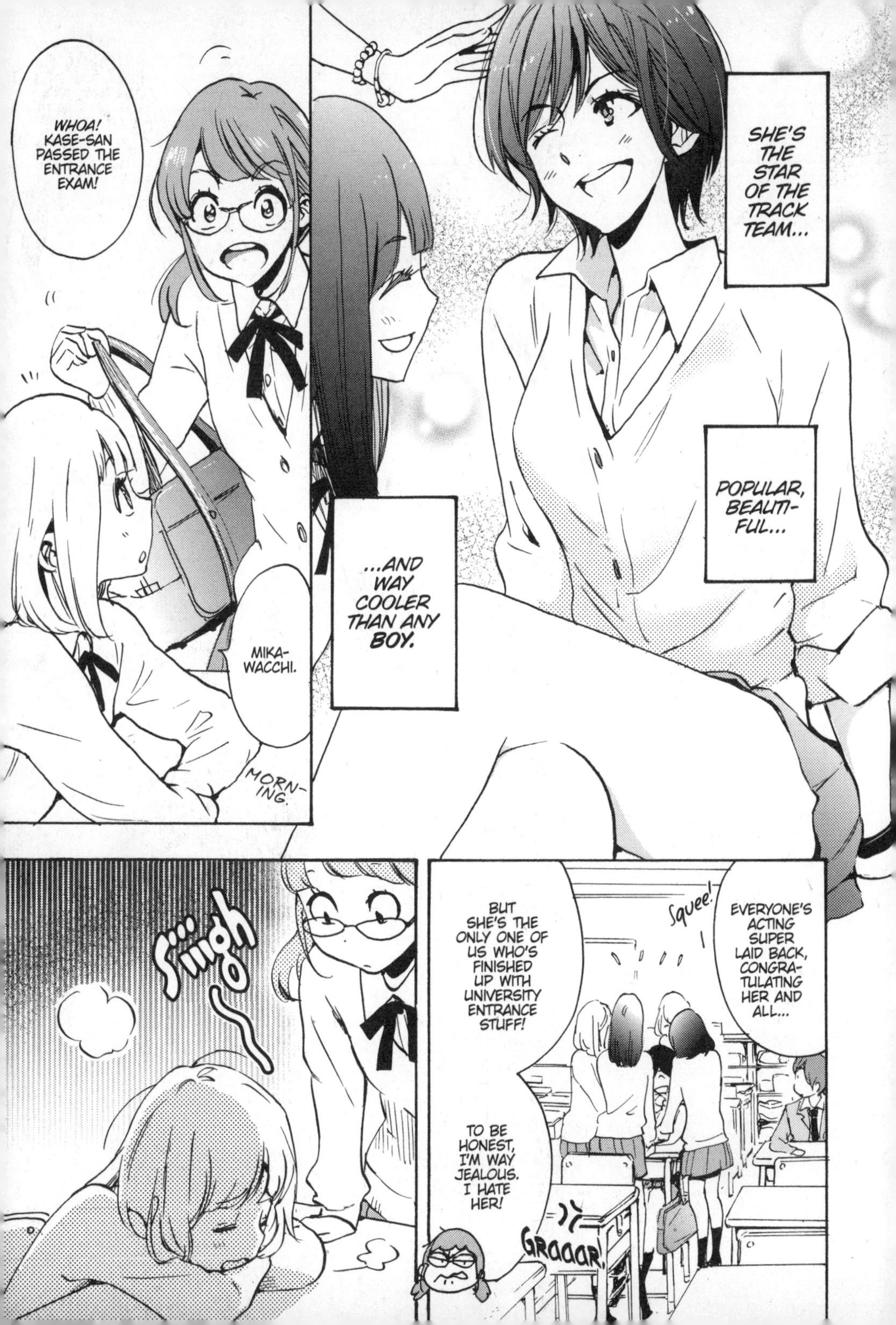

SHE'S THE STAR OF THE TRACK TEAM...
POPULAR, BEAUTIFUL...
...AND WAY COOLER THAN ANY BOY.
WHOA! KASE-SAN PASSED THE ENTRANCE EXAM!
MIKA-WACCHI.
MORNING.
EVERYONE'S ACTING SUPER LAID BACK, CONGRATULATING HER AND ALL...
Squee!
BUT SHE'S THE ONLY ONE OF US WHO'S FINISHED UP WITH UNIVERSITY ENTRANCE STUFF!
TO BE HONEST, I'M WAY JEALOUS. I HATE HER!
GRAAAR!
SIIIGH

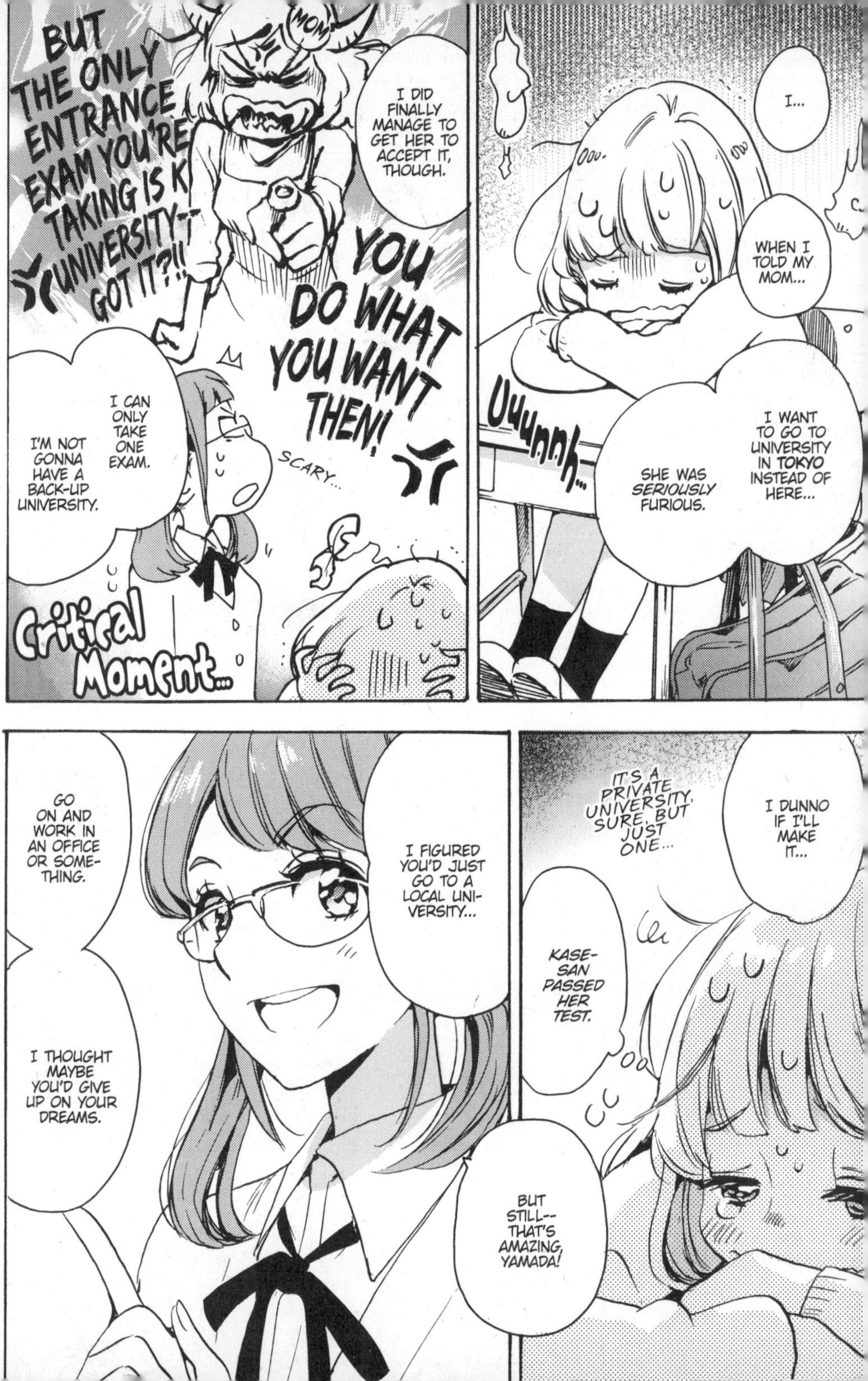
I...
WHEN I TOLD MY MOM...
I WANT TO GO TO UNIVERSITY IN TOKYO INSTEAD OF HERE...
SHE WAS SERIOUSLY FURIOUS.
Uuunnh...
MOM
I DID FINALLY MANAGE TO GET HER TO ACCEPT IT, THOUGH.
BUT THE ONLY ENTRANCE EXAM YOU'RE TAKING IS K UNIVERSITY--GOT IT?!!
YOU DO WHAT YOU WANT THEN!
I CAN ONLY TAKE ONE EXAM.
I'M NOT GONNA HAVE A BACK-UP UNIVERSITY.
SCARY...
Critical Moment...
I DUNNO IF I'LL MAKE IT...
IT'S A PRIVATE UNIVERSITY, SURE, BUT JUST ONE...
KASE-SAN PASSED HER TEST.
BUT STILL--THAT'S AMAZING, YAMADA!
I FIGURED YOU'D JUST GO TO A LOCAL UNIVERSITY...
GO ON AND WORK IN AN OFFICE OR SOMETHING.
I THOUGHT MAYBE YOU'D GIVE UP ON YOUR DREAMS.

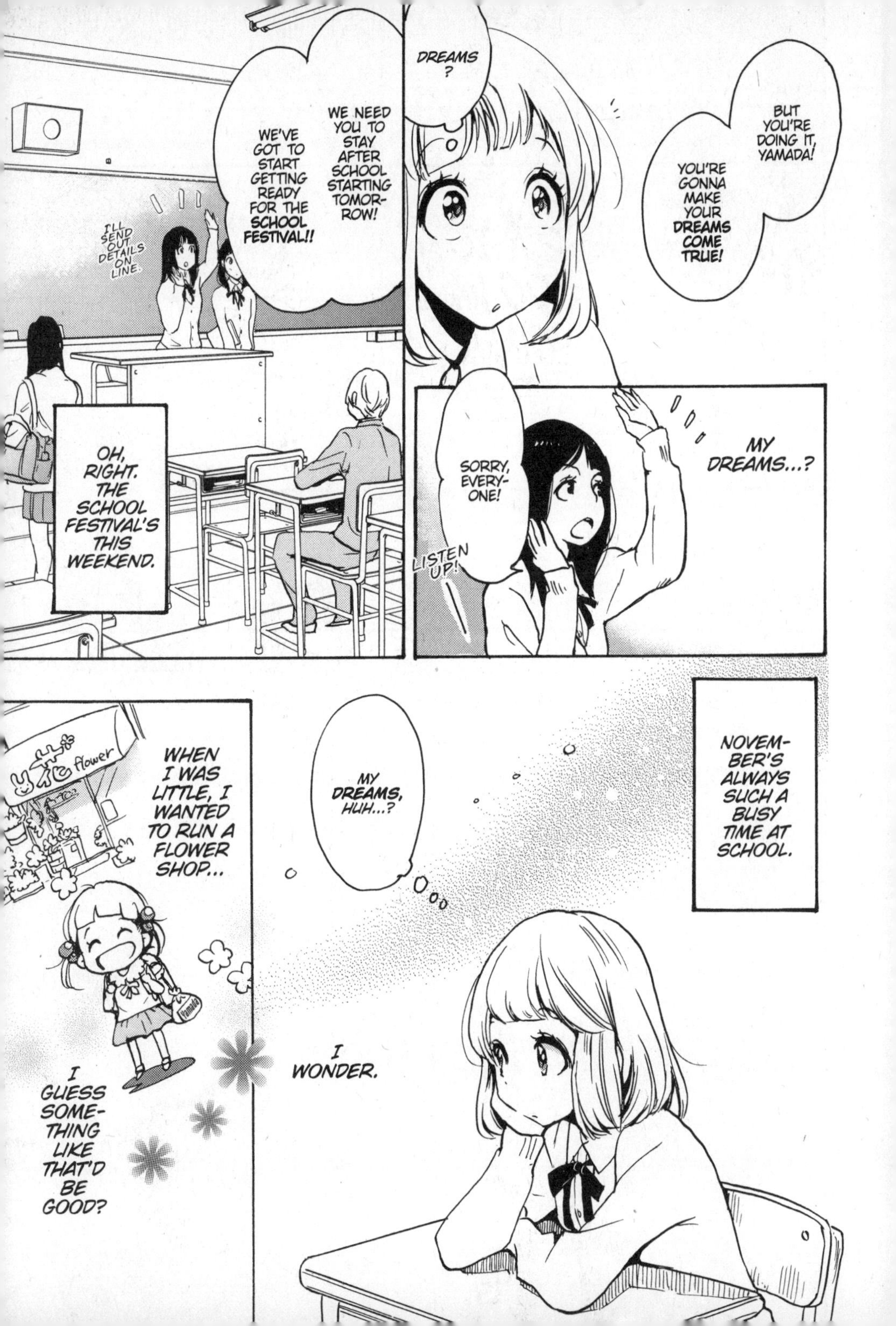
BUT YOU'RE DOING IT, YAMADA!
YOU'RE GONNA MAKE YOUR DREAMS COME TRUE!
DREAMS?
MY DREAMS...?
SORRY, EVERY-ONE!
LISTEN UP!
WE NEED YOU TO STAY AFTER SCHOOL STARTING TOMOR-ROW!
WE'VE GOT TO START GETTING READY FOR THE SCHOOL FESTIVAL!!
I'LL SEND OUT DETAILS ON LINE.
OH, RIGHT. THE SCHOOL FESTIVAL'S THIS WEEKEND.
NOVEM-BER'S ALWAYS SUCH A BUSY TIME AT SCHOOL.
MY DREAMS, HUH...?
I WONDER.
flower
WHEN I WAS LITTLE, I WANTED TO RUN A FLOWER SHOP...
Yamada
I GUESS SOME-THING LIKE THAT'D BE GOOD?

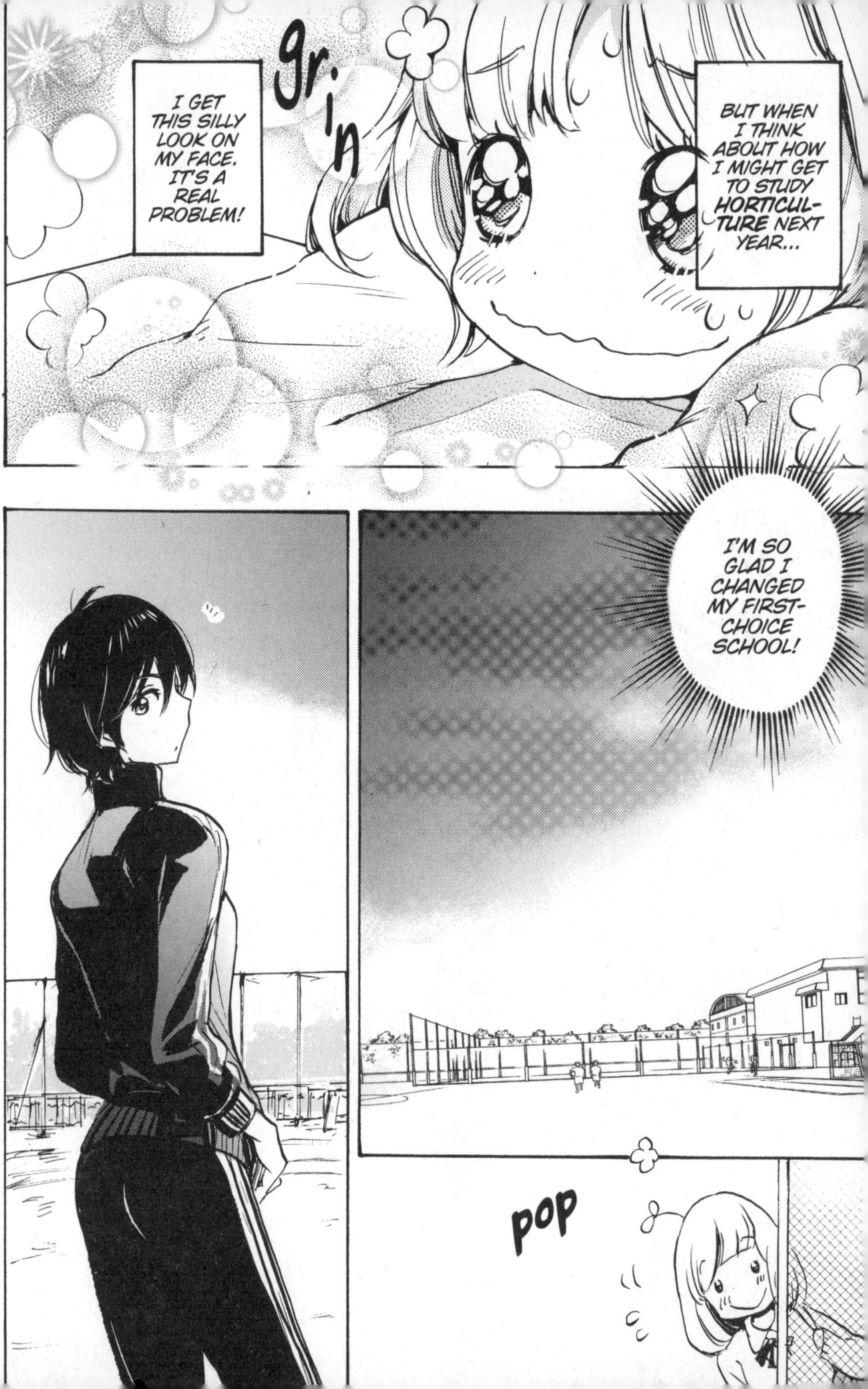
BUT WHEN I THINK ABOUT HOW I MIGHT GET TO STUDY HORTICULTURE NEXT YEAR...
I GET THIS SILLY LOOK ON MY FACE. IT'S A REAL PROBLEM!
grin
I'M SO GLAD I CHANGED MY FIRST-CHOICE SCHOOL!
pop

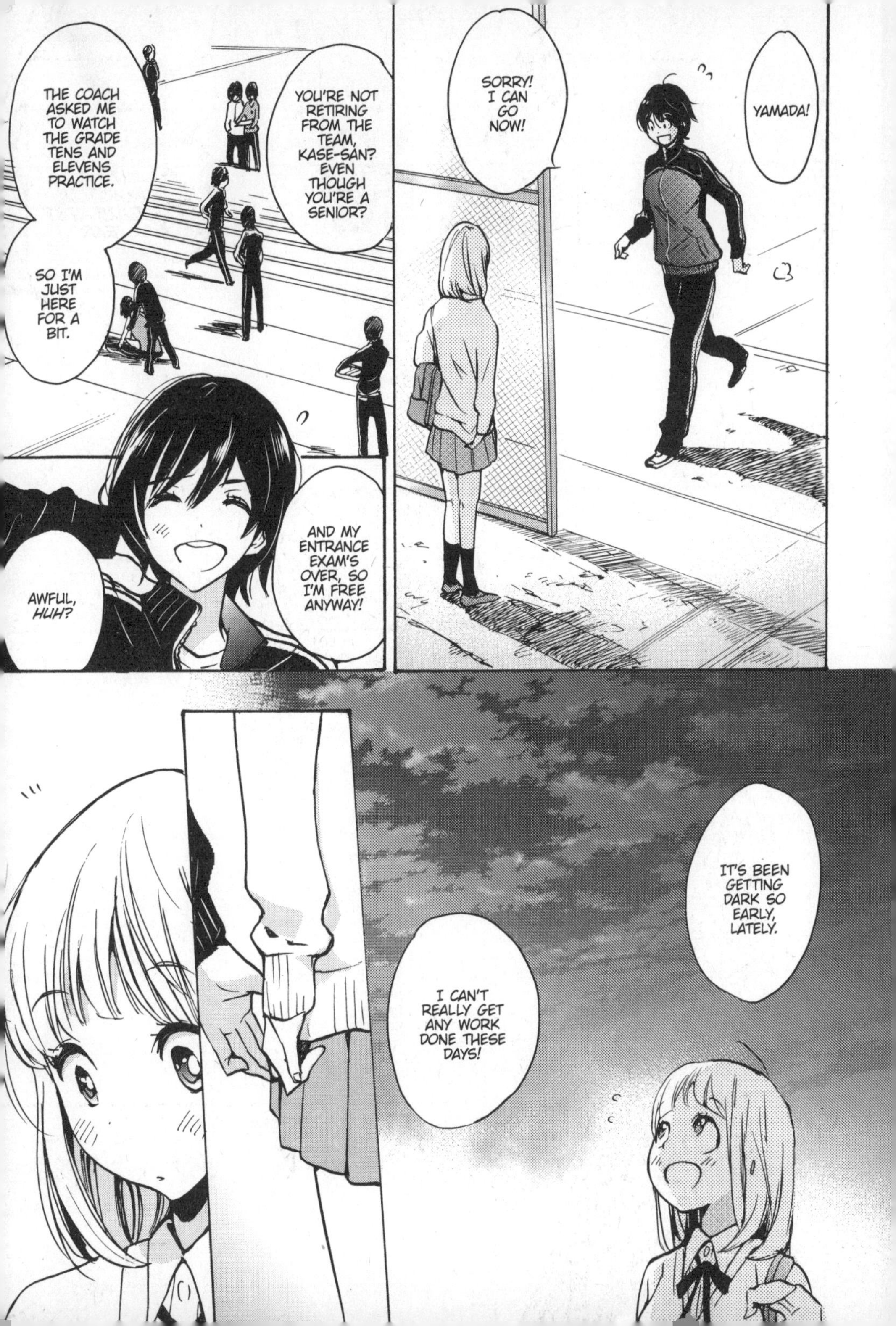
YAMADA!
SORRY! I CAN GO NOW!
YOU'RE NOT RETIRING FROM THE TEAM, KASE-SAN? EVEN THOUGH YOU'RE A SENIOR?
THE COACH ASKED ME TO WATCH THE GRADE TENS AND ELEVENS PRACTICE.
SO I'M JUST HERE FOR A BIT.
AND MY ENTRANCE EXAM'S OVER, SO I'M FREE ANYWAY!
AWFUL, HUH?
IT'S BEEN GETTING DARK SO EARLY, LATELY.
I CAN'T REALLY GET ANY WORK DONE THESE DAYS!

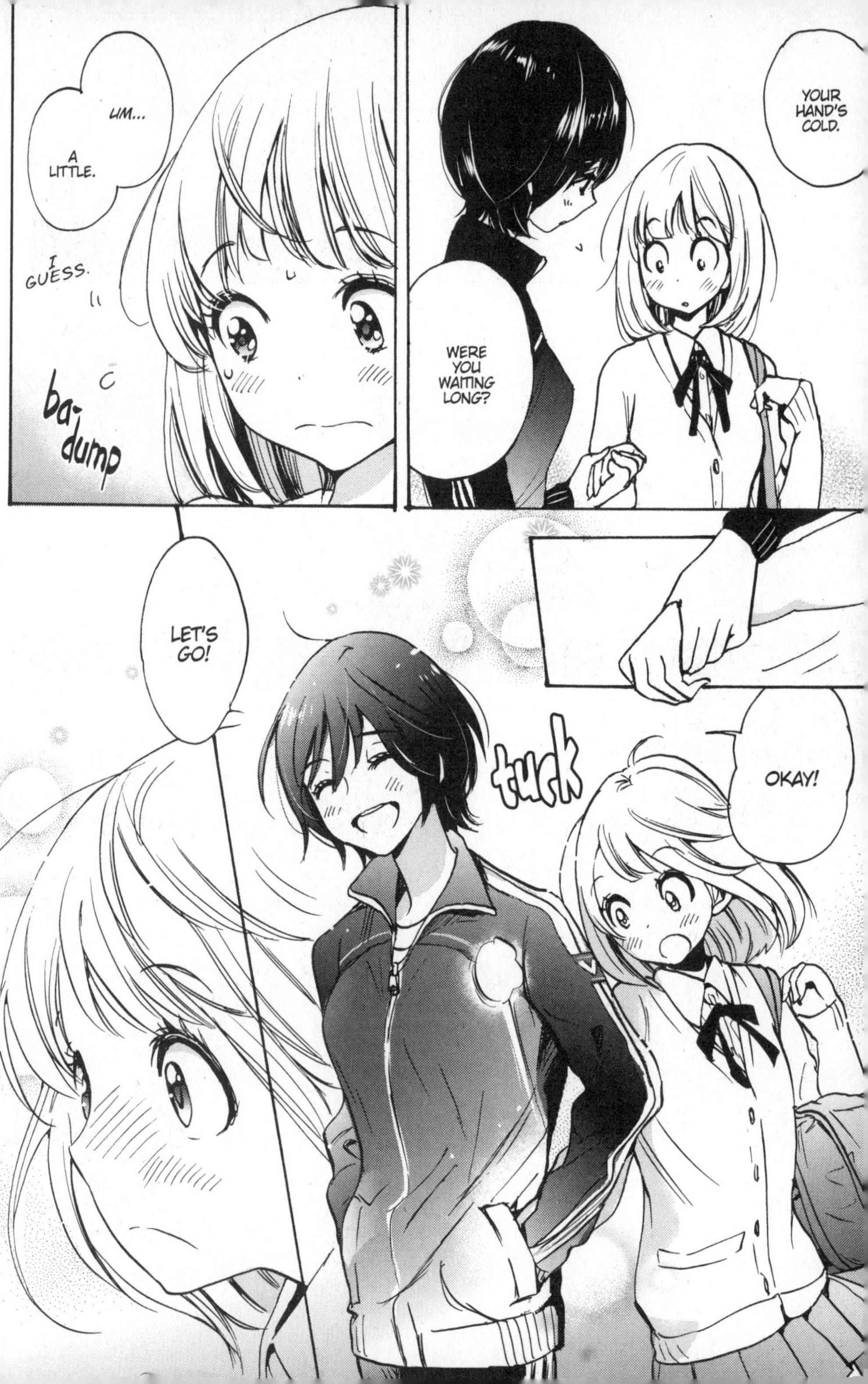
YOUR HAND'S COLD.
WERE YOU WAITING LONG?
UM... A LITTLE.
I GUESS.
ba-dump
LET'S GO!
tuck
OKAY!

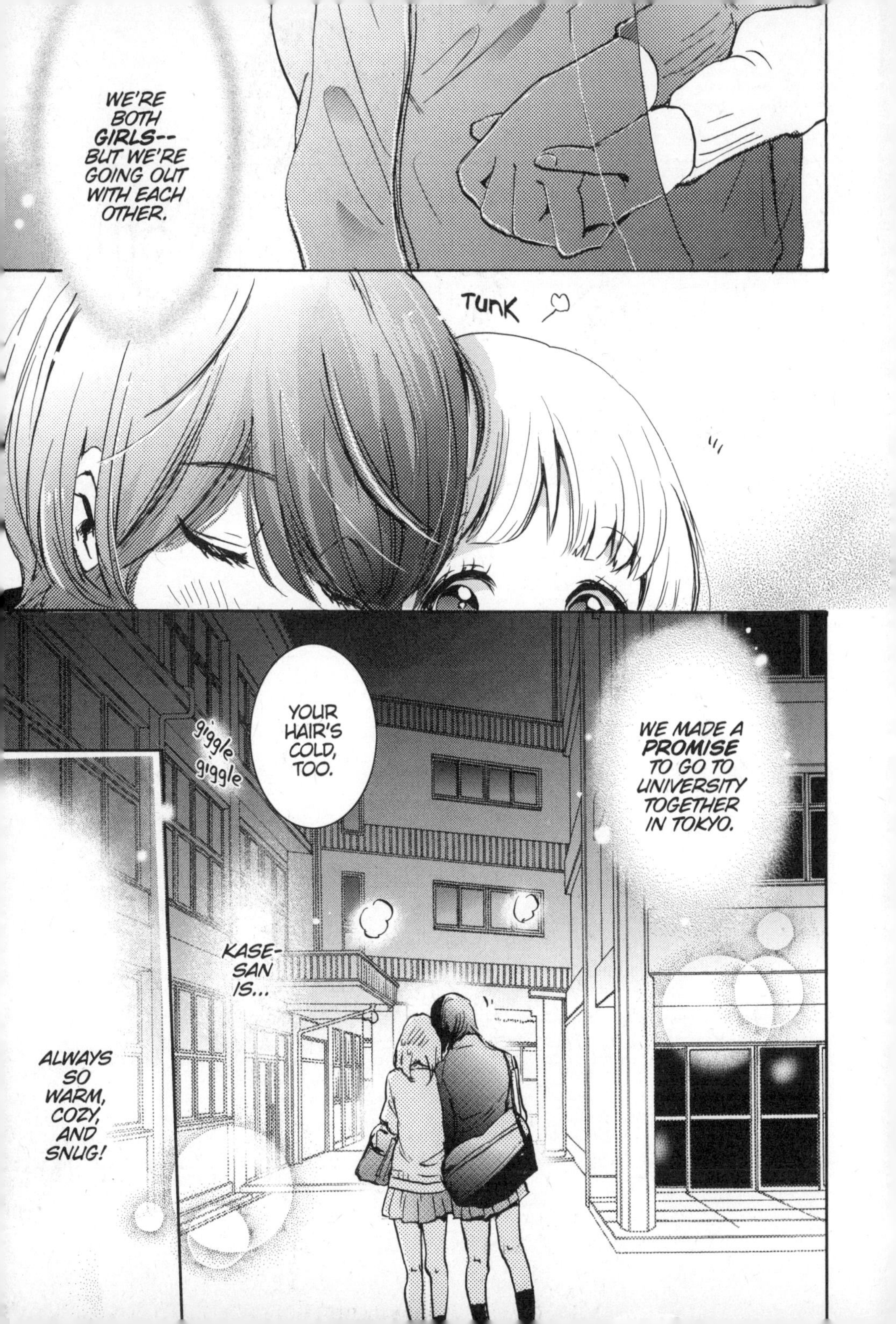
WE'RE BOTH GIRLS-- BUT WE'RE GOING OUT WITH EACH OTHER.
TUNK
WE MADE A PROMISE TO GO TO UNIVERSITY TOGETHER IN TOKYO.
YOUR HAIR'S COLD, TOO.
giggle giggle
KASE-SAN IS...
ALWAYS SO WARM, COZY, AND SNUG!

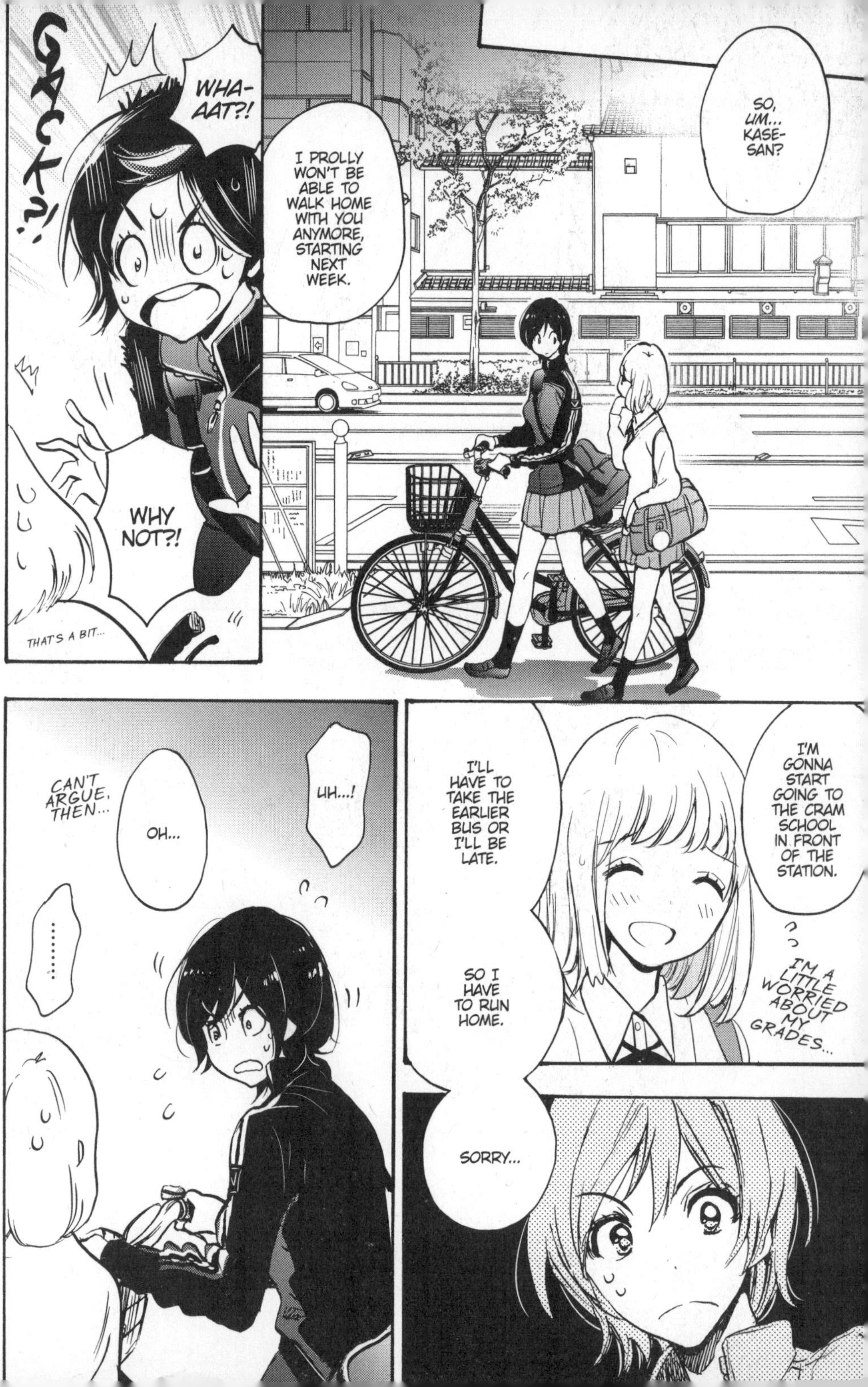
SO, UM... KASE-SAN?
I PROLLY WON'T BE ABLE TO WALK HOME WITH YOU ANYMORE, STARTING NEXT WEEK.
WHA-AAT?!
GACK?!
WHY NOT?!
THAT'S A BIT...
I'M GONNA START GOING TO THE CRAM SCHOOL IN FRONT OF THE STATION.
I'M A LITTLE WORRIED ABOUT MY GRADES...
I'LL HAVE TO TAKE THE EARLIER BUS OR I'LL BE LATE.
SO I HAVE TO RUN HOME.
SORRY...
UH...!
OH...
CAN'T ARGUE, THEN...
....

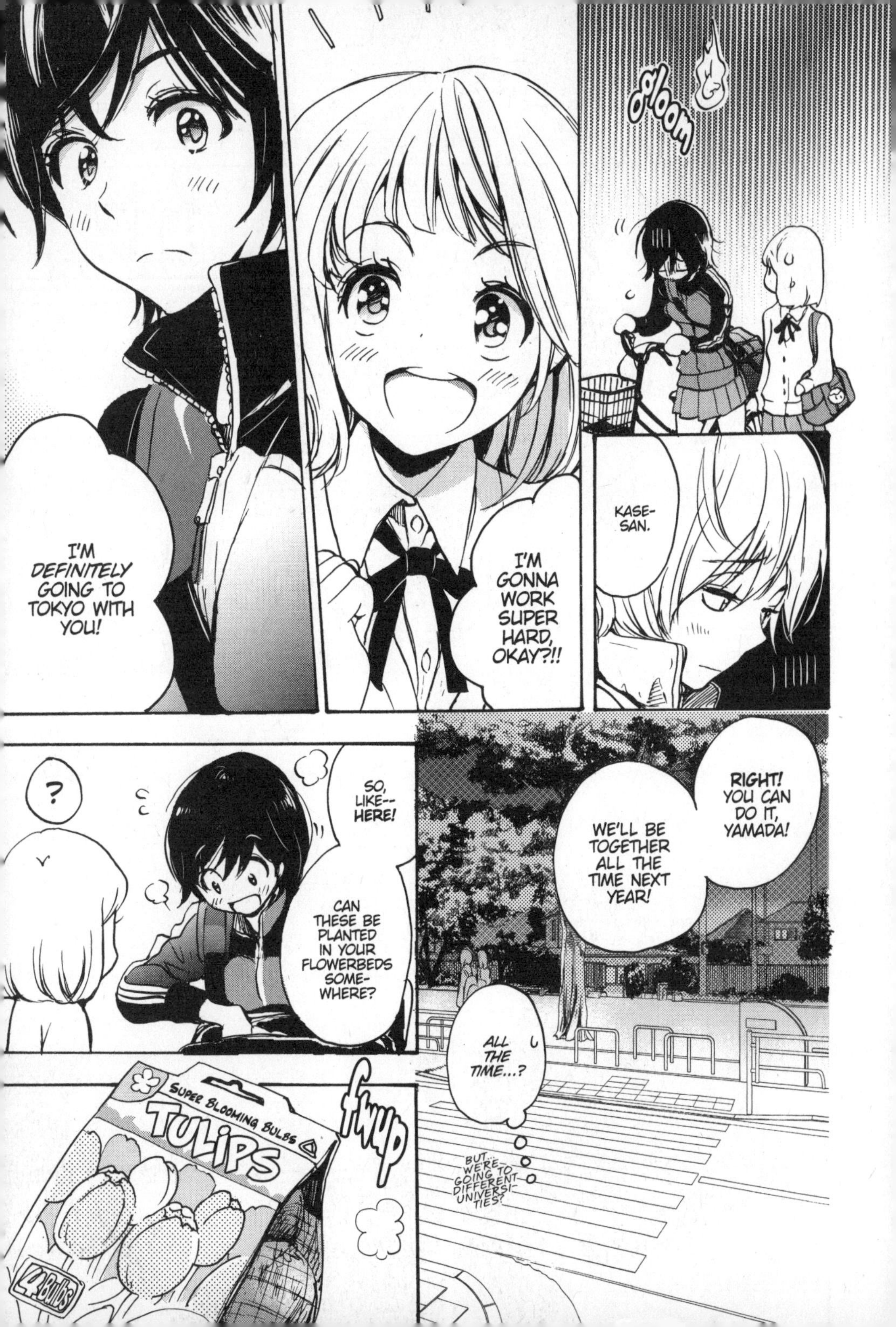
gloom
KASE-SAN.
I'M GONNA WORK SUPER HARD, OKAY?!!
I'M DEFINITELY GOING TO TOKYO WITH YOU!
RIGHT! YOU CAN DO IT, YAMADA!
WE'LL BE TOGETHER ALL THE TIME NEXT YEAR!
ALL THE TIME...?
BUT... WE'RE GOING TO DIFFERENT UNIVERSITIES?
SO, LIKE-- HERE!
CAN THESE BE PLANTED IN YOUR FLOWERBEDS SOMEWHERE?
?
fwup
SUPER BLOOMING BULBS
TULIPS
4 Bulbs

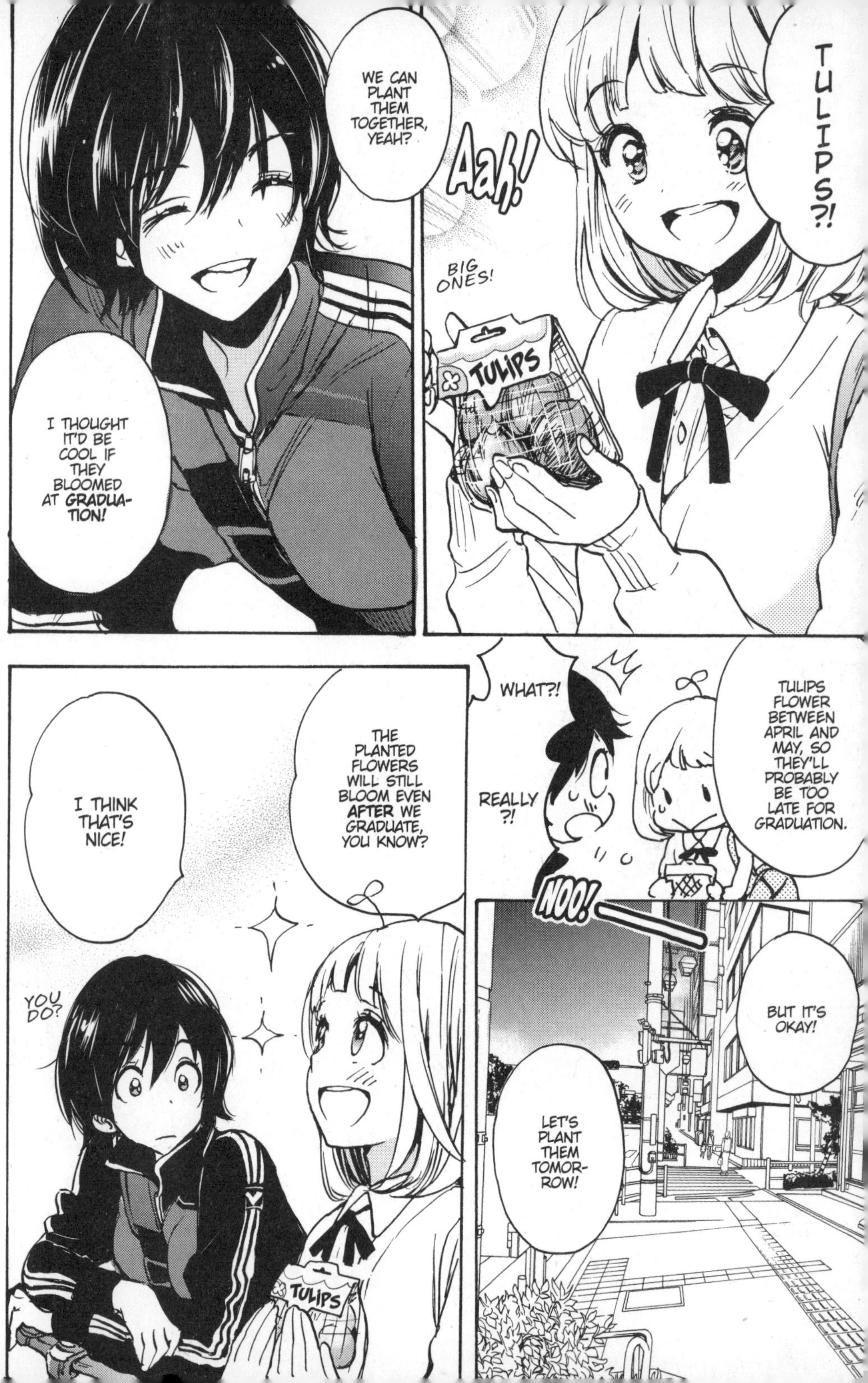
TULIPS?!
Aah!
BIG ONES!
TULIPS
WE CAN PLANT THEM TOGETHER, YEAH?
I THOUGHT IT'D BE COOL IF THEY BLOOMED AT GRADUATION!
TULIPS FLOWER BETWEEN APRIL AND MAY, SO THEY'LL PROBABLY BE TOO LATE FOR GRADUATION.
WHAT?!
REALLY?!
NOO!
BUT IT'S OKAY!
LET'S PLANT THEM TOMORROW!
THE PLANTED FLOWERS WILL STILL BLOOM EVEN AFTER WE GRADUATE, YOU KNOW?
I THINK THAT'S NICE!
YOU DO?
TULIPS

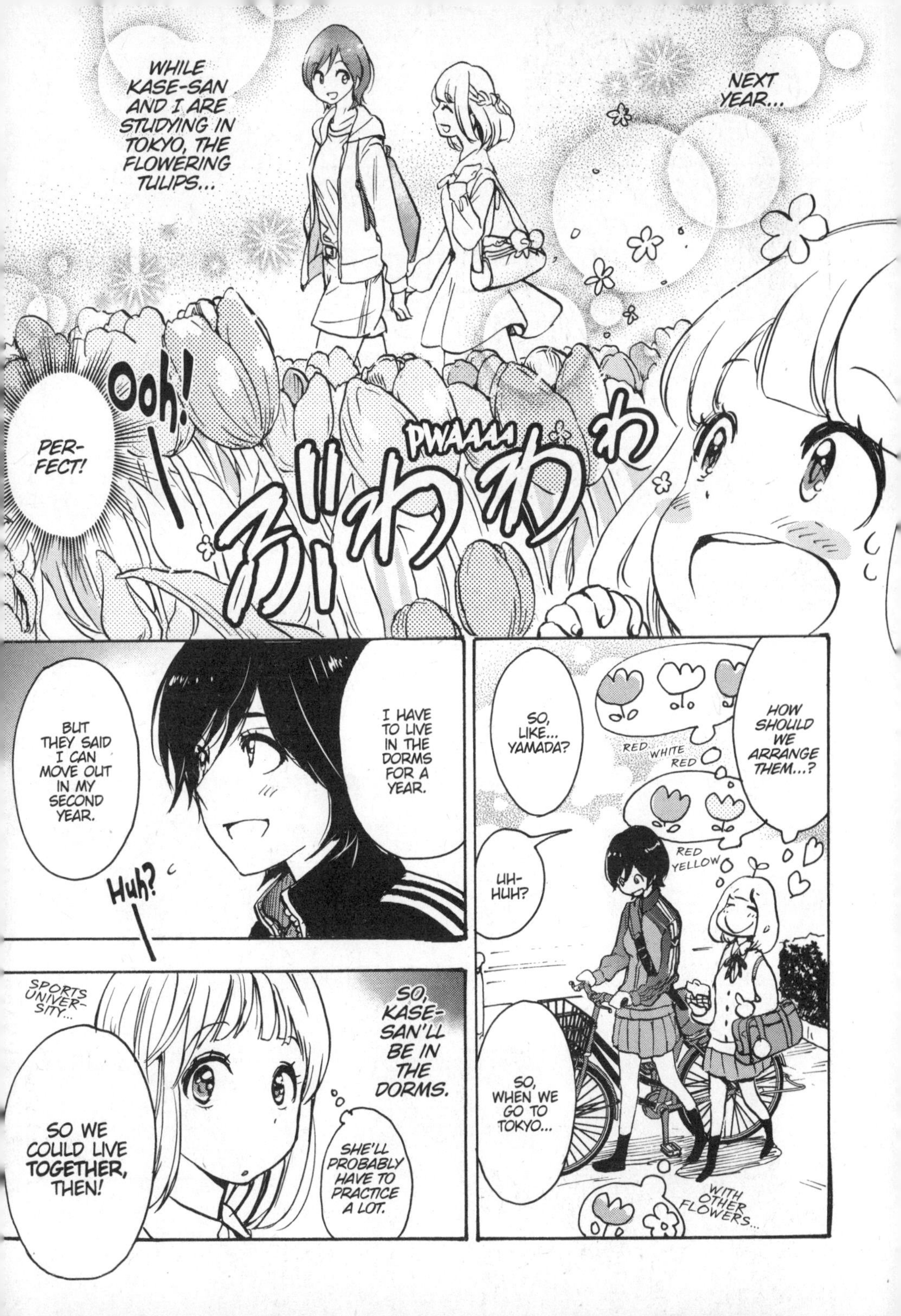
NEXT YEAR...
WHILE KASE-SAN AND I ARE STUDYING IN TOKYO, THE FLOWERING TULIPS...
PWAAA
ふわわわ
Ooh!
PER-FECT!
HOW SHOULD WE ARRANGE THEM...?
RED WHITE RED
SO, LIKE... YAMADA?
RED YELLOW
UH-HUH?
SO, WHEN WE GO TO TOKYO...
WITH OTHER FLOWERS...
I HAVE TO LIVE IN THE DORMS FOR A YEAR.
BUT THEY SAID I CAN MOVE OUT IN MY SECOND YEAR.
Huh?
SO, KASE-SAN'LL BE IN THE DORMS.
SHE'LL PROBABLY HAVE TO PRACTICE A LOT.
SPORTS UNIVERSITY...
SO WE COULD LIVE TOGETHER, THEN!

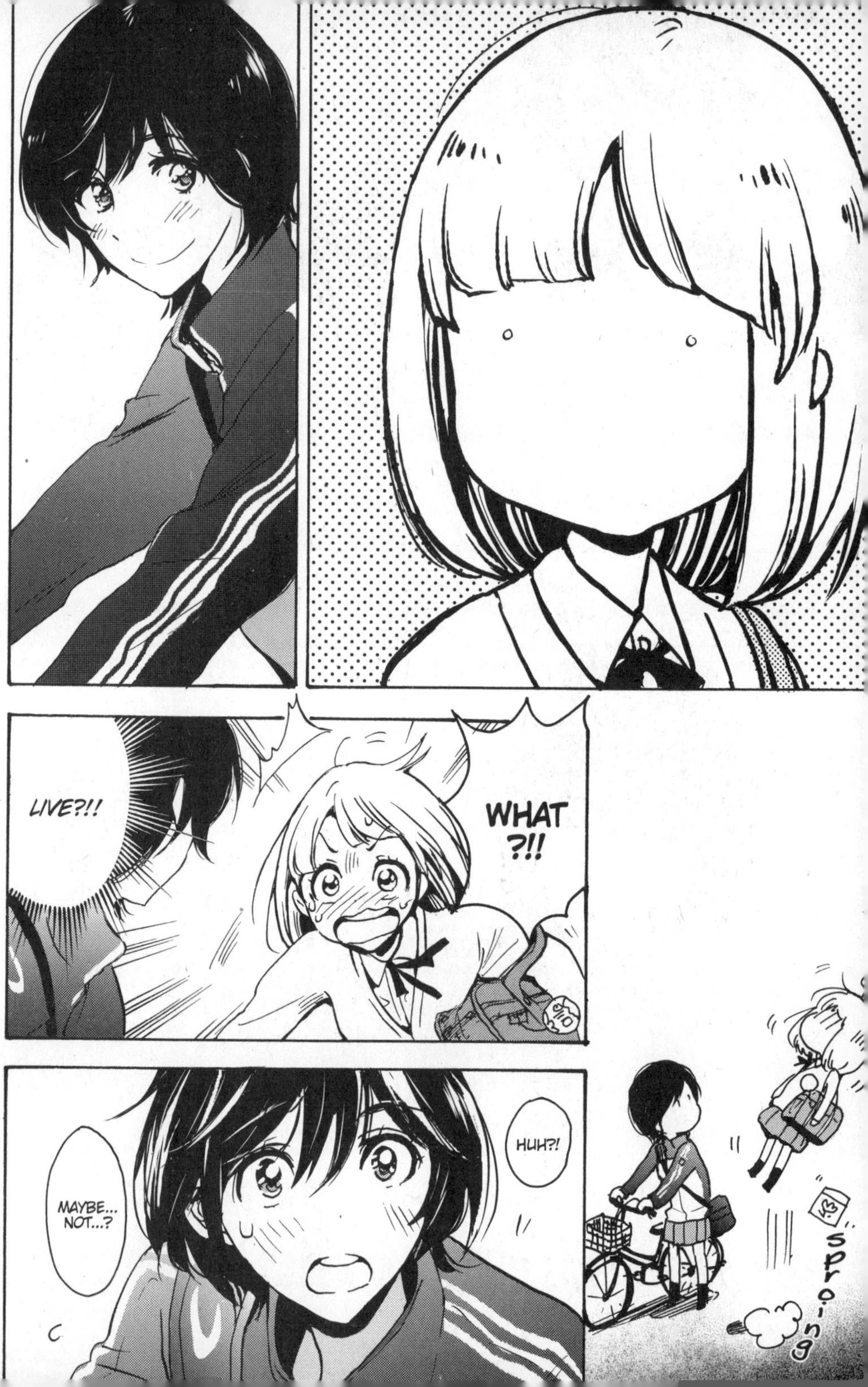
WHAT ?!!
LIVE?!!
sproing
HUH?!
MAYBE... NOT...?

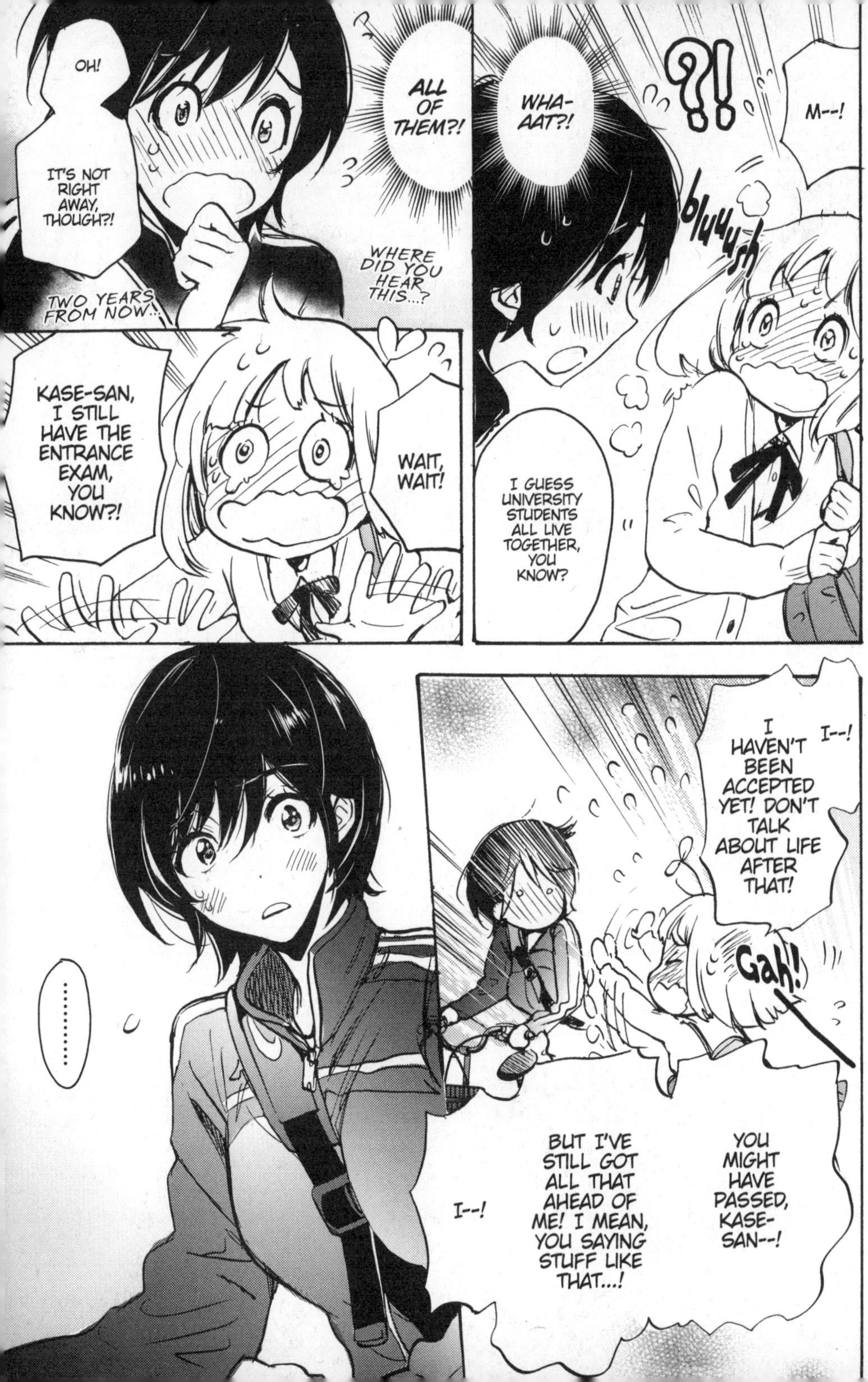
M--!
?!
bluuush
WHA-AAT?!
I GUESS UNIVERSITY STUDENTS ALL LIVE TOGETHER, YOU KNOW?
ALL OF THEM?!
OH!
IT'S NOT RIGHT AWAY, THOUGH?!
WHERE DID YOU HEAR THIS...?
TWO YEARS FROM NOW...
WAIT, WAIT!
KASE-SAN, I STILL HAVE THE ENTRANCE EXAM, YOU KNOW?!
I--!
I HAVEN'T BEEN ACCEPTED YET! DON'T TALK ABOUT LIFE AFTER THAT!
Gah!
YOU MIGHT HAVE PASSED, KASE-SAN--!
BUT I'VE STILL GOT ALL THAT AHEAD OF ME! I MEAN, YOU SAYING STUFF LIKE THAT...!
I--!
....

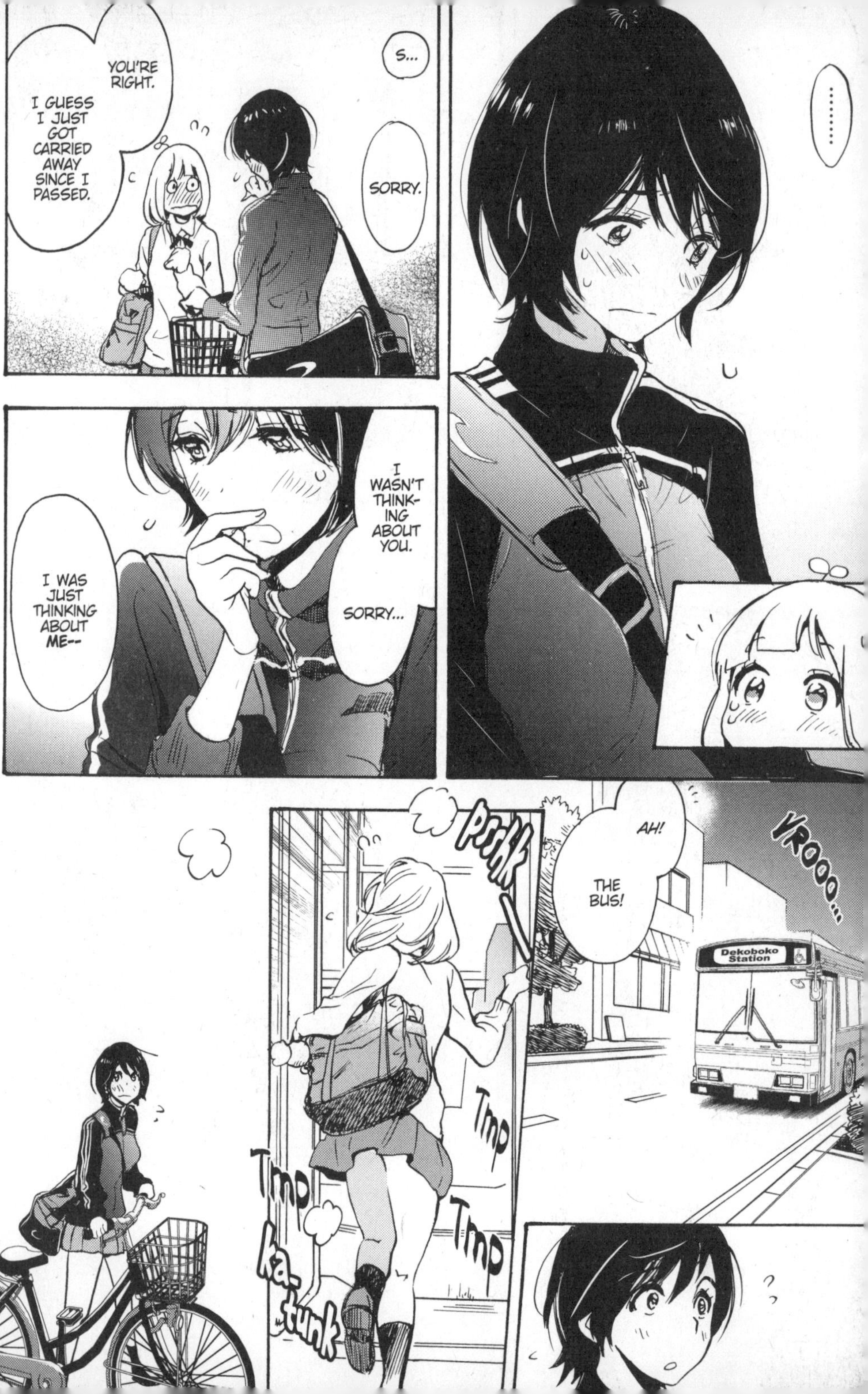
......
S...
SORRY.
YOU'RE RIGHT. I GUESS I JUST GOT CARRIED AWAY SINCE I PASSED.
I WASN'T THINKING ABOUT YOU.
SORRY...
I WAS JUST THINKING ABOUT ME--
VROOOO...
Dekoboko Station
AH! THE BUS!
Psshk
Tmp
Tmp
Tmp
Tmp
ka-tunk

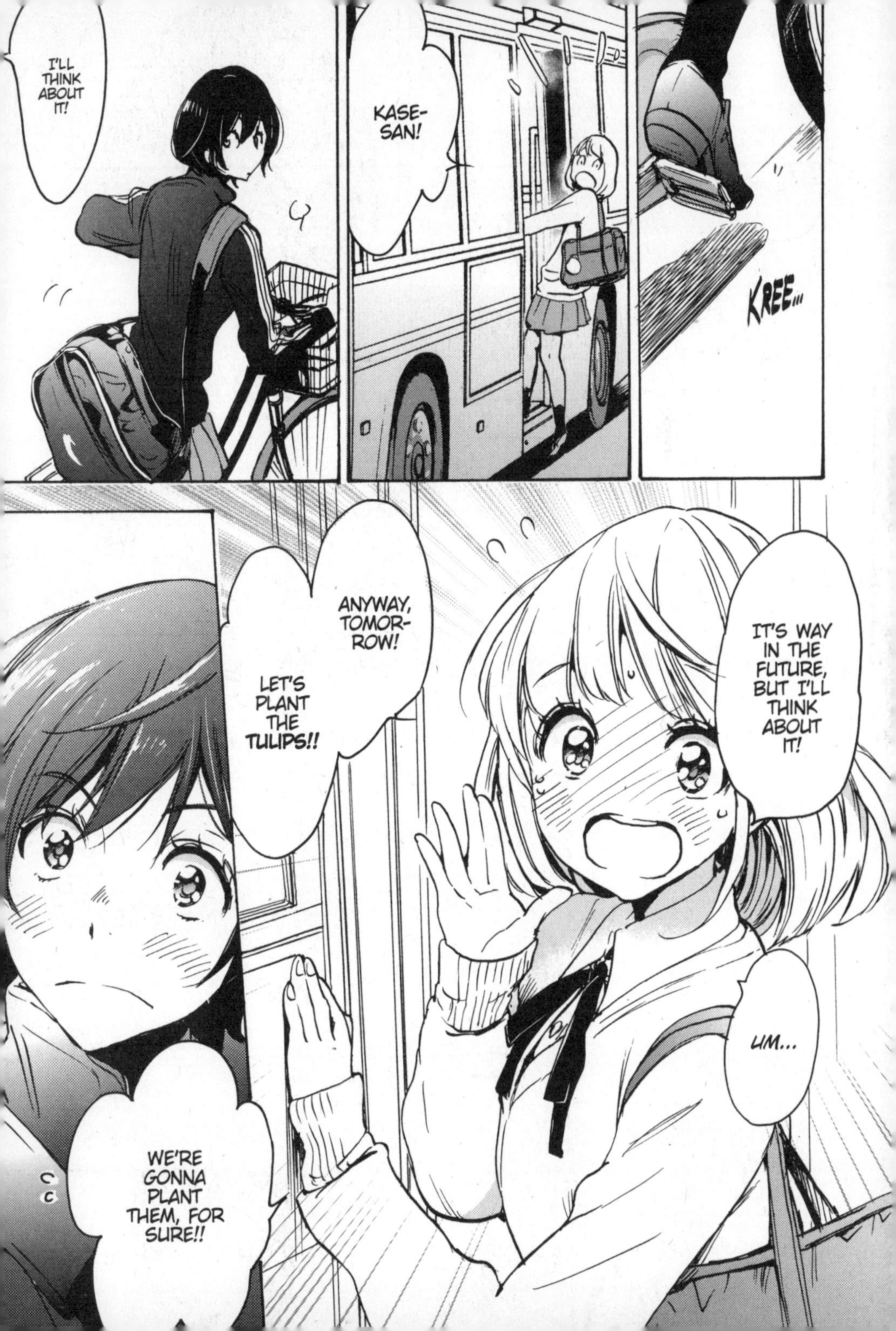
KREE...
KASE-SAN!
I'LL THINK ABOUT IT!
IT'S WAY IN THE FUTURE, BUT I'LL THINK ABOUT IT!
ANYWAY, TOMORROW!
LET'S PLANT THE TULIPS!!
UM...
WE'RE GONNA PLANT THEM, FOR SURE!!

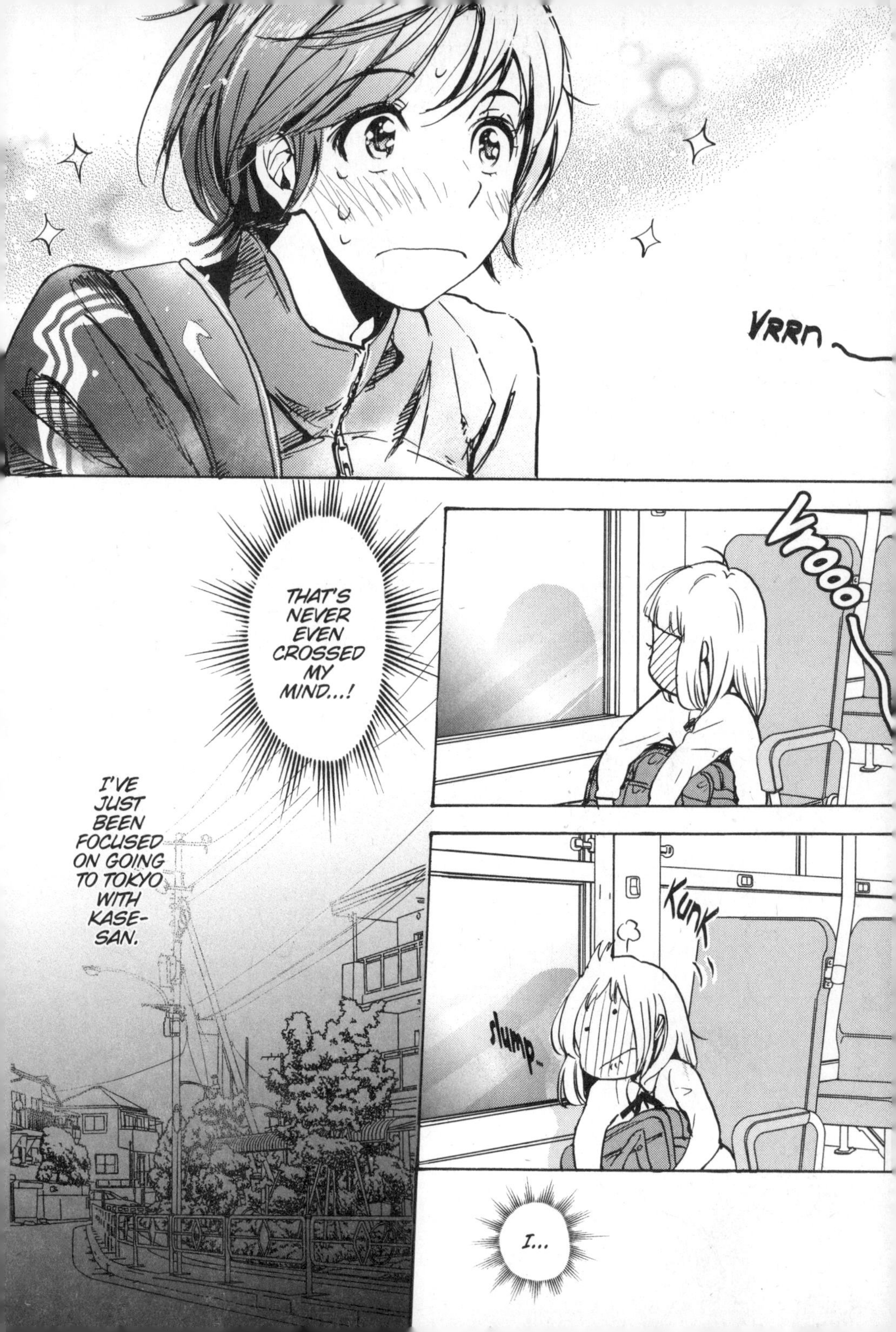
VRRN~
Vroooo
Kunk
slump
I...
THAT'S NEVER EVEN CROSSED MY MIND...!
I'VE JUST BEEN FOCUSED ON GOING TO TOKYO WITH KASE-SAN.

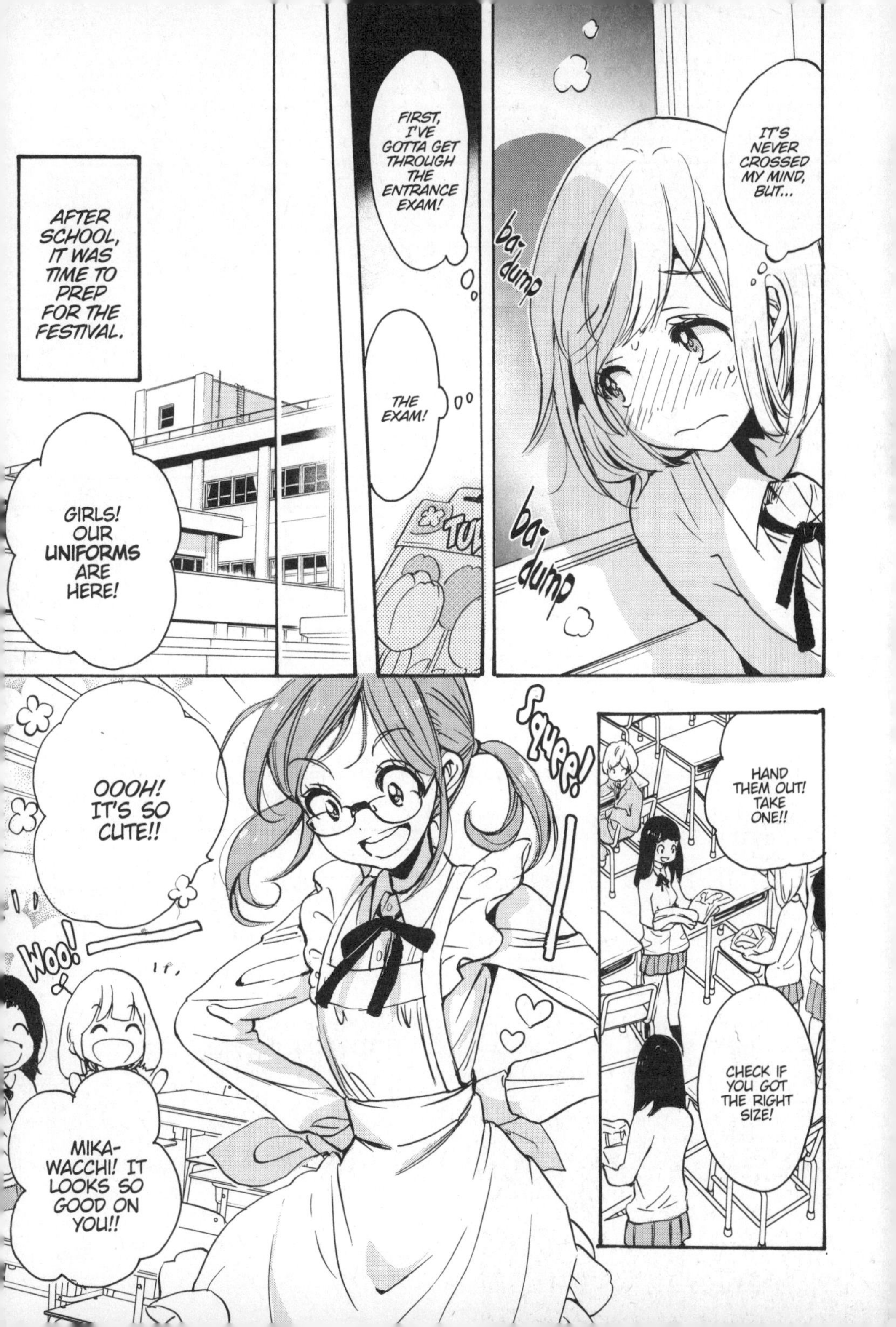
IT'S NEVER CROSSED MY MIND, BUT...
ba-dump
ba-dump
FIRST, I'VE GOTTA GET THROUGH THE ENTRANCE EXAM!
THE EXAM!
AFTER SCHOOL, IT WAS TIME TO PREP FOR THE FESTIVAL.
GIRLS! OUR UNIFORMS ARE HERE!
HAND THEM OUT! TAKE ONE!!
CHECK IF YOU GOT THE RIGHT SIZE!
Squee!
OOOH! IT'S SO CUTE!!
Woo!
MIKA-WACCHI! IT LOOKS SO GOOD ON YOU!!

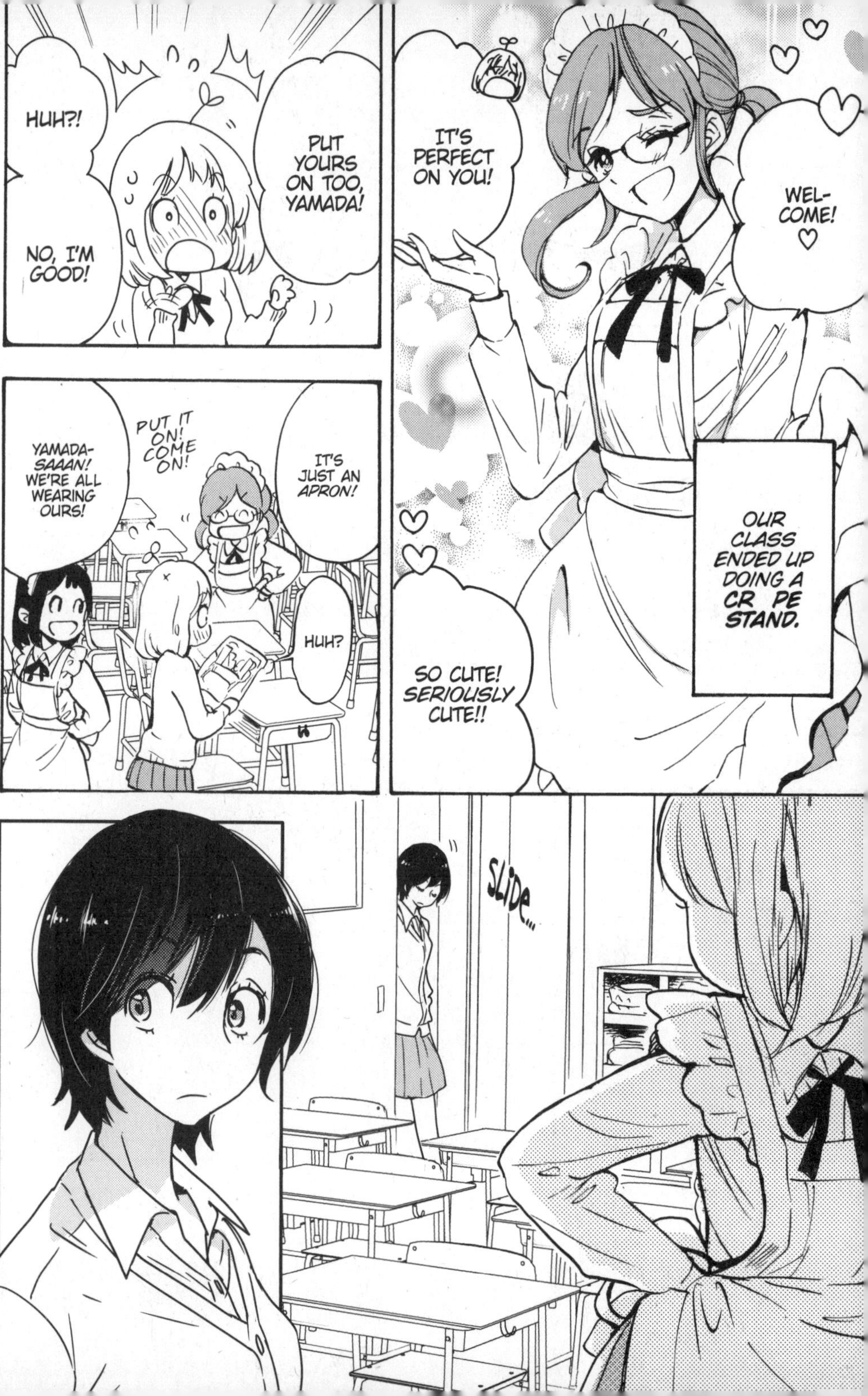
WEL-COME!
IT'S PERFECT ON YOU!
OUR CLASS ENDED UP DOING A CR PE STAND.
SO CUTE! SERIOUSLY CUTE!!
PUT YOURS ON TOO, YAMADA!
HUH?!
NO, I'M GOOD!
IT'S JUST AN APRON!
PUT IT ON! COME ON!
YAMADA-SAAAN! WE'RE ALL WEARING OURS!
HUH?
SLIDE...

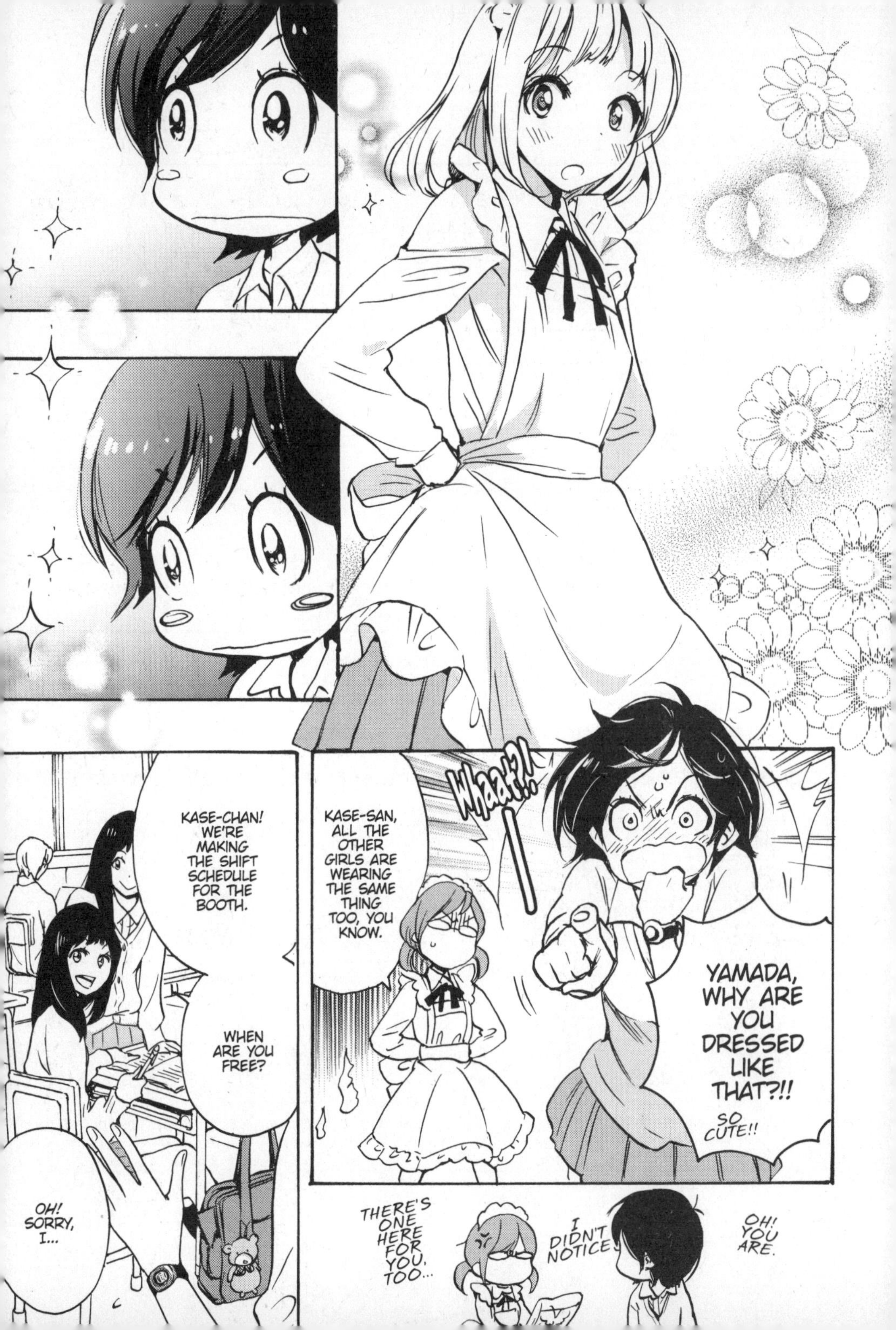

YAMADA, WHY ARE YOU DRESSED LIKE THAT?!!
Whaat?!!
SO CUTE!!
KASE-SAN, ALL THE OTHER GIRLS ARE WEARING THE SAME THING TOO, YOU KNOW.
OH! YOU ARE.
I DIDN'T NOTICE
THERE'S ONE HERE FOR YOU, TOO...
KASE-CHAN! WE'RE MAKING THE SHIFT SCHEDULE FOR THE BOOTH.
WHEN ARE YOU FREE?
OH! SORRY, I...

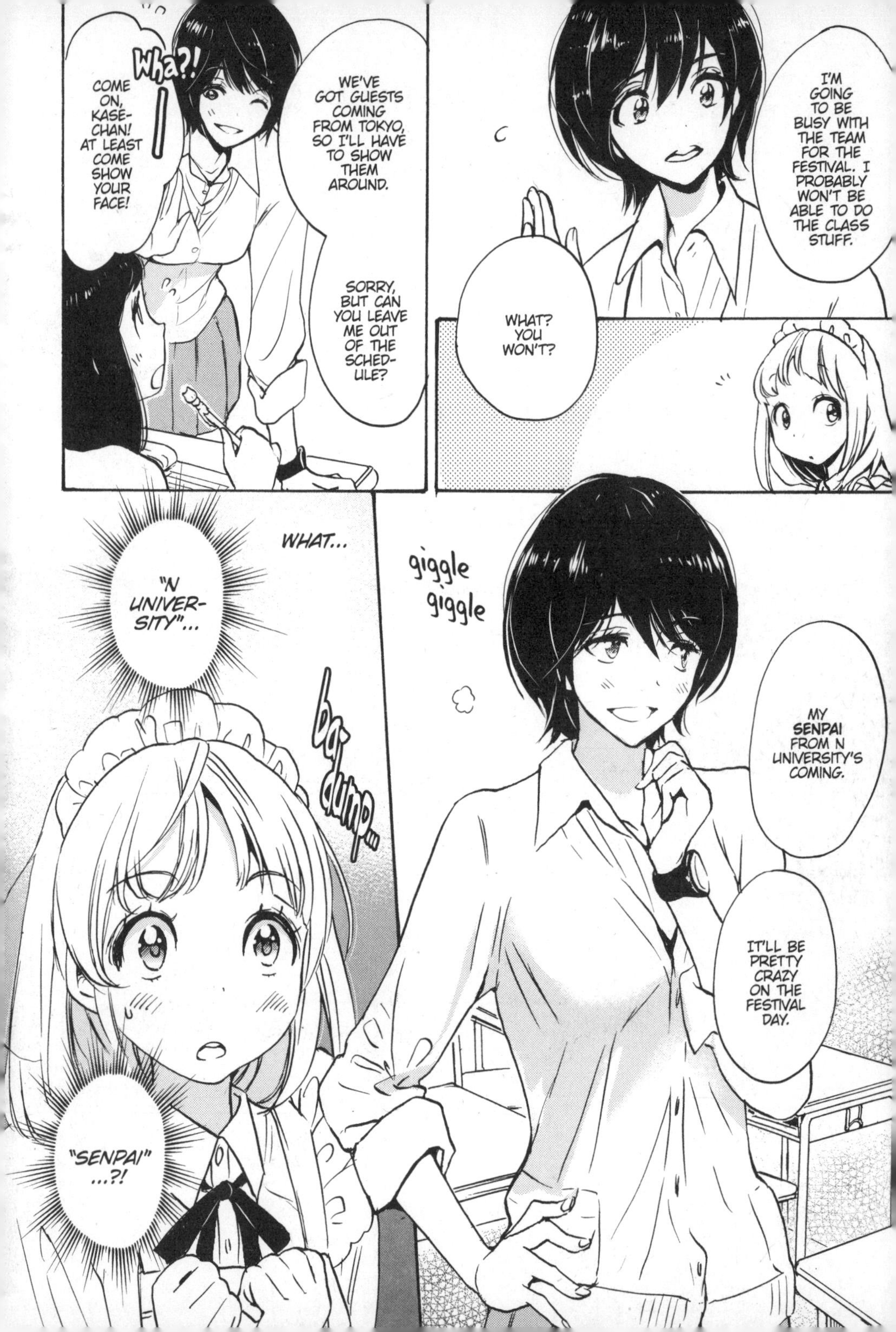

I'M GOING TO BE BUSY WITH THE TEAM FOR THE FESTIVAL. I PROBABLY WON'T BE ABLE TO DO THE CLASS STUFF.
WHAT? YOU WON'T?
SORRY, BUT CAN YOU LEAVE ME OUT OF THE SCHED-ULE?
WE'VE GOT GUESTS COMING FROM TOKYO, SO I'LL HAVE TO SHOW THEM AROUND.
COME ON, KASE-CHAN! AT LEAST COME SHOW YOUR FACE!
Wha?!
giggle giggle
MY SENPAI FROM N UNIVERSITY'S COMING.
IT'LL BE PRETTY CRAZY ON THE FESTIVAL DAY.
WHAT...
"N UNIVER-SITY"...
ba-dump...
"SENPAI" ...?!

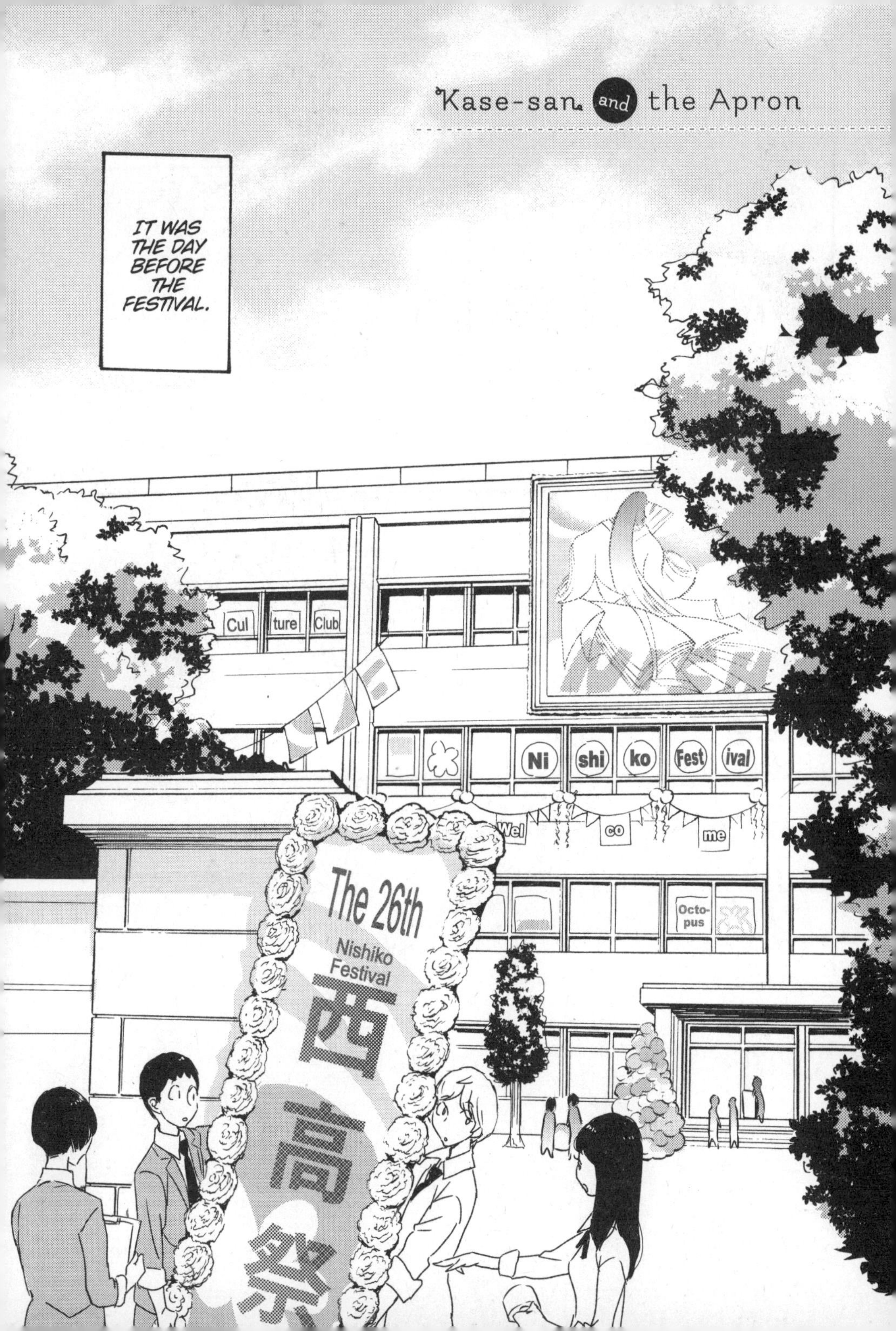
Kase-san and the Apron
IT WAS THE DAY BEFORE THE FESTIVAL.
Cul ture Club
Ni shi ko Fest ival
Wel co me
Octo-pus
The 26th
Nishiko Festival
西高祭

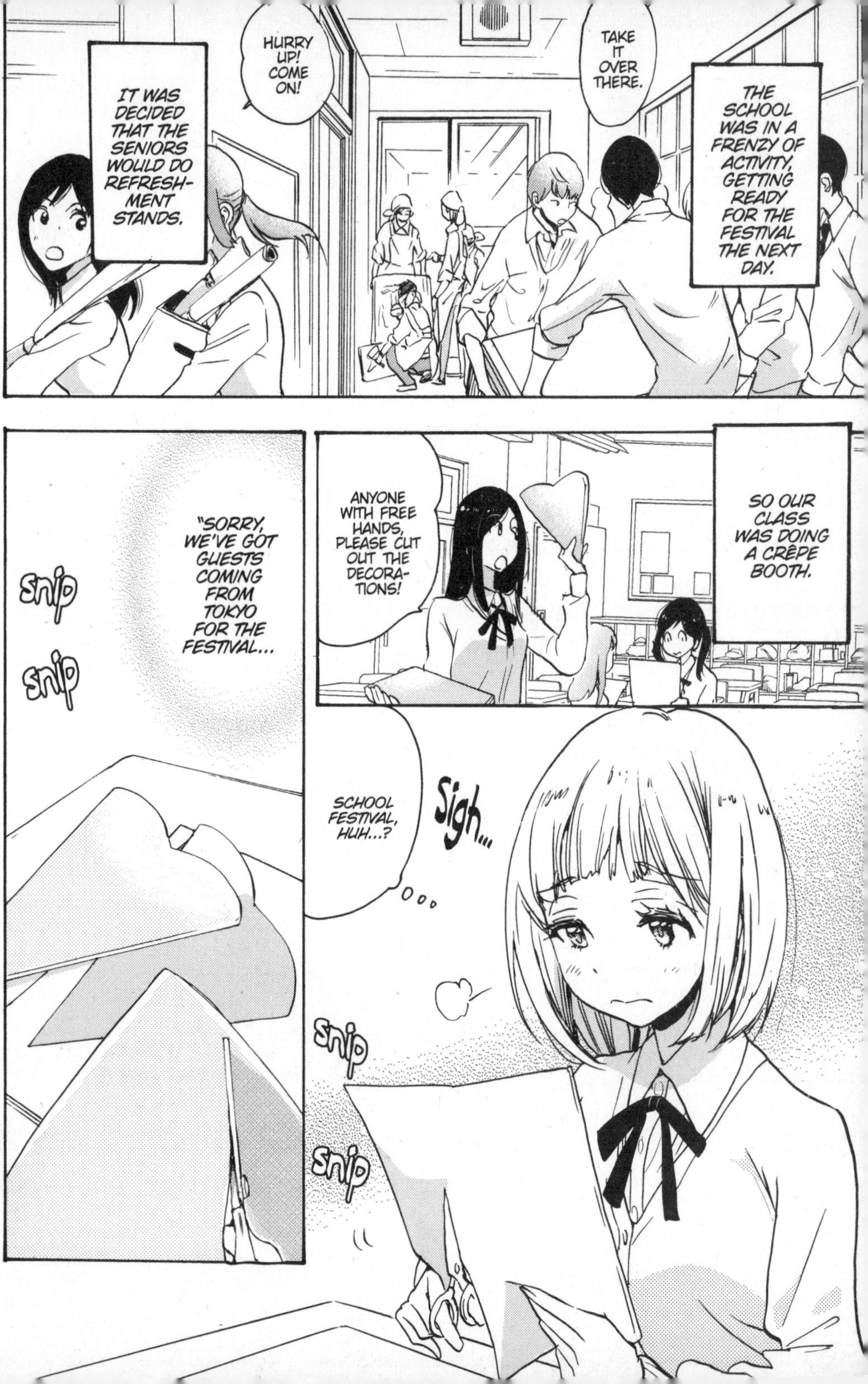
THE SCHOOL WAS IN A FRENZY OF ACTIVITY, GETTING READY FOR THE FESTIVAL THE NEXT DAY.
TAKE IT OVER THERE.
HURRY UP! COME ON!
IT WAS DECIDED THAT THE SENIORS WOULD DO REFRESHMENT STANDS.
SO OUR CLASS WAS DOING A CRÊPE BOOTH.
ANYONE WITH FREE HANDS, PLEASE CUT OUT THE DECORATIONS!
Sigh...
SCHOOL FESTIVAL, HUH...?
snip
snip
"SORRY, WE'VE GOT GUESTS COMING FROM TOKYO FOR THE FESTIVAL...
snip
snip

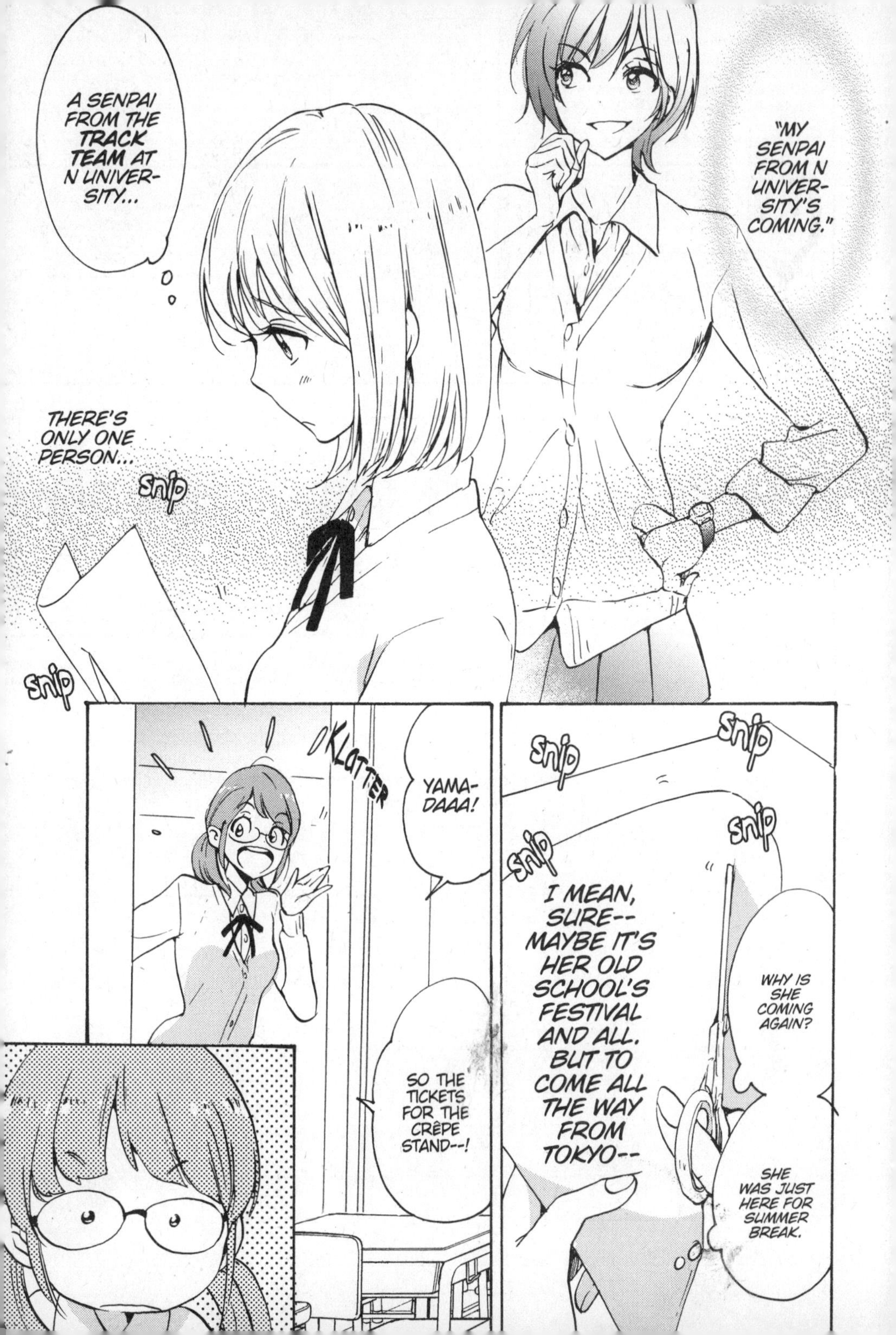
"MY SENPAI FROM N UNIVERSITY'S COMING."
A SENPAI FROM THE TRACK TEAM AT N UNIVERSITY...
THERE'S ONLY ONE PERSON...
snip
snip
snip
snip
snip
snip
WHY IS SHE COMING AGAIN?
SHE WAS JUST HERE FOR SUMMER BREAK.
I MEAN, SURE-- MAYBE IT'S HER OLD SCHOOL'S FESTIVAL AND ALL. BUT TO COME ALL THE WAY FROM TOKYO--
KLATTER
YAMADAAA!
SO THE TICKETS FOR THE CRÊPE STAND--!

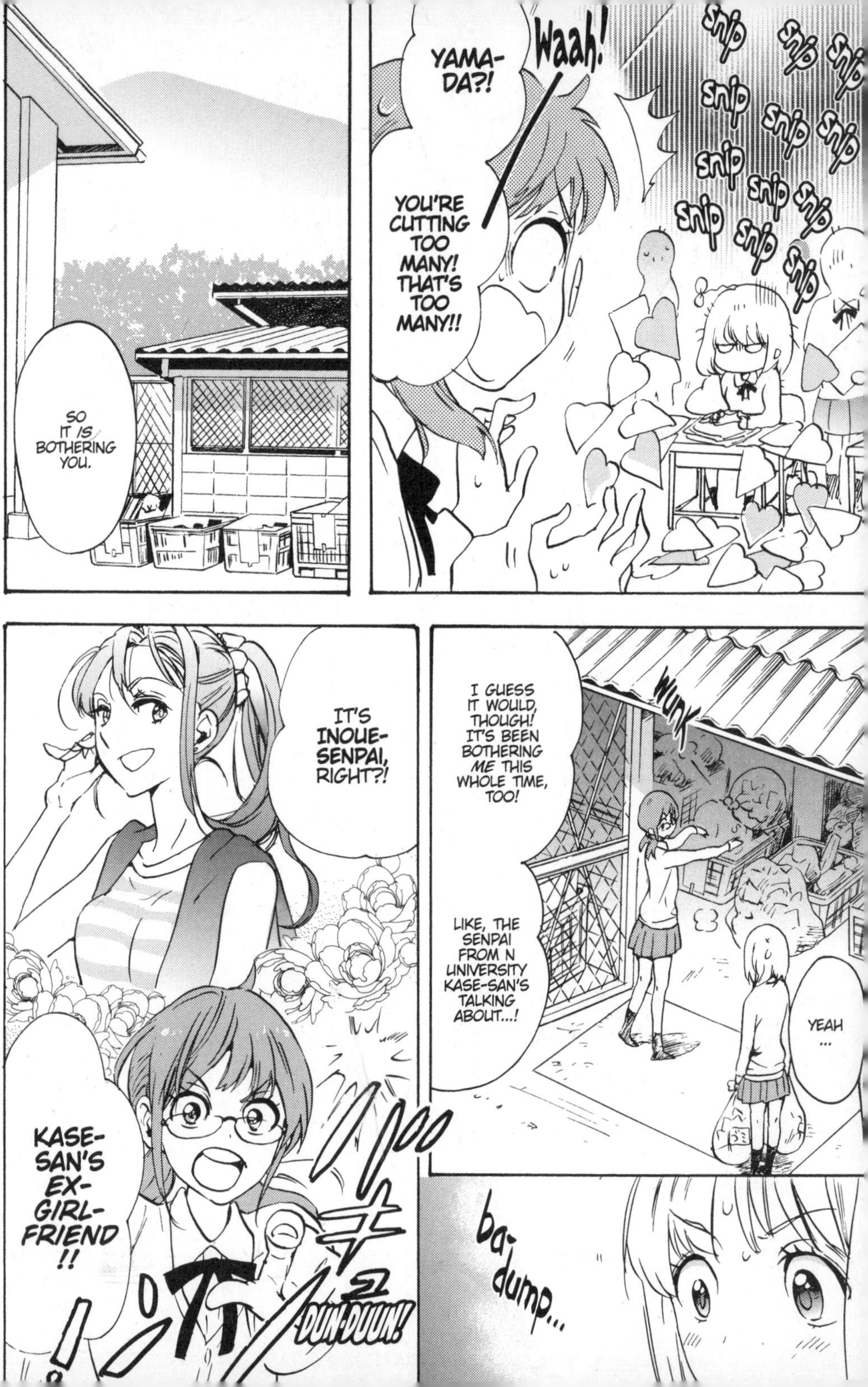
snip snip snip snip snip snip snip snip snip snip snip snip
Waah!
YAMA-DA?!
YOU'RE CUTTING TOO MANY! THAT'S TOO MANY!!
SO IT *IS* BOTHERING YOU.
I GUESS IT WOULD, THOUGH! IT'S BEEN BOTHERING *ME* THIS WHOLE TIME, TOO!
WUNK
LIKE, THE SENPAI FROM N UNIVERSITY KASE-SAN'S TALKING ABOUT...!
YEAH ...
ba-dump...
IT'S INOUE-SENPAI, RIGHT?!
KASE-SAN'S EX-GIRLFRIEND!!
DUN-DUUN!

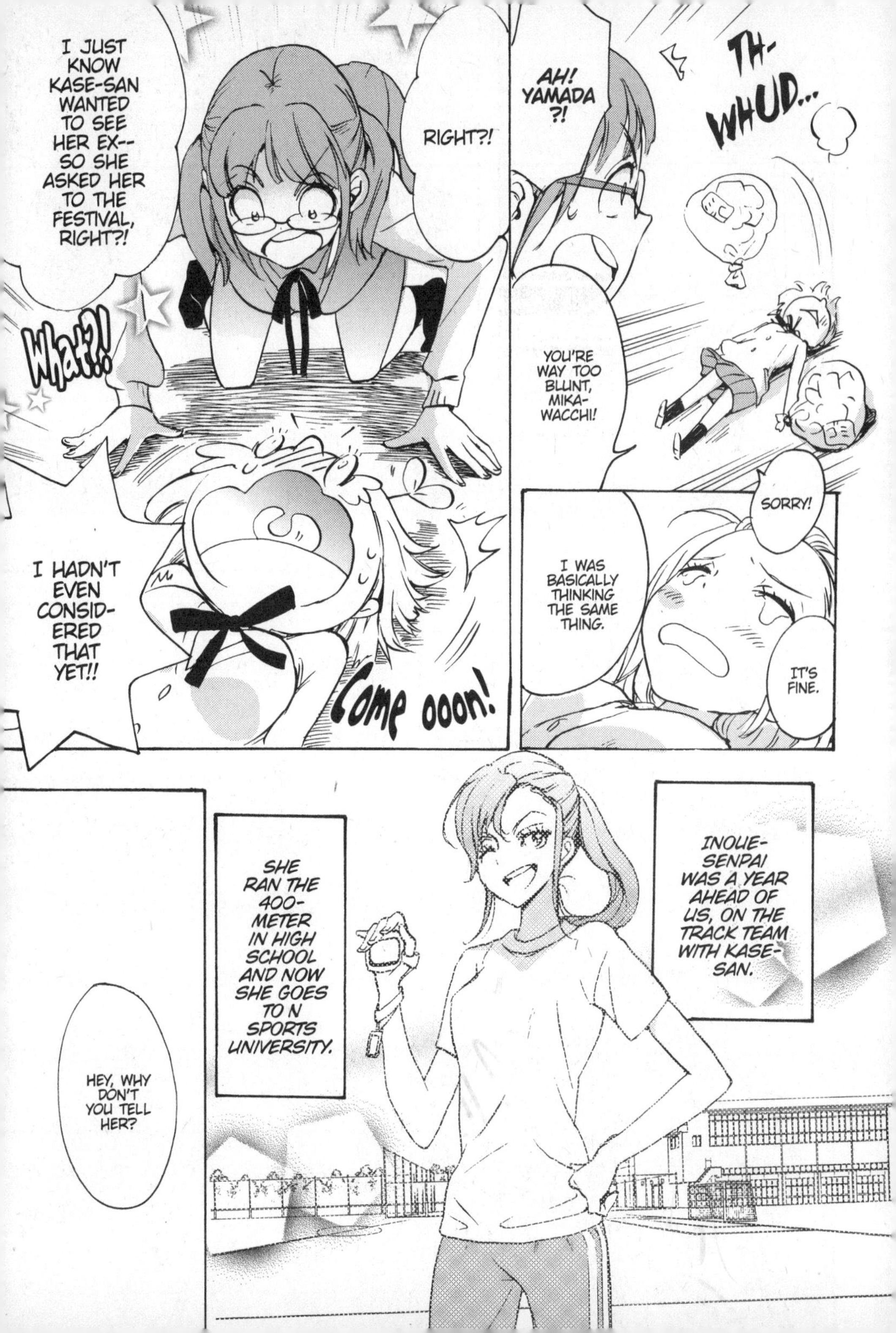

AH! YAMADA?!
TH-WHUD...
YOU'RE WAY TOO BLUNT, MIKA-WACCHI!
SORRY!
I WAS BASICALLY THINKING THE SAME THING.
IT'S FINE.
RIGHT?!
I JUST KNOW KASE-SAN WANTED TO SEE HER EX-- SO SHE ASKED HER TO THE FESTIVAL, RIGHT?!
What?!
Come ooon!
I HADN'T EVEN CONSIDERED THAT YET!!
INOUE-SENPAI WAS A YEAR AHEAD OF US, ON THE TRACK TEAM WITH KASE-SAN.
SHE RAN THE 400-METER IN HIGH SCHOOL AND NOW SHE GOES TO N SPORTS UNIVERSITY.
HEY, WHY DON'T YOU TELL HER?

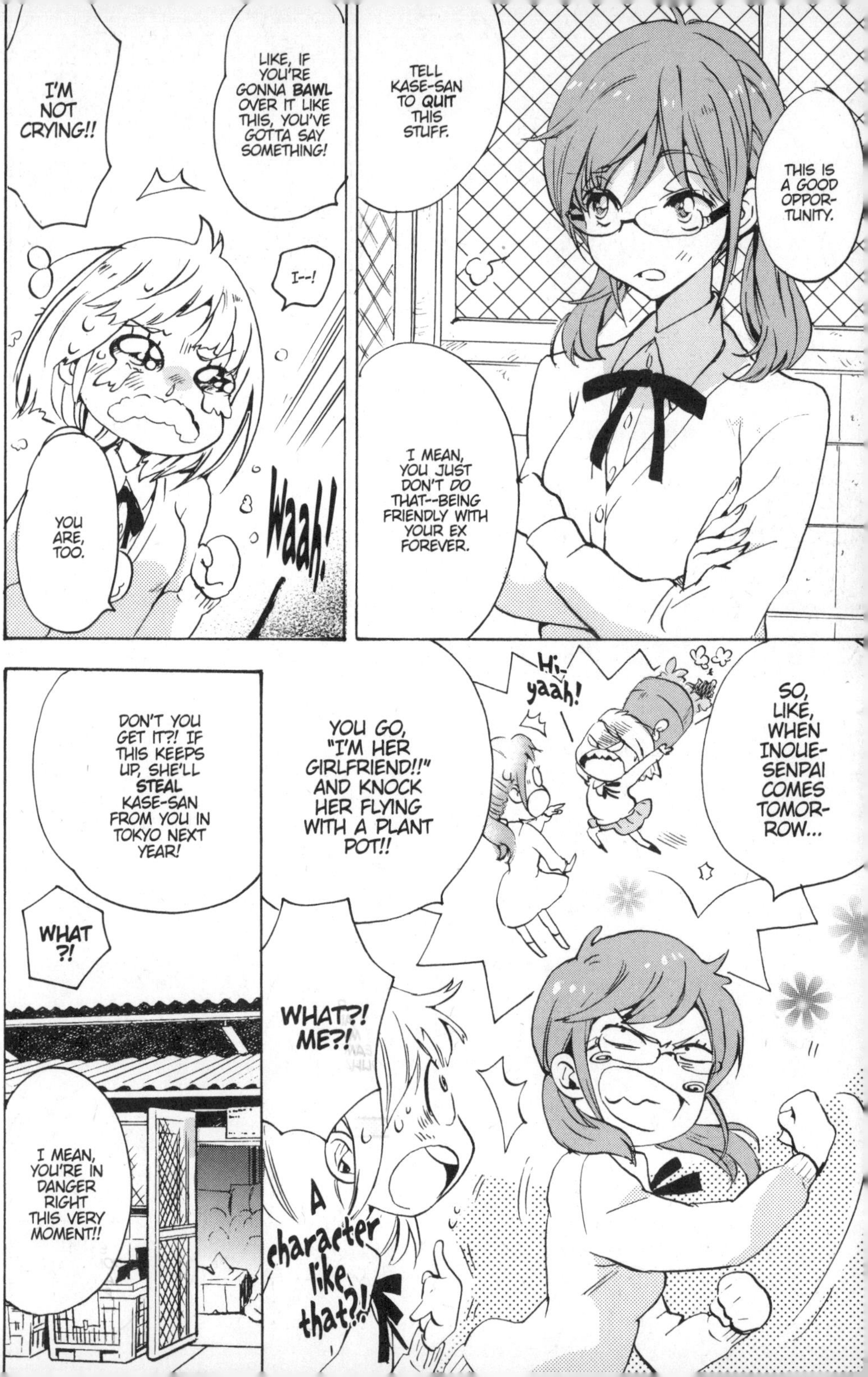
THIS IS A GOOD OPPORTUNITY.
TELL KASE-SAN TO QUIT THIS STUFF.
I MEAN, YOU JUST DON'T DO THAT--BEING FRIENDLY WITH YOUR EX FOREVER.
LIKE, IF YOU'RE GONNA BAWL OVER IT LIKE THIS, YOU'VE GOTTA SAY SOMETHING!
I'M NOT CRYING!!
I--!
Waah!
YOU ARE, TOO.
SO, LIKE, WHEN INOUE-SENPAI COMES TOMORROW...
Hi-yaah!
YOU GO, "I'M HER GIRLFRIEND!!" AND KNOCK HER FLYING WITH A PLANT POT!!
WHAT?! ME?!
A character like that?!
DON'T YOU GET IT?! IF THIS KEEPS UP, SHE'LL STEAL KASE-SAN FROM YOU IN TOKYO NEXT YEAR!
WHAT?!
I MEAN, YOU'RE IN DANGER RIGHT THIS VERY MOMENT!!

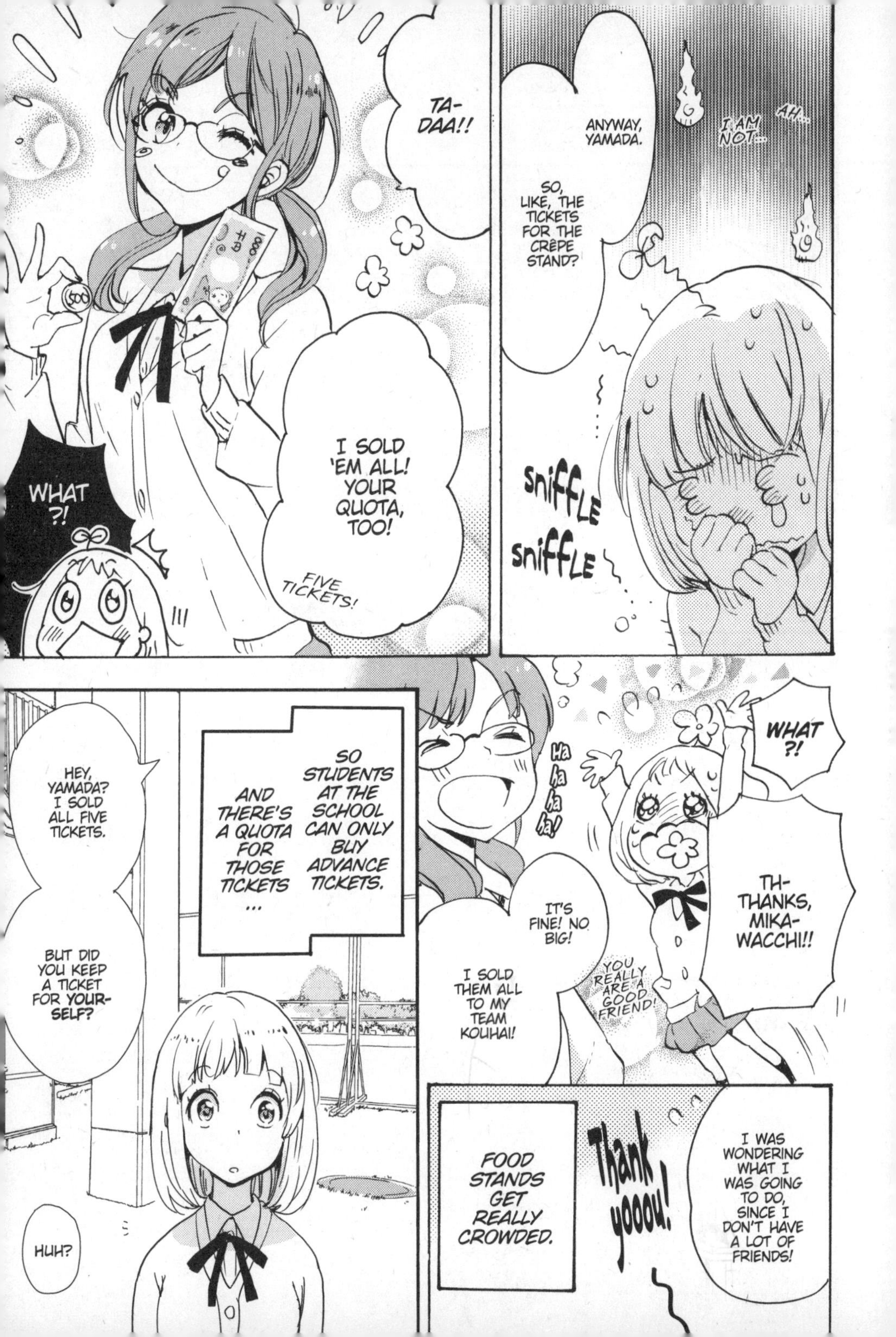
AH... I AM NOT...
ANYWAY, YAMADA.
SO, LIKE, THE TICKETS FOR THE CRÊPE STAND?
sniffLE sniffLE
TA-DAA!!
I SOLD 'EM ALL! YOUR QUOTA, TOO!
FIVE TICKETS!
WHAT ?!
WHAT ?!
TH-THANKS, MIKA-WACCHI!!
Ha ha ha ha ha!
IT'S FINE! NO BIG!
YOU REALLY ARE A GOOD FRIEND!
I SOLD THEM ALL TO MY TEAM KOUHAI!
I WAS WONDERING WHAT I WAS GOING TO DO, SINCE I DON'T HAVE A LOT OF FRIENDS!
Thank yooou!
FOOD STANDS GET REALLY CROWDED.
SO STUDENTS AT THE SCHOOL CAN ONLY BUY ADVANCE TICKETS.
AND THERE'S A QUOTA FOR THOSE TICKETS ...
HEY, YAMADA? I SOLD ALL FIVE TICKETS.
BUT DID YOU KEEP A TICKET FOR YOURSELF?
HUH?

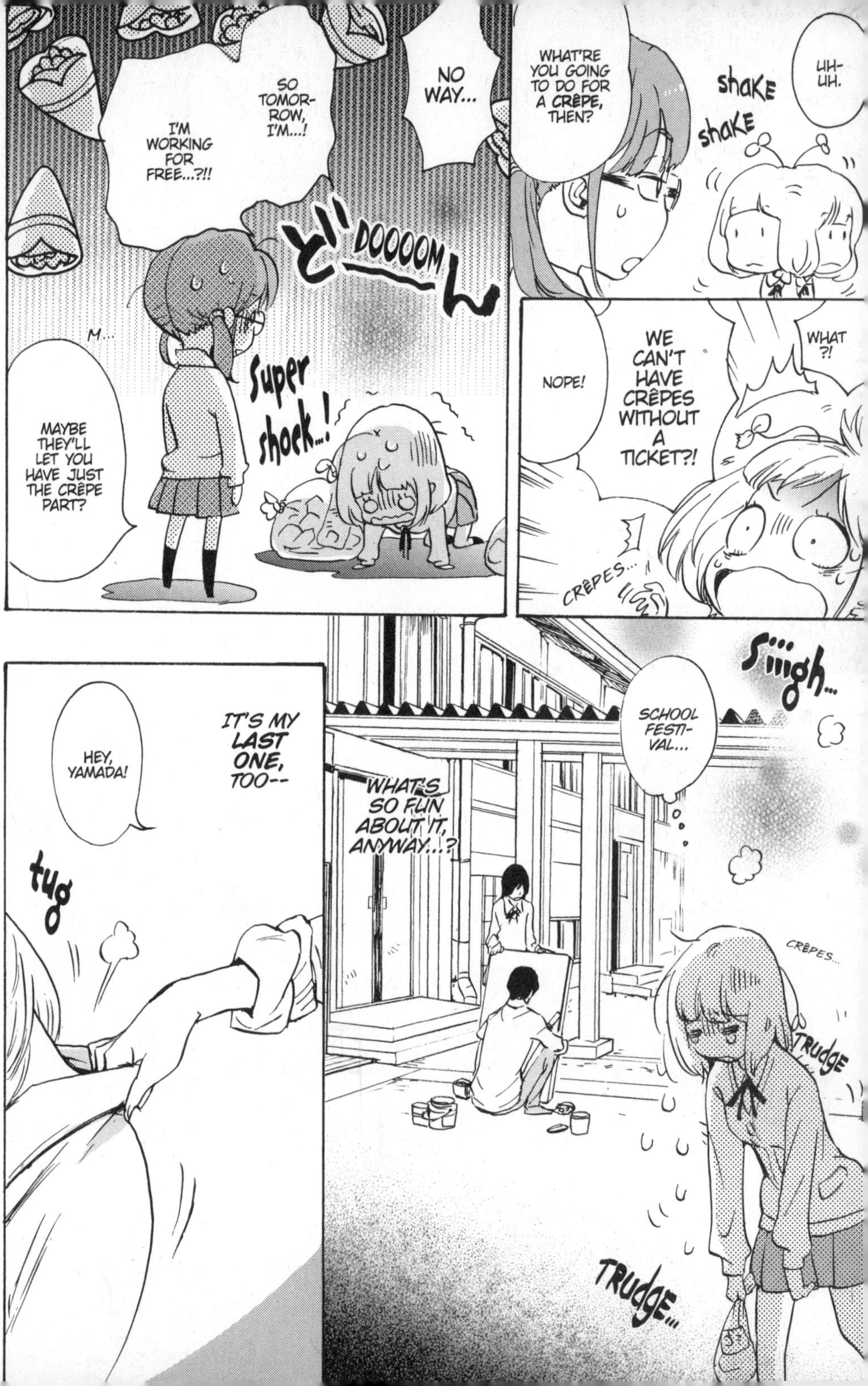

UH-UH.
shake
shake
WHAT'RE YOU GOING TO DO FOR A CRÊPE, THEN?
WHAT ?!
WE CAN'T HAVE CRÊPES WITHOUT A TICKET?!
NOPE!
CRÊPES...
NO WAY...
SO TOMORROW, I'M...!
I'M WORKING FOR FREE...?!!
DOOOOM
Super shock...!
M...
MAYBE THEY'LL LET YOU HAVE JUST THE CRÊPE PART?
Siiigh...
SCHOOL FESTIVAL...
WHAT'S SO FUN ABOUT IT, ANYWAY...?
CRÊPES...
TRUDGE
TRUDGE...
IT'S MY LAST ONE, TOO--
HEY, YAMADA!
tug

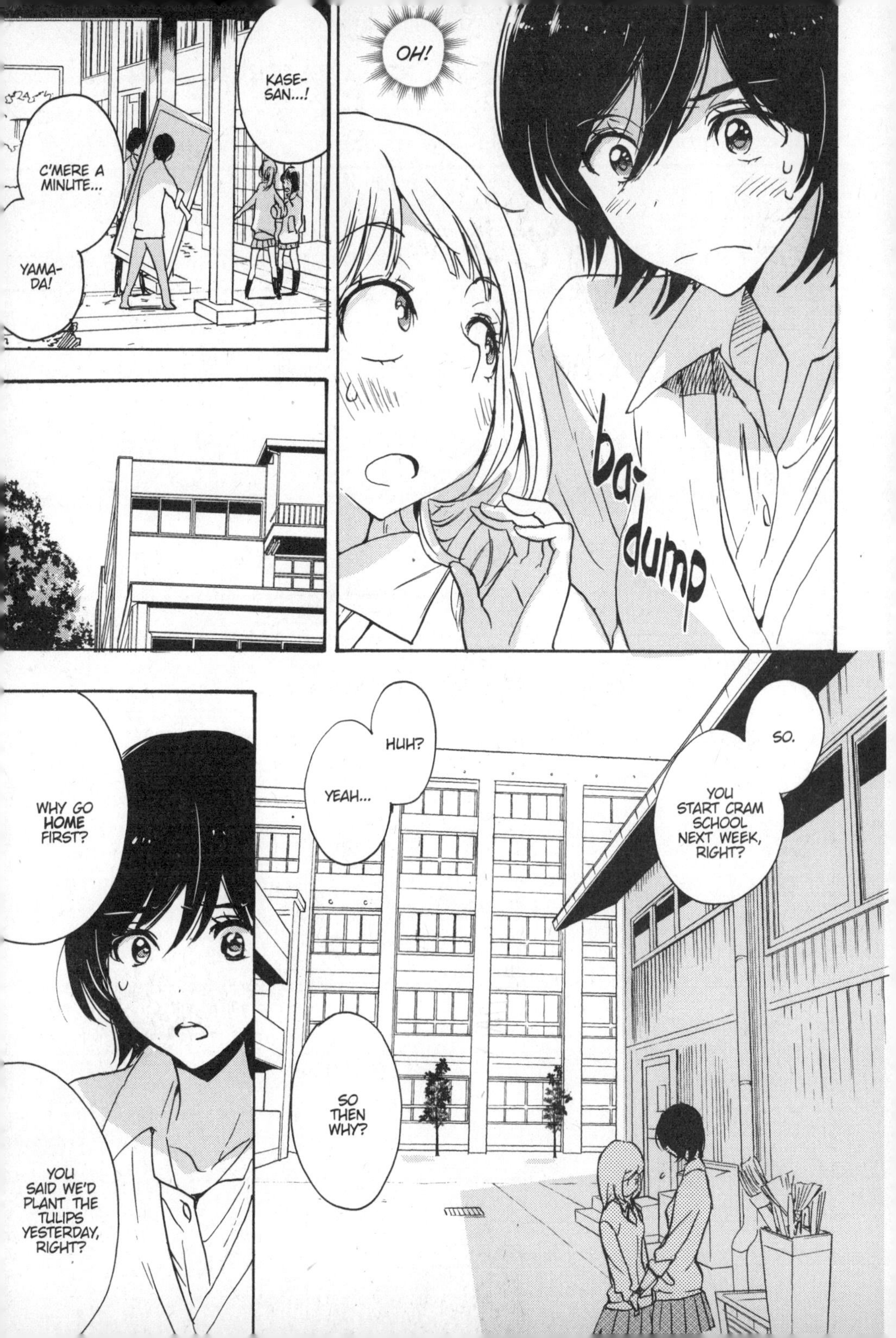
OH!
ba-dump
KASE-SAN...!
C'MERE A MINUTE...
YAMADA!
SO.
YOU START CRAM SCHOOL NEXT WEEK, RIGHT?
HUH?
YEAH...
SO THEN WHY?
WHY GO HOME FIRST?
YOU SAID WE'D PLANT THE TULIPS YESTERDAY, RIGHT?

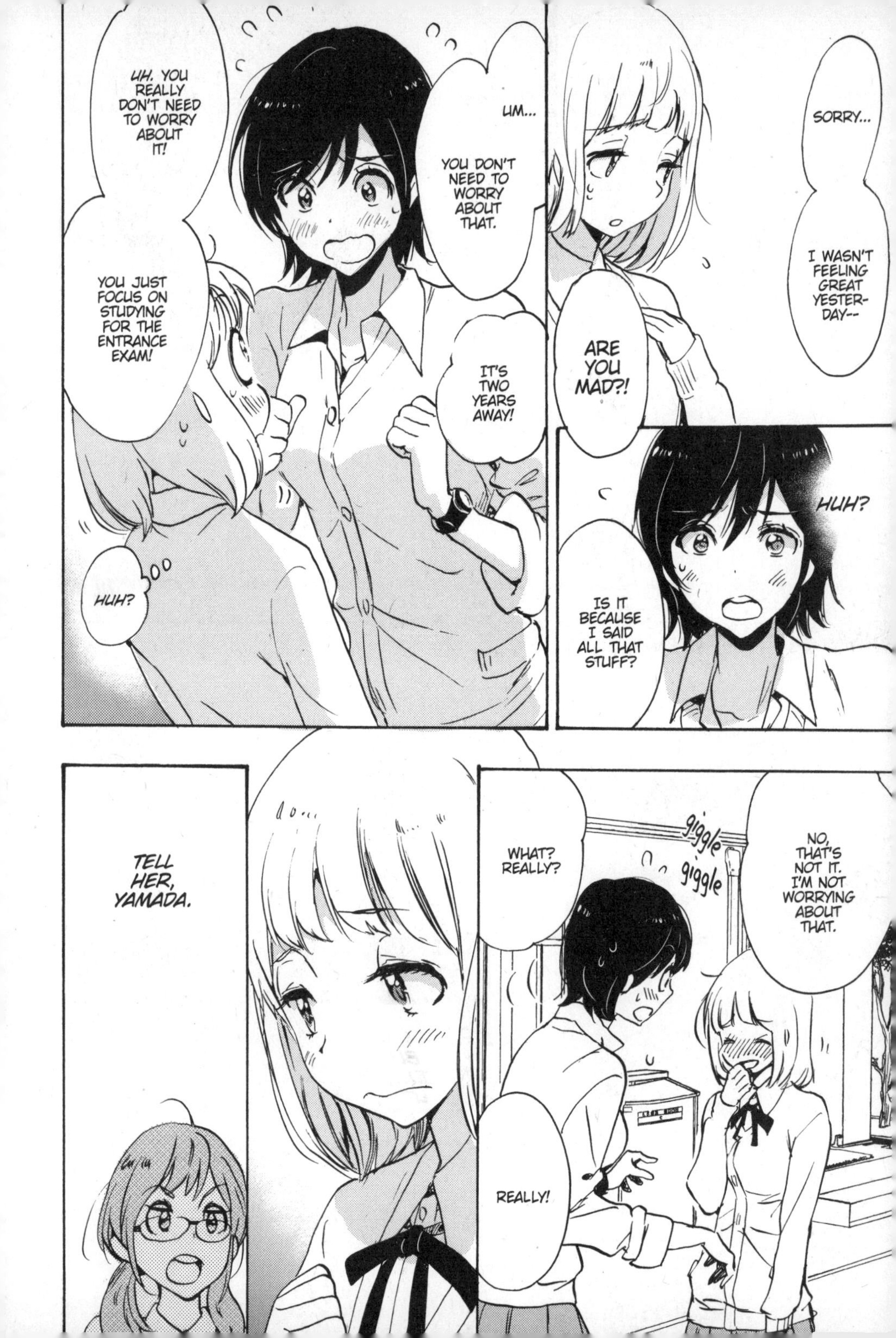
SORRY...
I WASN'T FEELING GREAT YESTER-DAY--
ARE YOU MAD?!
HUH?
IS IT BECAUSE I SAID ALL THAT STUFF?
UM...
YOU DON'T NEED TO WORRY ABOUT THAT.
IT'S TWO YEARS AWAY!
UH. YOU REALLY DON'T NEED TO WORRY ABOUT IT!
YOU JUST FOCUS ON STUDYING FOR THE ENTRANCE EXAM!
HUH?
NO, THAT'S NOT IT. I'M NOT WORRYING ABOUT THAT.
giggle
giggle
WHAT? REALLY?
REALLY!
TELL HER, YAMADA.

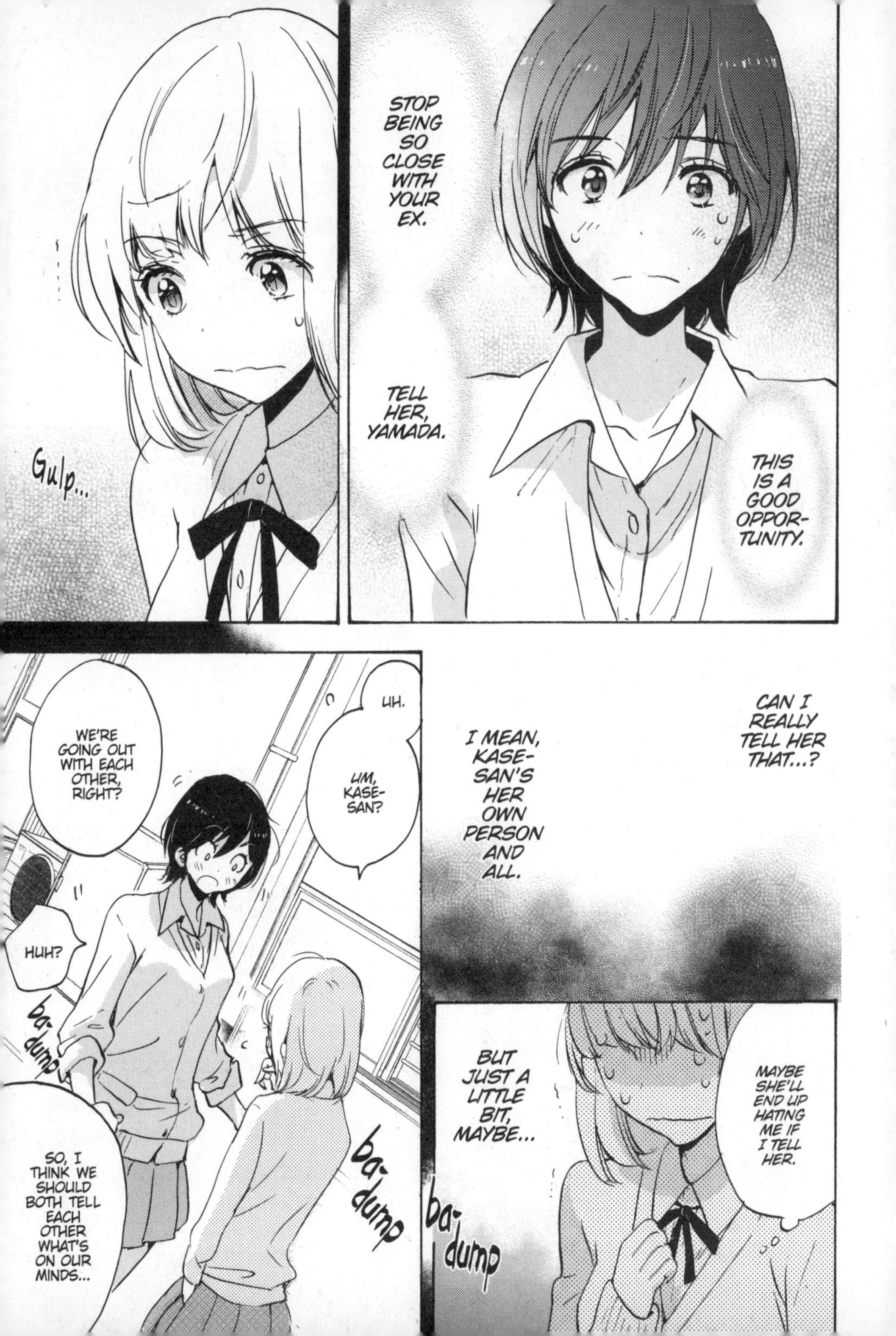
STOP BEING SO CLOSE WITH YOUR EX.
TELL HER, YAMADA.
THIS IS A GOOD OPPORTUNITY.
Gulp...
CAN I REALLY TELL HER THAT...?
I MEAN, KASE-SAN'S HER OWN PERSON AND ALL.
MAYBE SHE'LL END UP HATING ME IF I TELL HER.
BUT JUST A LITTLE BIT, MAYBE...
ba-dump
UH.
UM, KASE-SAN?
WE'RE GOING OUT WITH EACH OTHER, RIGHT?
HUH?
SO, I THINK WE SHOULD BOTH TELL EACH OTHER WHAT'S ON OUR MINDS...
ba-dump
ba-dump

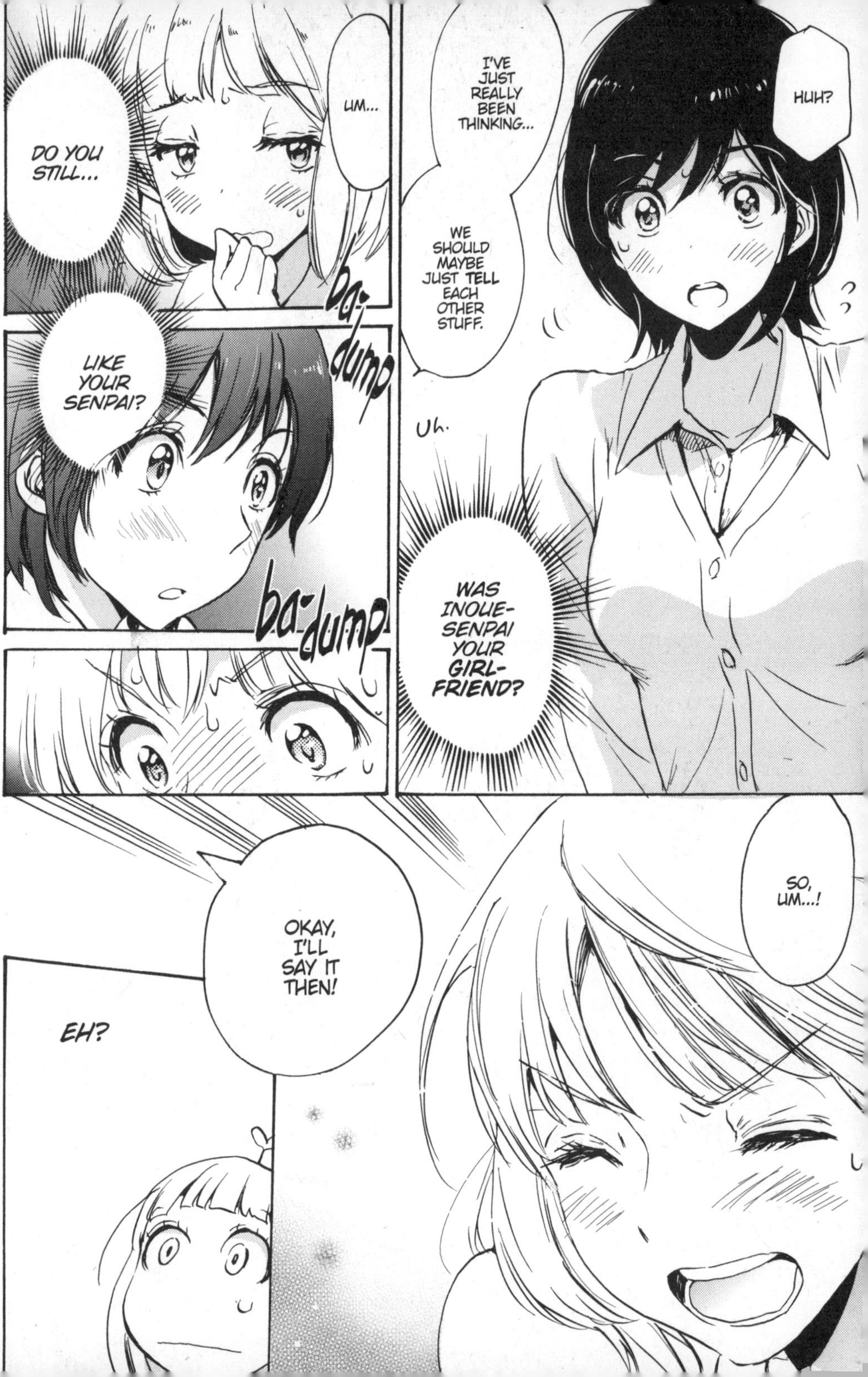
HUH?
I'VE JUST REALLY BEEN THINKING...
WE SHOULD MAYBE JUST TELL EACH OTHER STUFF.
Uh.
WAS INOUE-SENPAI YOUR GIRLFRIEND?
UM...
DO YOU STILL...
ba-dump
LIKE YOUR SENPAI?
ba-dump
SO, UM...!
OKAY, I'LL SAY IT THEN!
EH?

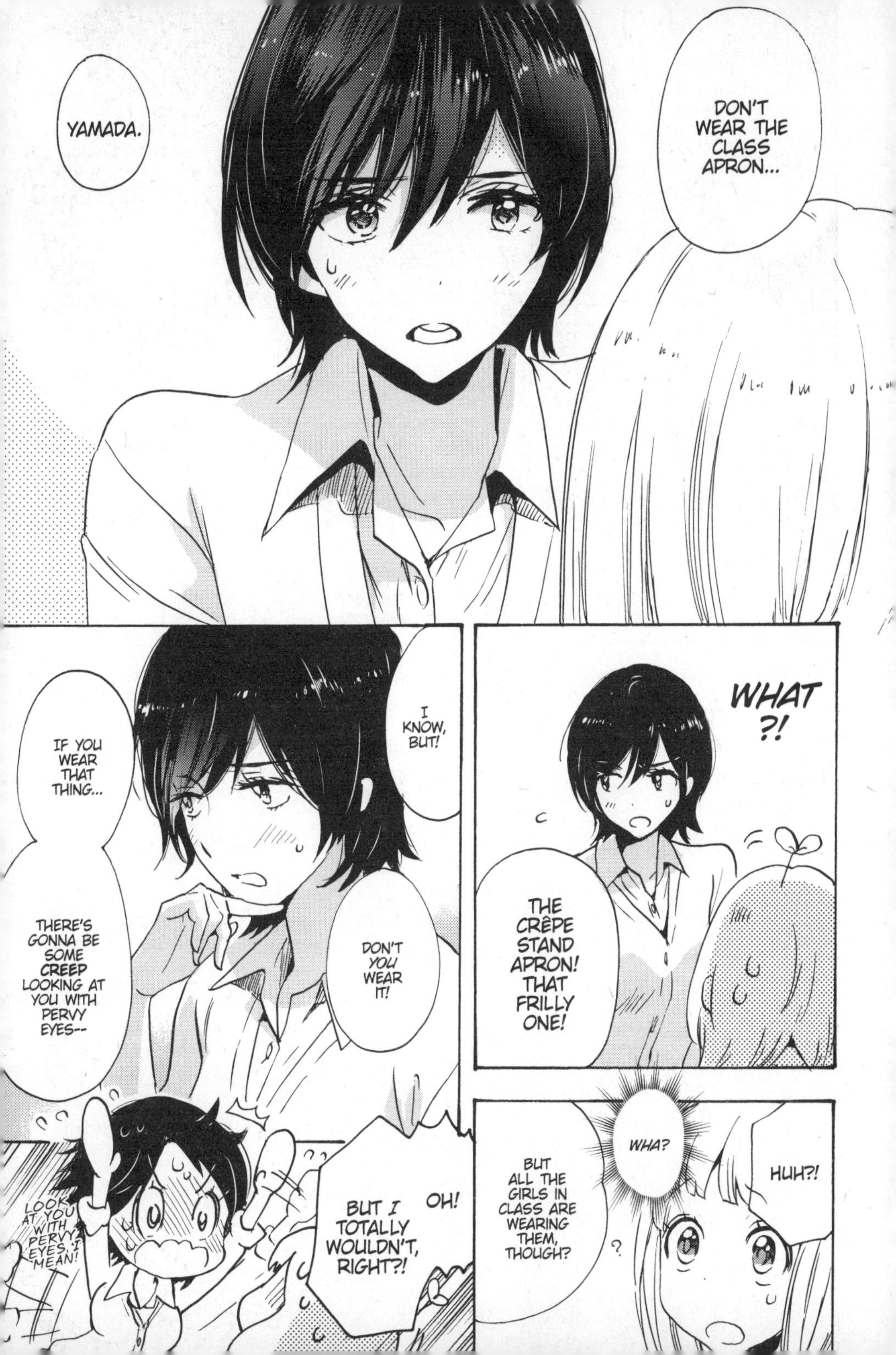
DON'T WEAR THE CLASS APRON...
YAMADA.
WHAT?!
THE CRÊPE STAND APRON! THAT FRILLY ONE!
HUH?!
WHA?
BUT ALL THE GIRLS IN CLASS ARE WEARING THEM, THOUGH?
I KNOW, BUT!
IF YOU WEAR THAT THING...
DON'T YOU WEAR IT!
THERE'S GONNA BE SOME CREEP LOOKING AT YOU WITH PERVY EYES--
OH!
BUT I TOTALLY WOULDN'T, RIGHT?!
LOOK AT YOU WITH PERVY EYES, I MEAN!

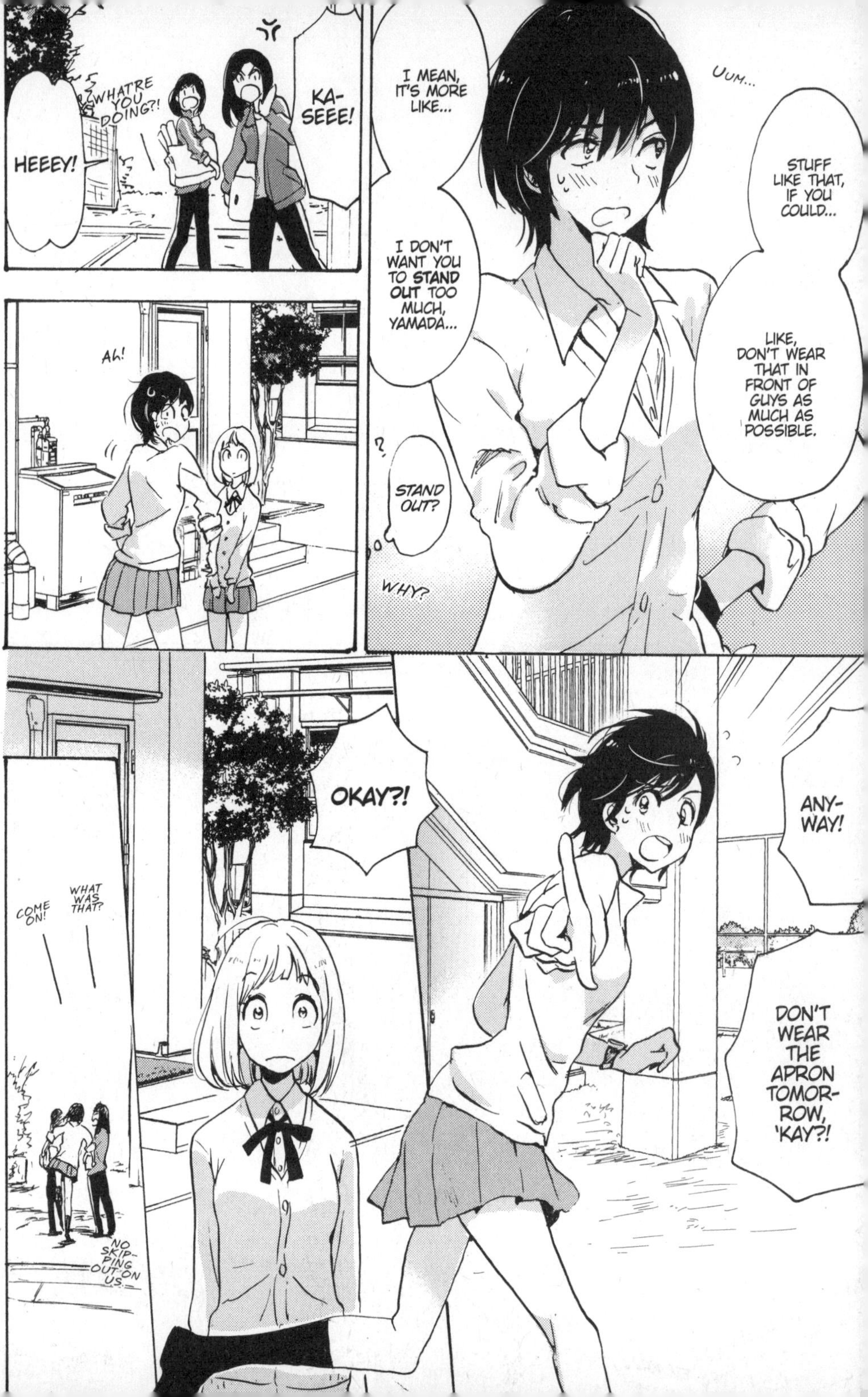
I MEAN, IT'S MORE LIKE...
I DON'T WANT YOU TO STAND OUT TOO MUCH, YAMADA...
STAND OUT?
WHY?
UUM...
LIKE, DON'T WEAR THAT IN FRONT OF GUYS AS MUCH AS POSSIBLE.
STUFF LIKE THAT, IF YOU COULD...
KA-SEEE!
WHAT'RE YOU DOING?!
HEEEY!
AH!
ANY-WAY!
DON'T WEAR THE APRON TOMOR-ROW, 'KAY?!
OKAY?!
WHAT WAS THAT?
COME ON!
NO SKIP-PING OUT ON US.

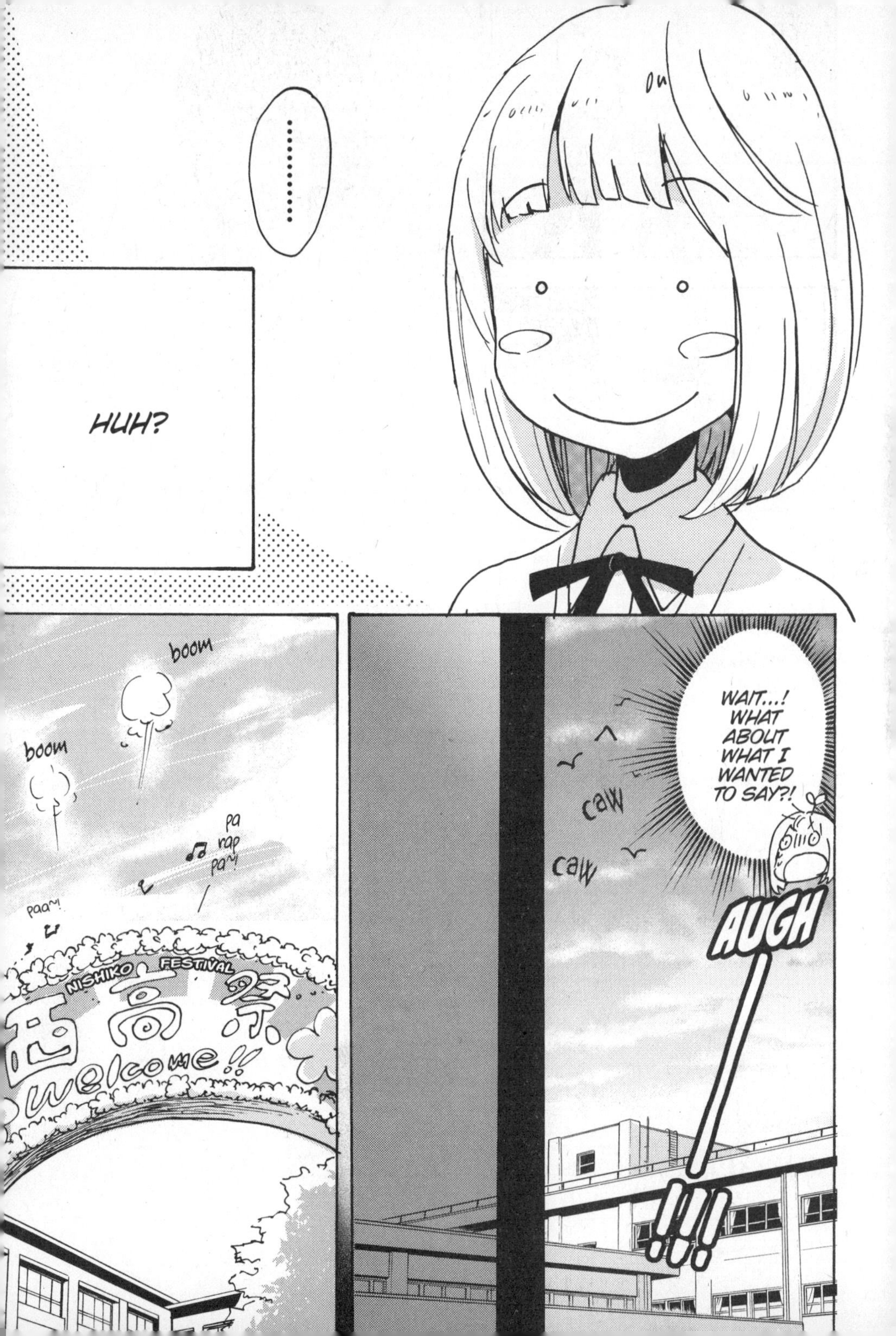
......
HUH?
WAIT...! WHAT ABOUT WHAT I WANTED TO SAY?!
caw
caw
AUGH
boom
boom
pa rap pa~!
paa~!
NISHIKO FESTIVAL
welcome!!

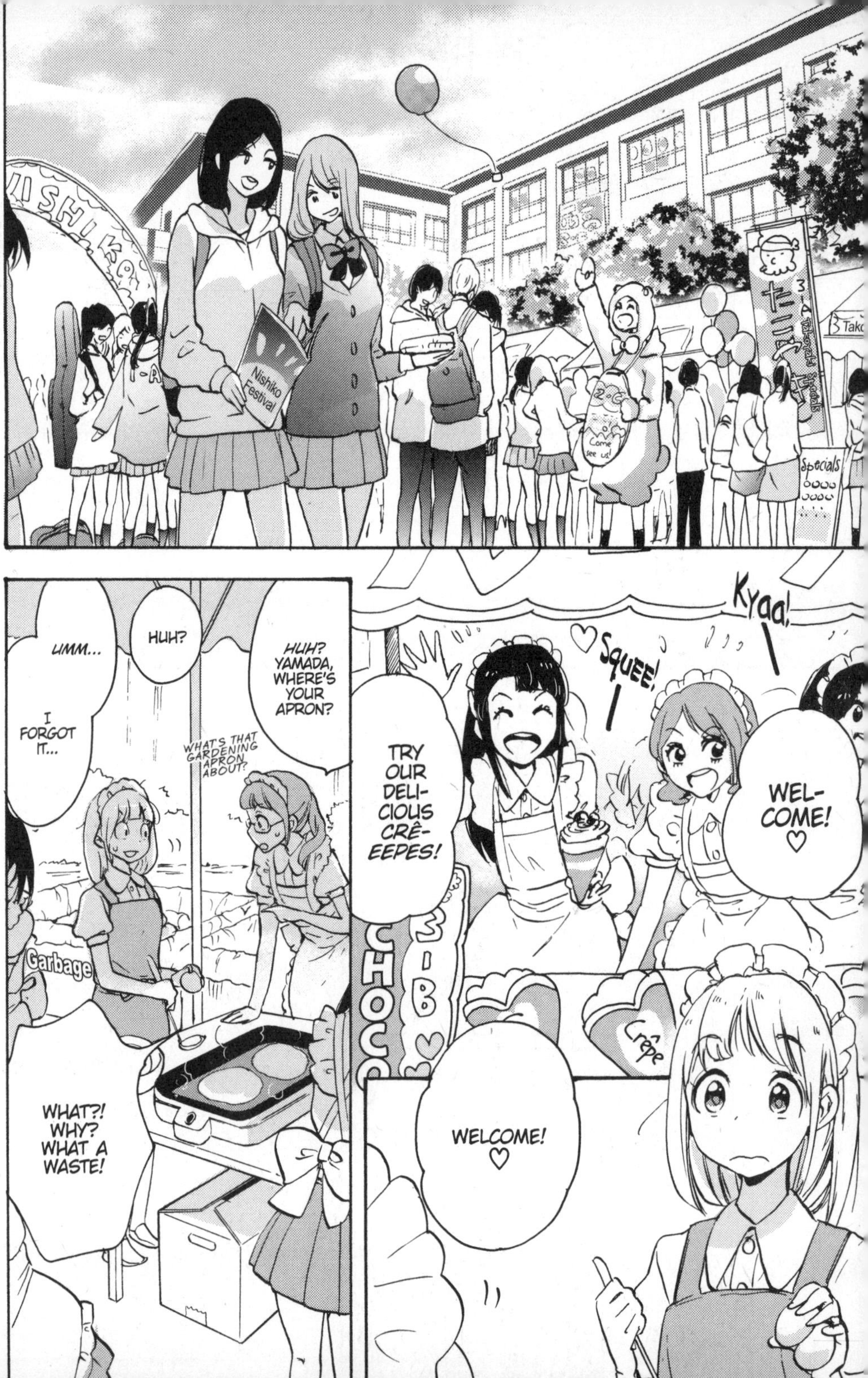
NISHIKO
Nishiko Festival
3-A Takoyaki Specials
3 Tako
Come see us!
Specials
Kyaa!
Squee!
WEL-COME! ♡
TRY OUR DELI-CIOUS CRÊ-EEPES!
CHOCO
Crêpe
WELCOME! ♡
HUH? YAMADA, WHERE'S YOUR APRON?
HUH?
UMM...
I FORGOT IT...
WHAT'S THAT GARDENING APRON ABOUT?
Garbage
WHAT?! WHY? WHAT A WASTE!

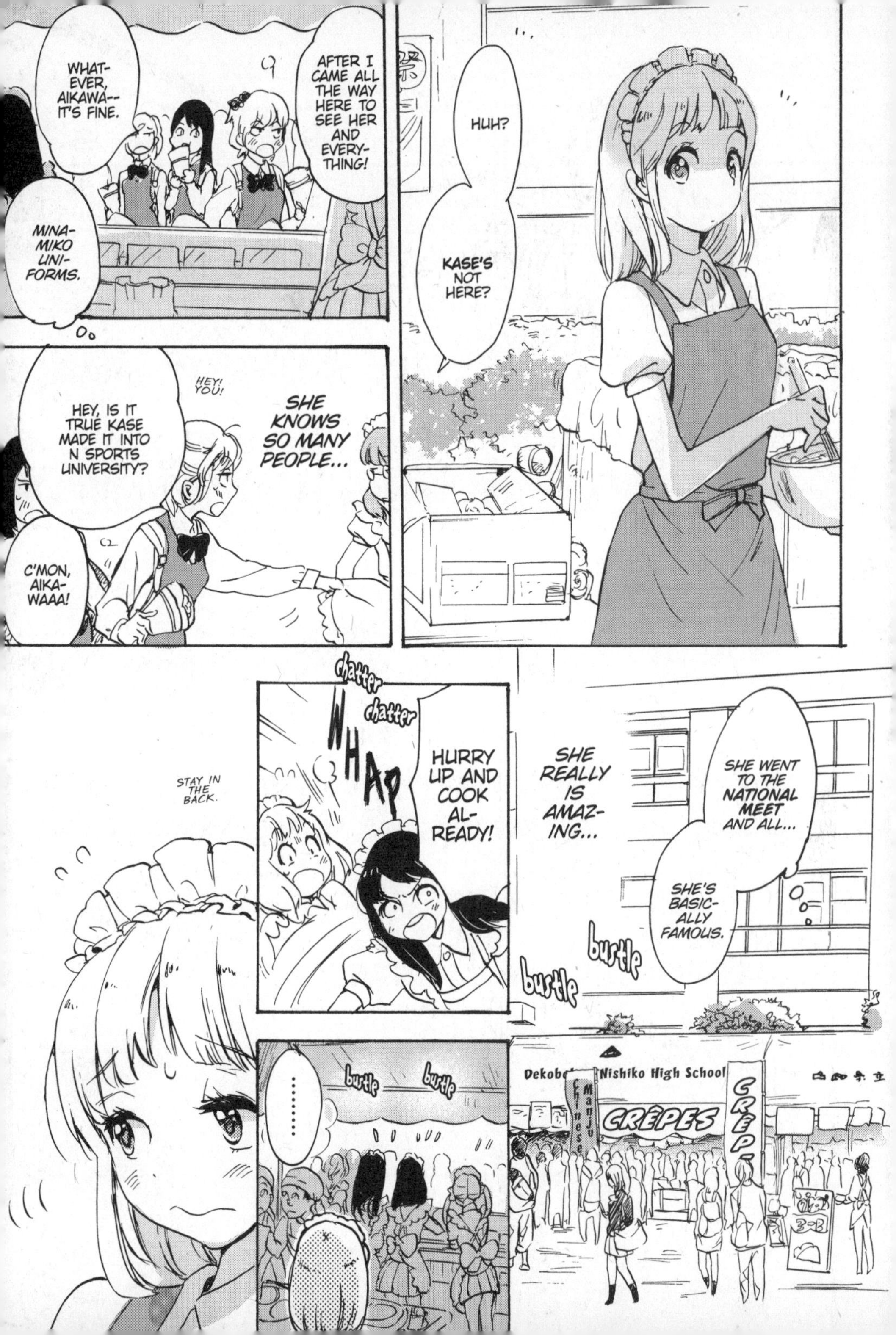
HUH?
KASE'S NOT HERE?
AFTER I CAME ALL THE WAY HERE TO SEE HER AND EVERYTHING!
WHATEVER, AIKAWA-- IT'S FINE.
MINAMIKO UNIFORMS.
SHE KNOWS SO MANY PEOPLE...
HEY! YOU!
HEY, IS IT TRUE KASE MADE IT INTO N SPORTS UNIVERSITY?
C'MON, AIKAWAAA!
SHE WENT TO THE NATIONAL MEET AND ALL...
SHE'S BASICALLY FAMOUS.
SHE REALLY IS AMAZING...
bustle
bustle
chatter
chatter
WHAP
HURRY UP AND COOK ALREADY!
STAY IN THE BACK.
......
bustle
bustle
Nishiko High School
Chinese Manju
CRÊPES
CRÊP-
3-B

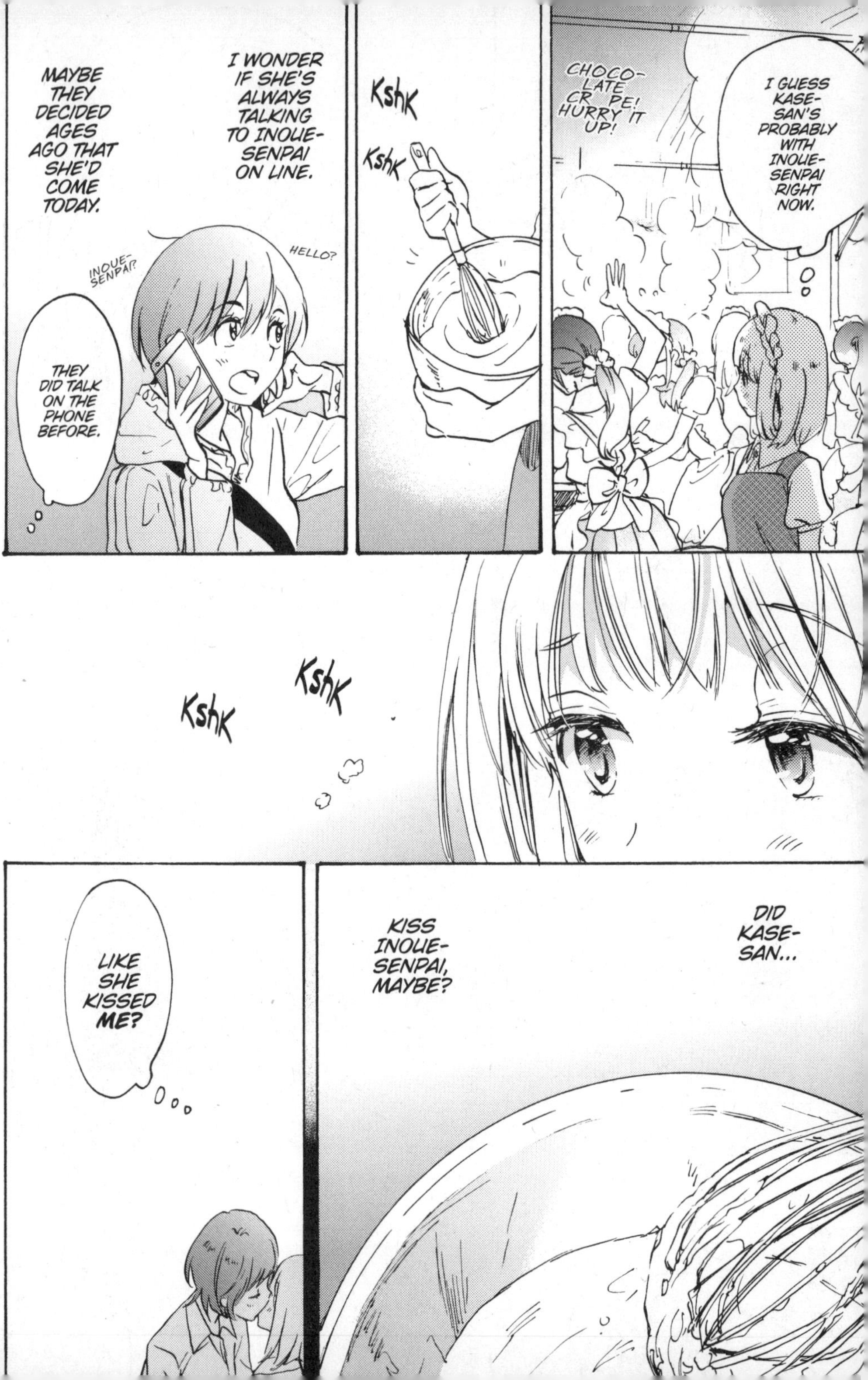
I GUESS KASE-SAN'S PROBABLY WITH INOUE-SENPAI RIGHT NOW.
CHOCO-LATE CR PE! HURRY IT UP!
Kshk
Kshk
I WONDER IF SHE'S ALWAYS TALKING TO INOUE-SENPAI ON LINE.
MAYBE THEY DECIDED AGES AGO THAT SHE'D COME TODAY.
HELLO?
INOUE-SENPAI!?
THEY DID TALK ON THE PHONE BEFORE.
Kshk
Kshk
DID KASE-SAN...
KISS INOUE-SENPAI, MAYBE?
LIKE SHE KISSED ME?

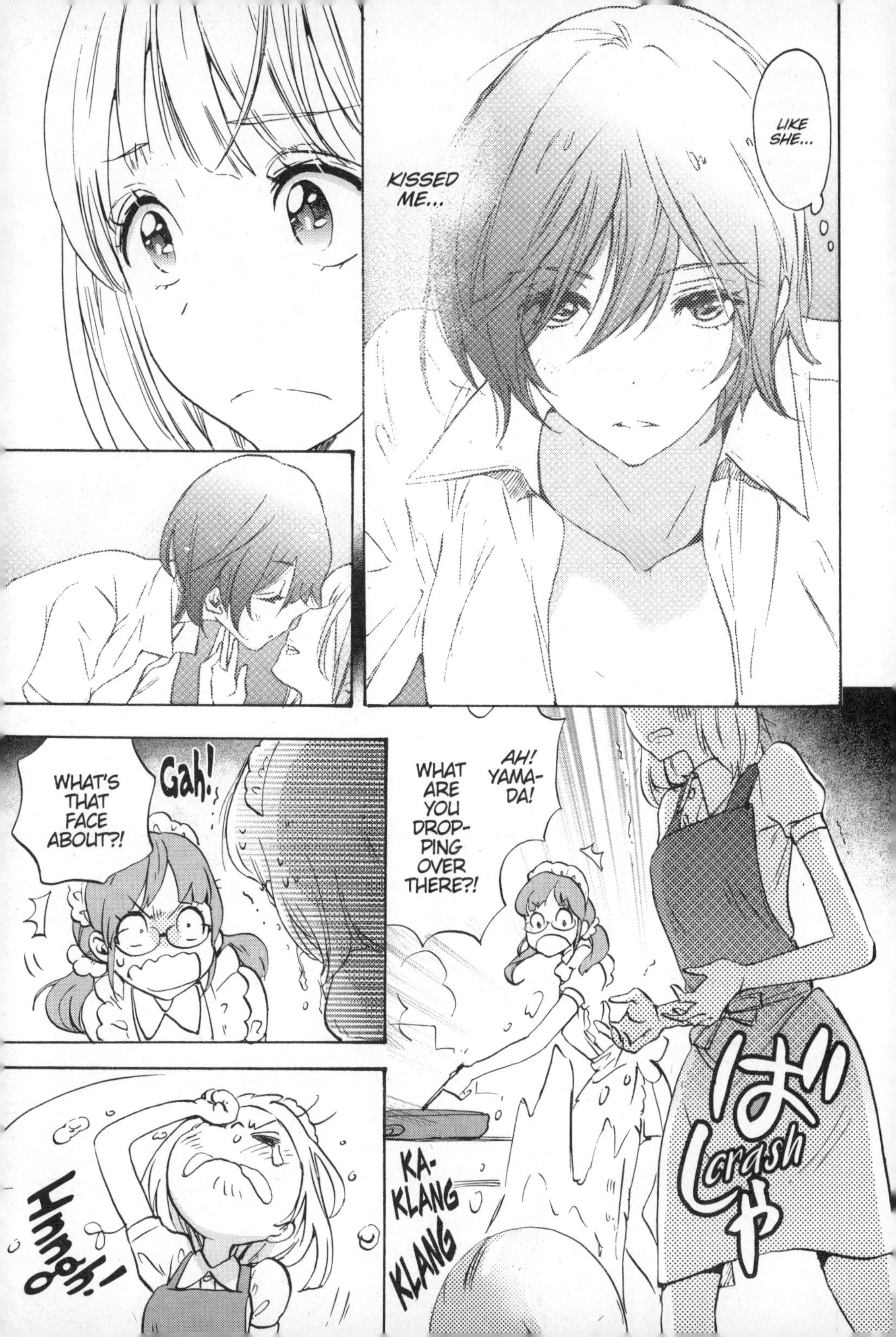
LIKE SHE...
KISSED ME...
AH! YAMA-DA!
WHAT ARE YOU DROP-PING OVER THERE?!
crash
KA-KLANG KLANG
WHAT'S THAT FACE ABOUT?!
Gah!
Hnngh!

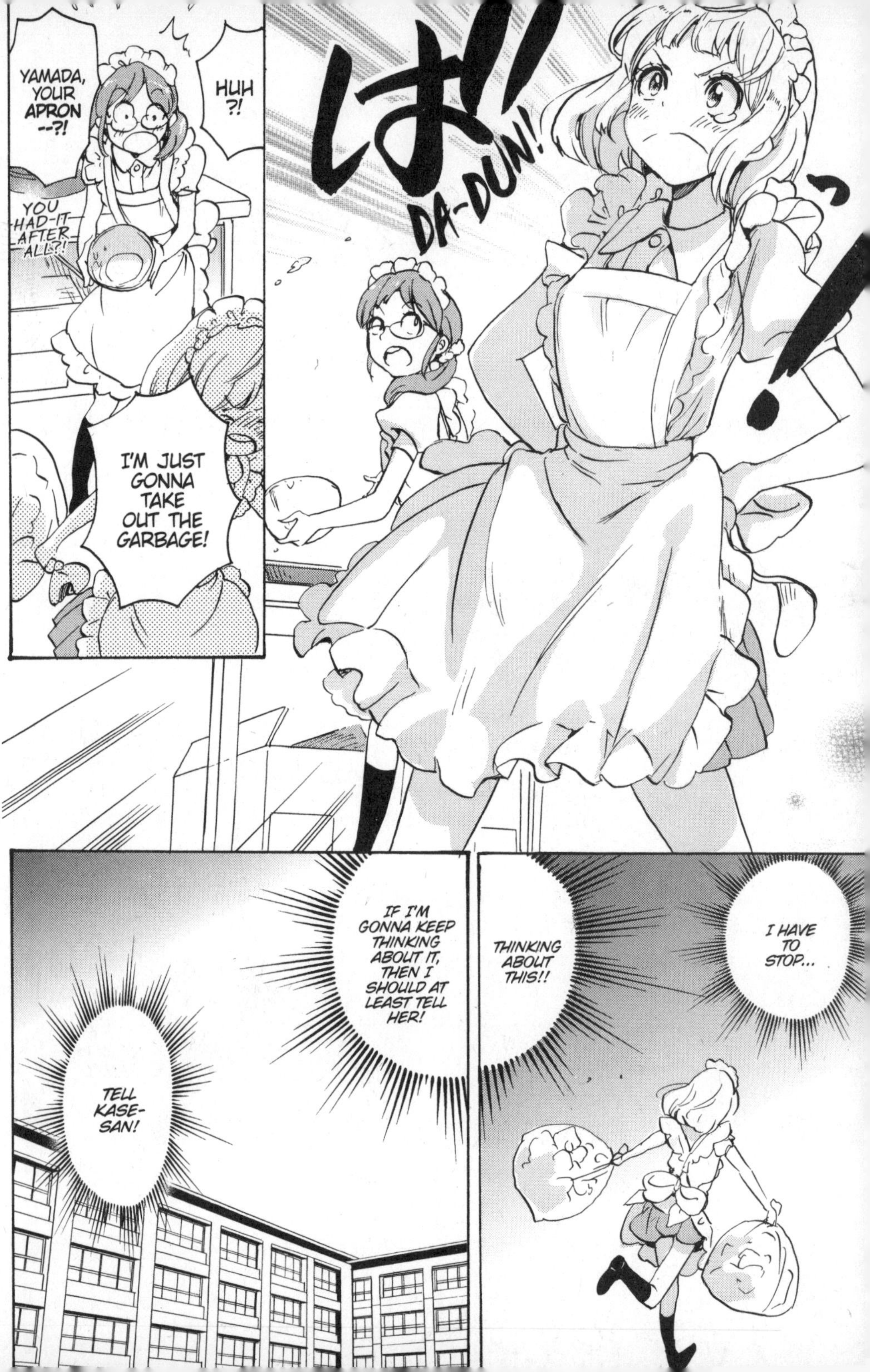

は!
DA-DUN!
YAMADA, YOUR APRON --?!
HUH ?!
YOU HAD IT AFTER ALL?!
I'M JUST GONNA TAKE OUT THE GARBAGE!
I HAVE TO STOP...
THINKING ABOUT THIS!!
IF I'M GONNA KEEP THINKING ABOUT IT, THEN I SHOULD AT LEAST TELL HER!
TELL KASE-SAN!

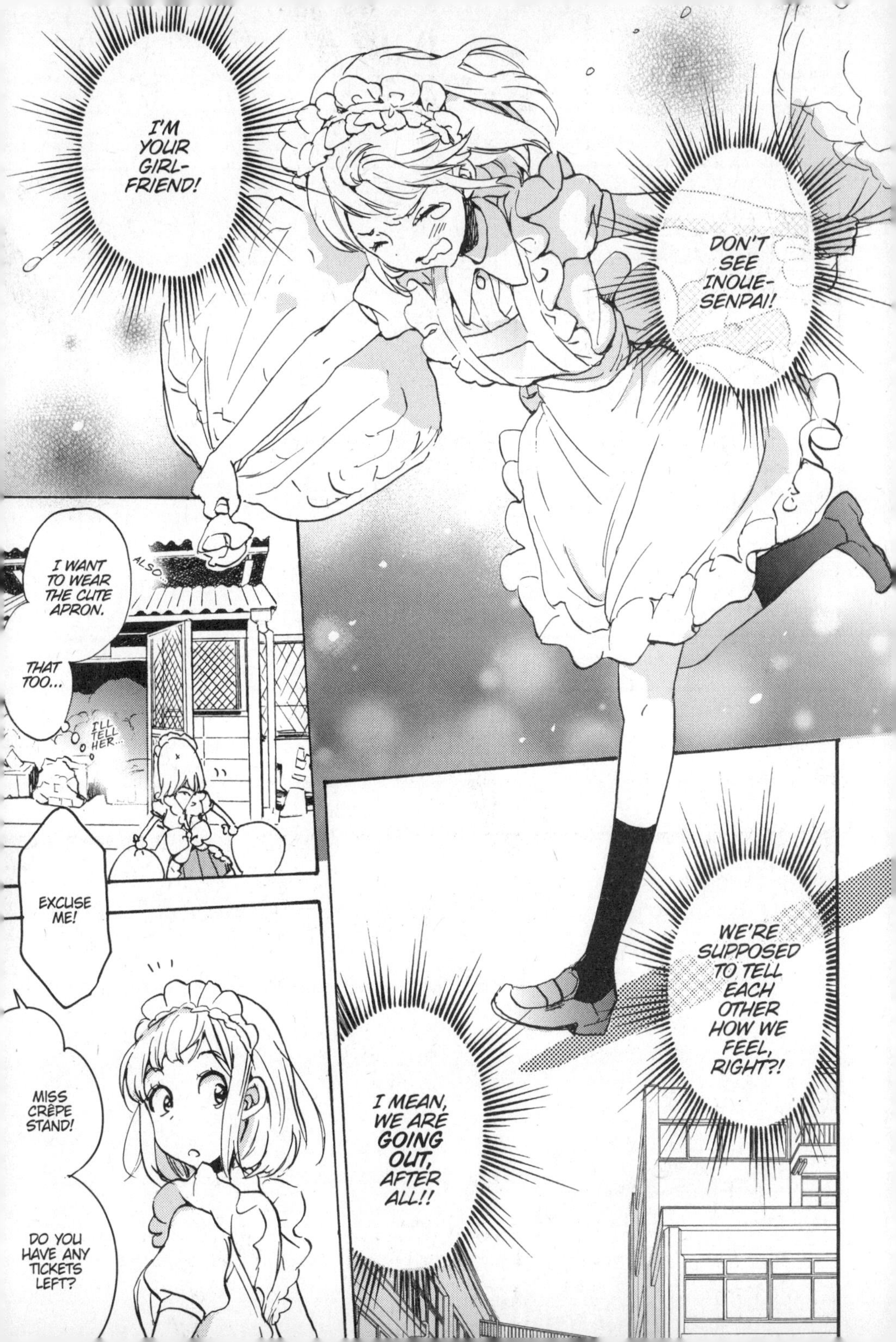
DON'T SEE INOUE-SENPAI!
I'M YOUR GIRL-FRIEND!
WE'RE SUPPOSED TO TELL EACH OTHER HOW WE FEEL, RIGHT?!
I MEAN, WE ARE GOING OUT, AFTER ALL!!
ALSO
I WANT TO WEAR THE CUTE APRON.
THAT TOO...
I'LL TELL HER...
EXCUSE ME!
MISS CRÊPE STAND!
DO YOU HAVE ANY TICKETS LEFT?

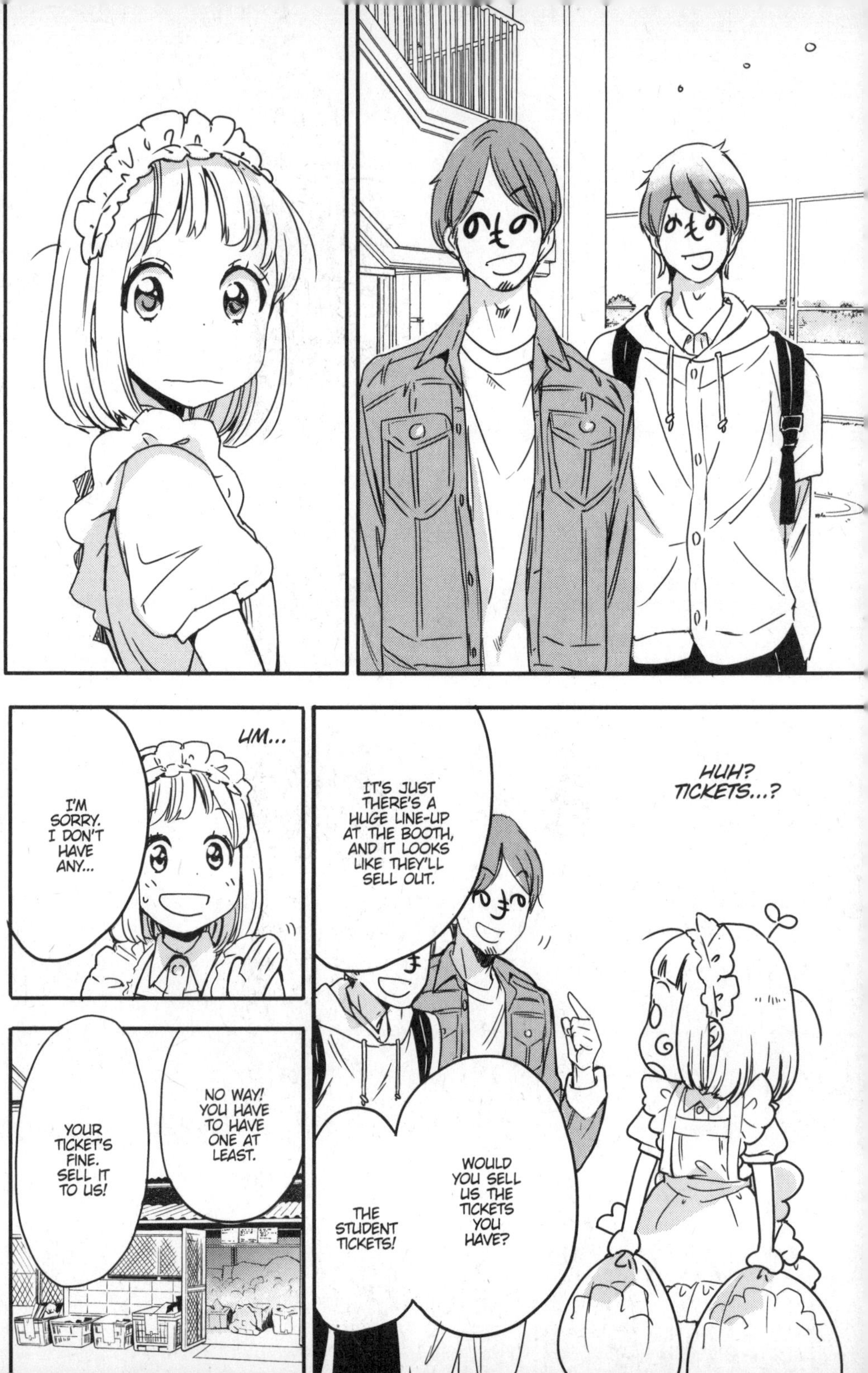
HUH? TICKETS...?
IT'S JUST THERE'S A HUGE LINE-UP AT THE BOOTH, AND IT LOOKS LIKE THEY'LL SELL OUT.
WOULD YOU SELL US THE TICKETS YOU HAVE?
THE STUDENT TICKETS!
UM...
I'M SORRY. I DON'T HAVE ANY...
NO WAY! YOU HAVE TO HAVE ONE AT LEAST.
YOUR TICKET'S FINE. SELL IT TO US!

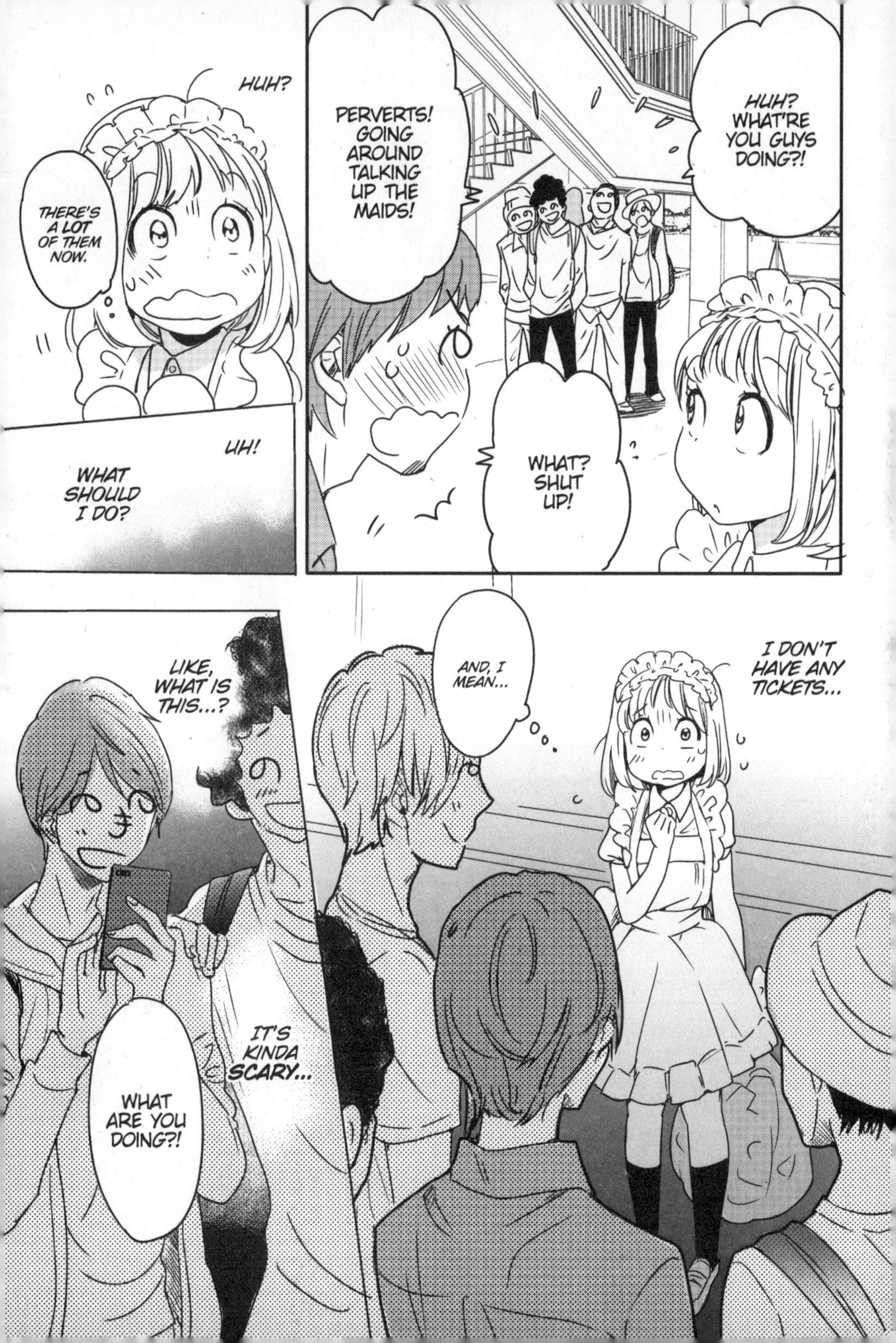
HUH? WHAT'RE YOU GUYS DOING?!
PERVERTS! GOING AROUND TALKING UP THE MAIDS!
WHAT? SHUT UP!
HUH?
THERE'S A LOT OF THEM NOW.
UH!
WHAT SHOULD I DO?
I DON'T HAVE ANY TICKETS...
AND, I MEAN...
LIKE, WHAT IS THIS...?
IT'S KINDA SCARY...
WHAT ARE YOU DOING?!

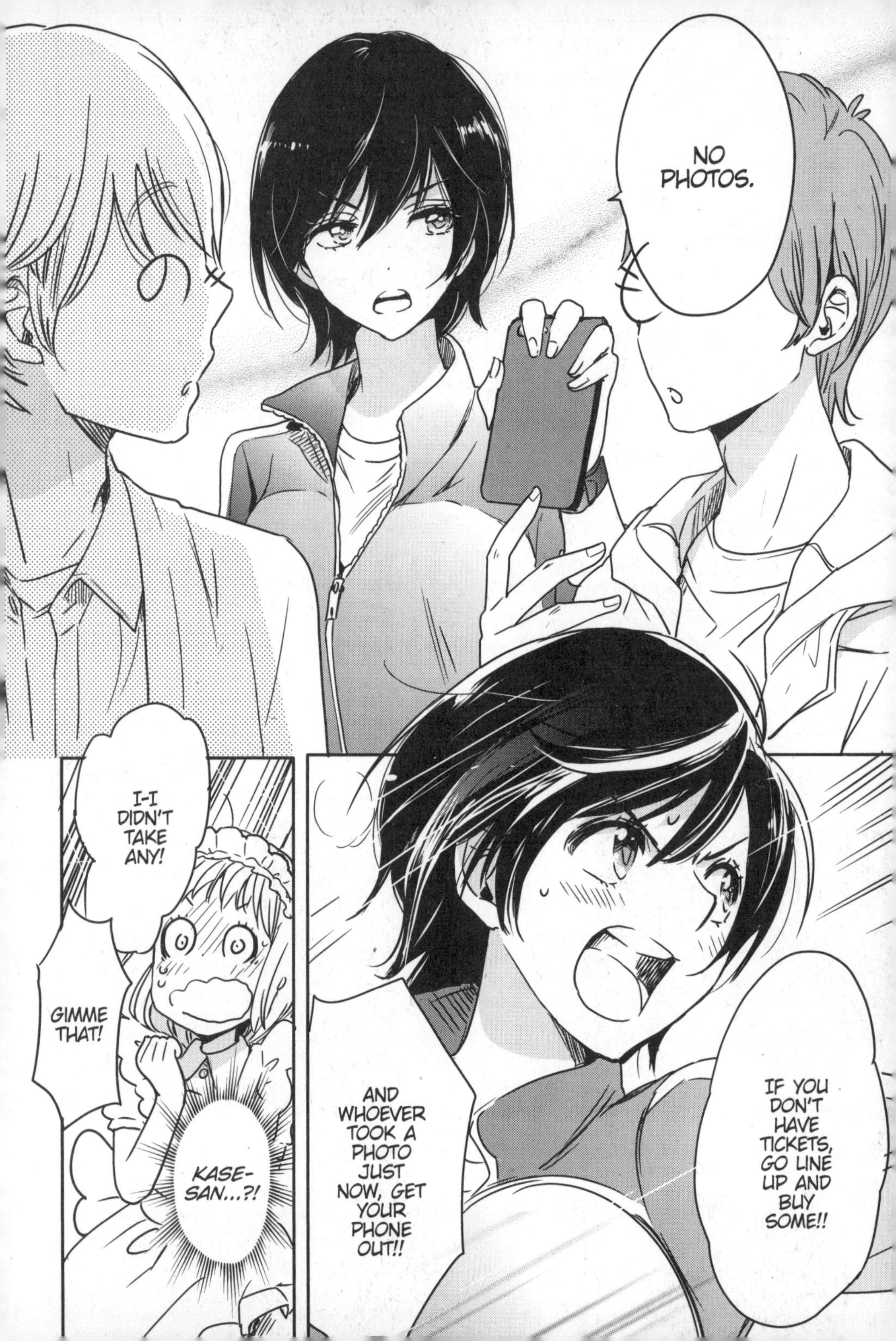
NO PHOTOS.
IF YOU DON'T HAVE TICKETS, GO LINE UP AND BUY SOME!!
AND WHOEVER TOOK A PHOTO JUST NOW, GET YOUR PHONE OUT!!
I-I DIDN'T TAKE ANY!
GIMME THAT!
KASE-SAN...?!

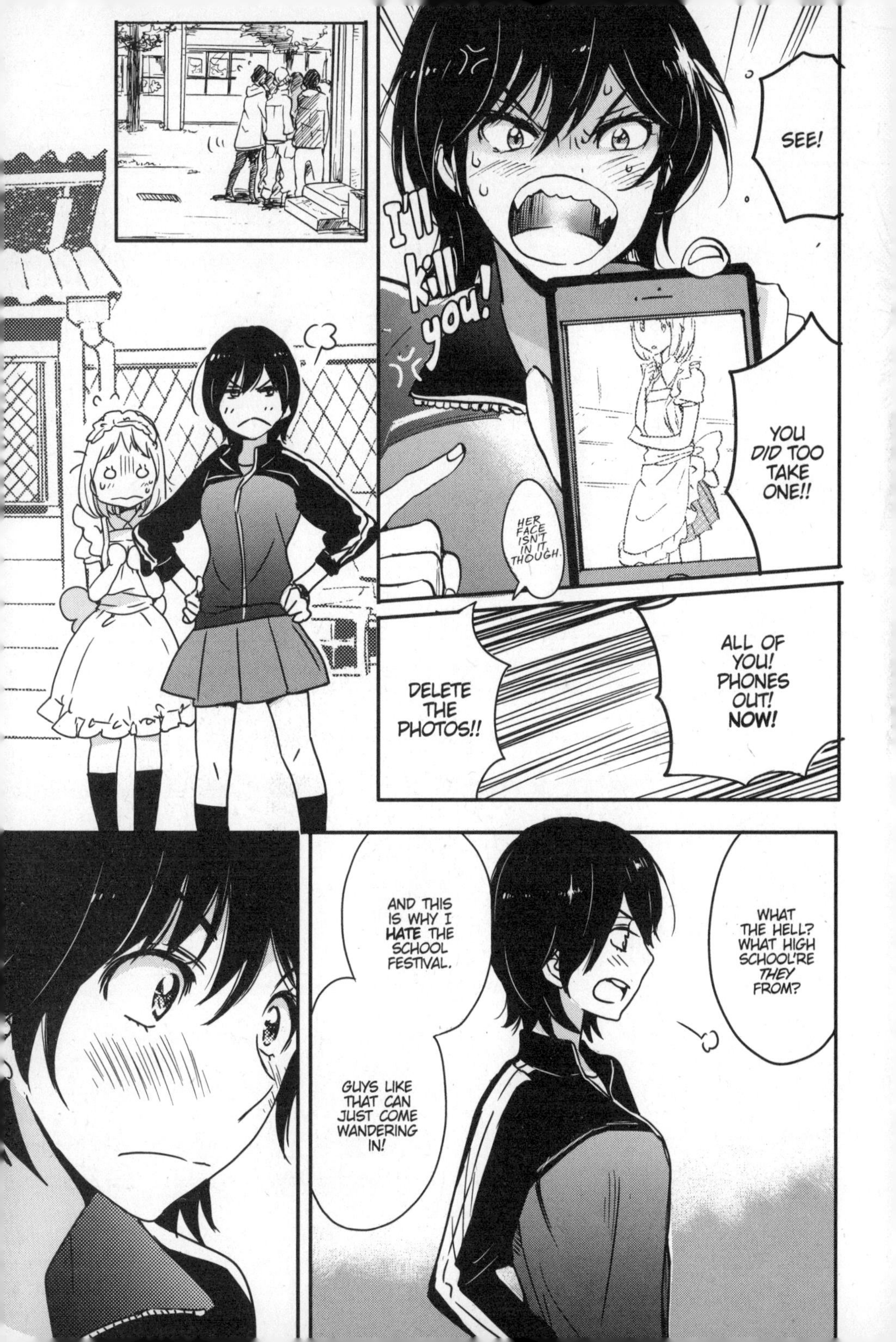
SEE!
I'll kill you!
YOU DID TOO TAKE ONE!!
HER FACE ISN'T IN IT THOUGH.
ALL OF YOU! PHONES OUT! NOW!
DELETE THE PHOTOS!!
WHAT THE HELL? WHAT HIGH SCHOOL'RE THEY FROM?
AND THIS IS WHY I HATE THE SCHOOL FESTIVAL.
GUYS LIKE THAT CAN JUST COME WANDERING IN!

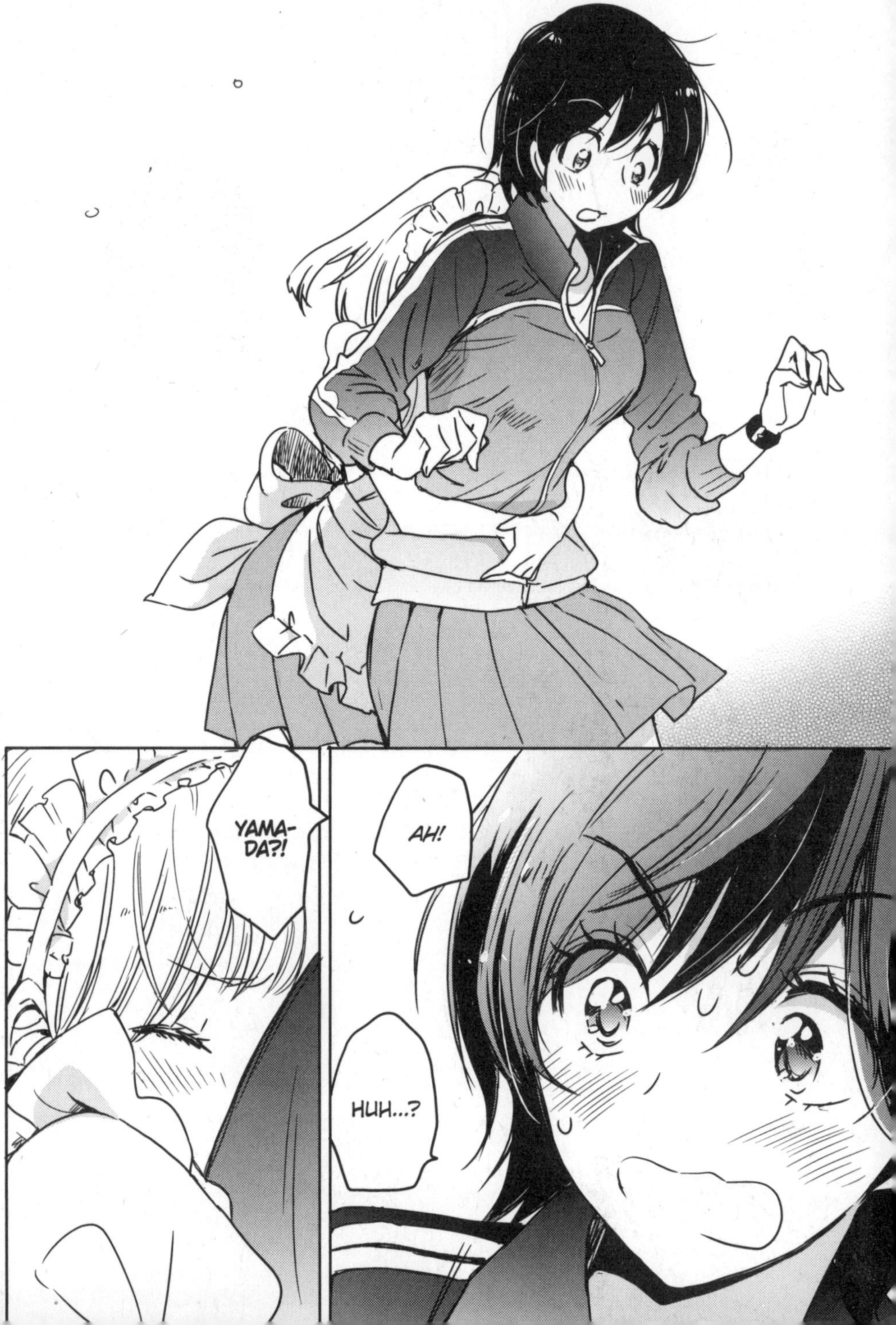
AH!
HUH...?
YAMA-DA?!

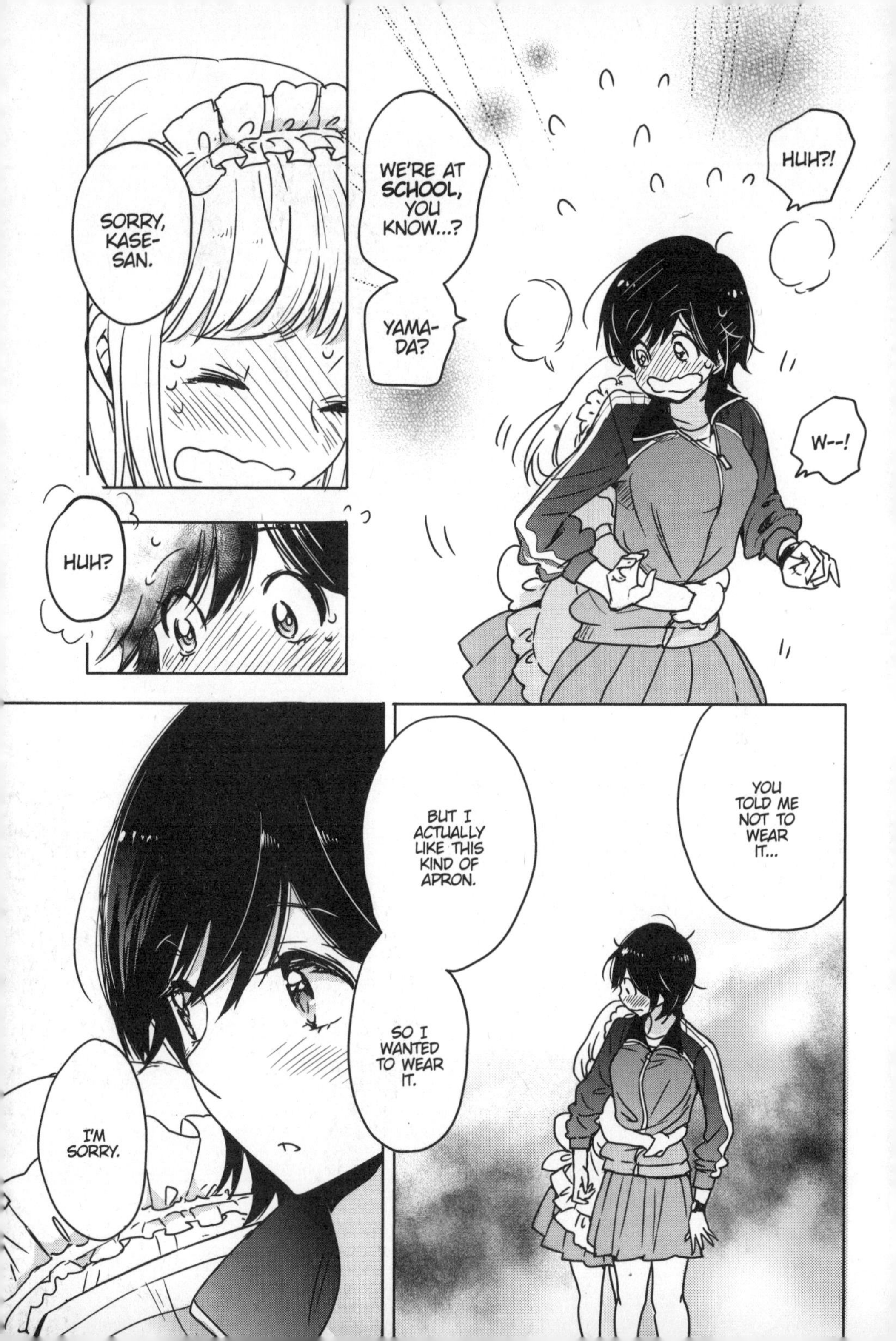
HUH?!
WE'RE AT SCHOOL, YOU KNOW...?
YAMADA?
W--!
SORRY, KASE-SAN.
HUH?
YOU TOLD ME NOT TO WEAR IT...
BUT I ACTUALLY LIKE THIS KIND OF APRON.
SO I WANTED TO WEAR IT.
I'M SORRY.

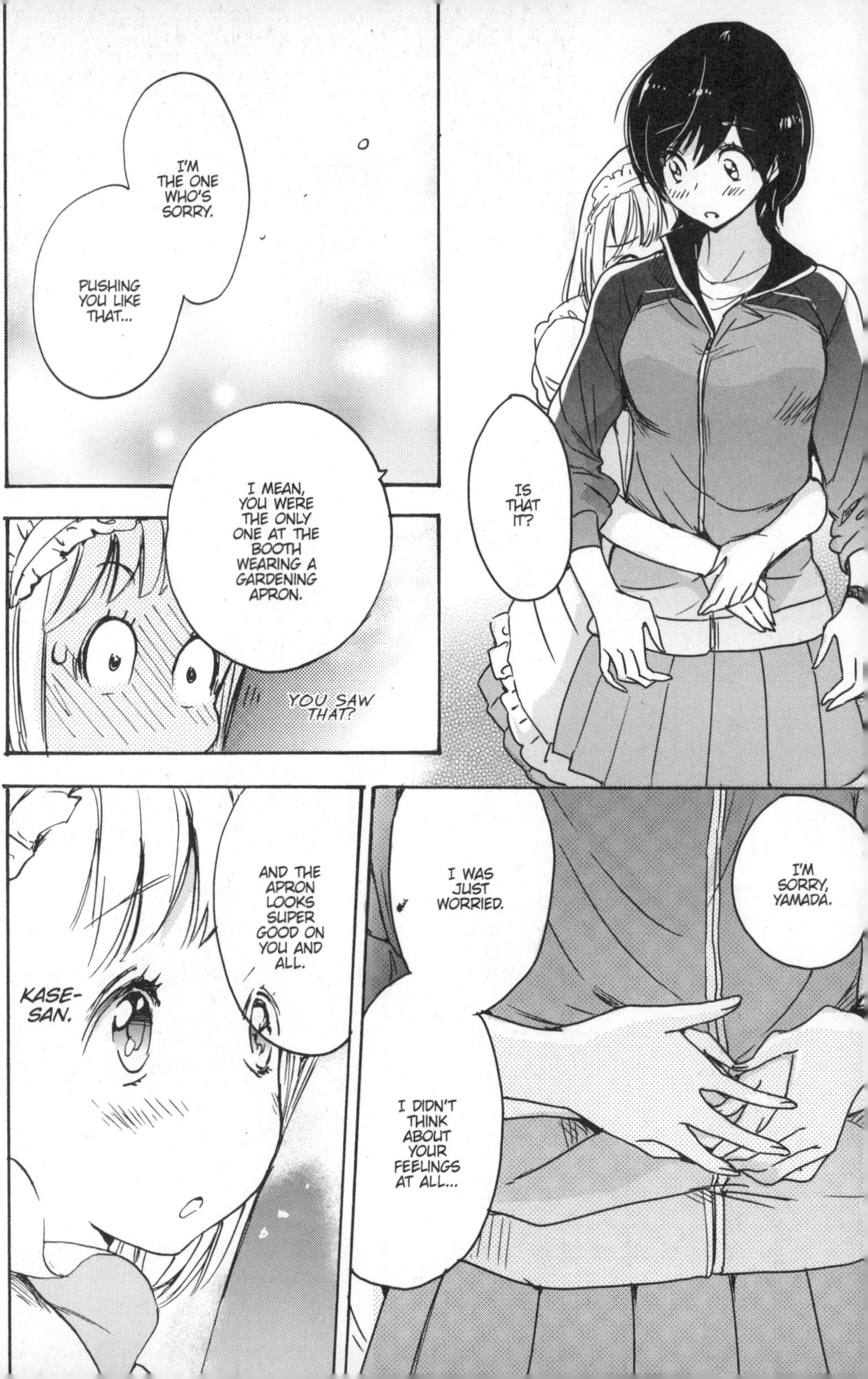
IS THAT IT?
I'M THE ONE WHO'S SORRY.
PUSHING YOU LIKE THAT...
I MEAN, YOU WERE THE ONLY ONE AT THE BOOTH WEARING A GARDENING APRON.
YOU SAW THAT?
I'M SORRY, YAMADA.
I WAS JUST WORRIED.
I DIDN'T THINK ABOUT YOUR FEELINGS AT ALL...
AND THE APRON LOOKS SUPER GOOD ON YOU AND ALL.
KASE-SAN.

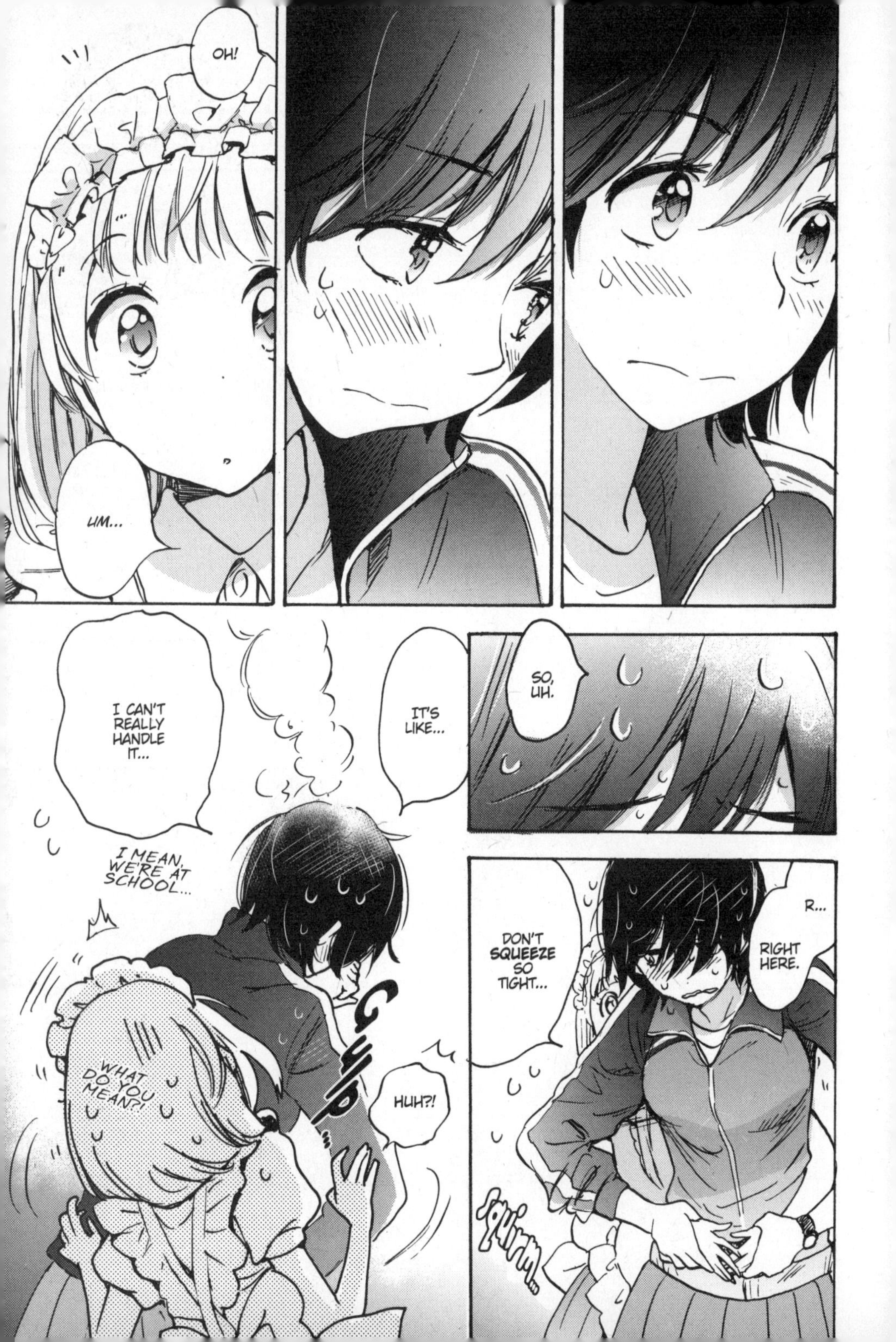OH!
...
UM...
SO, UH.
IT'S LIKE...
I CAN'T REALLY HANDLE IT...
R...
RIGHT HERE.
DON'T SQUEEZE SO TIGHT...
squirm...
I MEAN, WE'RE AT SCHOOL...
GULP...
HUH?!
WHAT DO YOU MEAN?!

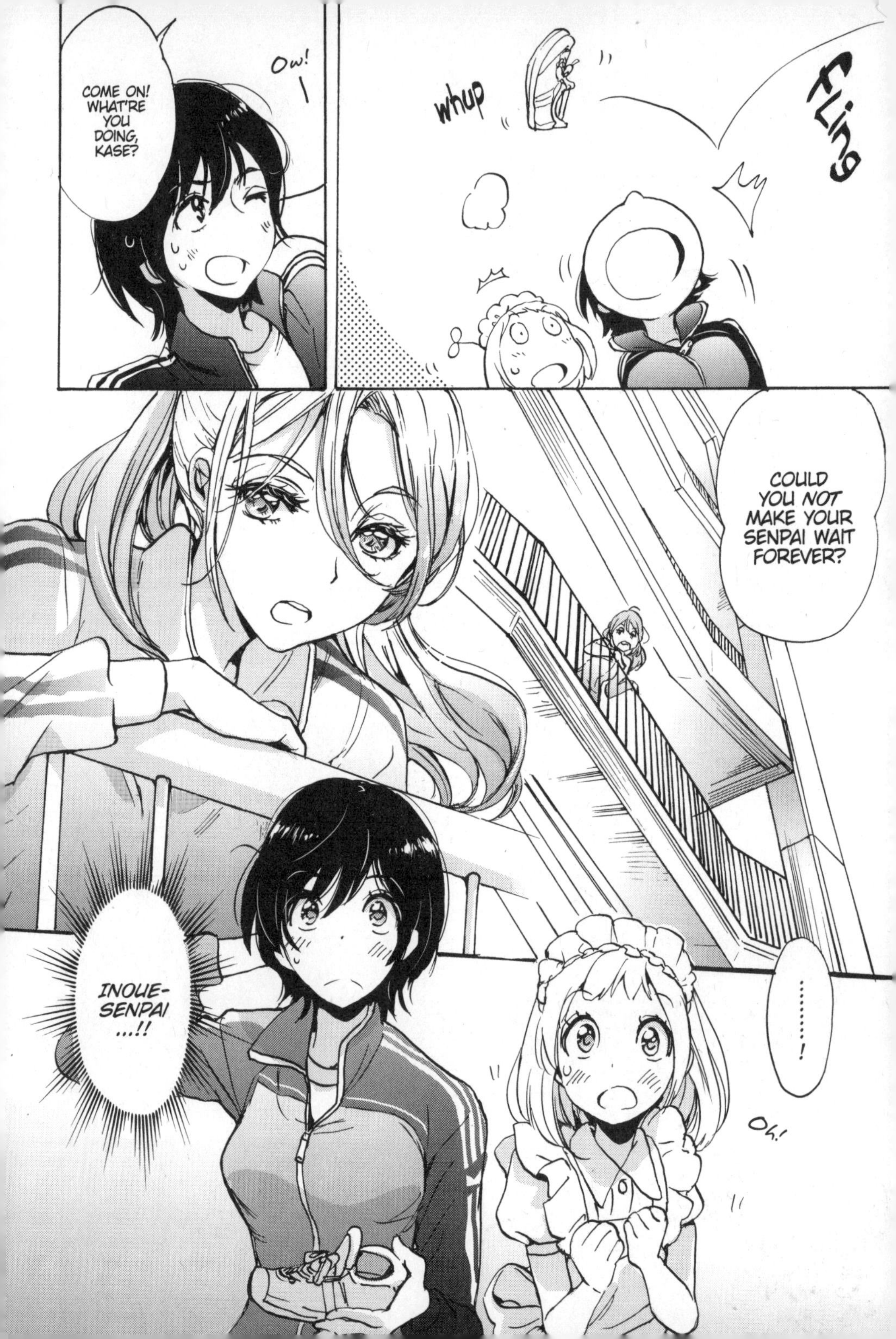
Fling
whup
COME ON! WHAT'RE YOU DOING, KASE?
Ow!
COULD YOU NOT MAKE YOUR SENPAI WAIT FOREVER?
........!
Oh!
INOUE-SENPAI ...!!

Kase-san and Crêpes

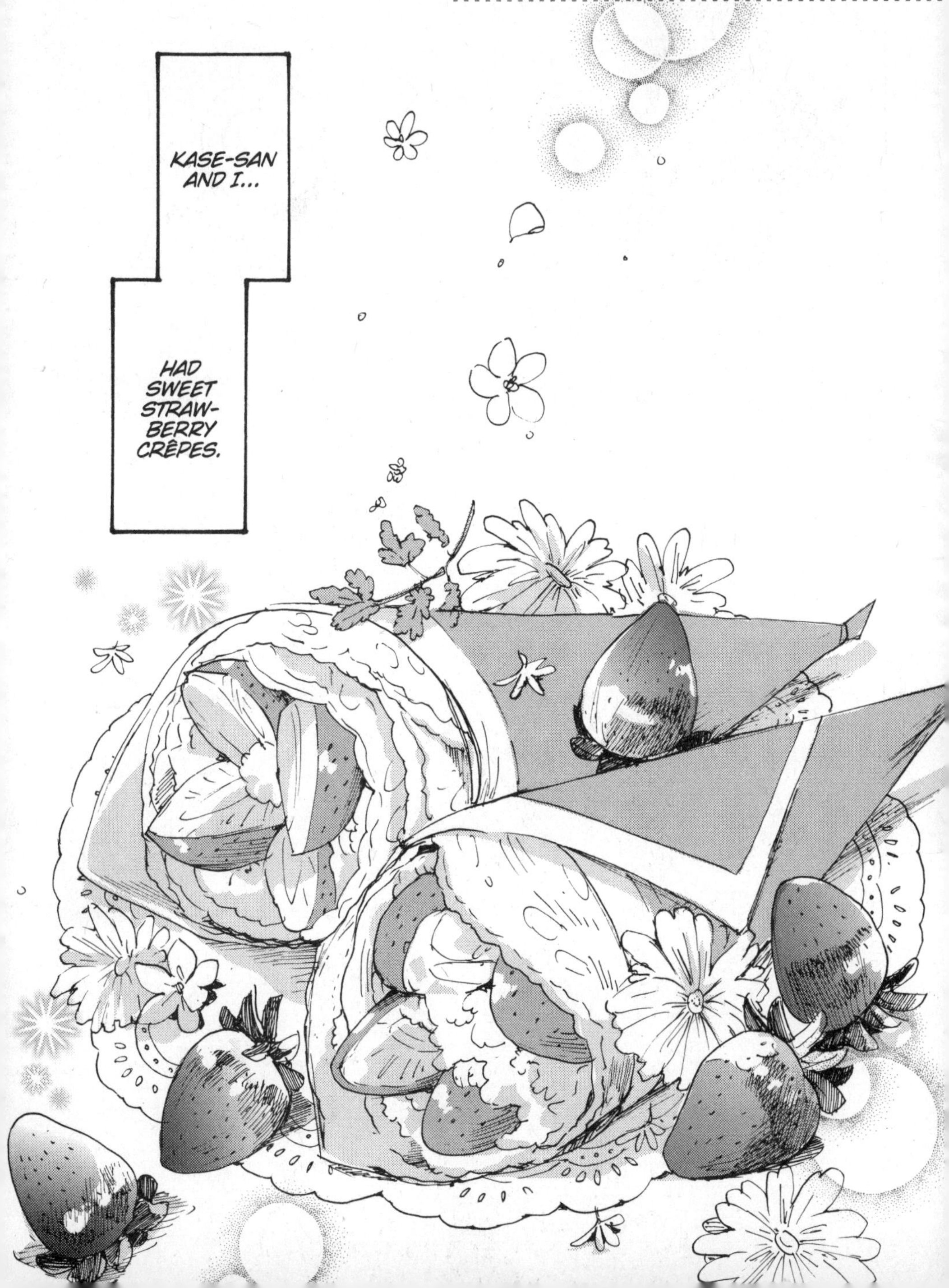
KASE-SAN AND I...
HAD SWEET STRAW-BERRY CRÊPES.

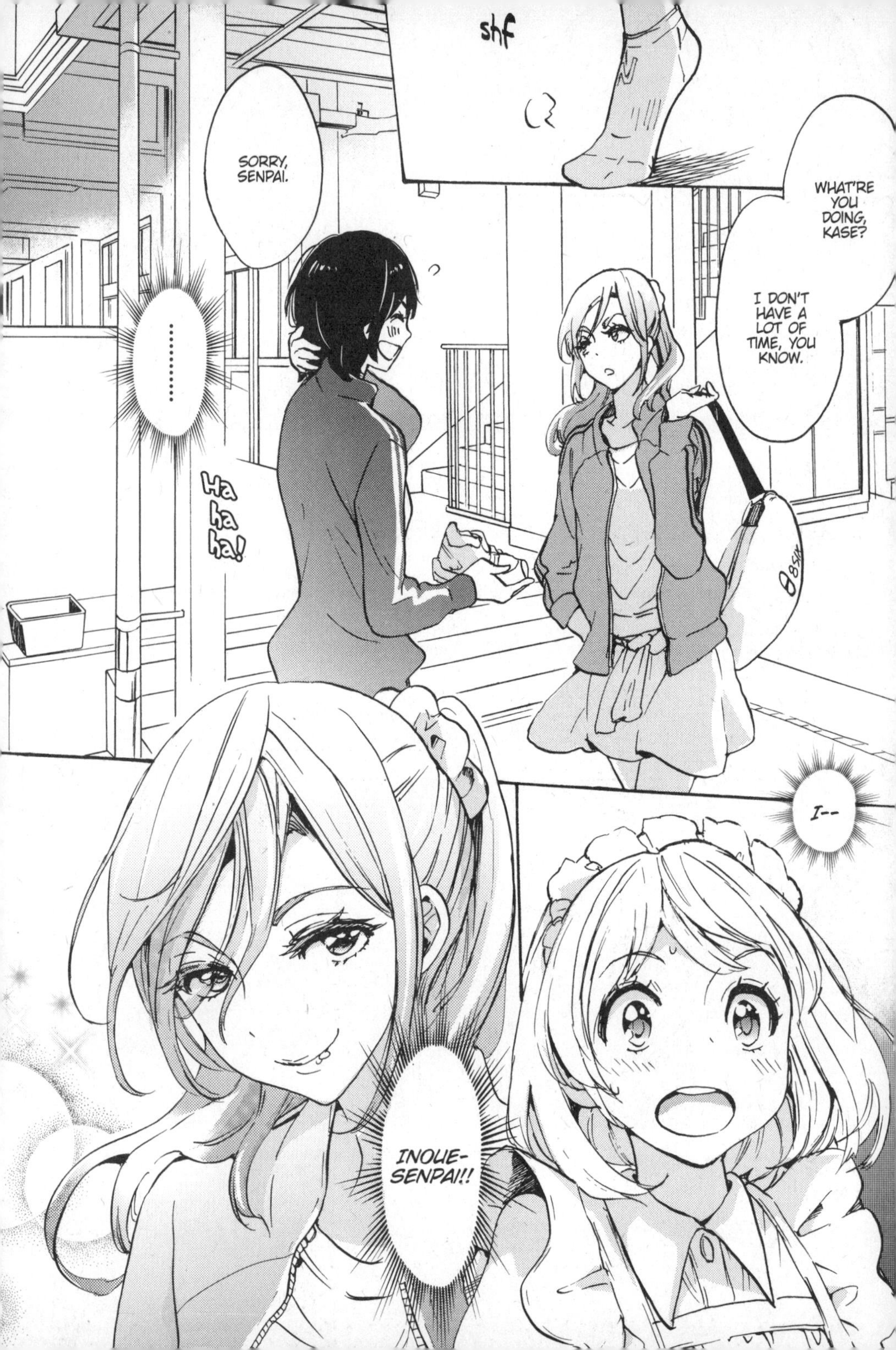
shf
WHAT'RE YOU DOING, KASE?
I DON'T HAVE A LOT OF TIME, YOU KNOW.
SORRY, SENPAI.
......
Ha ha ha!
I--
INOUE-SENPAI!!

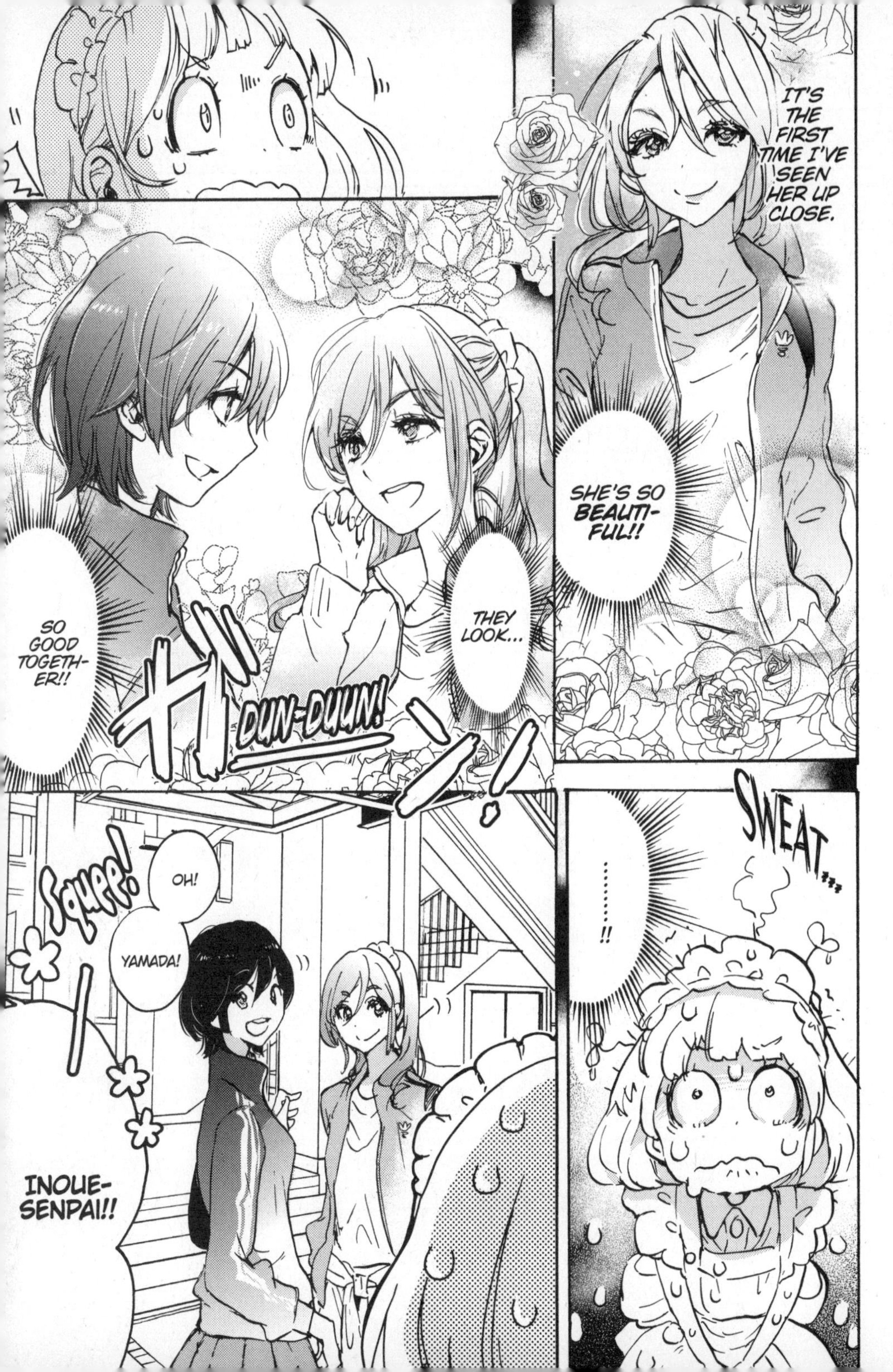
IT'S THE FIRST TIME I'VE SEEN HER UP CLOSE.
SHE'S SO BEAUTI-FUL!!
THEY LOOK...
SO GOOD TOGETHER!!
DUN-DUUN!
SWEAT...
......!!
Squee!
OH!
YAMADA!
INOUE-SENPAI!!

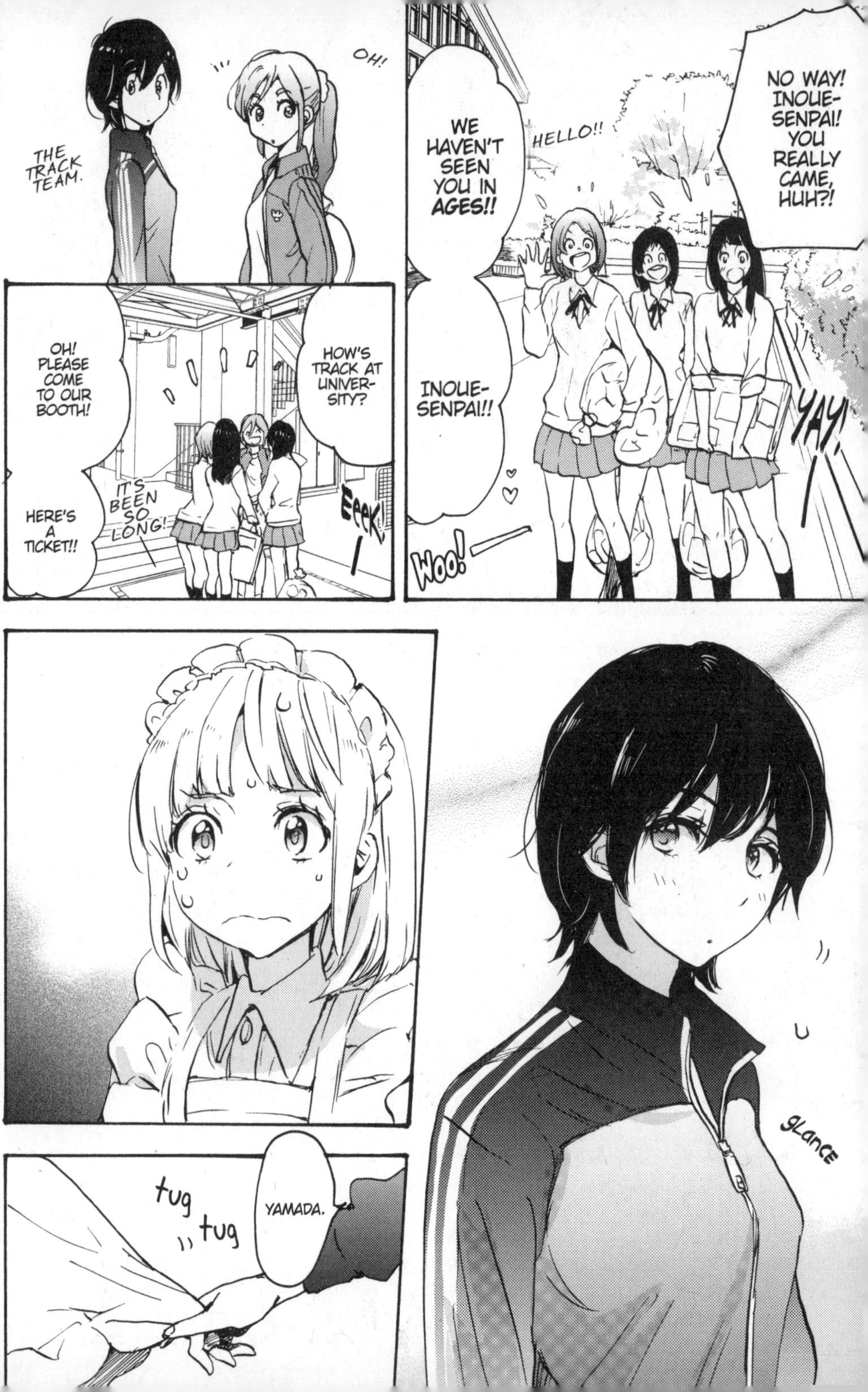
NO WAY! INOUE-SENPAI! YOU REALLY CAME, HUH?!
HELLO!!
WE HAVEN'T SEEN YOU IN AGES!!
INOUE-SENPAI!!
YAY!
WOO!
OH!
THE TRACK TEAM.
HOW'S TRACK AT UNIVERSITY?
OH! PLEASE COME TO OUR BOOTH!
IT'S BEEN SO LONG!
EEEK!
HERE'S A TICKET!!
glance
YAMADA.
tug tug

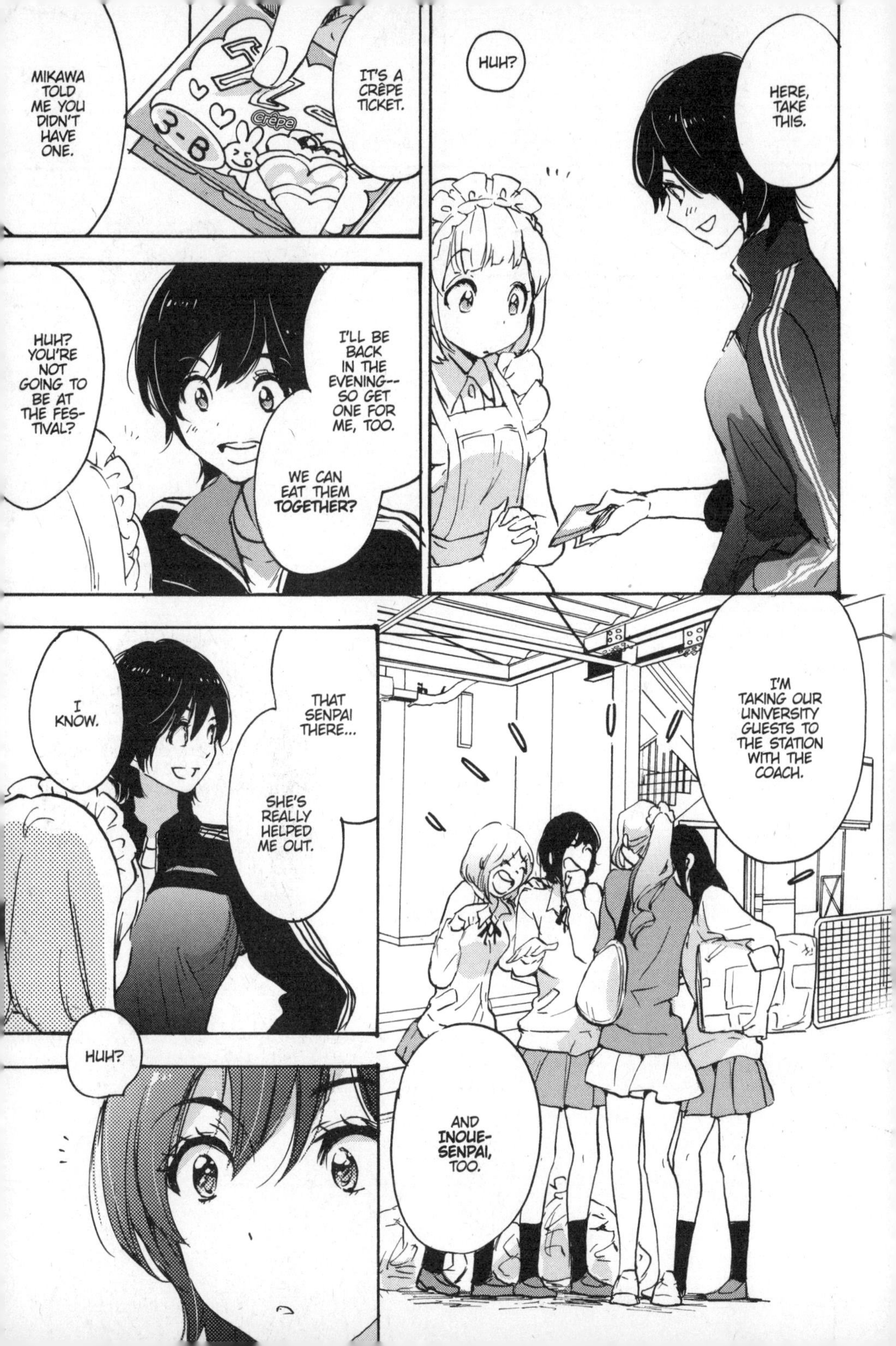
HERE, TAKE THIS.
HUH?
IT'S A CRÊPE TICKET.
MIKAWA TOLD ME YOU DIDN'T HAVE ONE.
I'LL BE BACK IN THE EVENING-- SO GET ONE FOR ME, TOO.
WE CAN EAT THEM TOGETHER?
HUH? YOU'RE NOT GOING TO BE AT THE FES-TIVAL?
I'M TAKING OUR UNIVERSITY GUESTS TO THE STATION WITH THE COACH.
AND INOUE-SENPAI, TOO.
THAT SENPAI THERE...
SHE'S REALLY HELPED ME OUT.
I KNOW.
HUH?

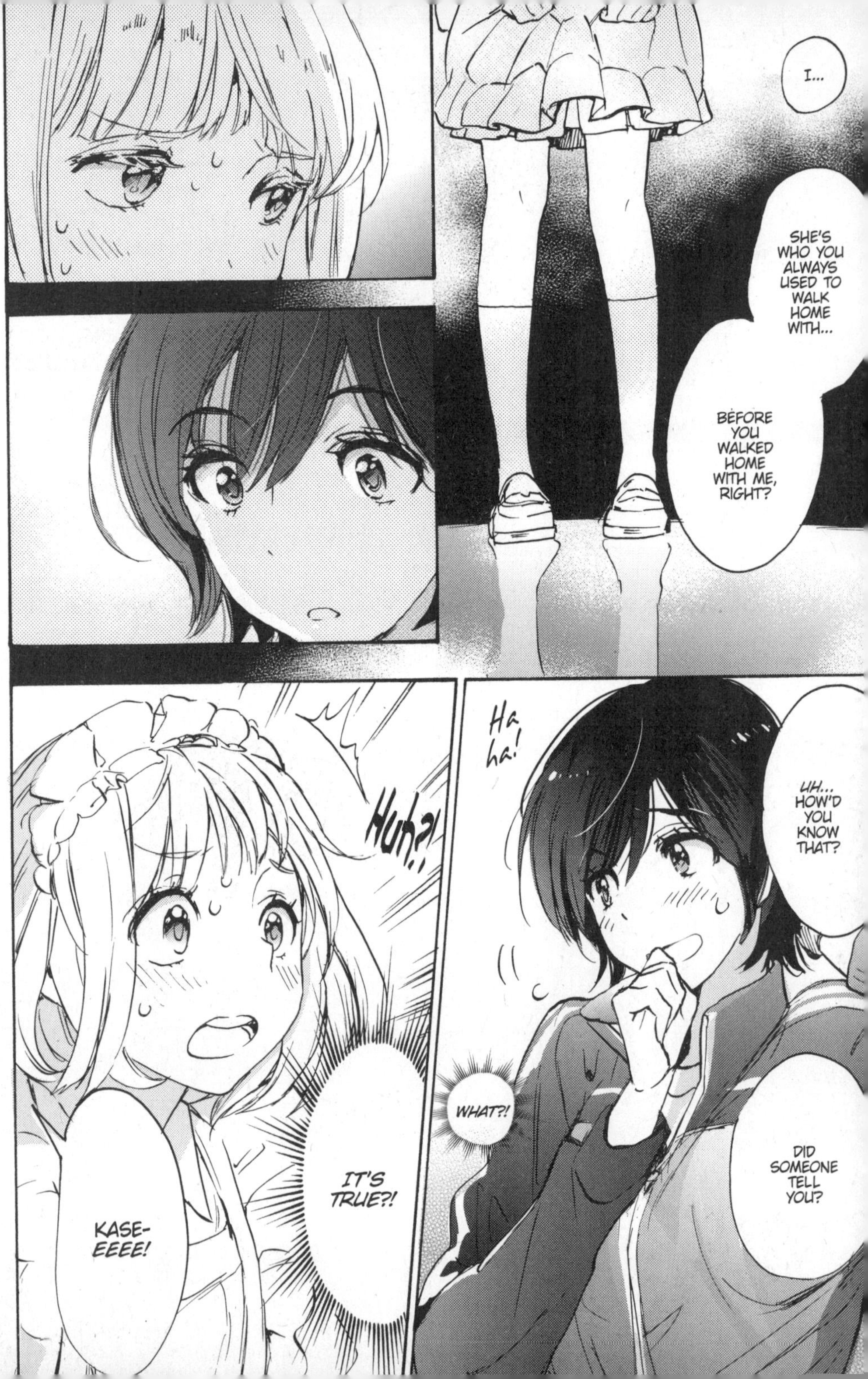
I...
SHE'S WHO YOU ALWAYS USED TO WALK HOME WITH...
BEFORE YOU WALKED HOME WITH ME, RIGHT?
Ha ha!
UH... HOW'D YOU KNOW THAT?
DID SOMEONE TELL YOU?
WHAT?!
Huh?!
IT'S TRUE?!
KASE-EEEE!

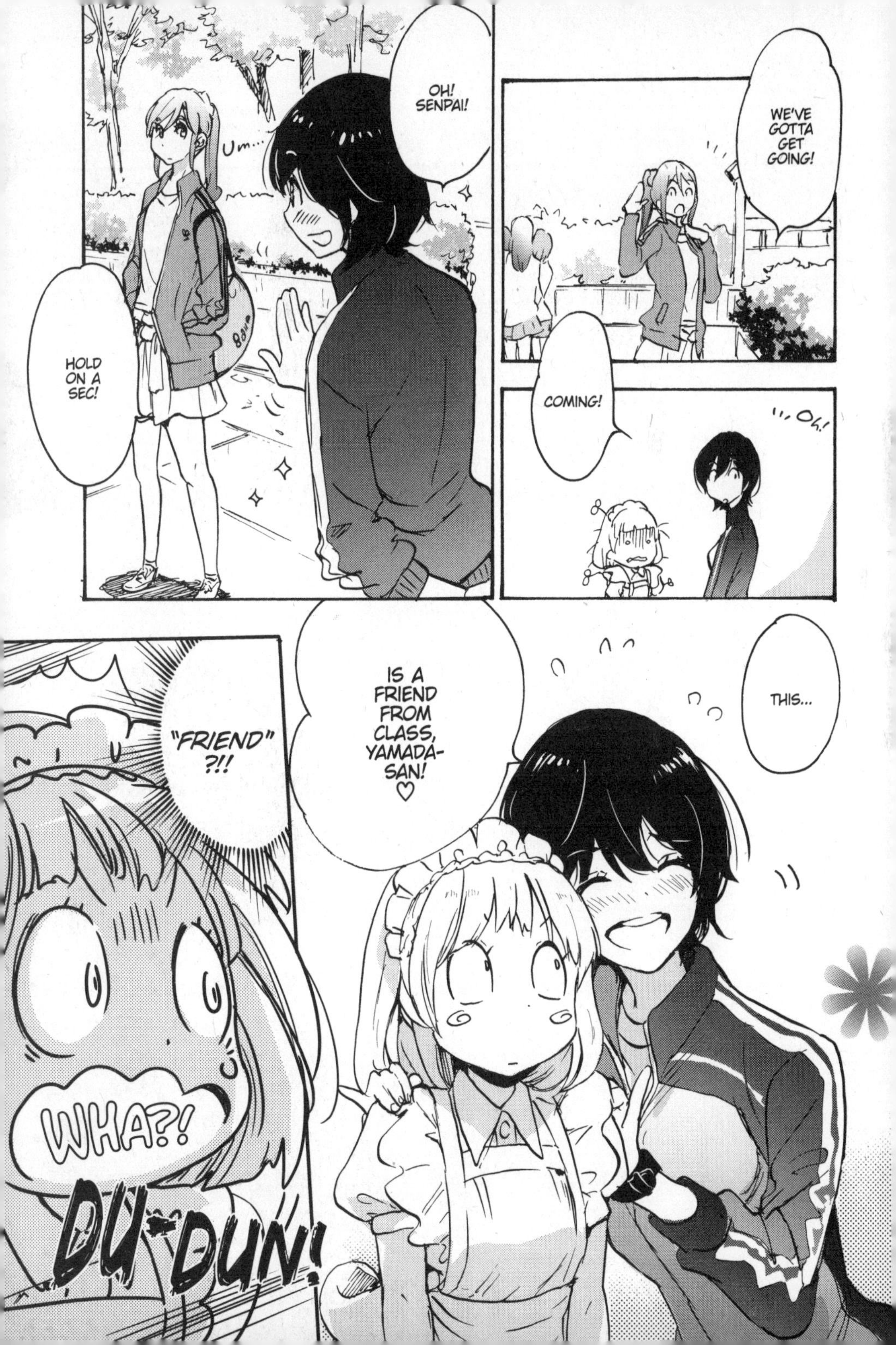

WE'VE GOTTA GET GOING!
COMING!
Oh!
OH! SENPAI!
Um...
HOLD ON A SEC!
THIS...
IS A FRIEND FROM CLASS, YAMADA-SAN! ♡
"FRIEND"?!!
WHA?!
DU-DUN!

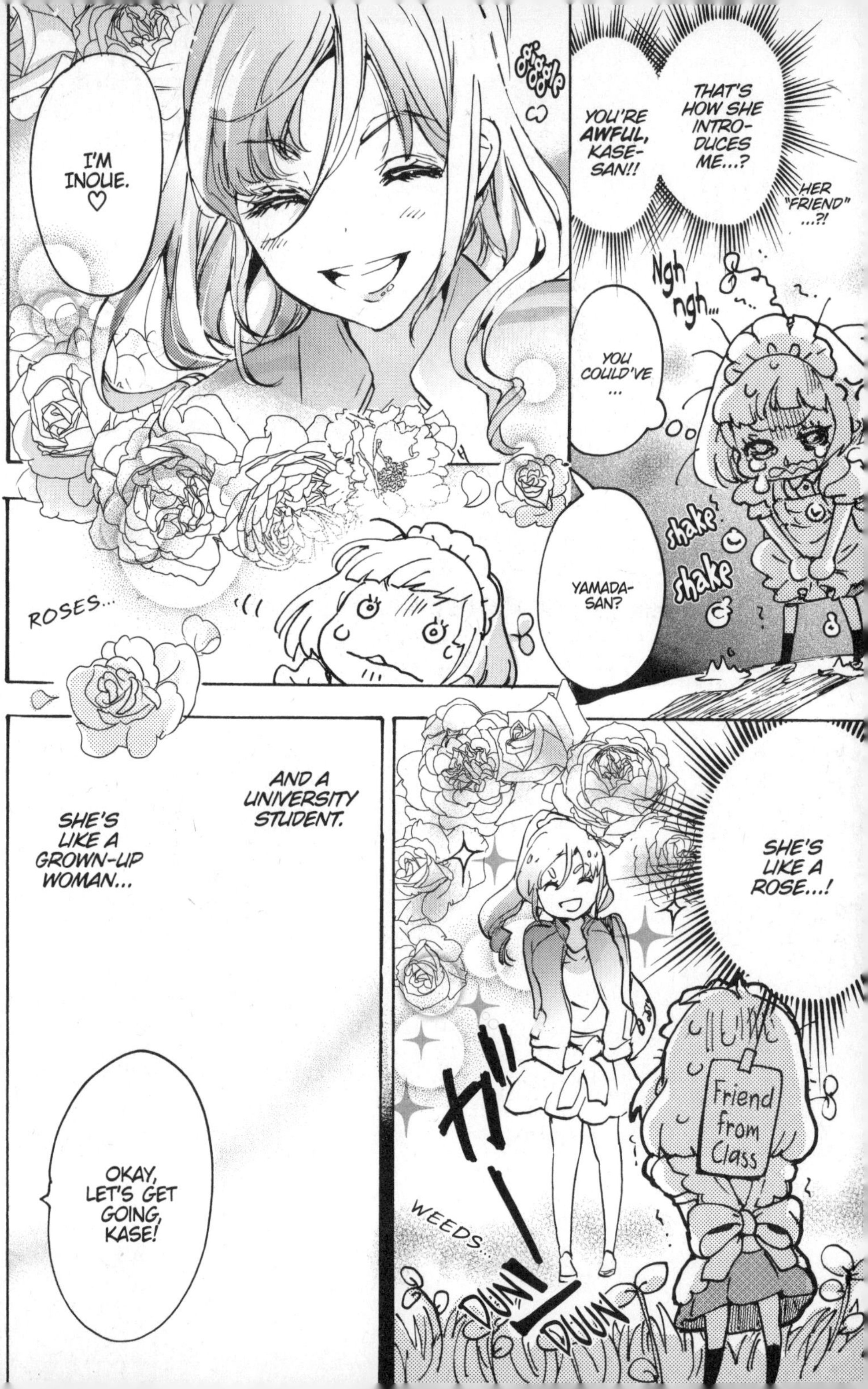
THAT'S HOW SHE INTRODUCES ME...?
YOU'RE AWFUL, KASE-SAN!!
HER "FRIEND"...?!
Ngh ngh...
YOU COULD'VE...
shake shake
YAMADA-SAN?
giggle
I'M INOUE. ♡
ROSES...
SHE'S LIKE A ROSE...!
Friend from Class
WEEDS...
DUN DUUN
AND A UNIVERSITY STUDENT.
SHE'S LIKE A GROWN-UP WOMAN...
OKAY, LET'S GET GOING, KASE!

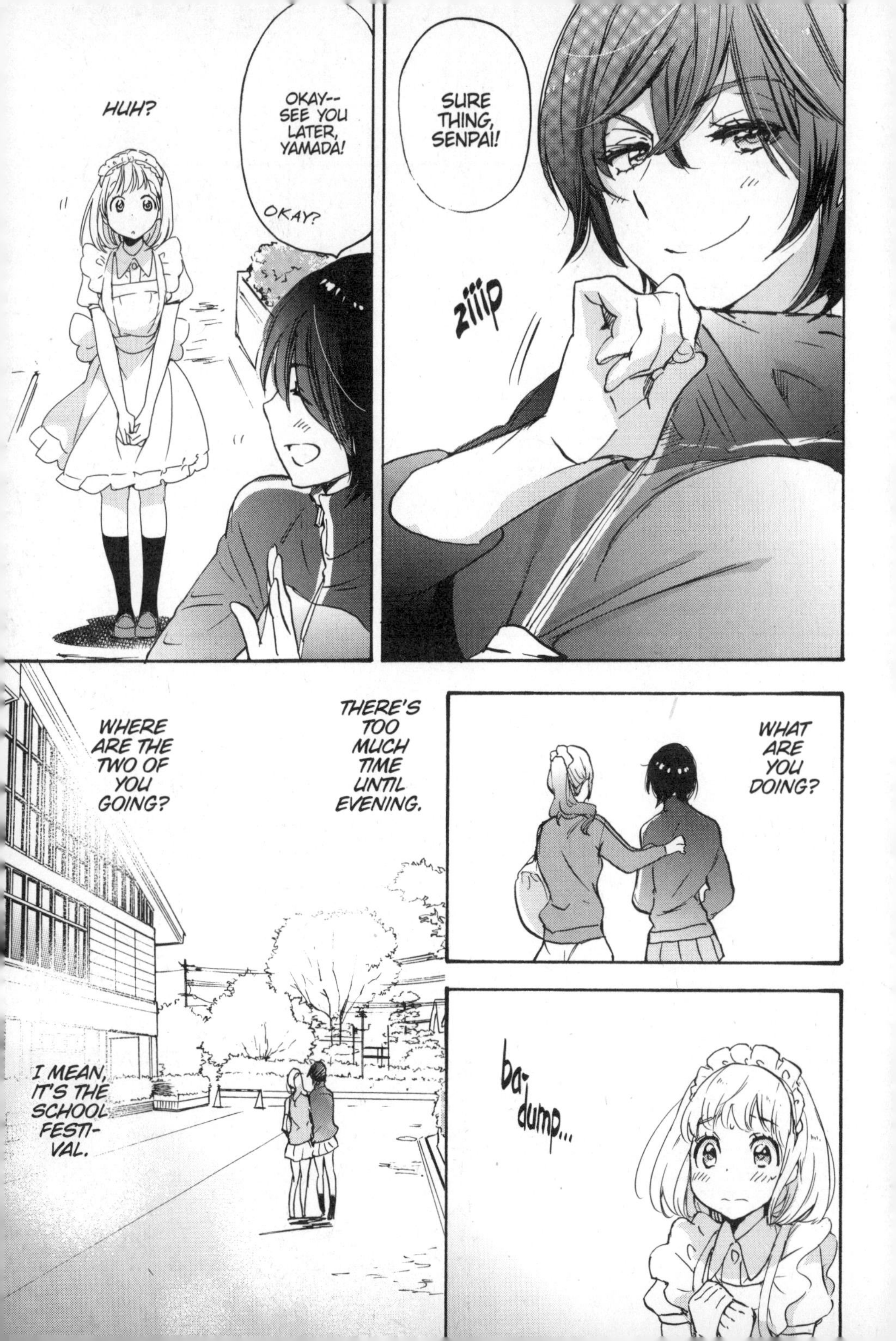
SURE THING, SENPAI!
ziiip
OKAY-- SEE YOU LATER, YAMADA!
OKAY?
HUH?
WHAT ARE YOU DOING?
ba-dump...
THERE'S TOO MUCH TIME UNTIL EVENING.
WHERE ARE THE TWO OF YOU GOING?
I MEAN, IT'S THE SCHOOL FESTIVAL.

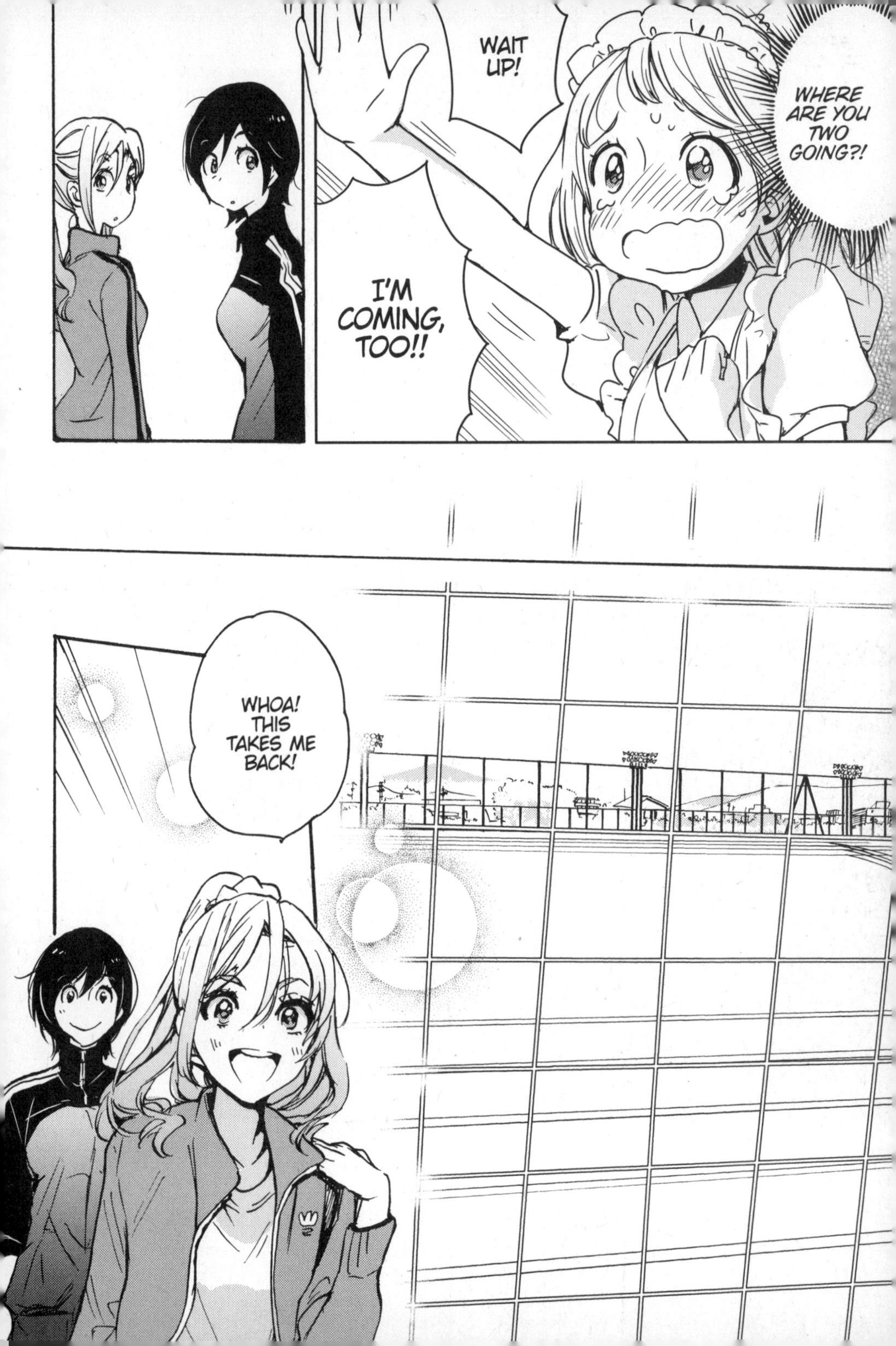
WHERE ARE YOU TWO GOING?!
WAIT UP!
I'M COMING, TOO!!
WHOA! THIS TAKES ME BACK!

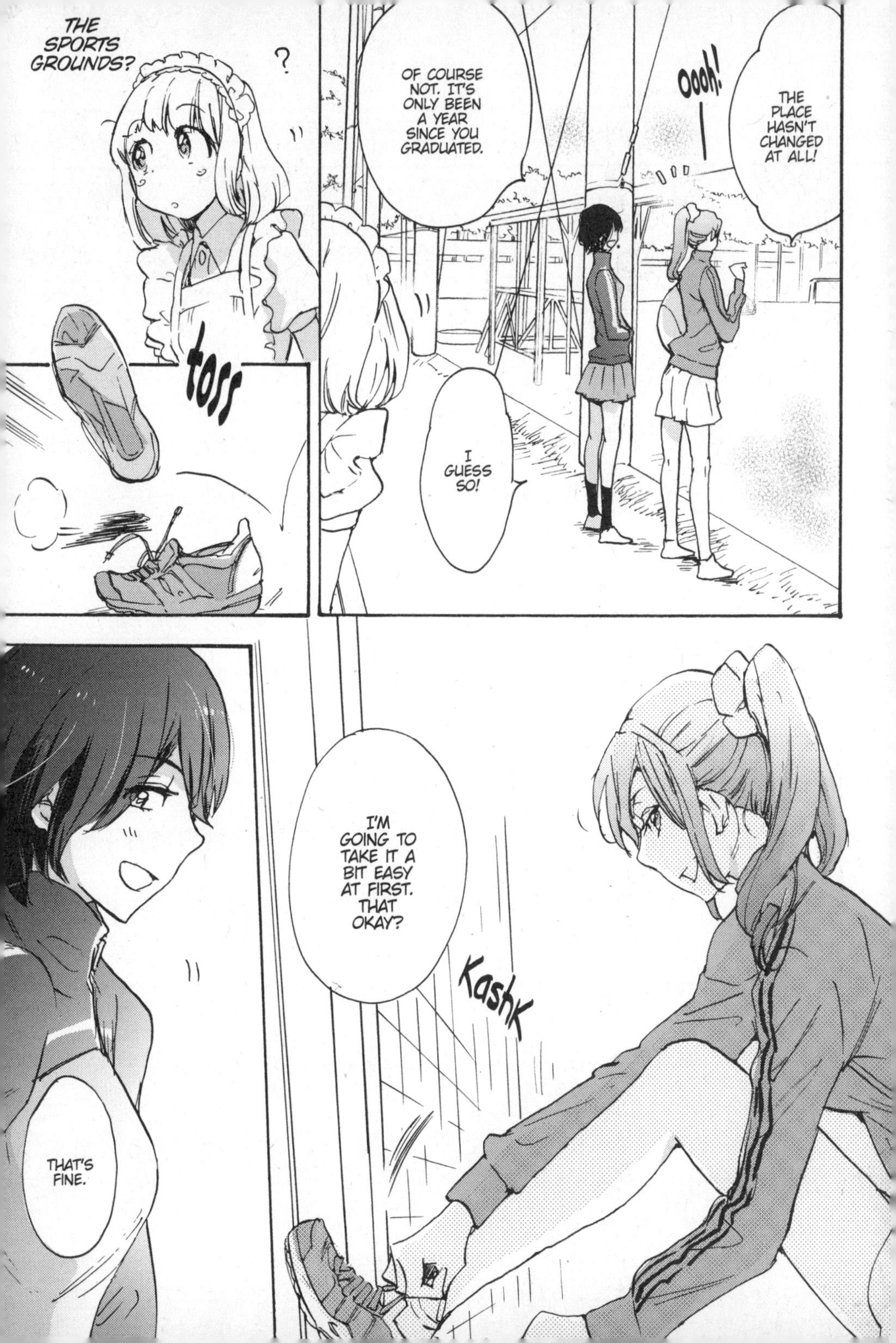

Oooh!
THE PLACE HASN'T CHANGED AT ALL!
OF COURSE NOT. IT'S ONLY BEEN A YEAR SINCE YOU GRADUATED.
I GUESS SO!
THE SPORTS GROUNDS?
?
toss
I'M GOING TO TAKE IT A BIT EASY AT FIRST. THAT OKAY?
Kashk
THAT'S FINE.

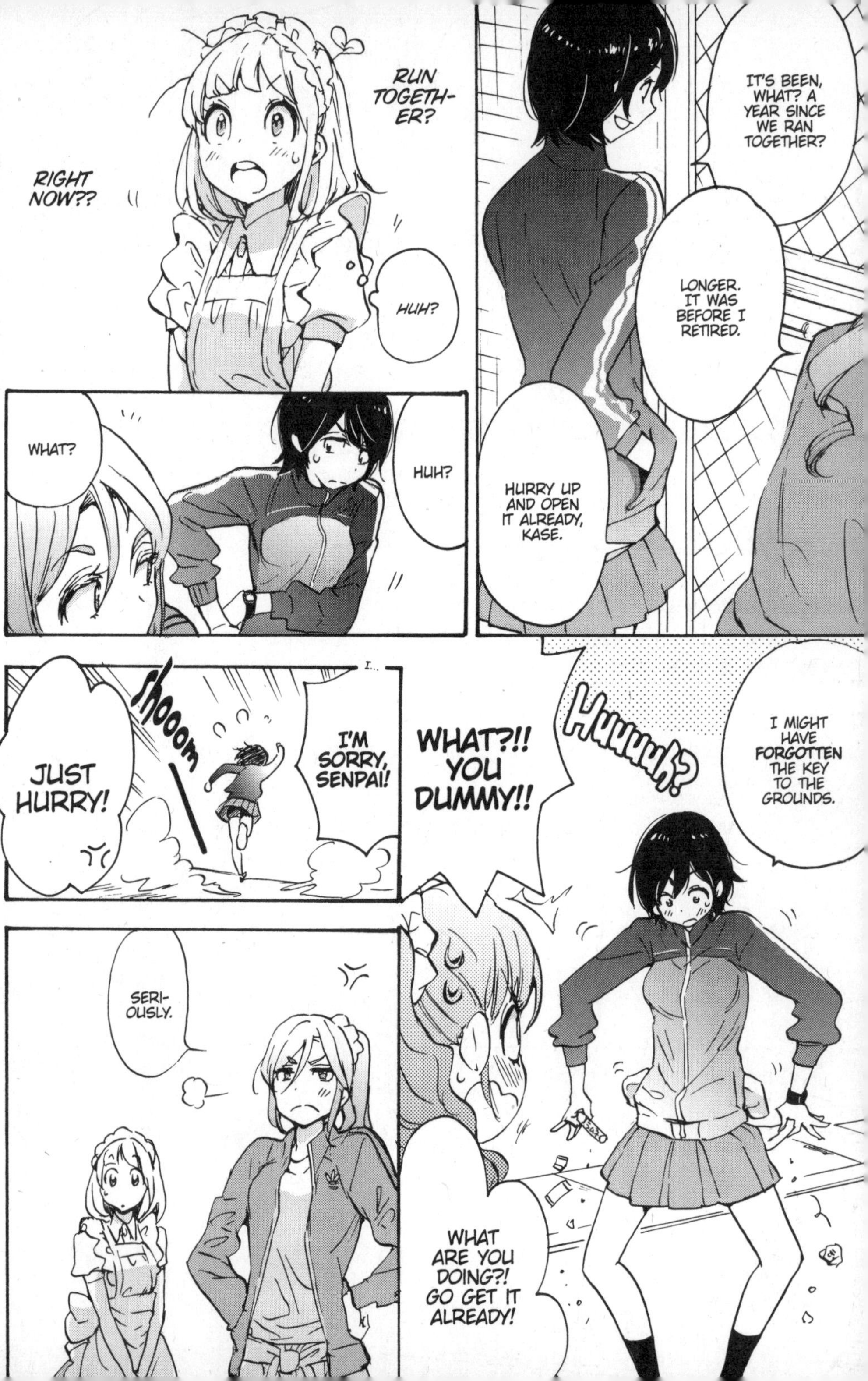

IT'S BEEN, WHAT? A YEAR SINCE WE RAN TOGETHER?
LONGER. IT WAS BEFORE I RETIRED.
HURRY UP AND OPEN IT ALREADY, KASE.
RUN TOGETH-ER?
RIGHT NOW??
HUH?
HUH?
WHAT?
I MIGHT HAVE FORGOTTEN THE KEY TO THE GROUNDS.
Huuuuh?
WHAT?!! YOU DUMMY!!
WHAT ARE YOU DOING?! GO GET IT ALREADY!
I...
I'M SORRY, SENPAI!
shooom
JUST HURRY!
SERI-OUSLY.

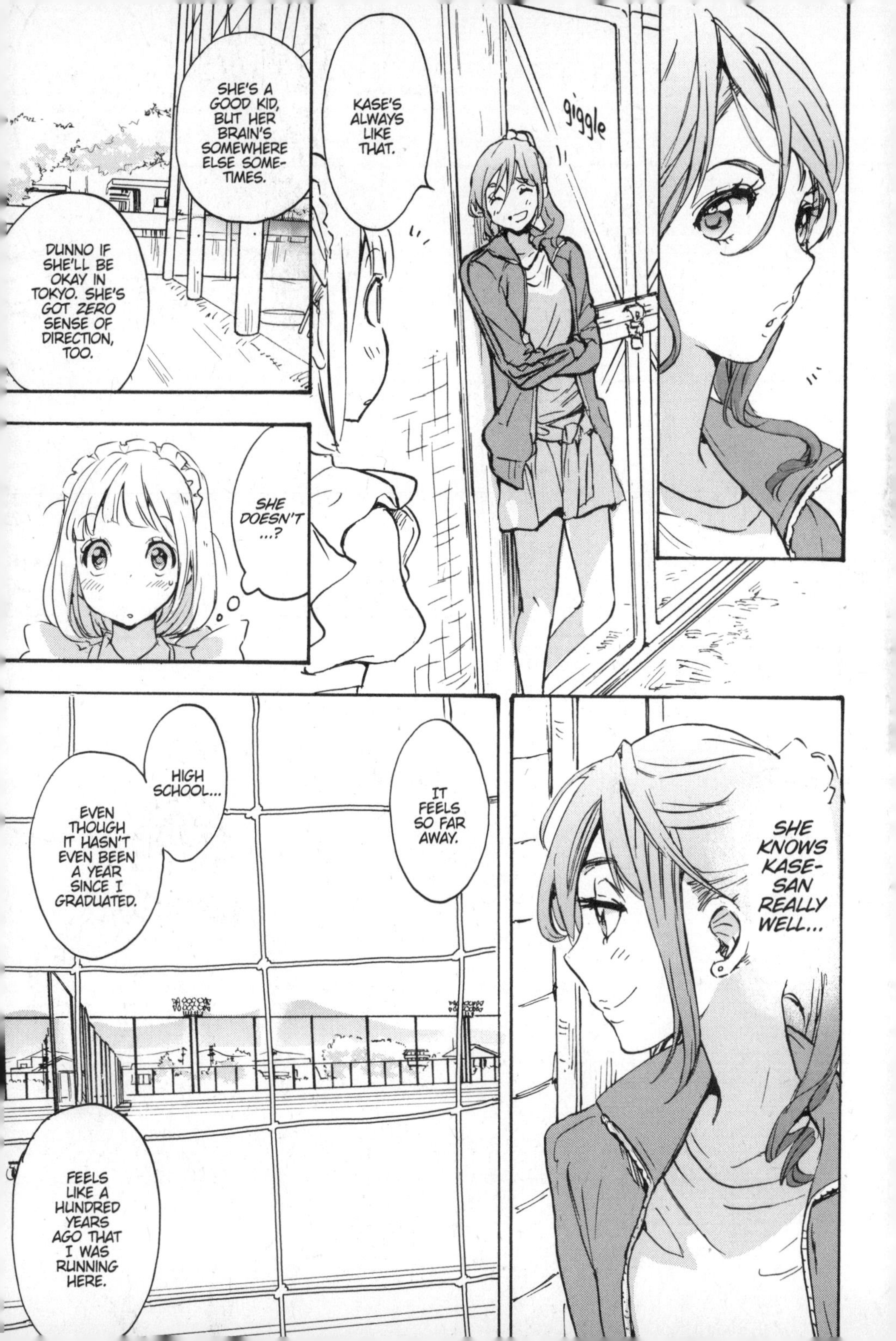
giggle
KASE'S ALWAYS LIKE THAT.
SHE'S A GOOD KID, BUT HER BRAIN'S SOMEWHERE ELSE SOME-TIMES.
DUNNO IF SHE'LL BE OKAY IN TOKYO. SHE'S GOT ZERO SENSE OF DIRECTION, TOO.
SHE DOESN'T ...?
SHE KNOWS KASE-SAN REALLY WELL...
IT FEELS SO FAR AWAY.
HIGH SCHOOL...
EVEN THOUGH IT HASN'T EVEN BEEN A YEAR SINCE I GRADUATED.
FEELS LIKE A HUNDRED YEARS AGO THAT I WAS RUNNING HERE.

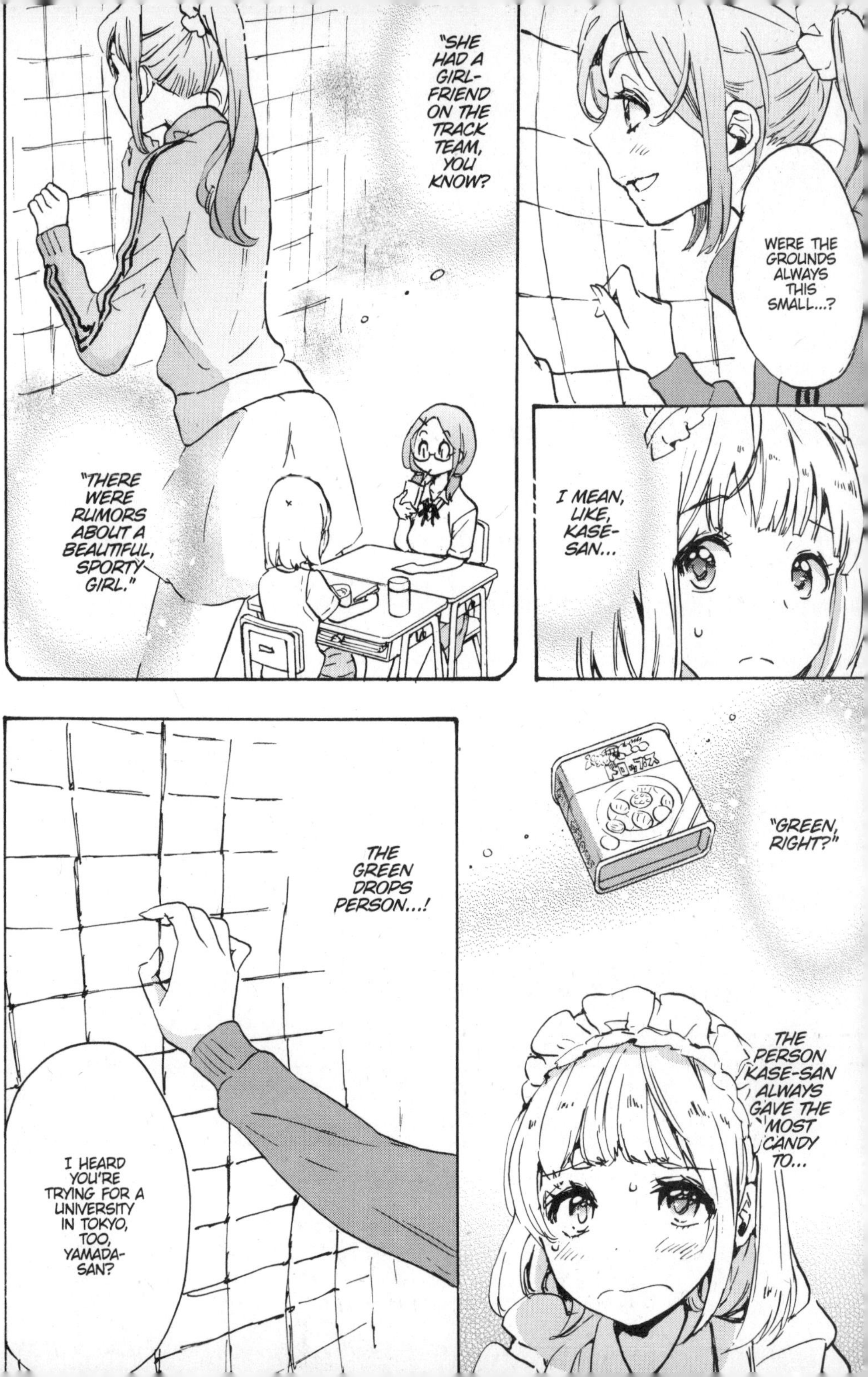
WERE THE GROUNDS ALWAYS THIS SMALL...?
I MEAN, LIKE, KASE-SAN...
"SHE HAD A GIRLFRIEND ON THE TRACK TEAM, YOU KNOW?
"THERE WERE RUMORS ABOUT A BEAUTIFUL, SPORTY GIRL."
"GREEN, RIGHT?"
THE PERSON KASE-SAN ALWAYS GAVE THE MOST CANDY TO...
THE GREEN DROPS PERSON...!
I HEARD YOU'RE TRYING FOR A UNIVERSITY IN TOKYO, TOO, YAMADA-SAN?

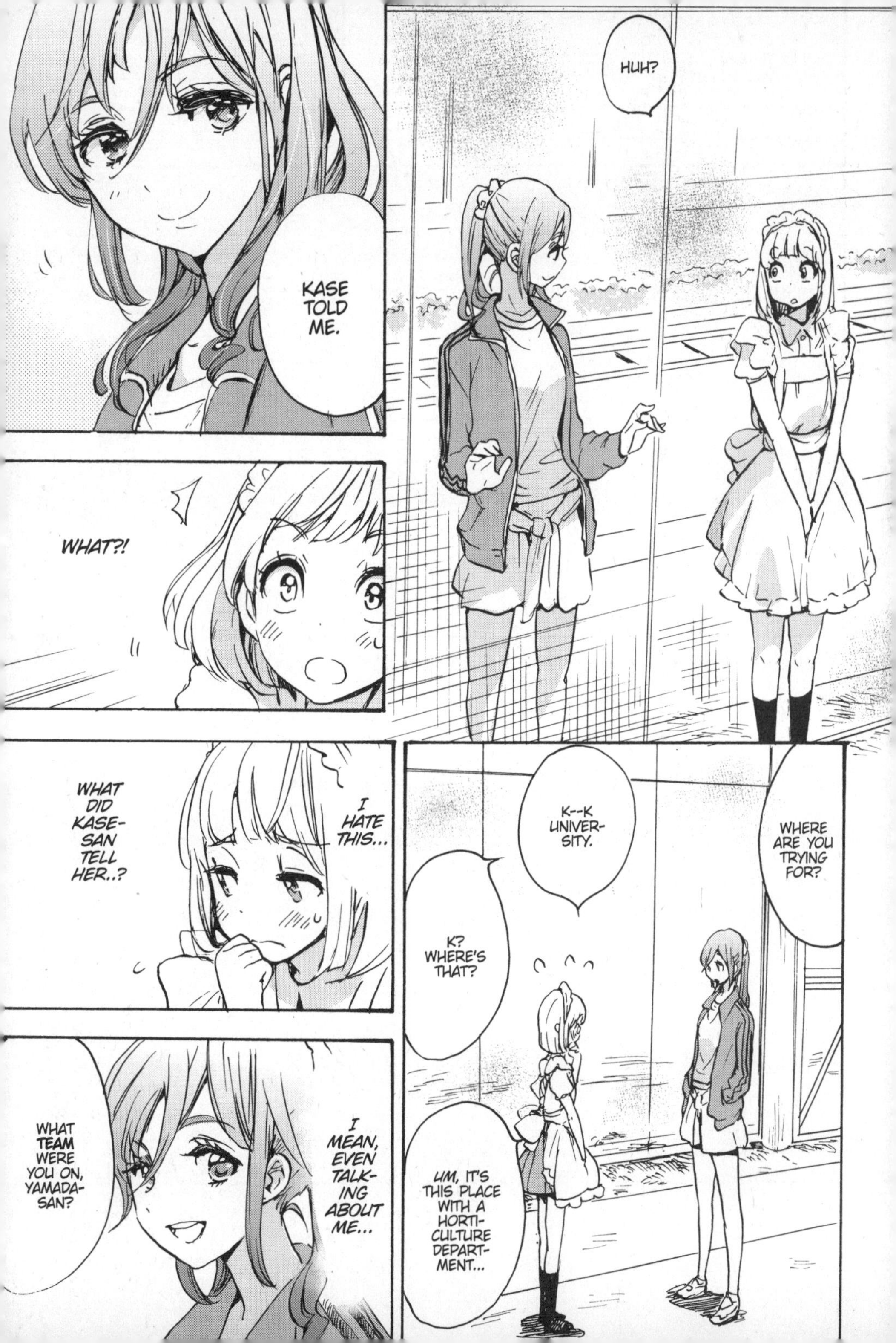
HUH?
KASE TOLD ME.
WHAT?!
I HATE THIS...
WHAT DID KASE-SAN TELL HER..?
I MEAN, EVEN TALKING ABOUT ME...
WHAT TEAM WERE YOU ON, YAMADA-SAN?
WHERE ARE YOU TRYING FOR?
K--K UNIVERSITY.
K? WHERE'S THAT?
UM, IT'S THIS PLACE WITH A HORTICULTURE DEPARTMENT...

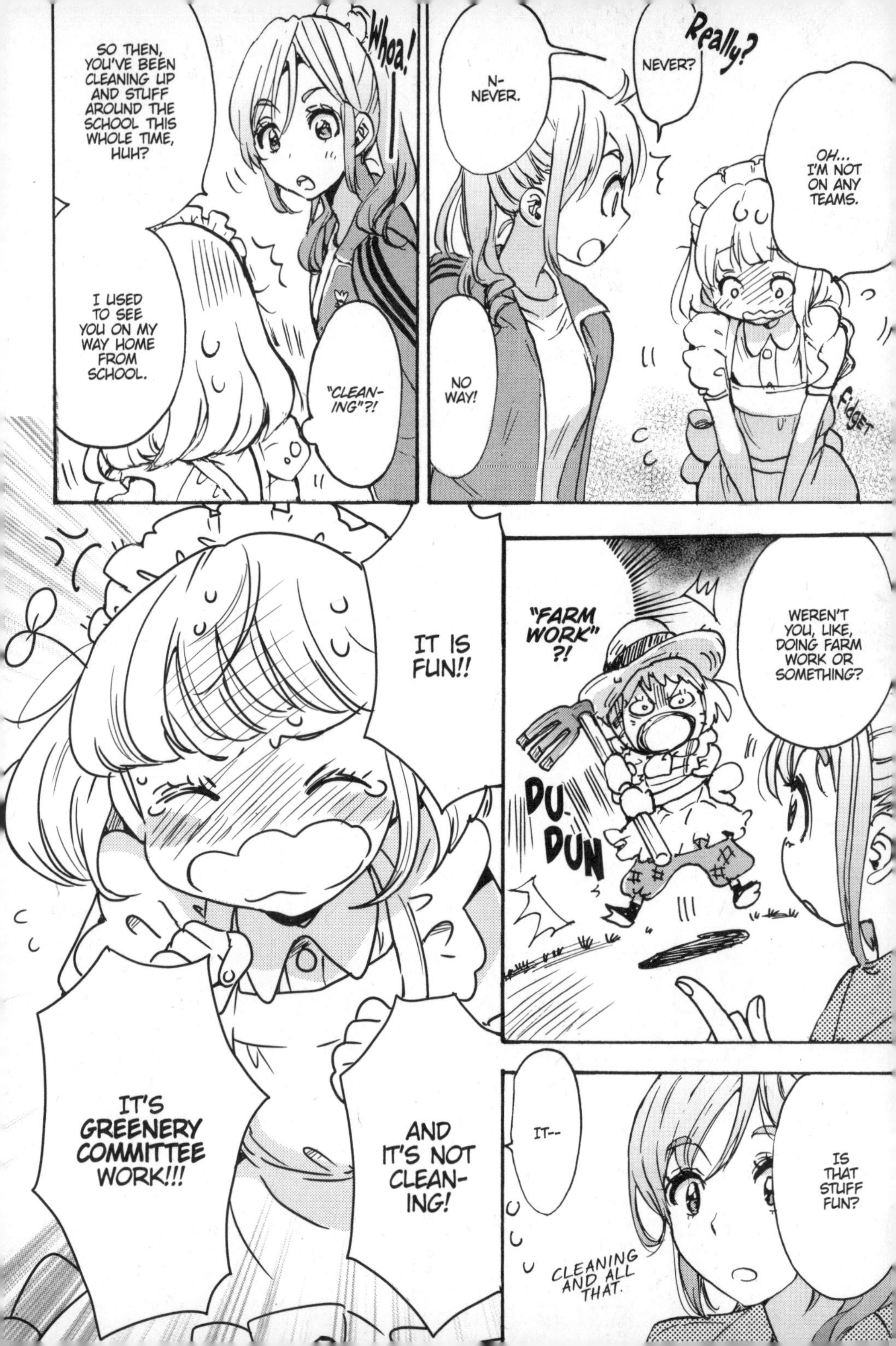
OH... I'M NOT ON ANY TEAMS.
Fidget
NO WAY!
Really?
NEVER?
N- NEVER.
Whoa!
SO THEN, YOU'VE BEEN CLEANING UP AND STUFF AROUND THE SCHOOL THIS WHOLE TIME, HUH?
I USED TO SEE YOU ON MY WAY HOME FROM SCHOOL.
"CLEAN- ING"?!
WEREN'T YOU, LIKE, DOING FARM WORK OR SOMETHING?
"FARM WORK"?!
DU- DUN
IS THAT STUFF FUN?
CLEANING AND ALL THAT.
IT--
IT IS FUN!!
AND IT'S NOT CLEAN- ING!
IT'S GREENERY COMMITTEE WORK!!!

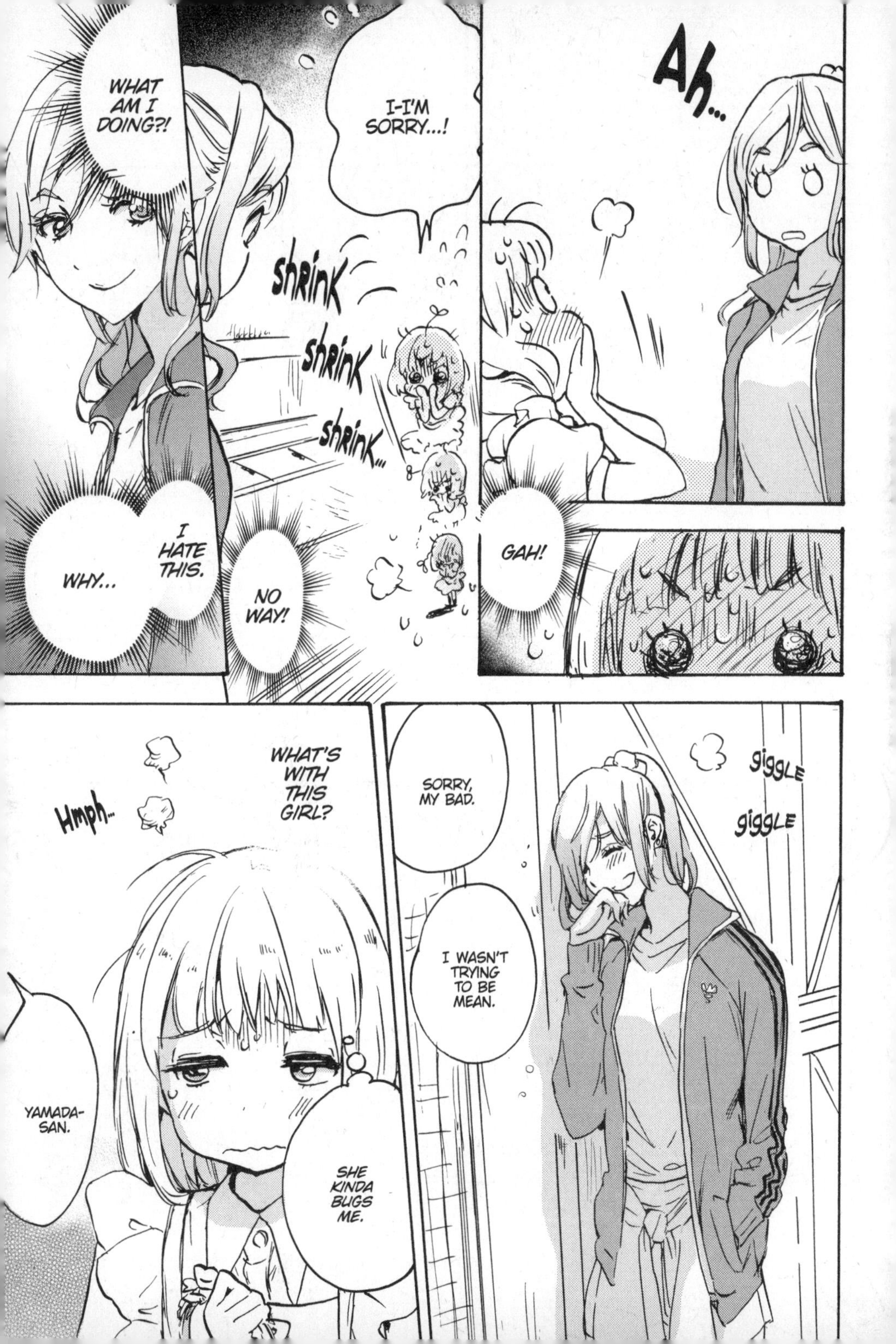
Ah...
GAH!
I-I'M SORRY...!
shrink
shrink
shrink...
NO WAY!
WHAT AM I DOING?!
I HATE THIS.
WHY...
giggle
giggle
SORRY, MY BAD.
I WASN'T TRYING TO BE MEAN.
WHAT'S WITH THIS GIRL?
Hmph...
SHE KINDA BUGS ME.
YAMADA-SAN.

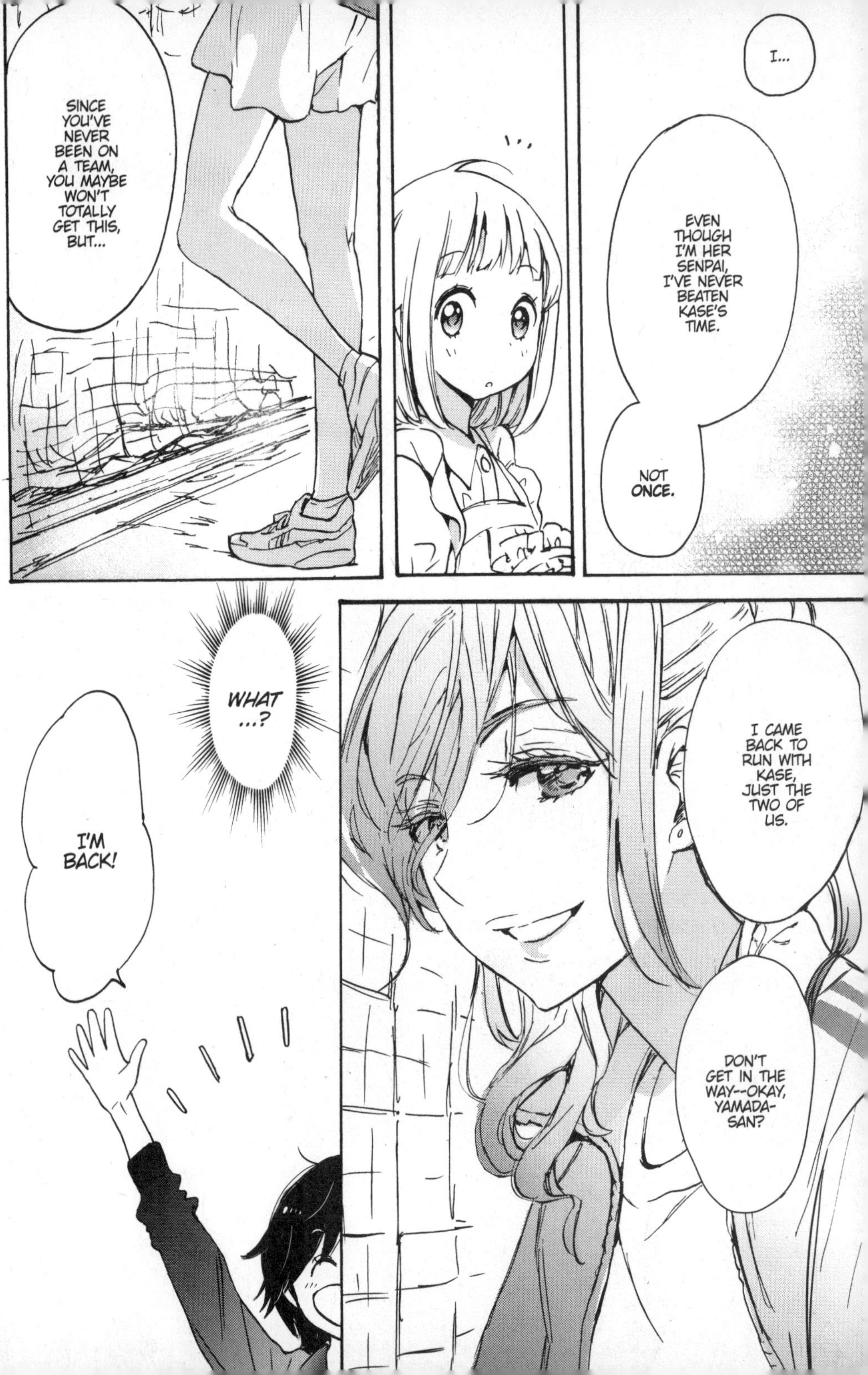
I...
EVEN THOUGH I'M HER SENPAI, I'VE NEVER BEATEN KASE'S TIME.
NOT ONCE.
SINCE YOU'VE NEVER BEEN ON A TEAM, YOU MAYBE WON'T TOTALLY GET THIS, BUT...
I CAME BACK TO RUN WITH KASE, JUST THE TWO OF US.
DON'T GET IN THE WAY--OKAY, YAMADA-SAN?
WHAT...?
I'M BACK!

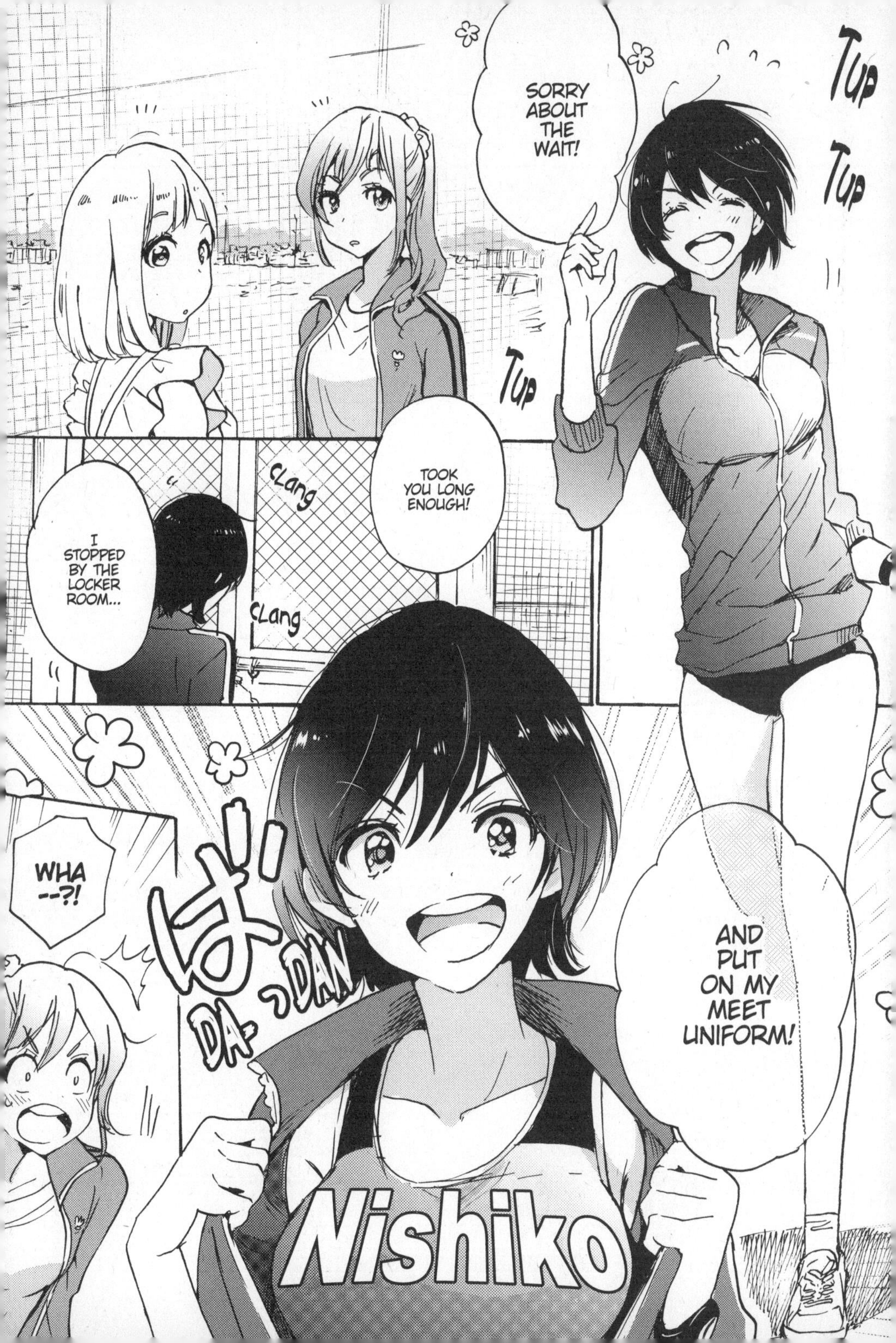
TUP
TUP
SORRY ABOUT THE WAIT!
TUP
TOOK YOU LONG ENOUGH!
CLANG
CLANG
I STOPPED BY THE LOCKER ROOM...
AND PUT ON MY MEET UNIFORM!
DA っDAN
WHA--?!
Nishiko

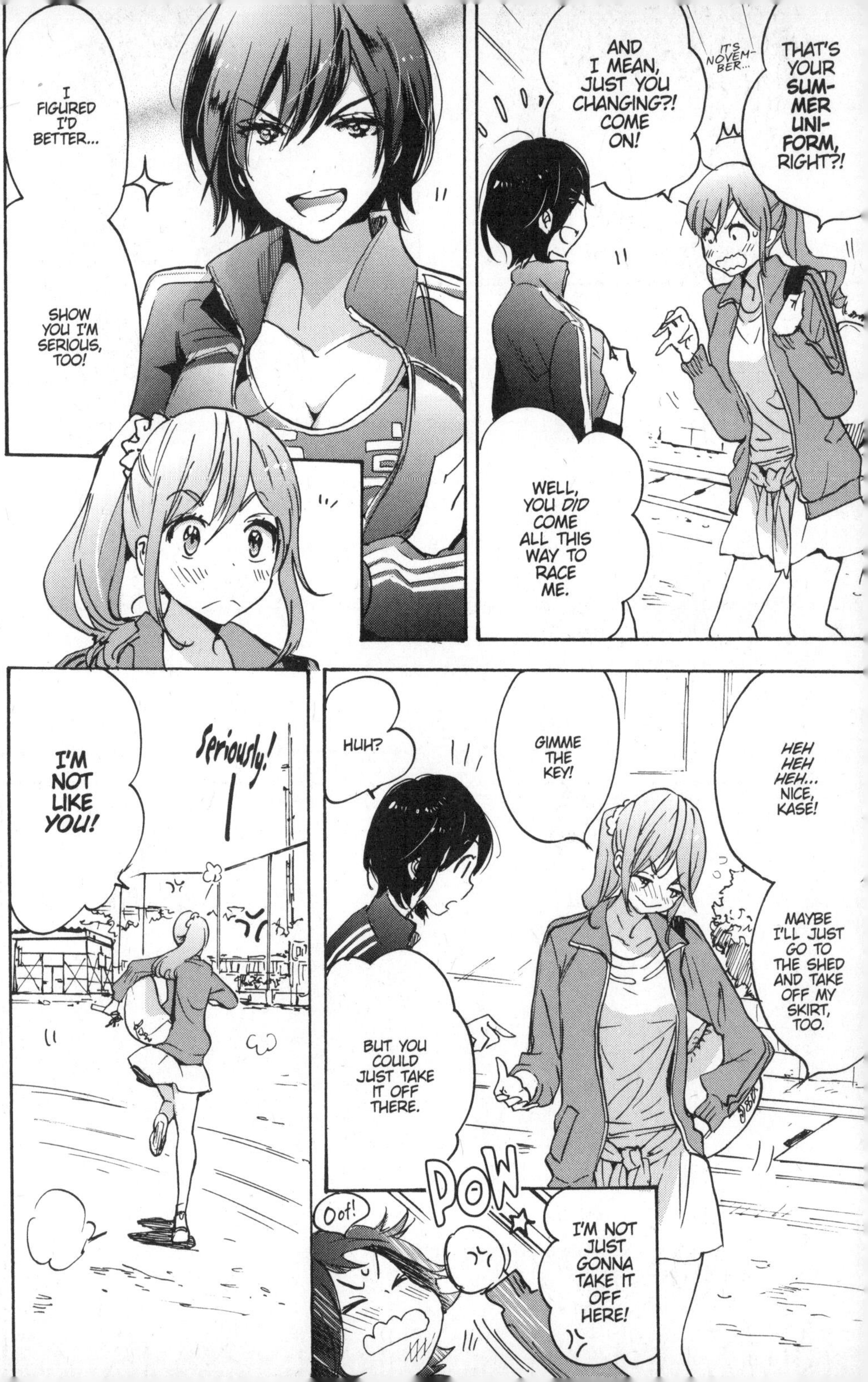
THAT'S YOUR SUMMER UNIFORM, RIGHT?!
IT'S NOVEMBER...
AND I MEAN, JUST YOU CHANGING?! COME ON!
WELL, YOU *DID* COME ALL THIS WAY TO RACE ME.
I FIGURED I'D BETTER...
SHOW YOU I'M SERIOUS, TOO!
HEH HEH HEH... NICE, KASE!
GIMME THE KEY!
HUH?
MAYBE I'LL JUST GO TO THE SHED AND TAKE OFF MY SKIRT, TOO.
BUT YOU COULD JUST TAKE IT OFF THERE.
POW
I'M NOT JUST GONNA TAKE IT OFF HERE!
Oof!
Seriously!
I'M NOT LIKE *YOU*!

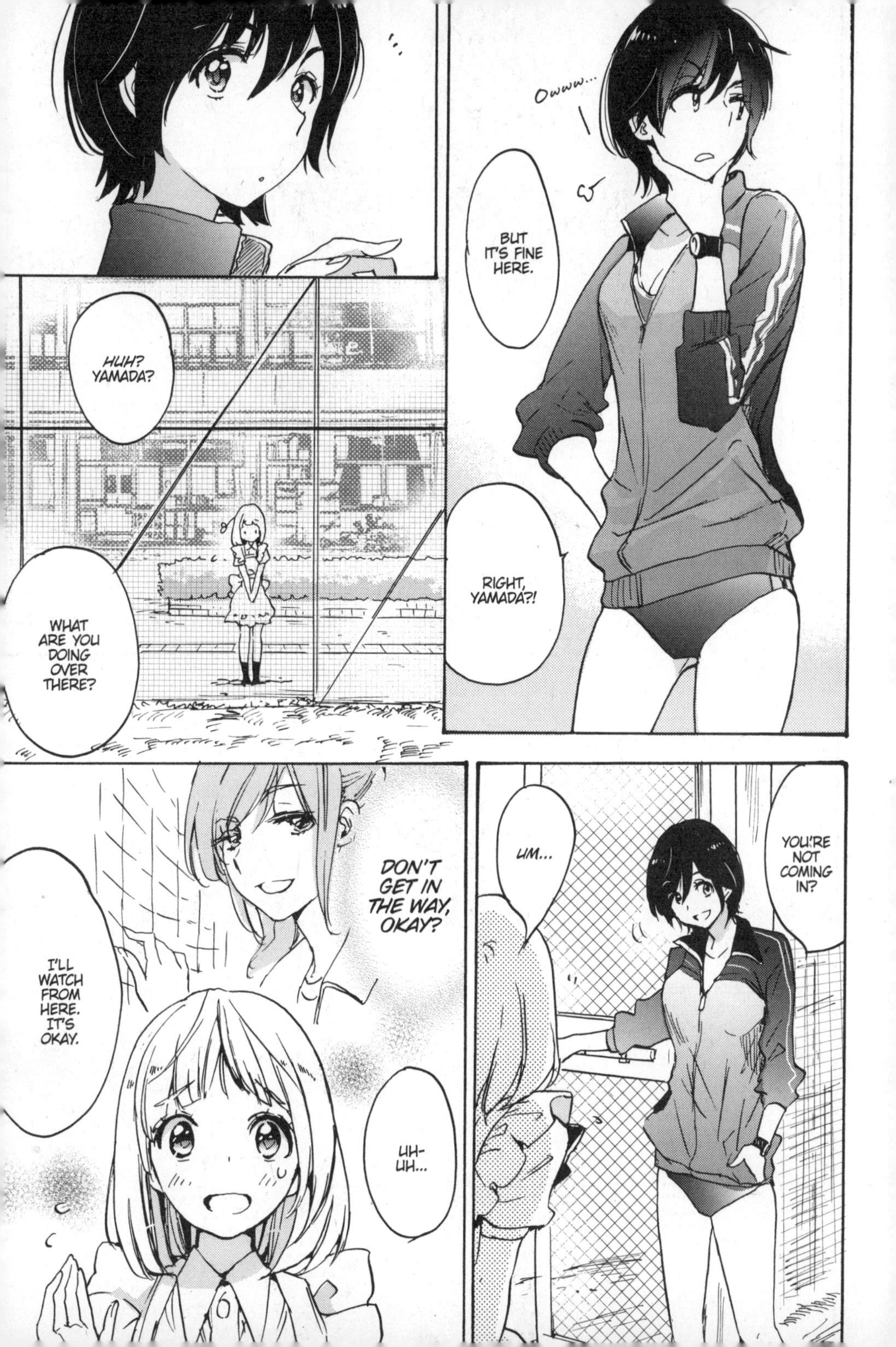
Owww...
BUT IT'S FINE HERE.
RIGHT, YAMADA?!
...
HUH? YAMADA?
WHAT ARE YOU DOING OVER THERE?
YOU'RE NOT COMING IN?
UM...
DON'T GET IN THE WAY, OKAY?
UH-UH...
I'LL WATCH FROM HERE. IT'S OKAY.

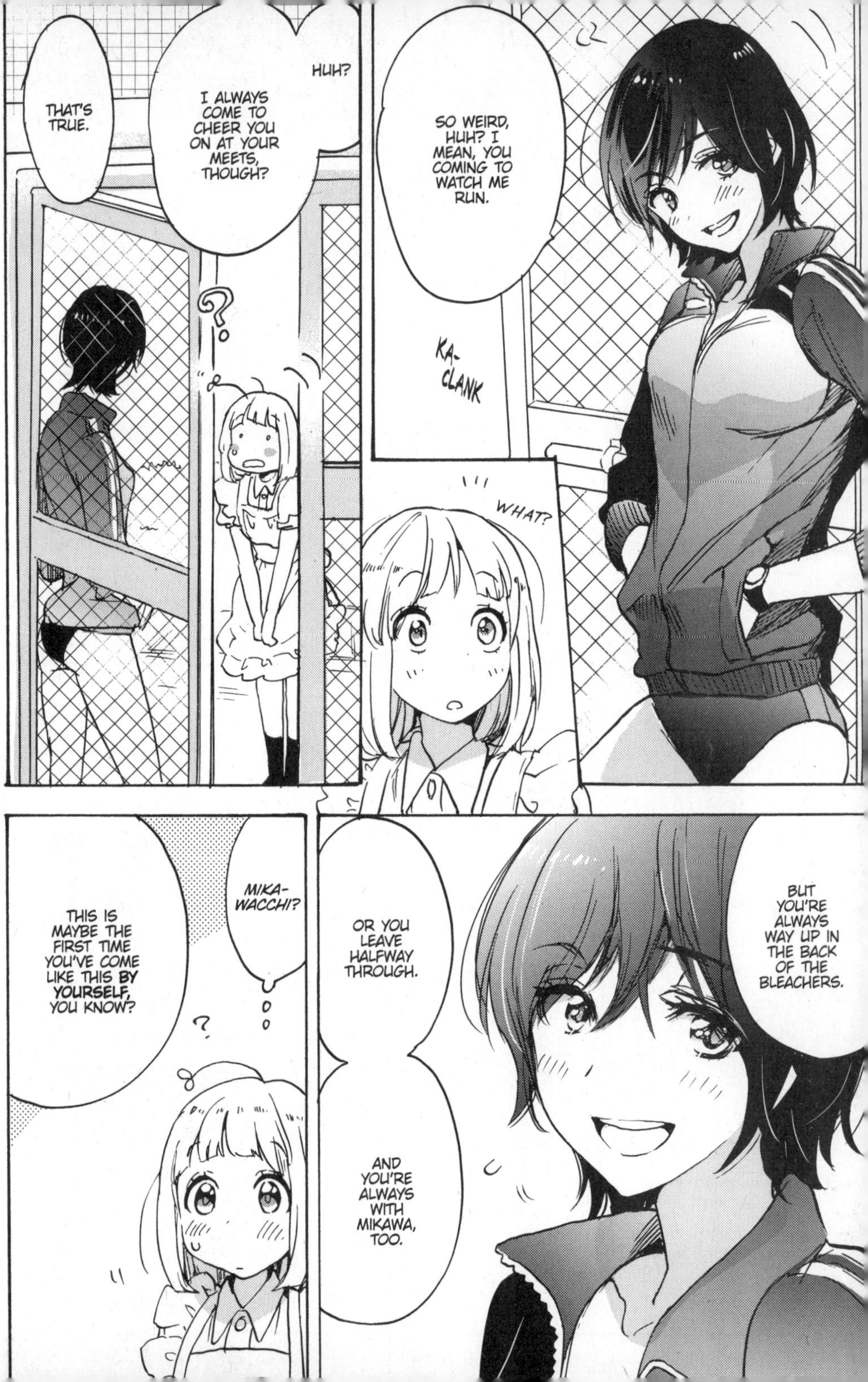
SO WEIRD, HUH? I MEAN, YOU COMING TO WATCH ME RUN.
KA-CLANK
WHAT?
HUH?
I ALWAYS COME TO CHEER YOU ON AT YOUR MEETS, THOUGH?
THAT'S TRUE.
BUT YOU'RE ALWAYS WAY UP IN THE BACK OF THE BLEACHERS.
OR YOU LEAVE HALFWAY THROUGH.
AND YOU'RE ALWAYS WITH MIKAWA, TOO.
MIKA-WACCHI?
THIS IS MAYBE THE FIRST TIME YOU'VE COME LIKE THIS BY YOURSELF, YOU KNOW?

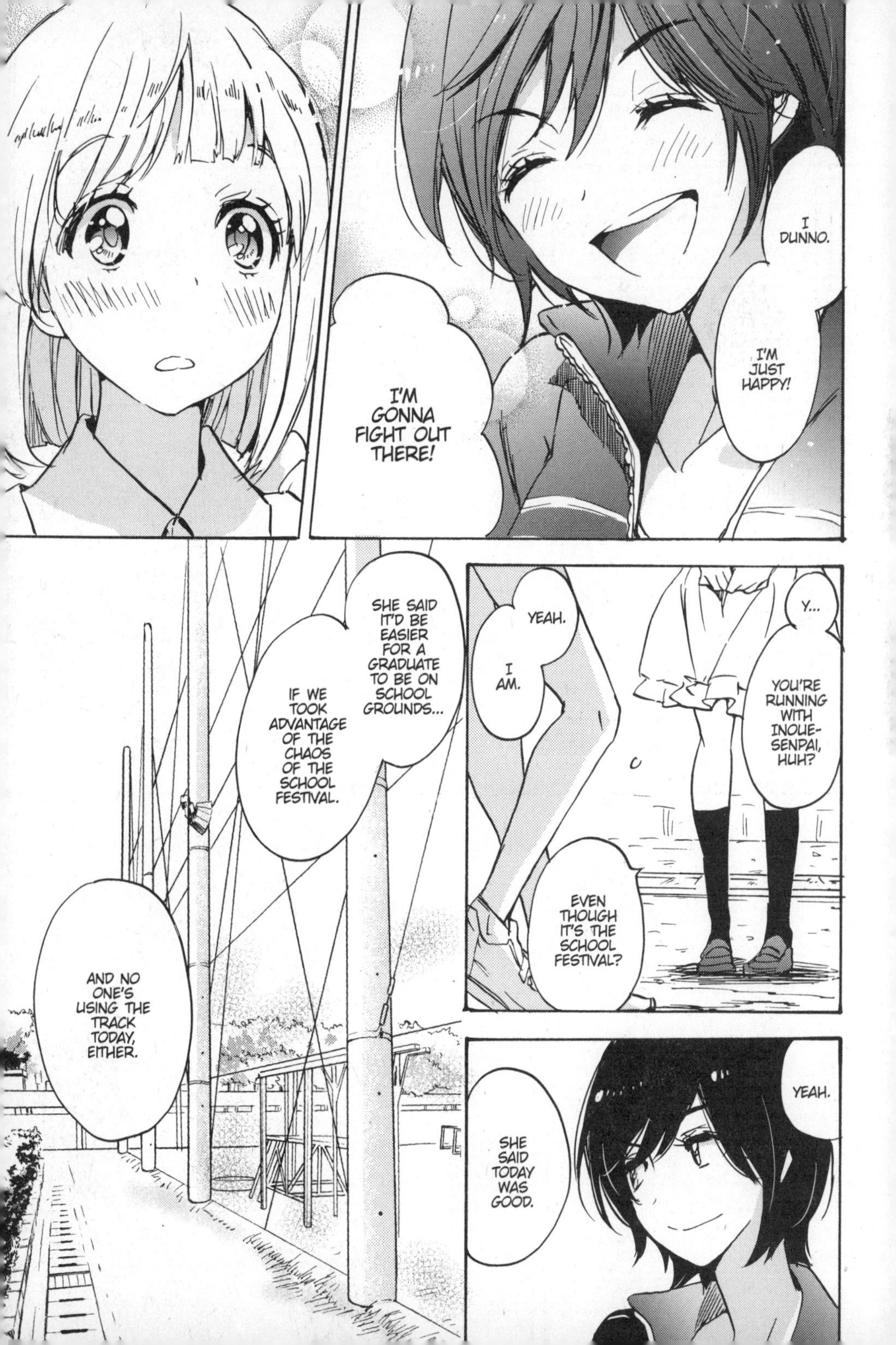
I DUNNO.
I'M JUST HAPPY!
I'M GONNA FIGHT OUT THERE!
Y...
YOU'RE RUNNING WITH INOUE-SENPAI, HUH?
EVEN THOUGH IT'S THE SCHOOL FESTIVAL?
YEAH.
I AM.
YEAH.
SHE SAID TODAY WAS GOOD.
SHE SAID IT'D BE EASIER FOR A GRADUATE TO BE ON SCHOOL GROUNDS...
IF WE TOOK ADVANTAGE OF THE CHAOS OF THE SCHOOL FESTIVAL.
AND NO ONE'S USING THE TRACK TODAY, EITHER.

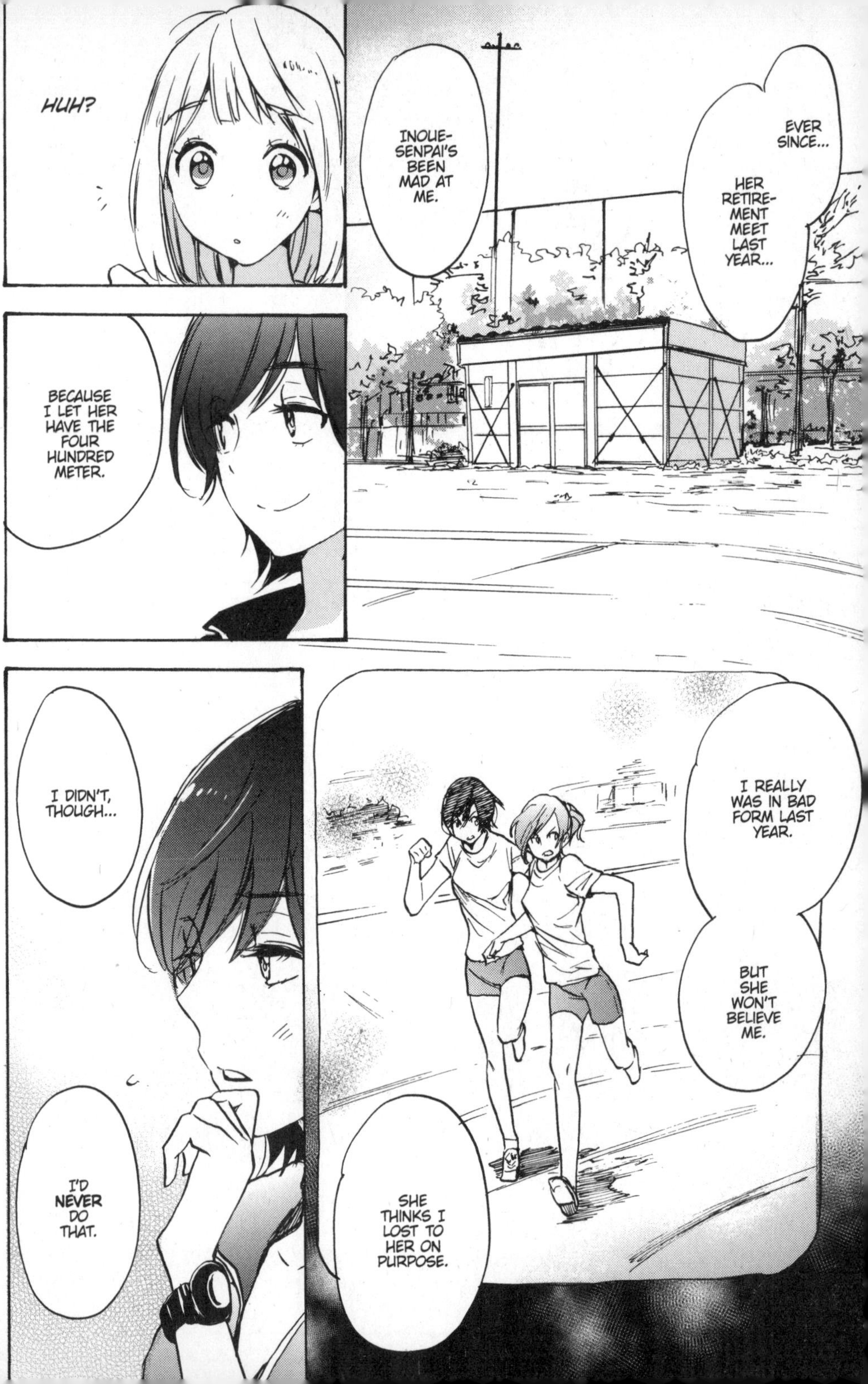
EVER SINCE... HER RETIREMENT MEET LAST YEAR...
INOUE-SENPAI'S BEEN MAD AT ME.
HUH?
BECAUSE I LET HER HAVE THE FOUR HUNDRED METER.
I REALLY WAS IN BAD FORM LAST YEAR.
BUT SHE WON'T BELIEVE ME.
SHE THINKS I LOST TO HER ON PURPOSE.
I DIDN'T, THOUGH...
I'D NEVER DO THAT.

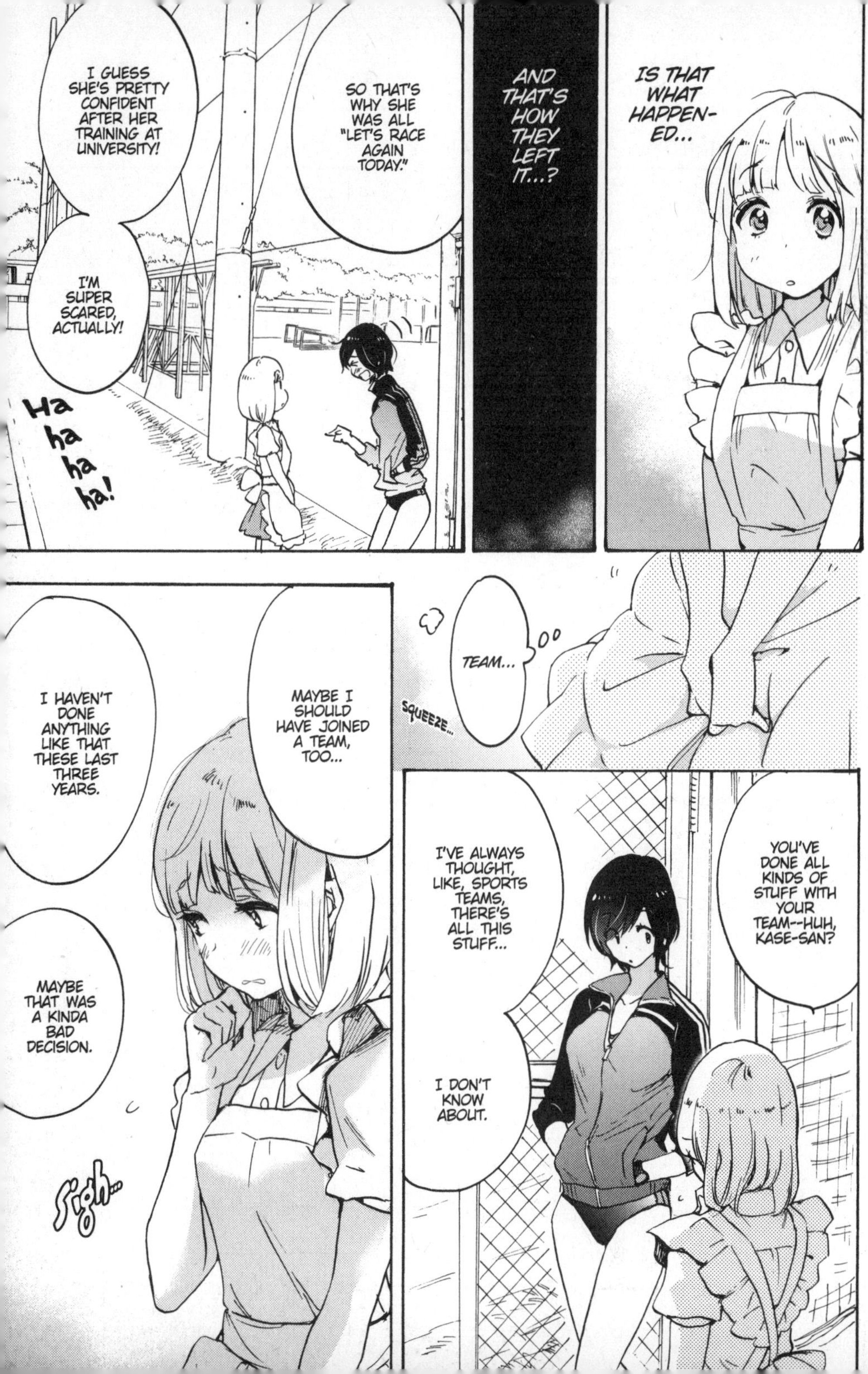
IS THAT WHAT HAPPEN-ED...
AND THAT'S HOW THEY LEFT IT...?
SO THAT'S WHY SHE WAS ALL "LET'S RACE AGAIN TODAY."
I GUESS SHE'S PRETTY CONFIDENT AFTER HER TRAINING AT UNIVERSITY!
I'M SUPER SCARED, ACTUALLY!
Ha ha ha ha!
TEAM...
SQUEEZE...
YOU'VE DONE ALL KINDS OF STUFF WITH YOUR TEAM--HUH, KASE-SAN?
I'VE ALWAYS THOUGHT, LIKE, SPORTS TEAMS, THERE'S ALL THIS STUFF...
I DON'T KNOW ABOUT.
MAYBE I SHOULD HAVE JOINED A TEAM, TOO...
I HAVEN'T DONE ANYTHING LIKE THAT THESE LAST THREE YEARS.
MAYBE THAT WAS A KINDA BAD DECISION.
Sigh...

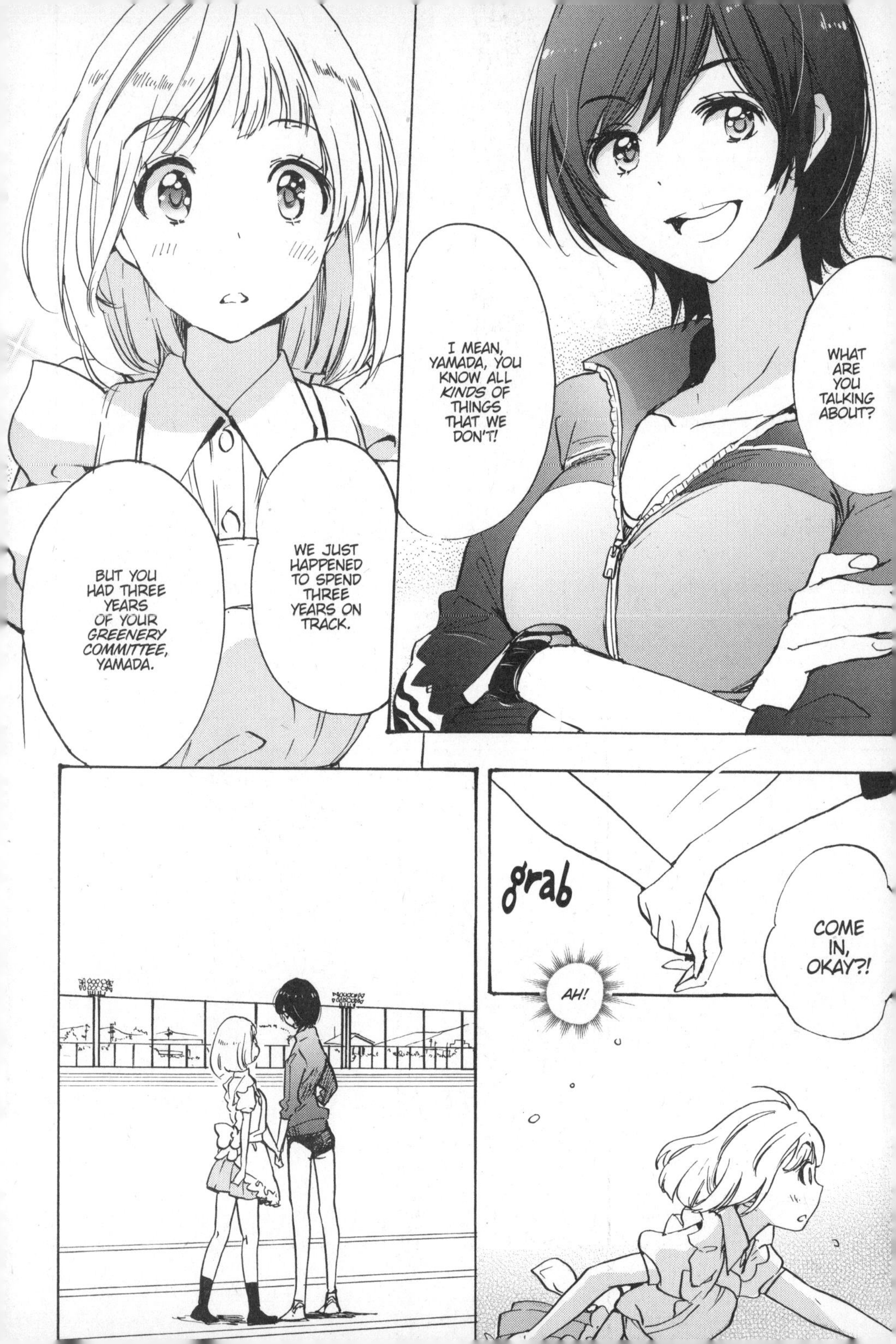
WHAT ARE YOU TALKING ABOUT?
I MEAN, YAMADA, YOU KNOW ALL *KINDS* OF THINGS THAT WE DON'T!
WE JUST HAPPENED TO SPEND THREE YEARS ON TRACK.
BUT YOU HAD THREE YEARS OF YOUR GREENERY COMMITTEE, YAMADA.
COME IN, OKAY?!
grab
AH!

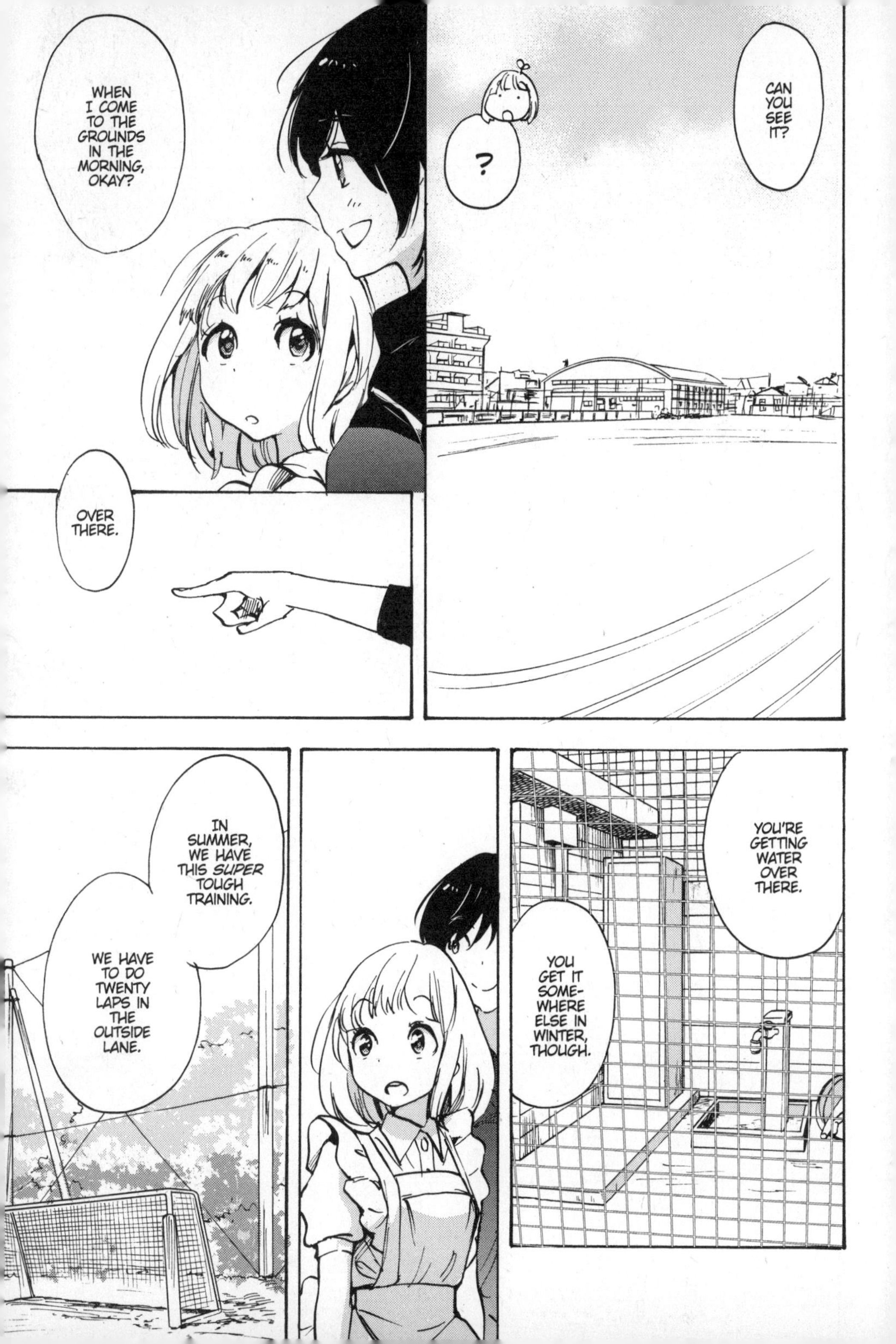
CAN YOU SEE IT?
?
WHEN I COME TO THE GROUNDS IN THE MORNING, OKAY?
OVER THERE.
YOU'RE GETTING WATER OVER THERE.
YOU GET IT SOMEWHERE ELSE IN WINTER, THOUGH.
IN SUMMER, WE HAVE THIS *SUPER* TOUGH TRAINING.
WE HAVE TO DO TWENTY LAPS IN THE OUTSIDE LANE.

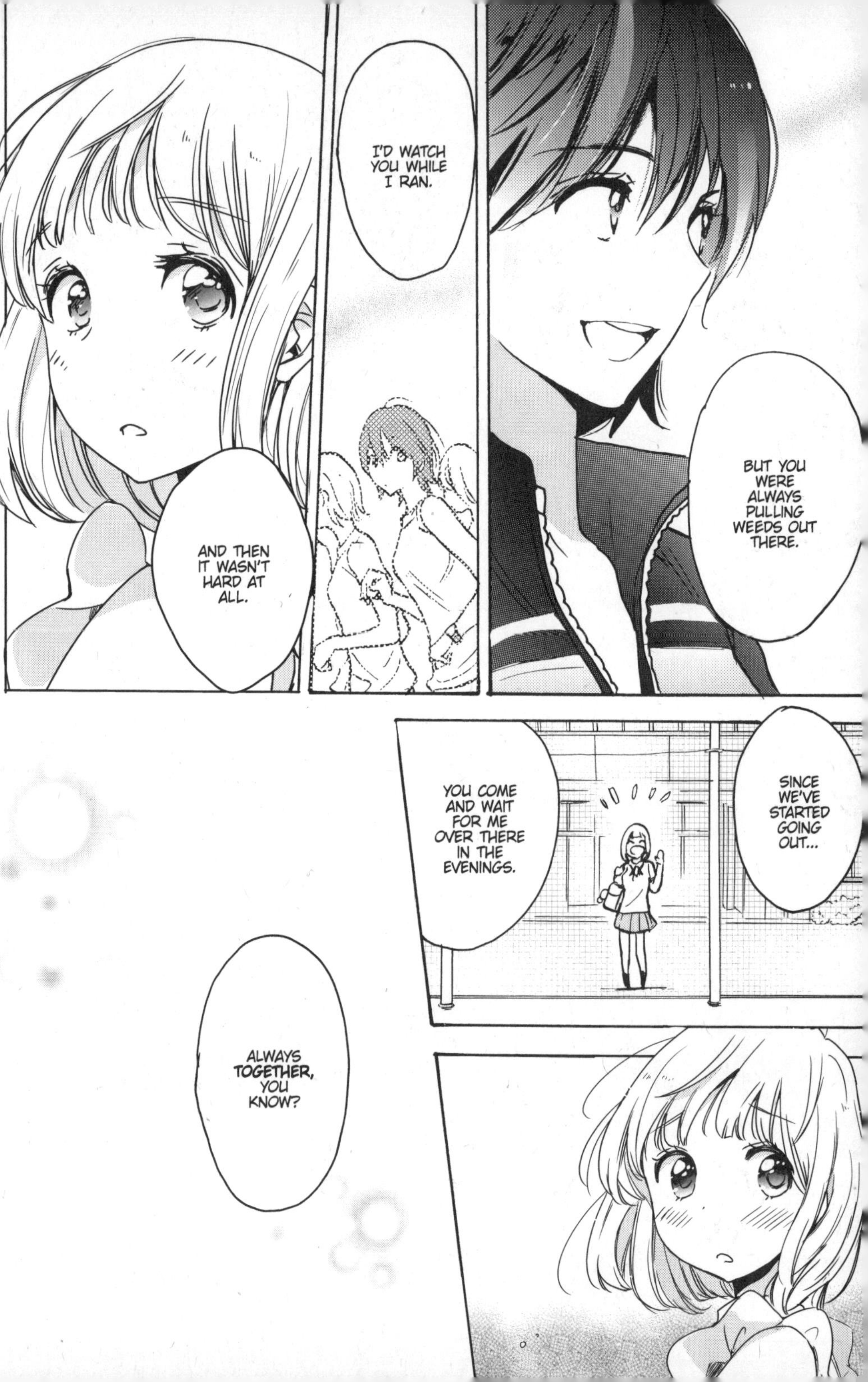
BUT YOU WERE ALWAYS PULLING WEEDS OUT THERE.
I'D WATCH YOU WHILE I RAN.
AND THEN IT WASN'T HARD AT ALL.
SINCE WE'VE STARTED GOING OUT...
YOU COME AND WAIT FOR ME OVER THERE IN THE EVENINGS.
ALWAYS TOGETHER, YOU KNOW?

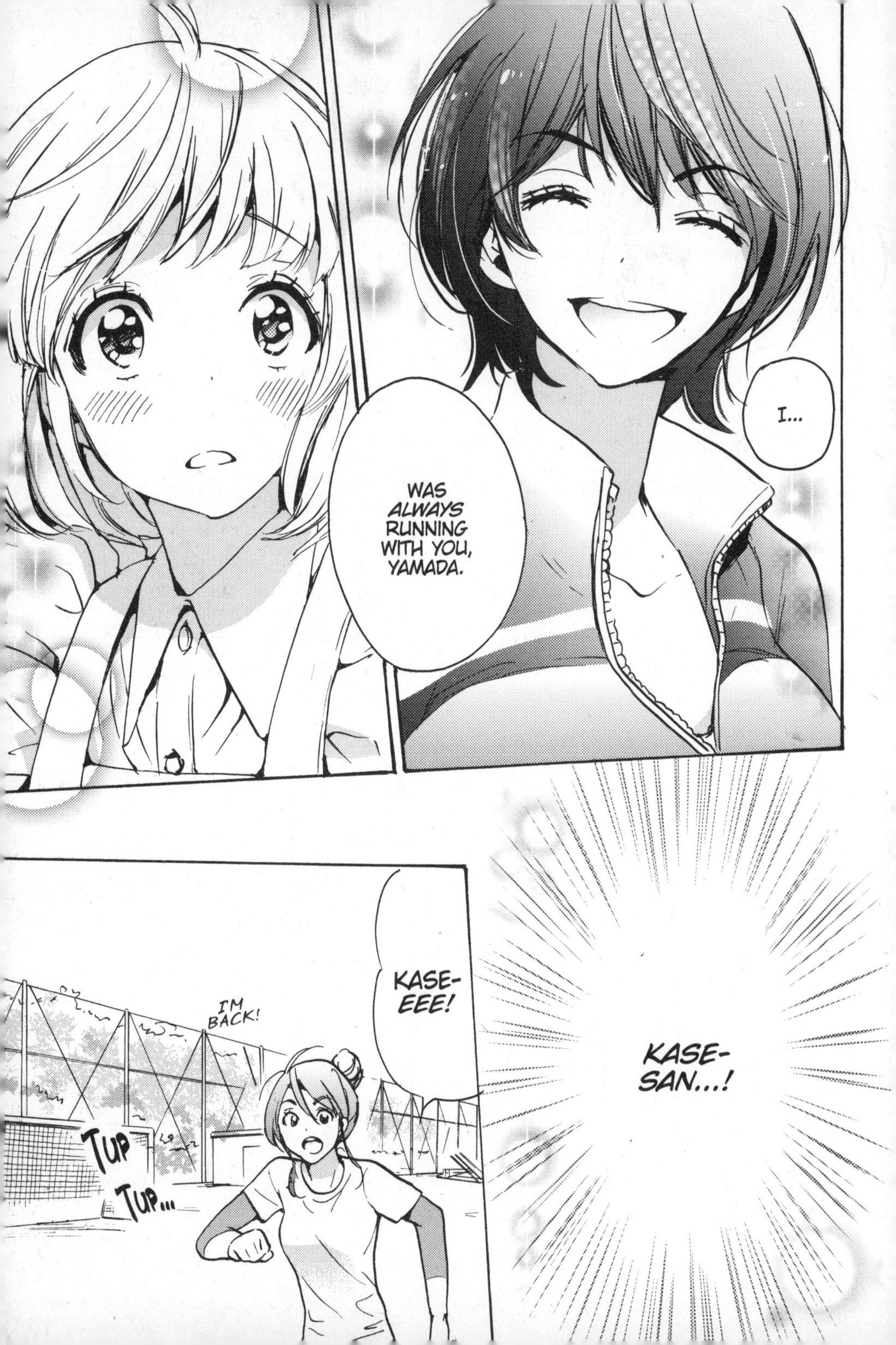
I...
WAS ALWAYS RUNNING WITH YOU, YAMADA.
KASE-SAN...!
KASE-EEE!
I'M BACK!
TUP TUP...

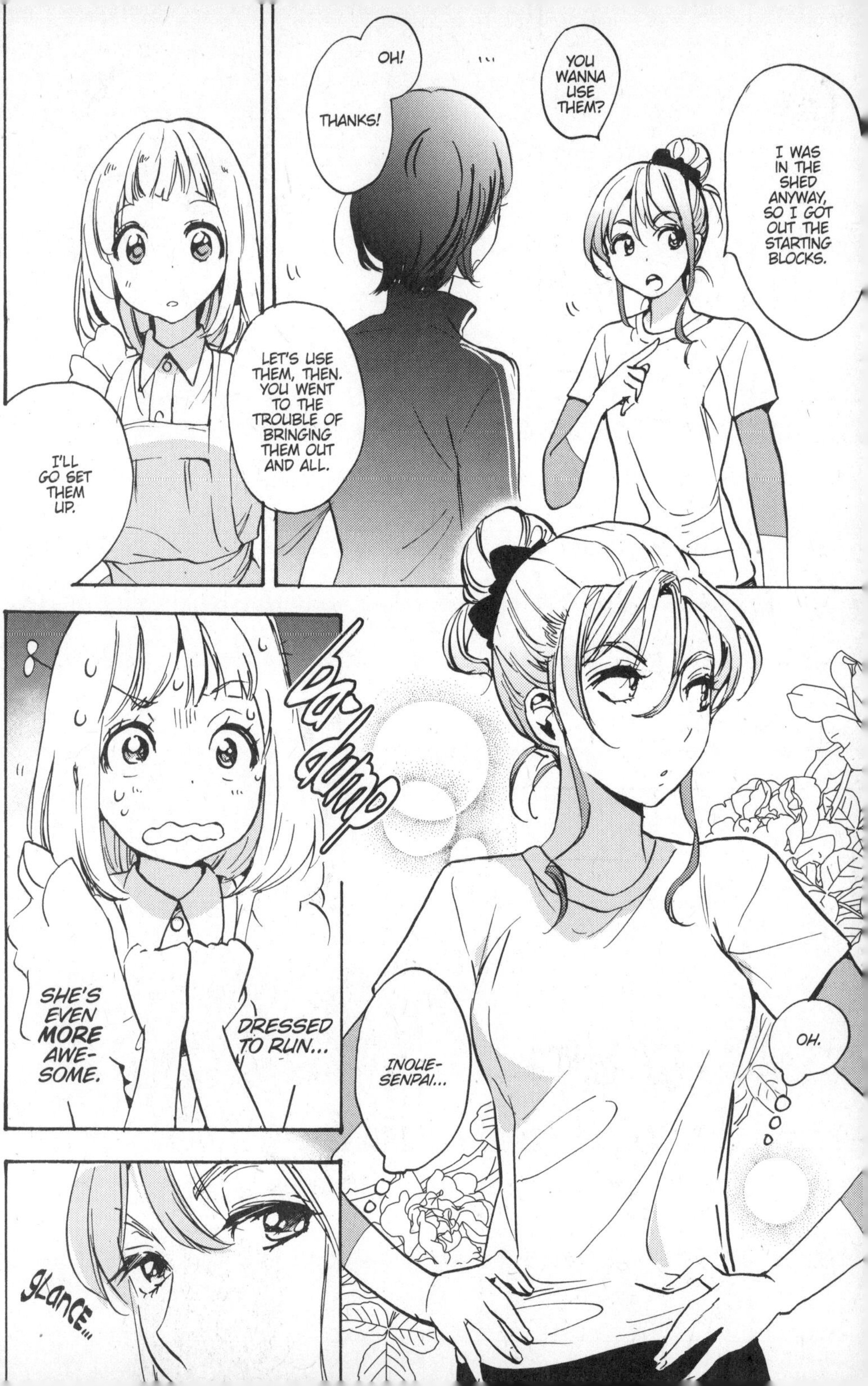

I WAS IN THE SHED ANYWAY, SO I GOT OUT THE STARTING BLOCKS.
YOU WANNA USE THEM?
...
OH!
THANKS!
LET'S USE THEM, THEN. YOU WENT TO THE TROUBLE OF BRINGING THEM OUT AND ALL.
I'LL GO SET THEM UP.
OH.
INOUE-SENPAI...
ba-dump
DRESSED TO RUN...
SHE'S EVEN MORE AWESOME.
glance...

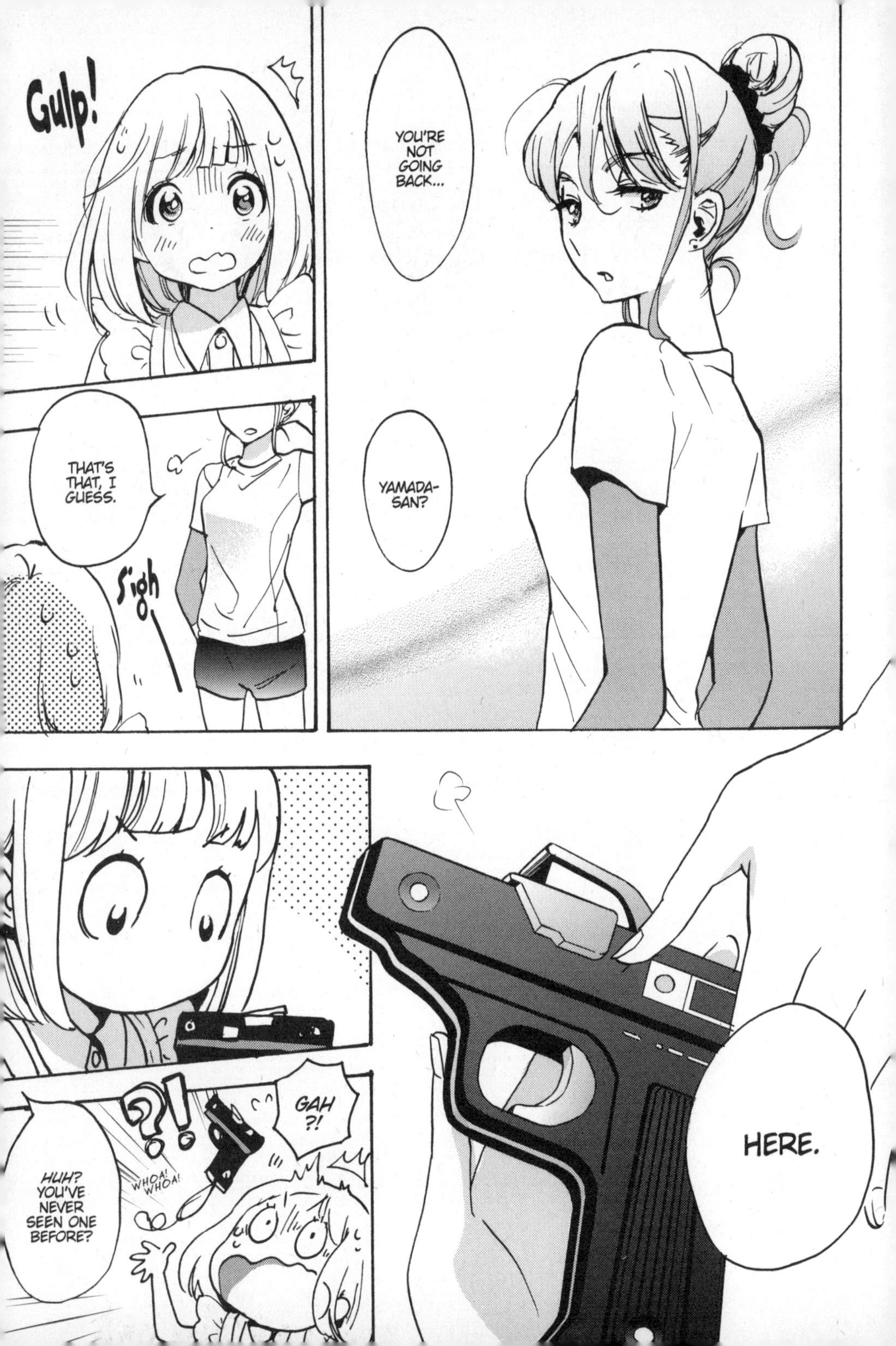
YOU'RE NOT GOING BACK...
YAMADA-SAN?
Gulp!
THAT'S THAT, I GUESS.
Sigh
HERE.
GAH ?!
WHOA! WHOA!
HUH? YOU'VE NEVER SEEN ONE BEFORE?

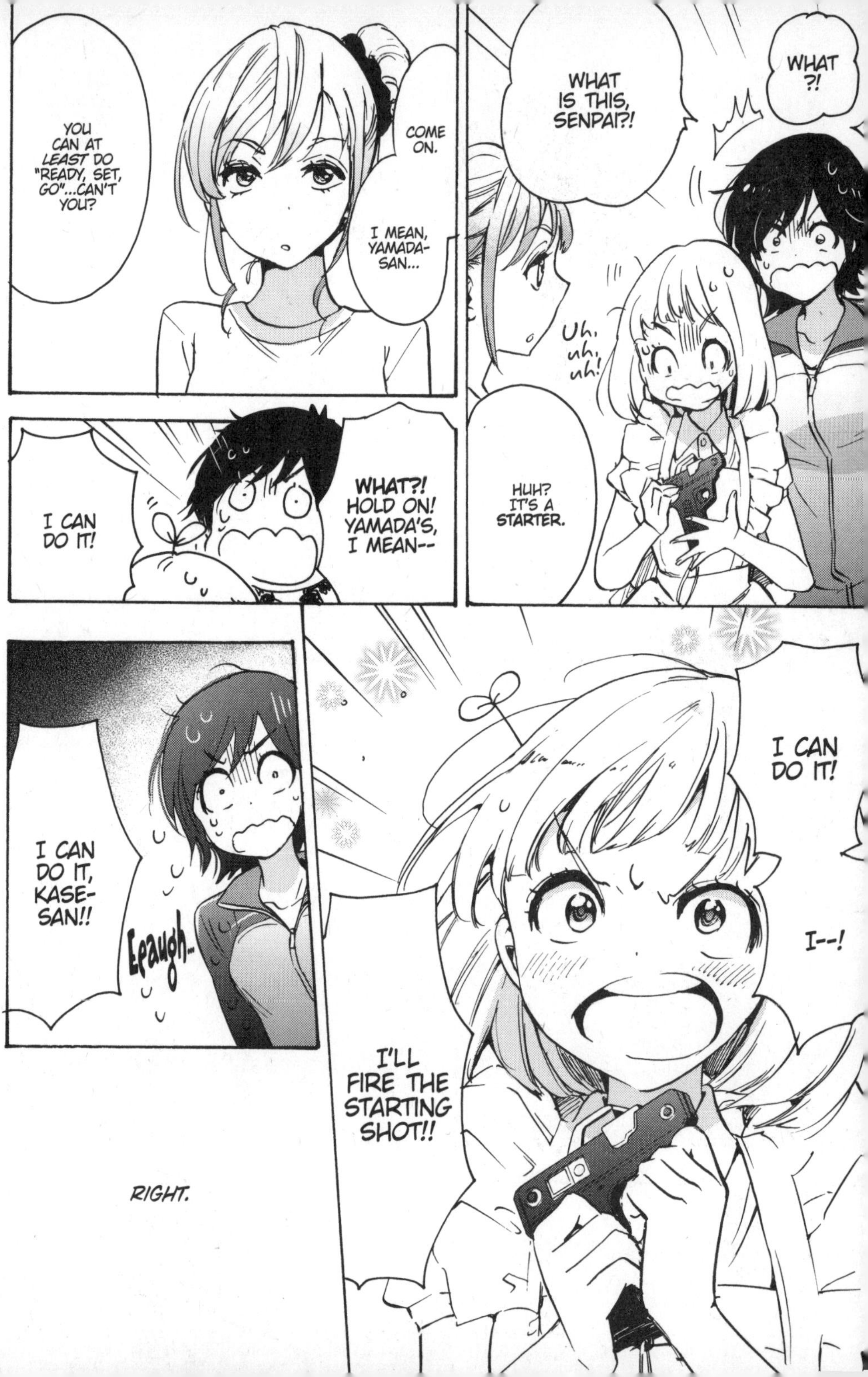
WHAT ?!
WHAT IS THIS, SENPAI?!
Uh, uh, uh!
HUH? IT'S A STARTER.
COME ON.
I MEAN, YAMADA-SAN...
YOU CAN AT LEAST DO "READY, SET, GO"...CAN'T YOU?
WHAT?! HOLD ON! YAMADA'S, I MEAN--
I CAN DO IT!
I CAN DO IT!
I--!
I'LL FIRE THE STARTING SHOT!!
I CAN DO IT, KASE-SAN!!
Eeaugh...
RIGHT.

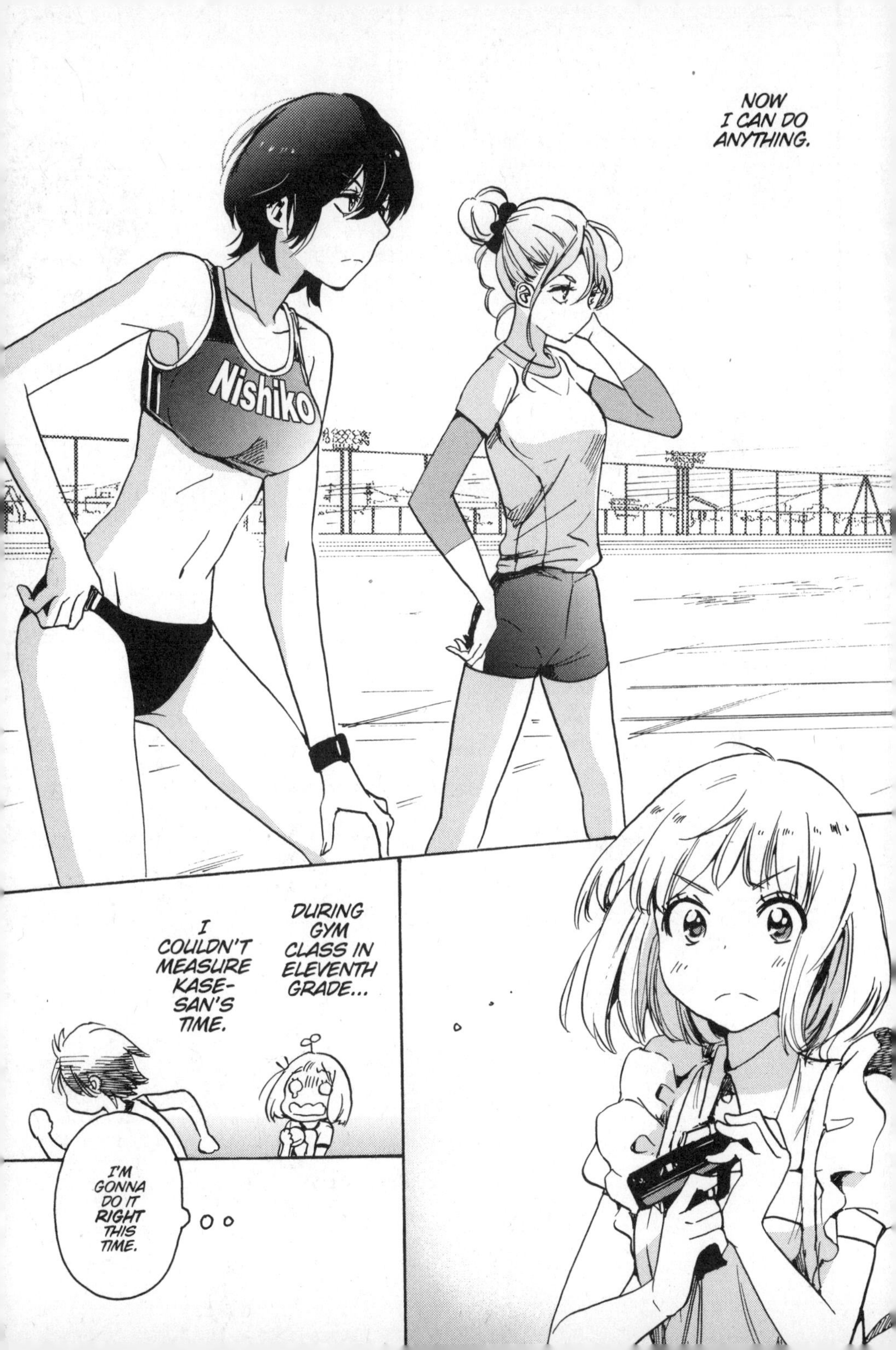
NOW I CAN DO ANYTHING.
Nishiko
DURING GYM CLASS IN ELEVENTH GRADE...
I COULDN'T MEASURE KASE-SAN'S TIME.
I'M GONNA DO IT RIGHT THIS TIME.

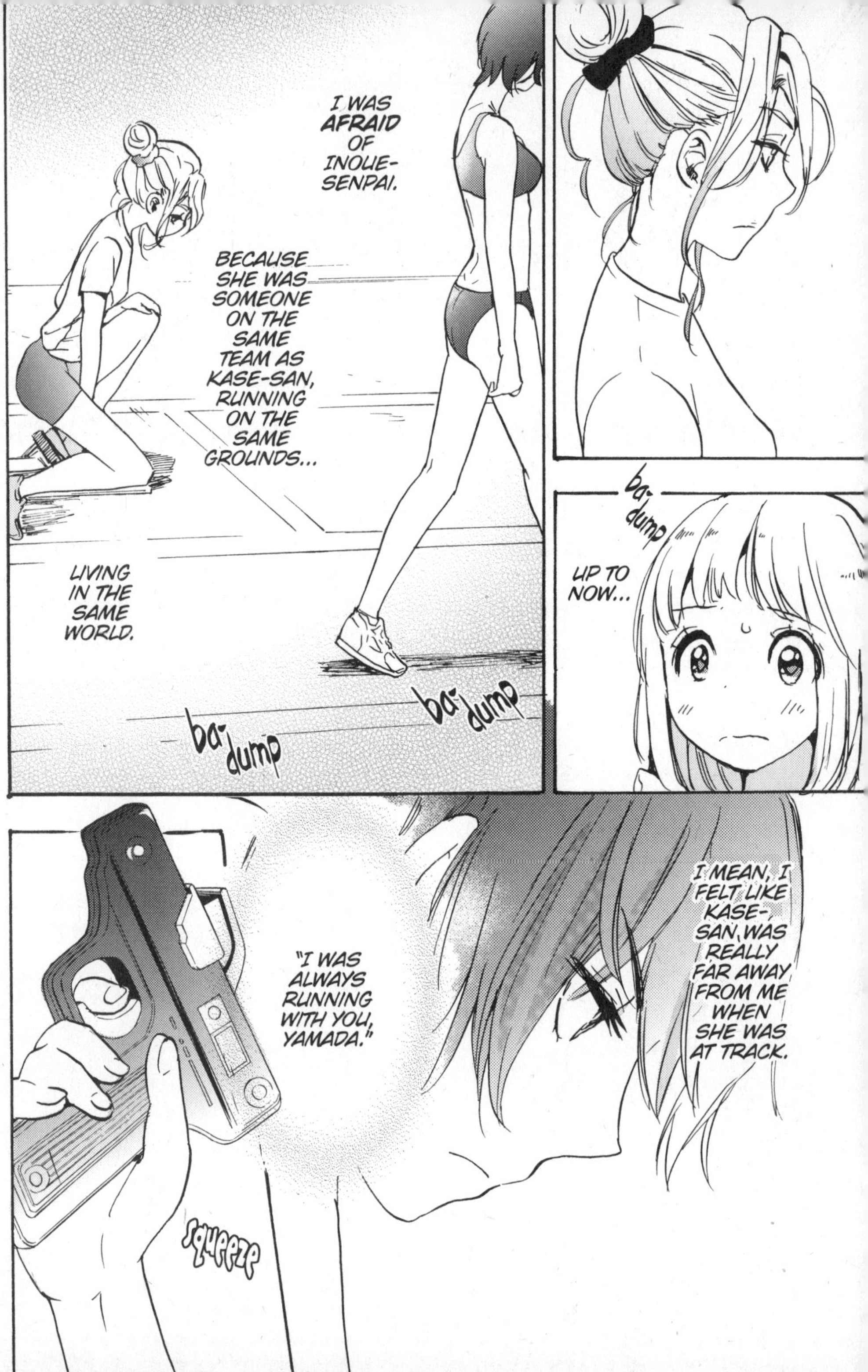
ba-dump
UP TO NOW...
I WAS AFRAID OF INOUE-SENPAI.
BECAUSE SHE WAS SOMEONE ON THE SAME TEAM AS KASE-SAN, RUNNING ON THE SAME GROUNDS...
LIVING IN THE SAME WORLD.
ba-dump
ba-dump
I MEAN, I FELT LIKE KASE-SAN WAS REALLY FAR AWAY FROM ME WHEN SHE WAS AT TRACK.
"I WAS ALWAYS RUNNING WITH YOU, YAMADA."
squeeze

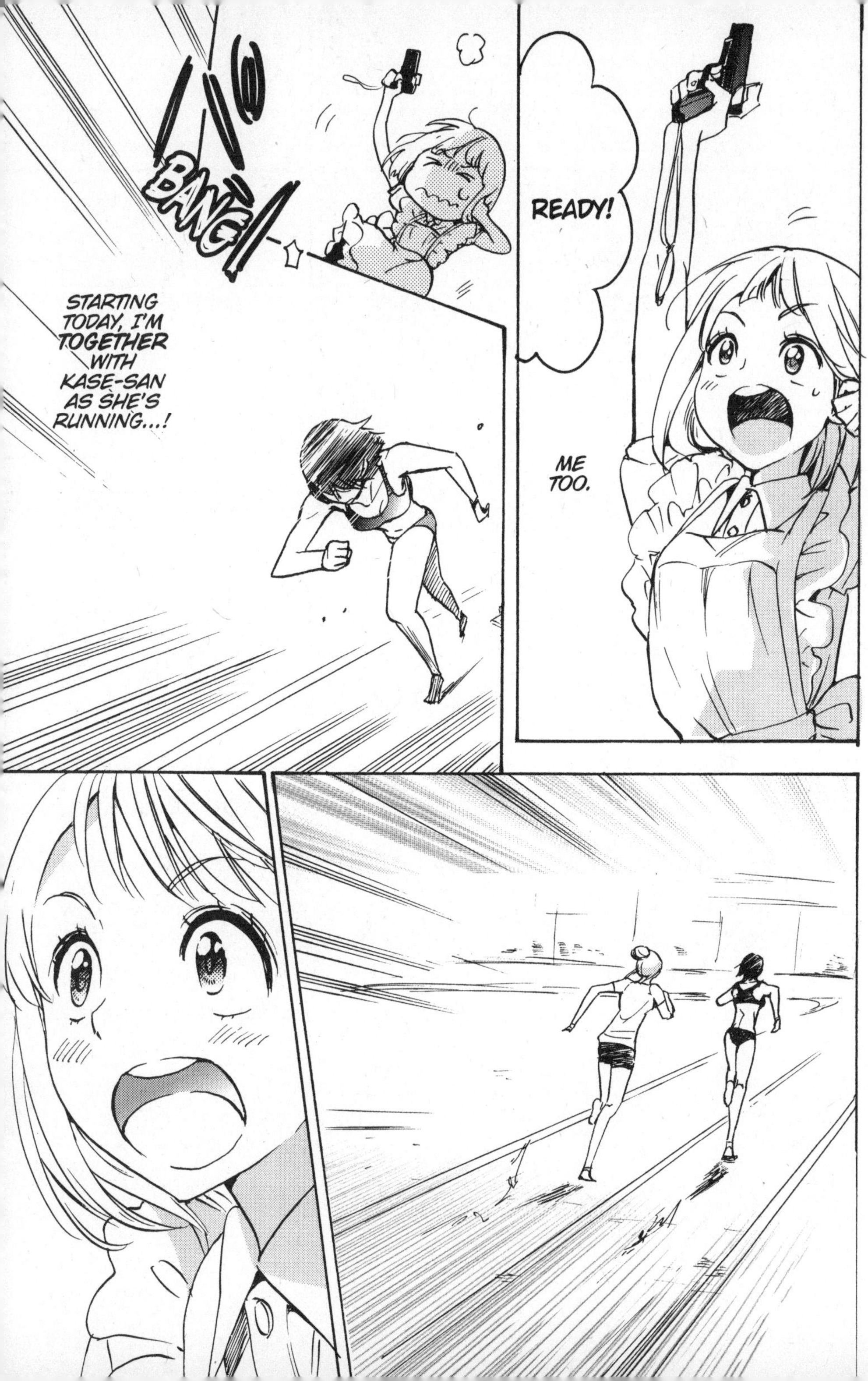
READY!
ME TOO.
BANG
STARTING TODAY, I'M TOGETHER WITH KASE-SAN AS SHE'S RUNNING...!

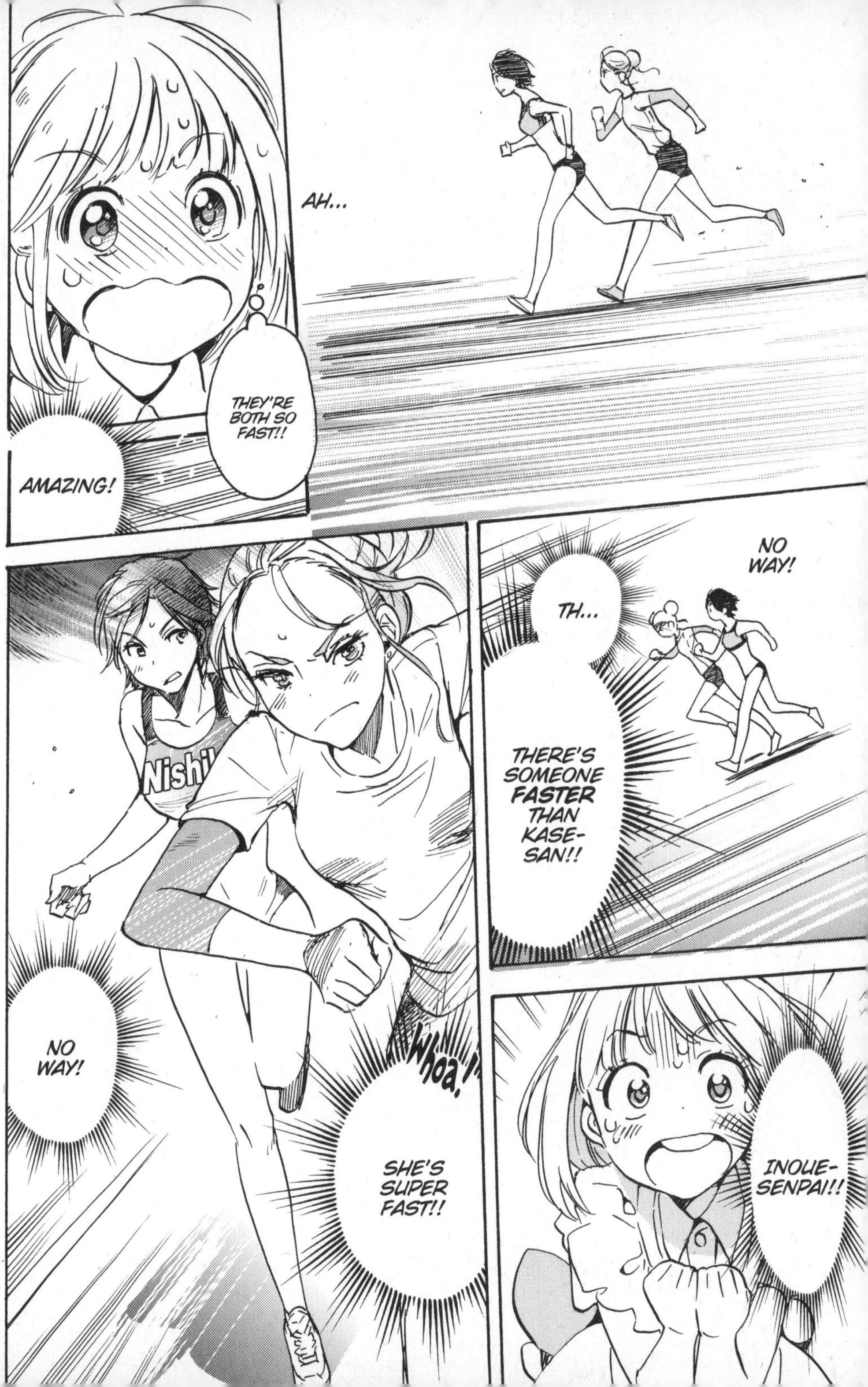
AH...
THEY'RE BOTH SO FAST!!
AMAZING!
NO WAY!
TH...
THERE'S SOMEONE FASTER THAN KASE-SAN!!
INOUE-SENPAI!!
Whoa!!
SHE'S SUPER FAST!!
NO WAY!

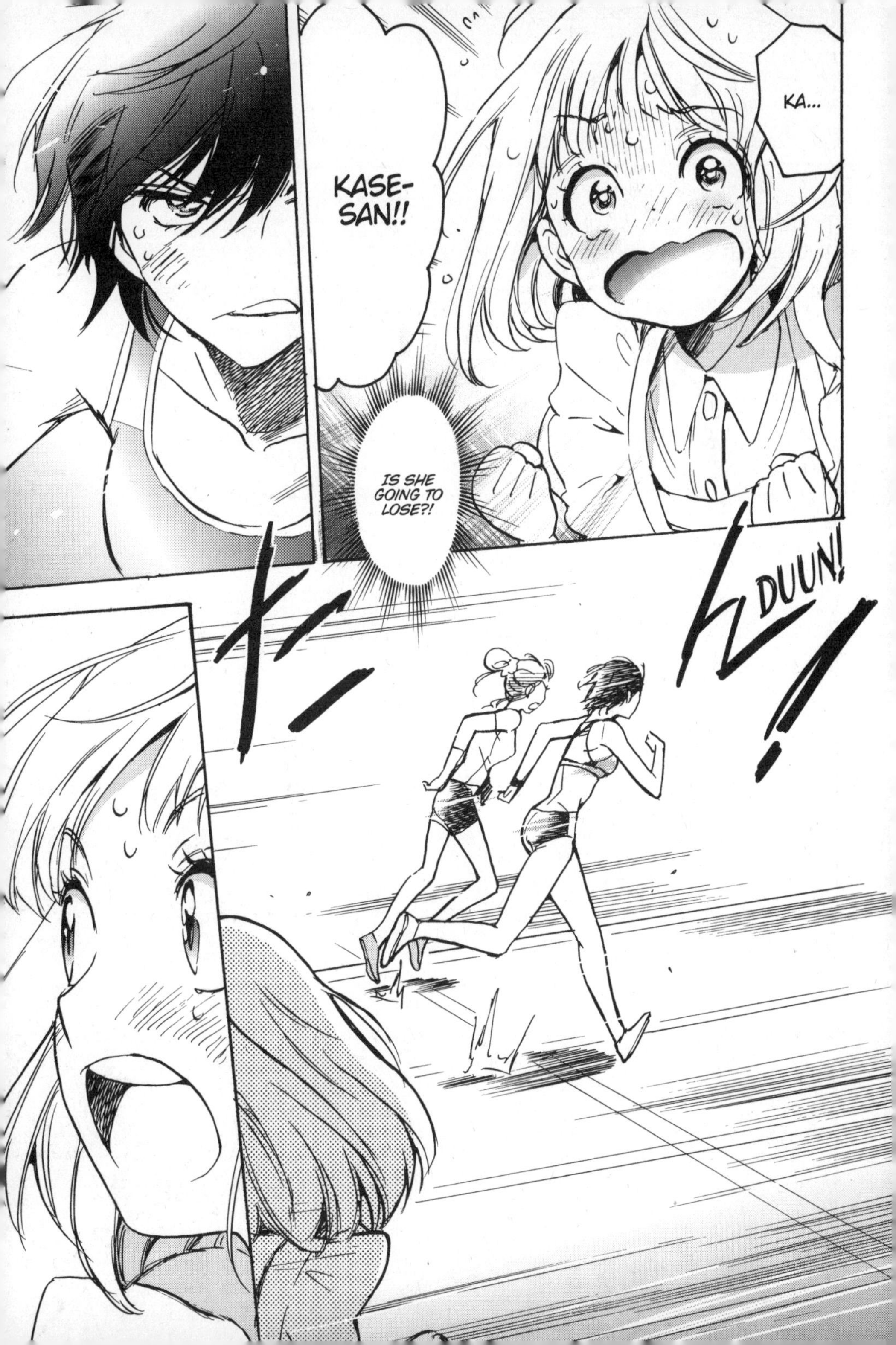
KA...
KASE-SAN!!
IS SHE GOING TO LOSE?!
DUUN!

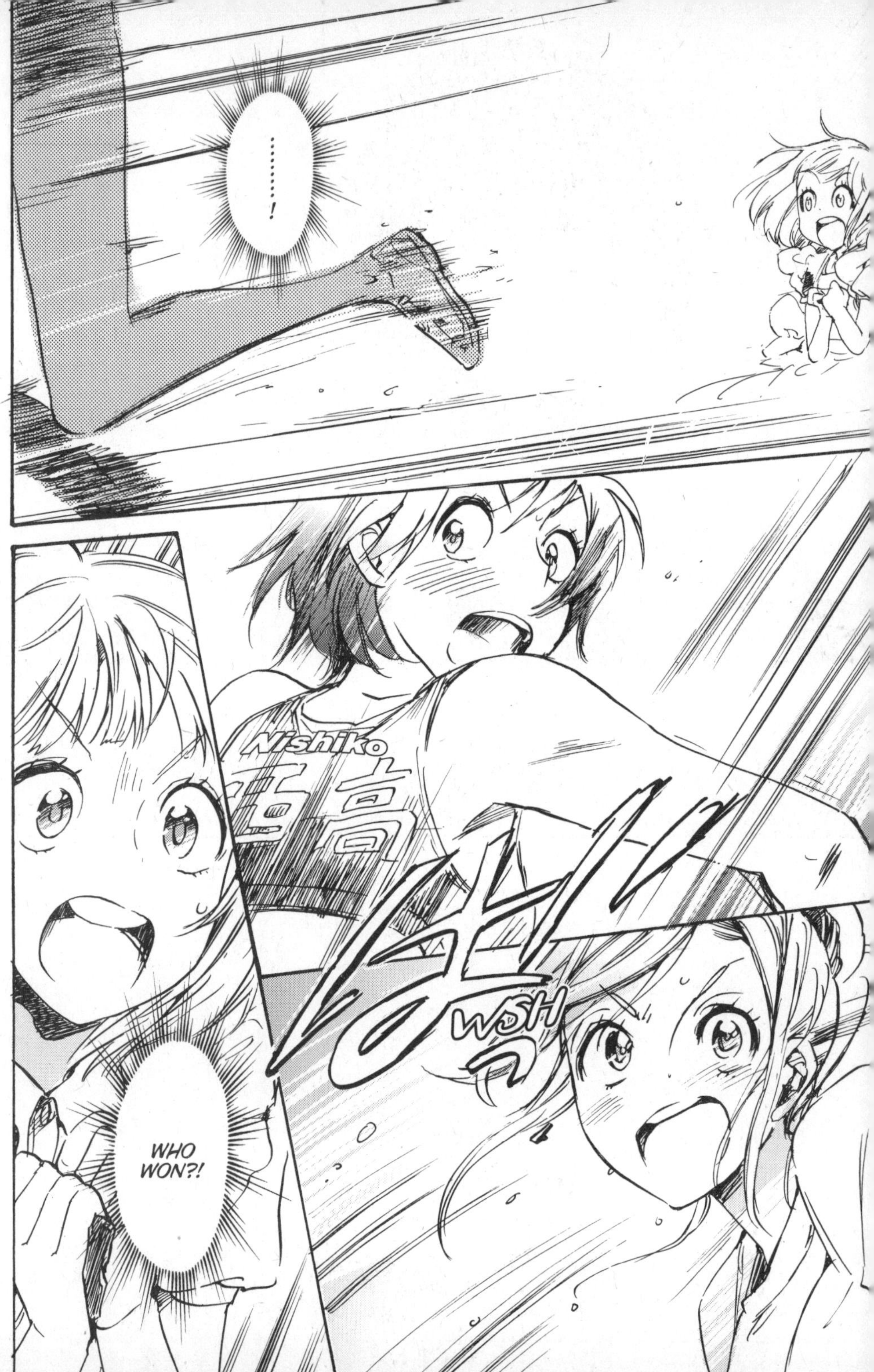
......!
Nishiko
WSH
WHO WON?!

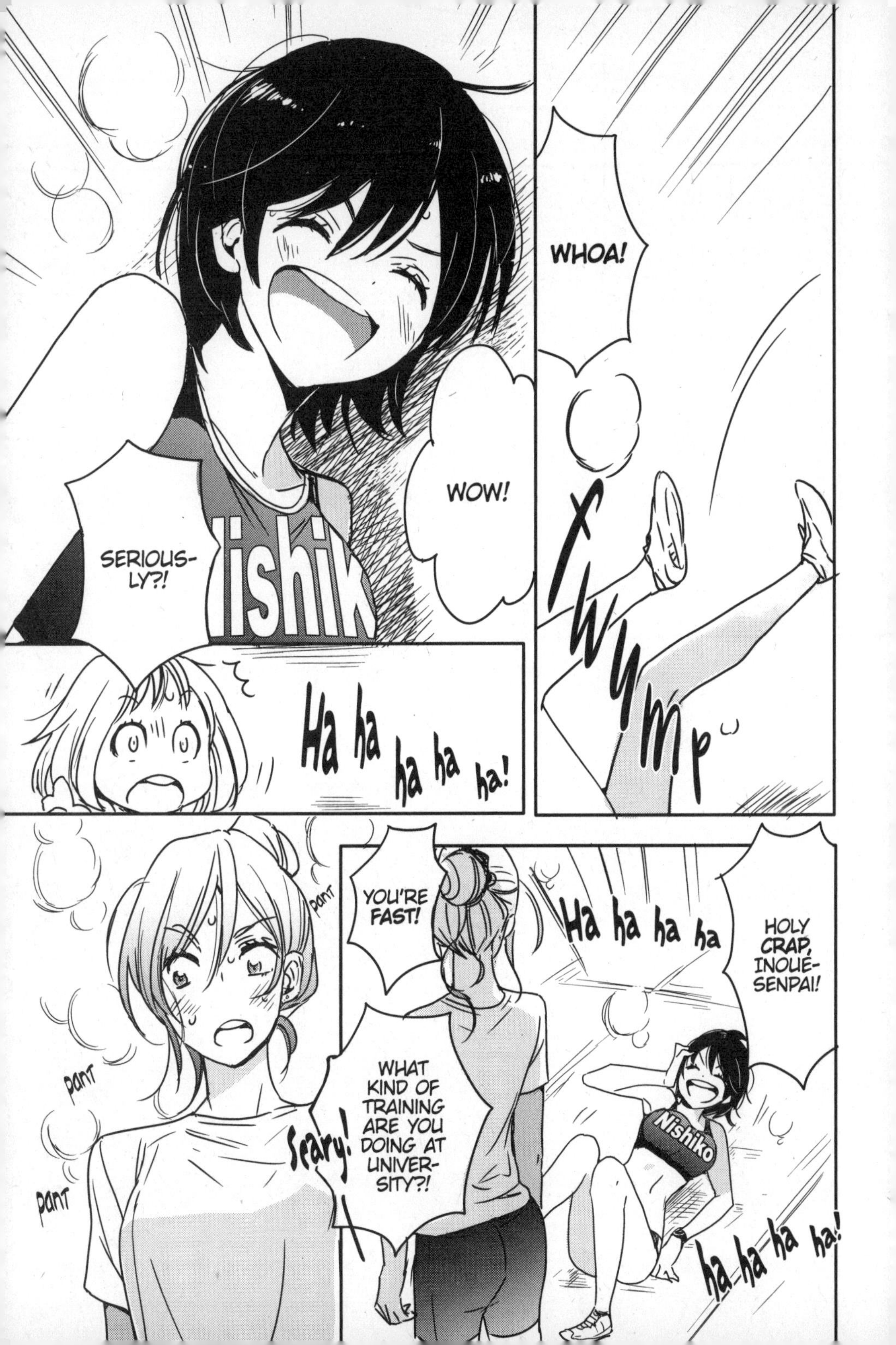
WHOA!
Fwump
WOW!
SERIOUSLY?!
Ha ha ha ha ha!
HOLY CRAP, INOUE-SENPAI!
Ha ha ha ha
YOU'RE FAST!
WHAT KIND OF TRAINING ARE YOU DOING AT UNIVERSITY?!
Scary!
Nishiko
ha ha ha ha ha!
pant
pant
pant

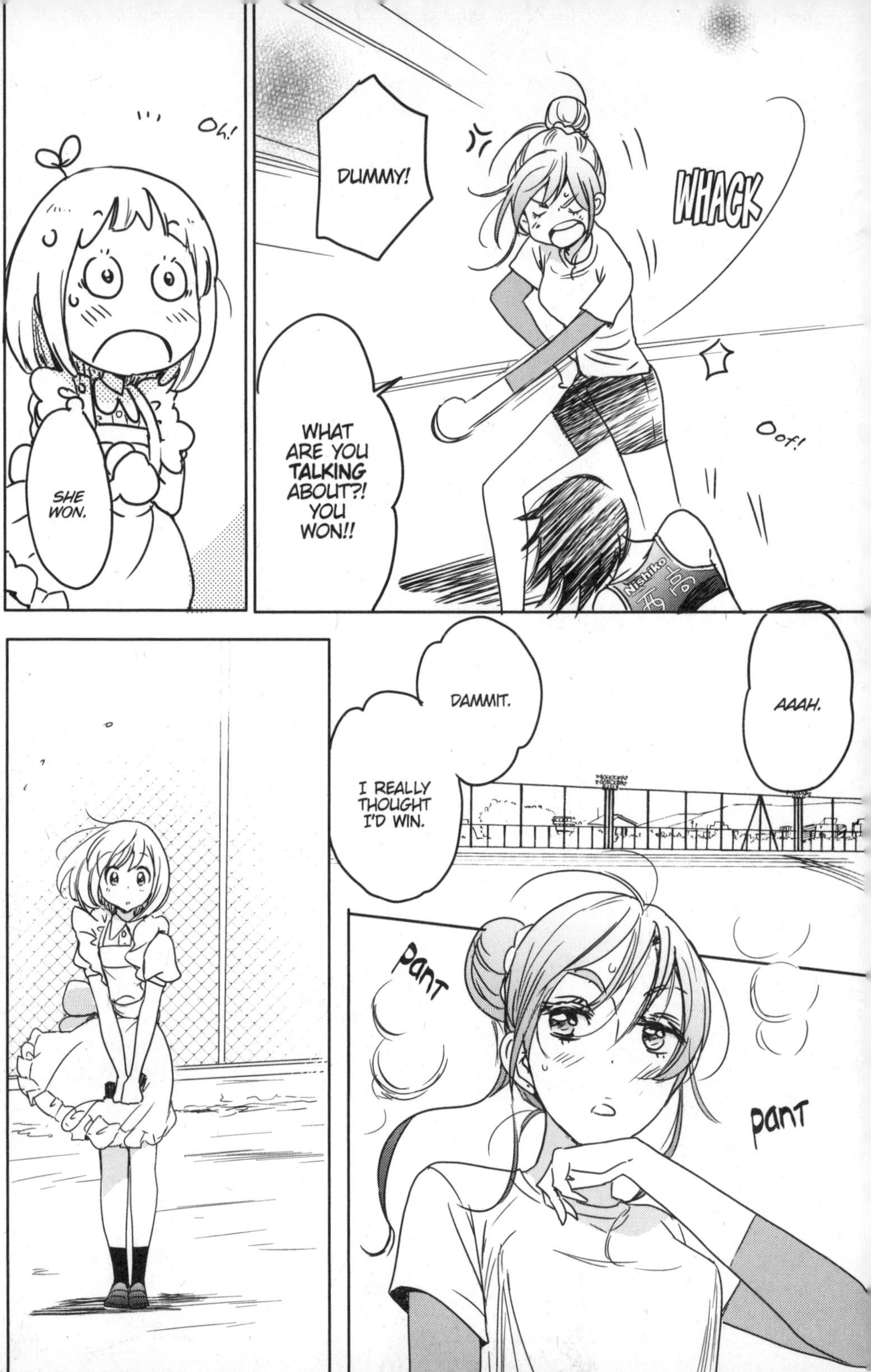
WHACK
DUMMY!
Oof!
WHAT ARE YOU TALKING ABOUT?! YOU WON!!
Oh!
SHE WON.
AAAH.
DAMMIT.
I REALLY THOUGHT I'D WIN.
pant
pant

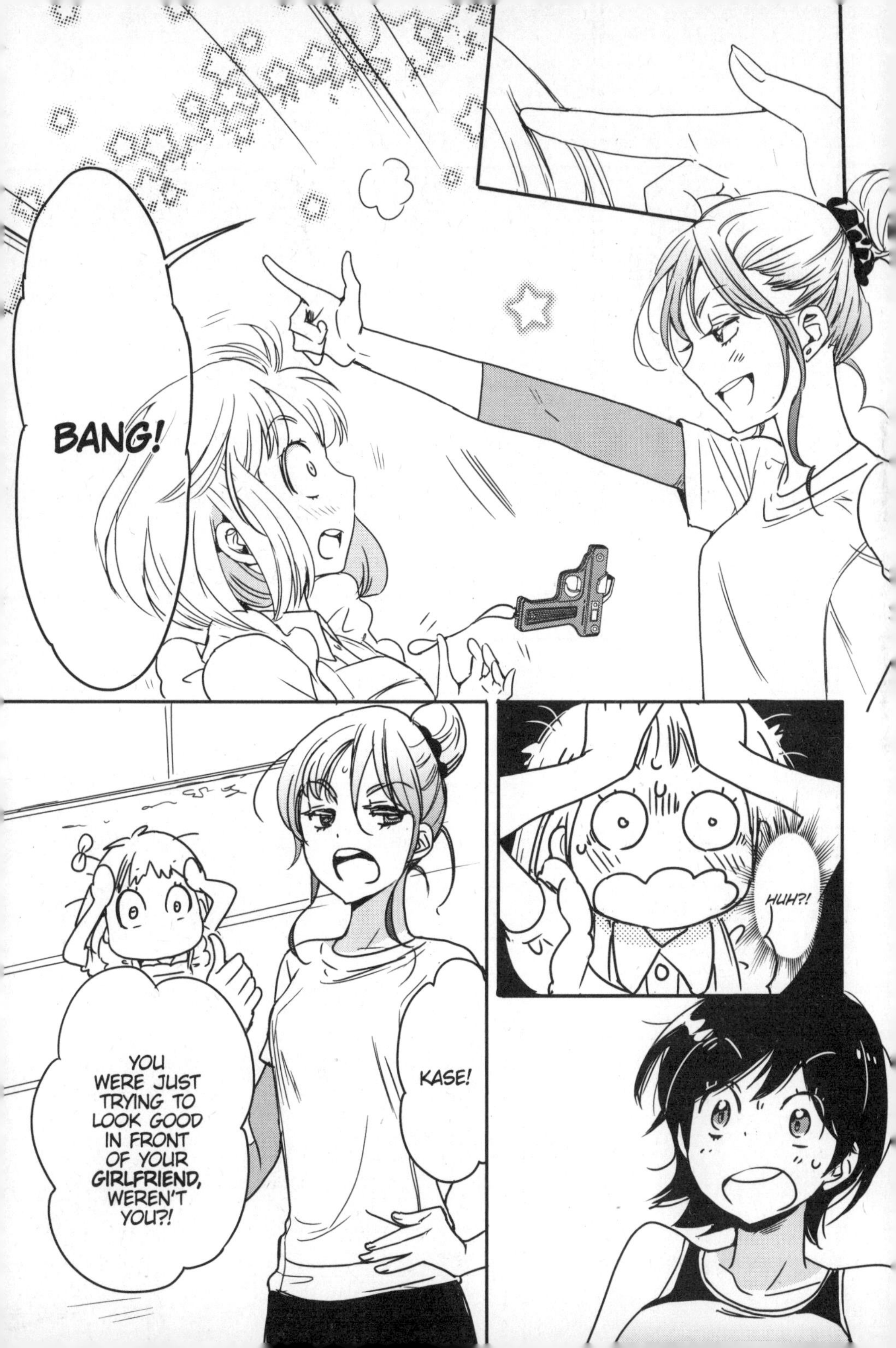
BANG!
HUH?!
KASE!
YOU WERE JUST TRYING TO LOOK GOOD IN FRONT OF YOUR GIRLFRIEND, WEREN'T YOU?!

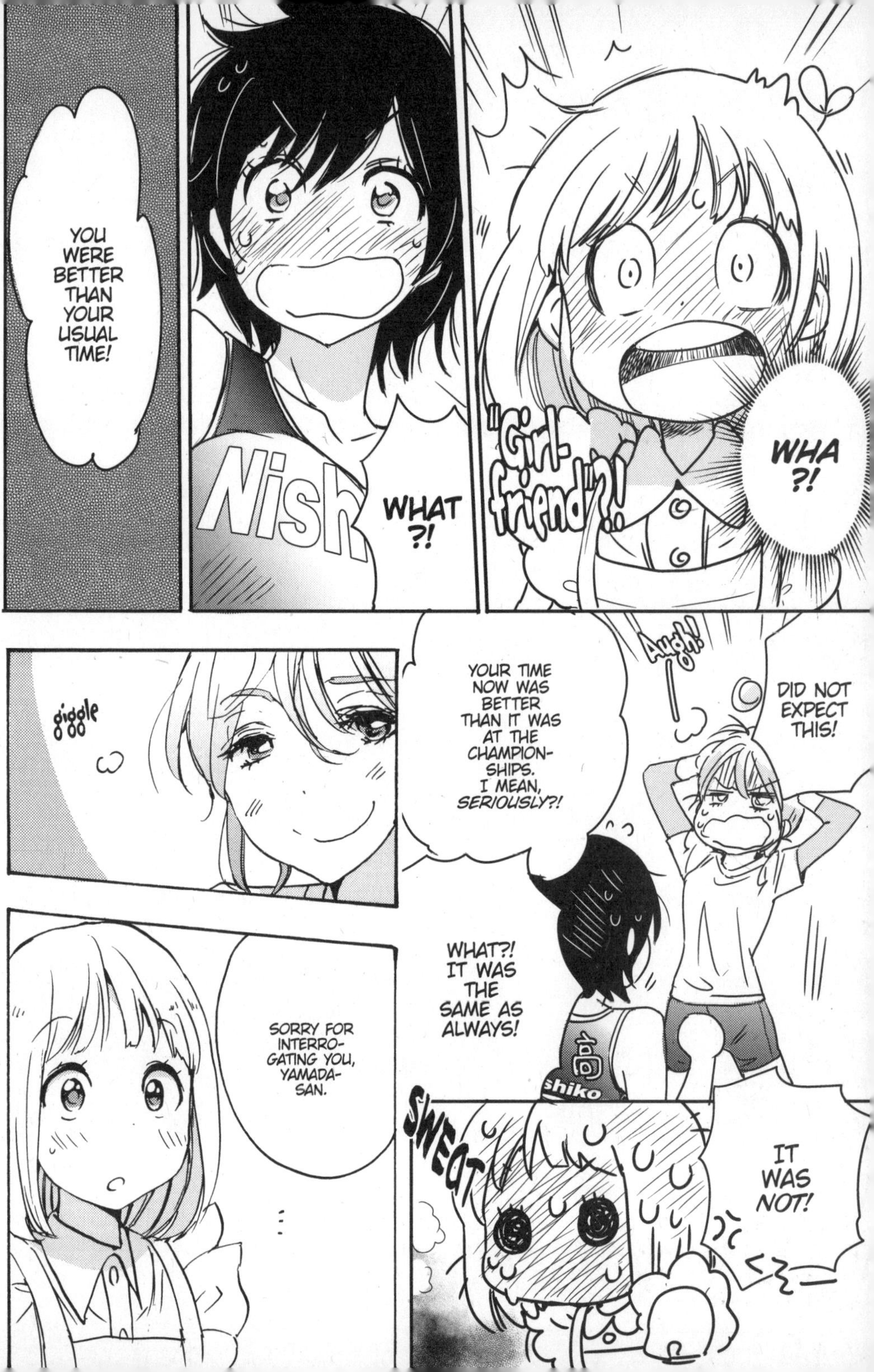
WHA?!
"Girl-friend"?!
WHAT?!
YOU WERE BETTER THAN YOUR USUAL TIME!
DID NOT EXPECT THIS!
Augh!
YOUR TIME NOW WAS BETTER THAN IT WAS AT THE CHAMPION-SHIPS. I MEAN, SERIOUSLY?!
WHAT?! IT WAS THE SAME AS ALWAYS!
IT WAS NOT!
SWEAT
giggle
SORRY FOR INTERRO-GATING YOU, YAMADA-SAN.
...

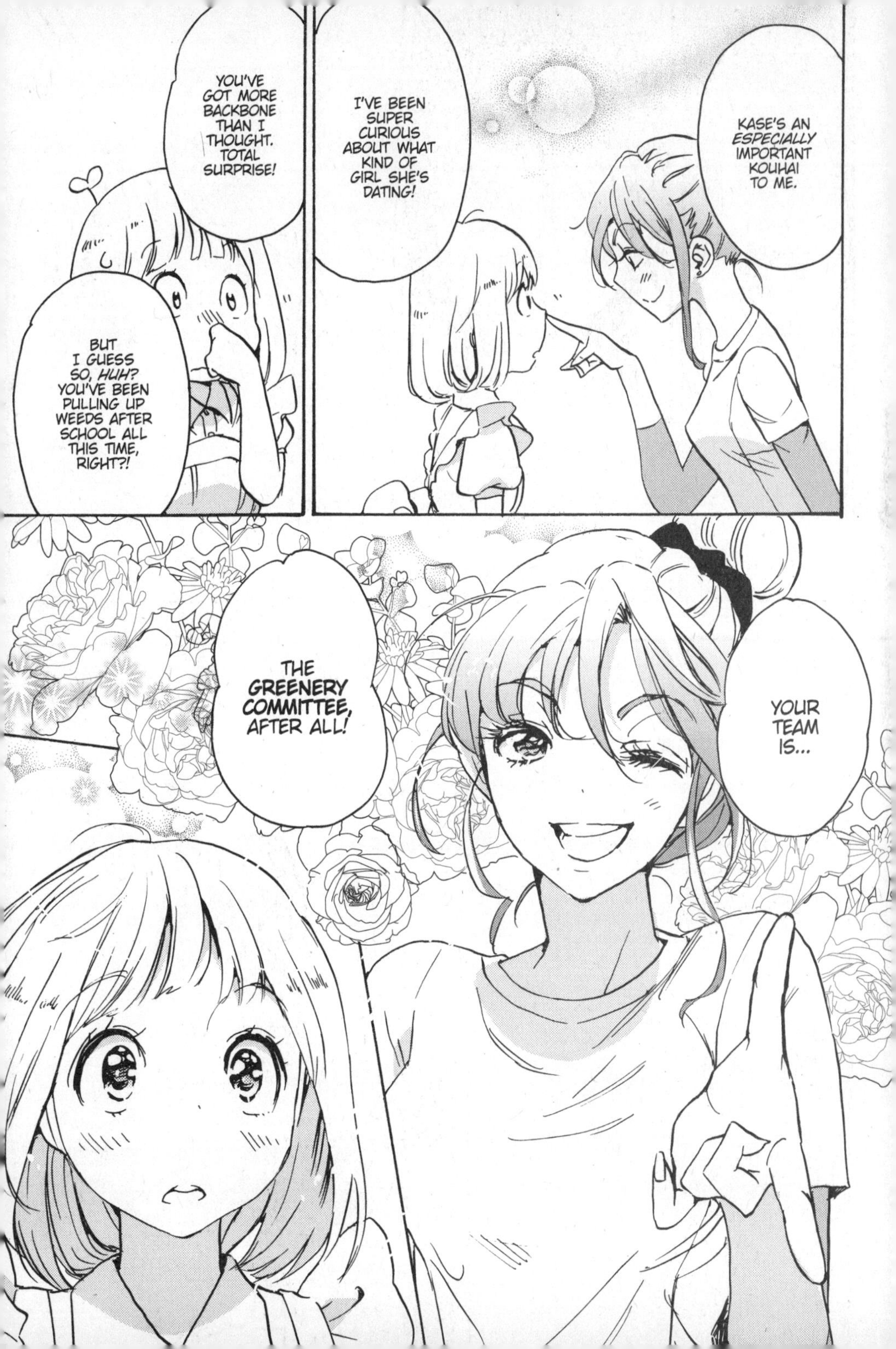
KASE'S AN *ESPECIALLY* IMPORTANT KOUHAI TO ME.
I'VE BEEN SUPER CURIOUS ABOUT WHAT KIND OF GIRL SHE'S DATING!
YOU'VE GOT MORE BACKBONE THAN I THOUGHT. TOTAL SURPRISE!
BUT I GUESS SO, *HUH*? YOU'VE BEEN PULLING UP WEEDS AFTER SCHOOL ALL THIS TIME, RIGHT?!
YOUR TEAM IS...
THE GREENERY COMMITTEE, AFTER ALL!

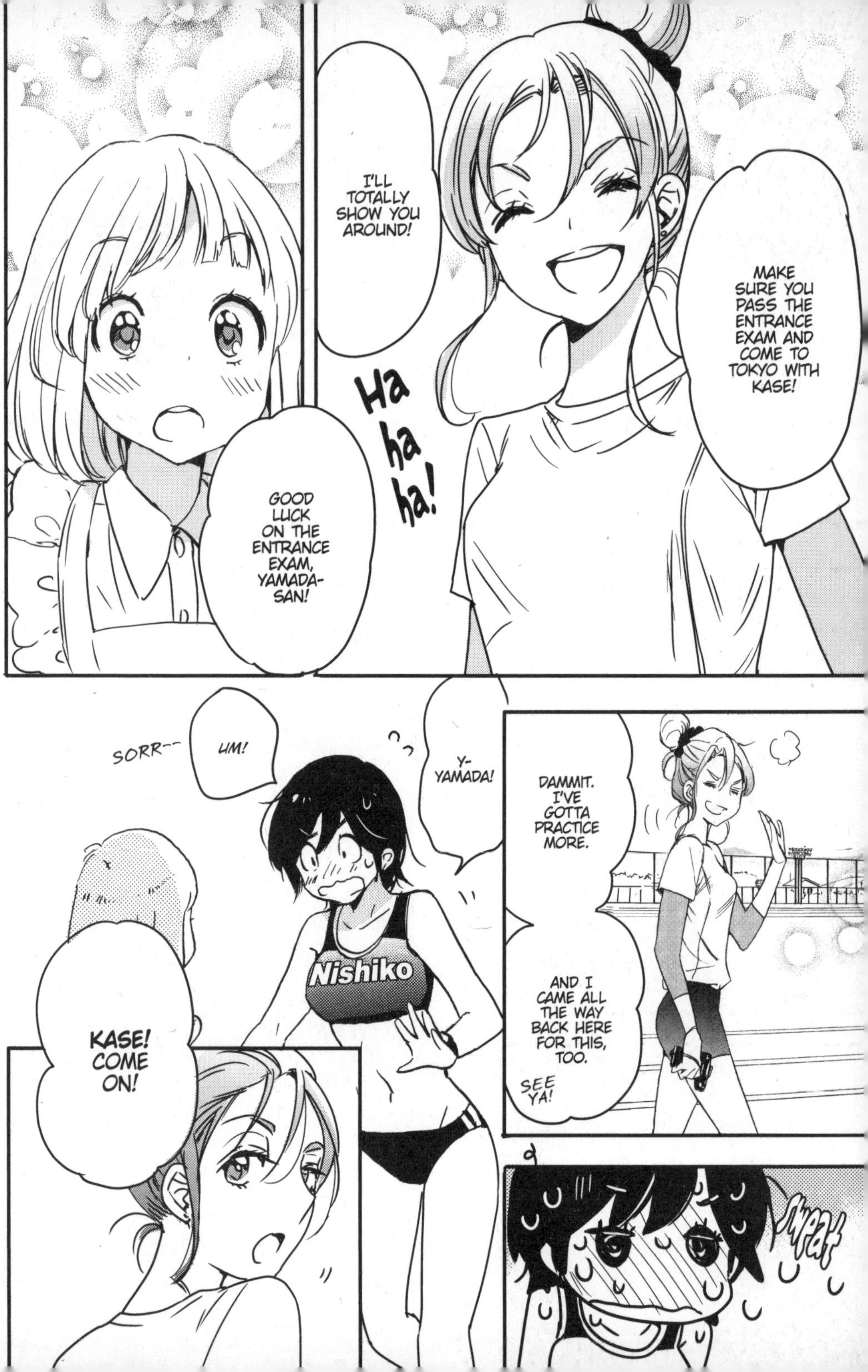

MAKE SURE YOU PASS THE ENTRANCE EXAM AND COME TO TOKYO WITH KASE!
I'LL TOTALLY SHOW YOU AROUND!
Ha ha ha!
GOOD LUCK ON THE ENTRANCE EXAM, YAMADA-SAN!
DAMMIT. I'VE GOTTA PRACTICE MORE.
AND I CAME ALL THE WAY BACK HERE FOR THIS, TOO.
SEE YA!
Y-YAMADA!
UM!
SORR--
Sweat
KASE! COME ON!

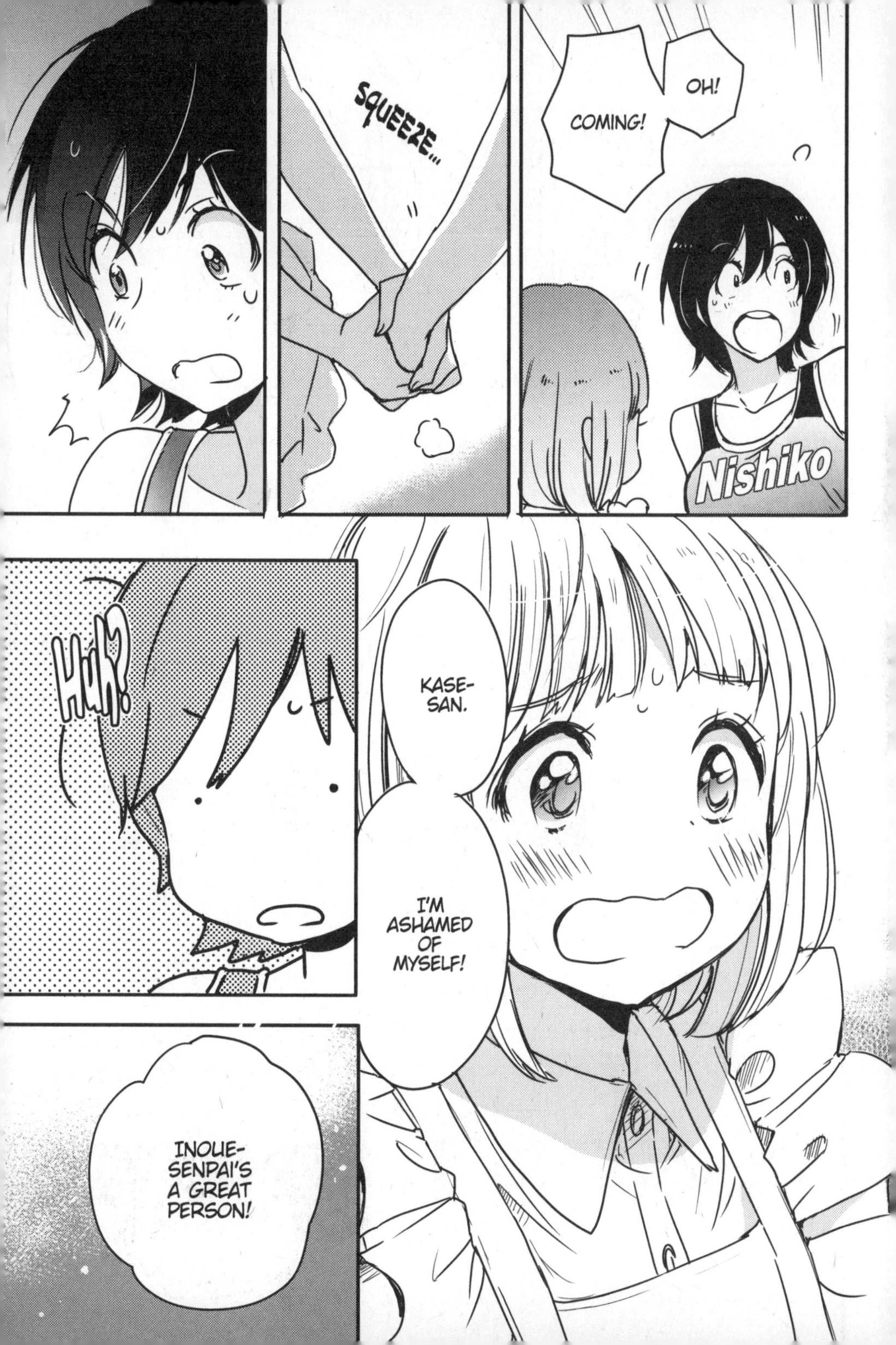
OH!
COMING!
SQUEEZE...
Nishiko
KASE-SAN.
I'M ASHAMED OF MYSELF!
HUH?
INOUE-SENPAI'S A GREAT PERSON!

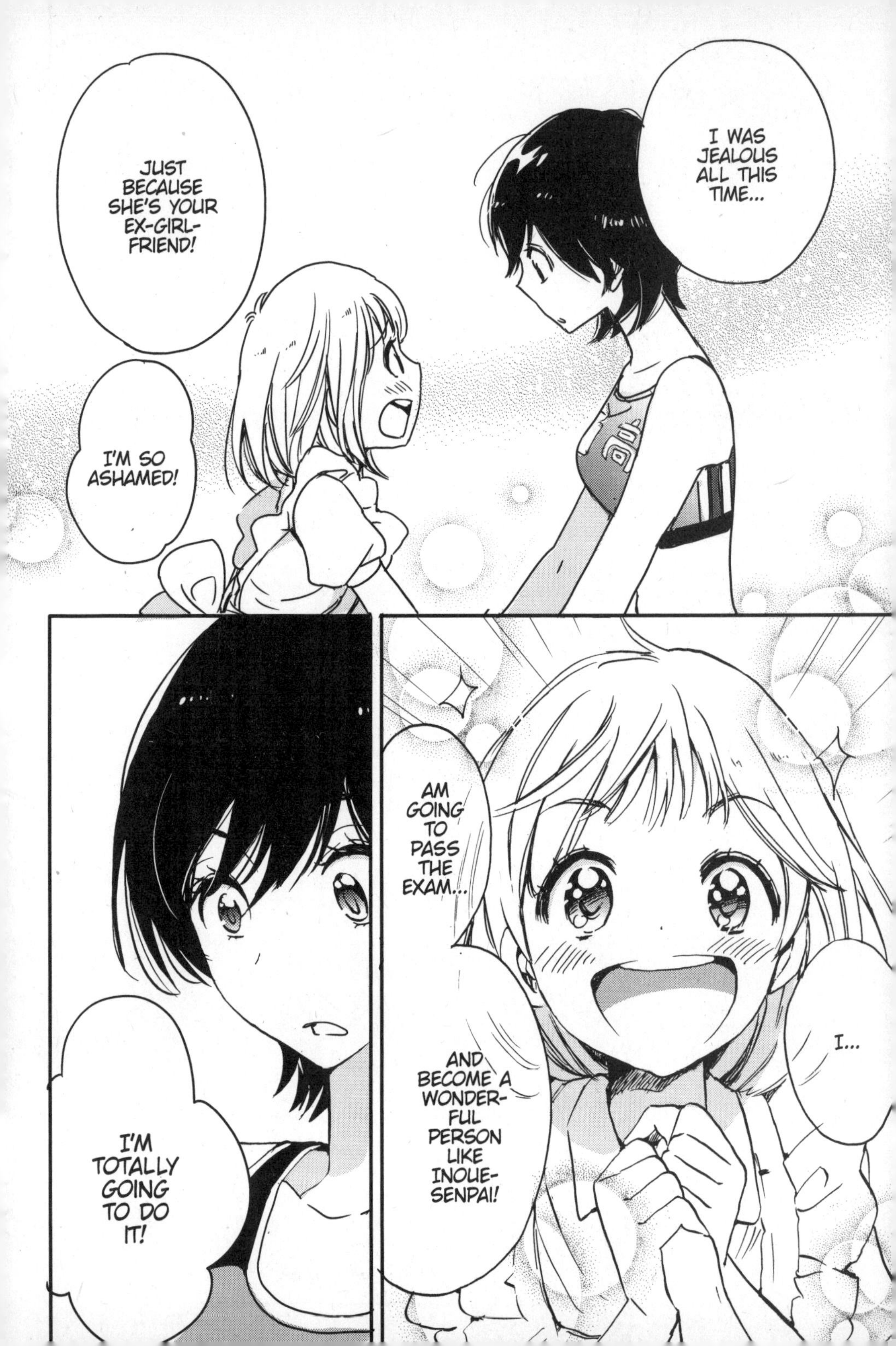
I WAS JEALOUS ALL THIS TIME...
JUST BECAUSE SHE'S YOUR EX-GIRL-FRIEND!
I'M SO ASHAMED!
I...
AM GOING TO PASS THE EXAM...
AND BECOME A WONDER-FUL PERSON LIKE INOUE-SENPAI!
I'M TOTALLY GOING TO DO IT!

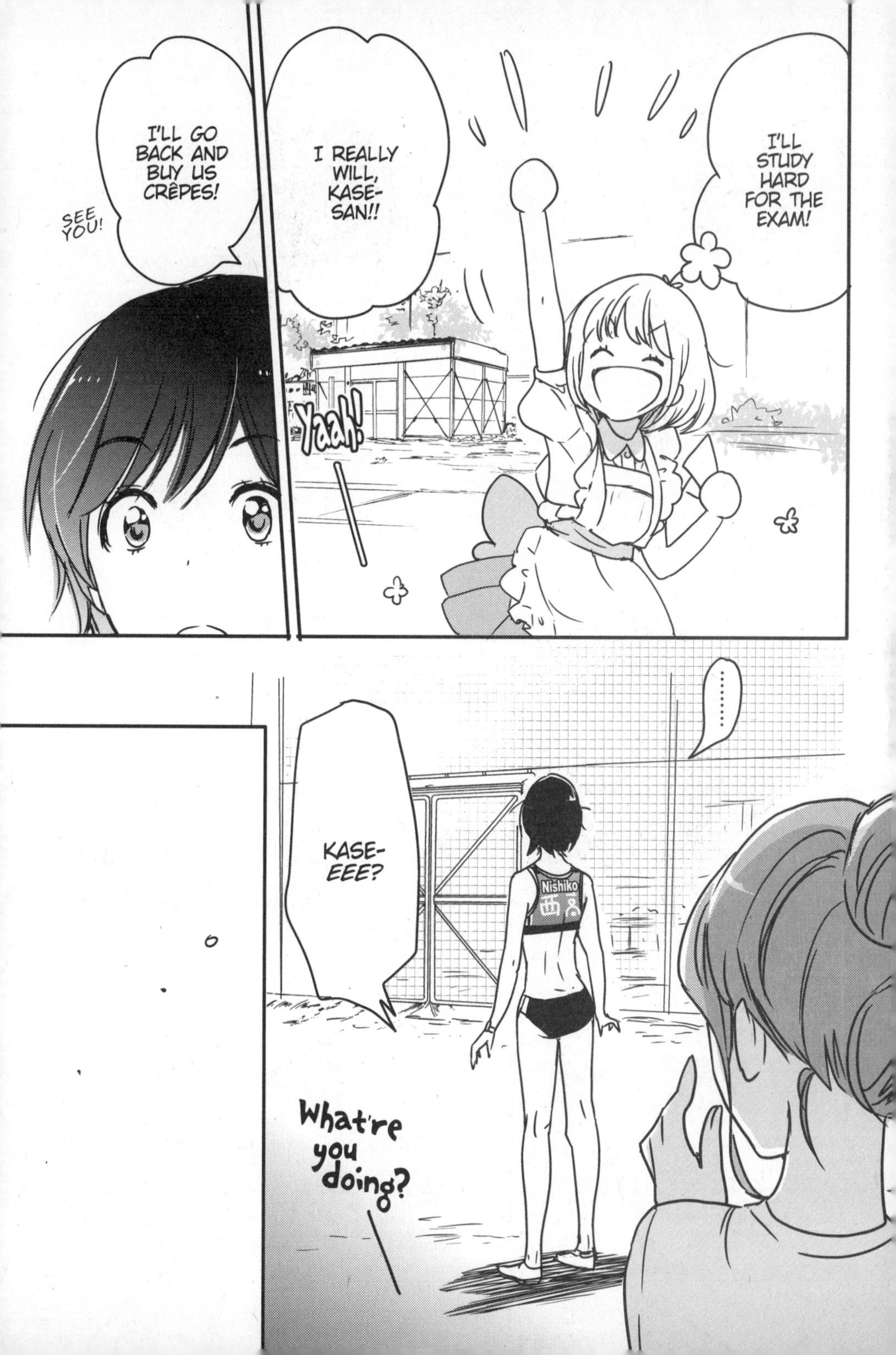
I'LL STUDY HARD FOR THE EXAM!
I REALLY WILL, KASE-SAN!!
Yaah!
I'LL GO BACK AND BUY US CRÊPES!
SEE YOU!
......
KASE-EEE?
What're you doing?

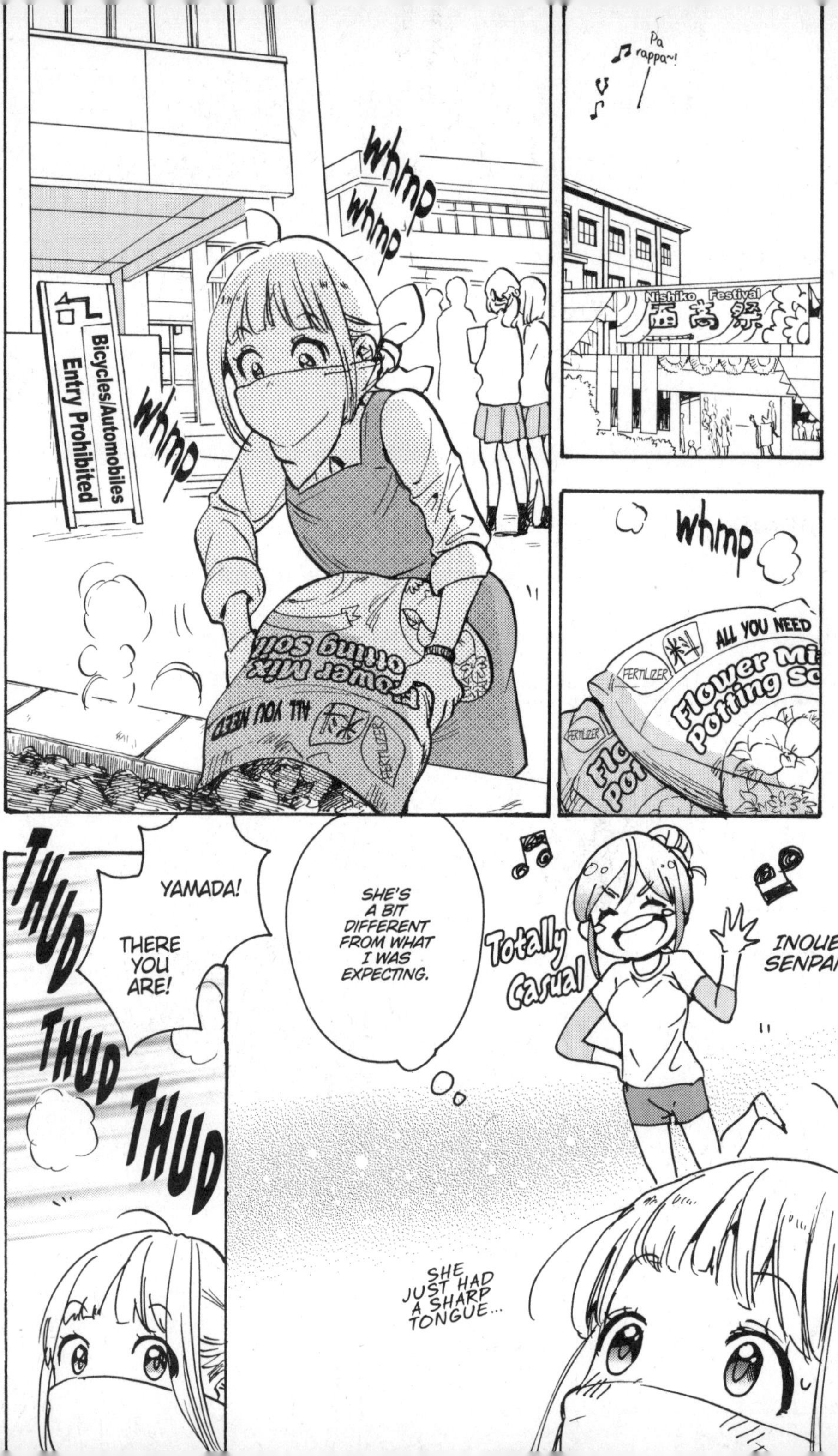

Pa rappa~!
Nishiko Festival
西高祭
whmp
ALL YOU NEED
FERTILIZER
Flower Mi
Potting So
whmp
whmp
Bicycles/Automobiles Entry Prohibited
whmp
INOUE-SENPAI...
Totally Casual
SHE'S A BIT DIFFERENT FROM WHAT I WAS EXPECTING.
YAMADA!
THERE YOU ARE!
THUD THUD THUD
SHE JUST HAD A SHARP TONGUE...

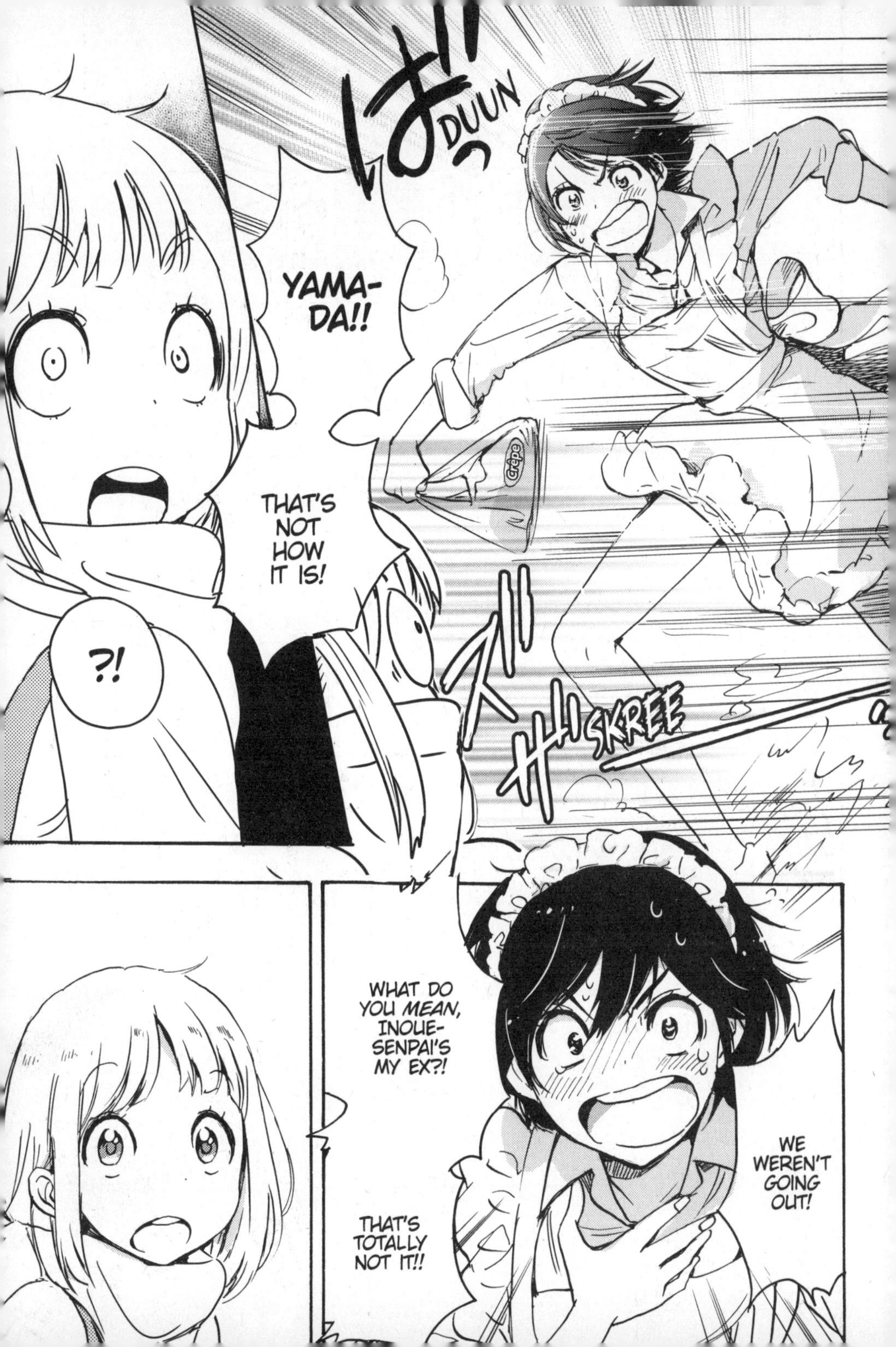
は!!
DUUN
YAMADA!!
THAT'S NOT HOW IT IS!
SKREE
?!
WHAT DO YOU *MEAN*, INOUE-SENPAI'S MY EX?!
WE WEREN'T GOING OUT!
THAT'S TOTALLY NOT IT!!

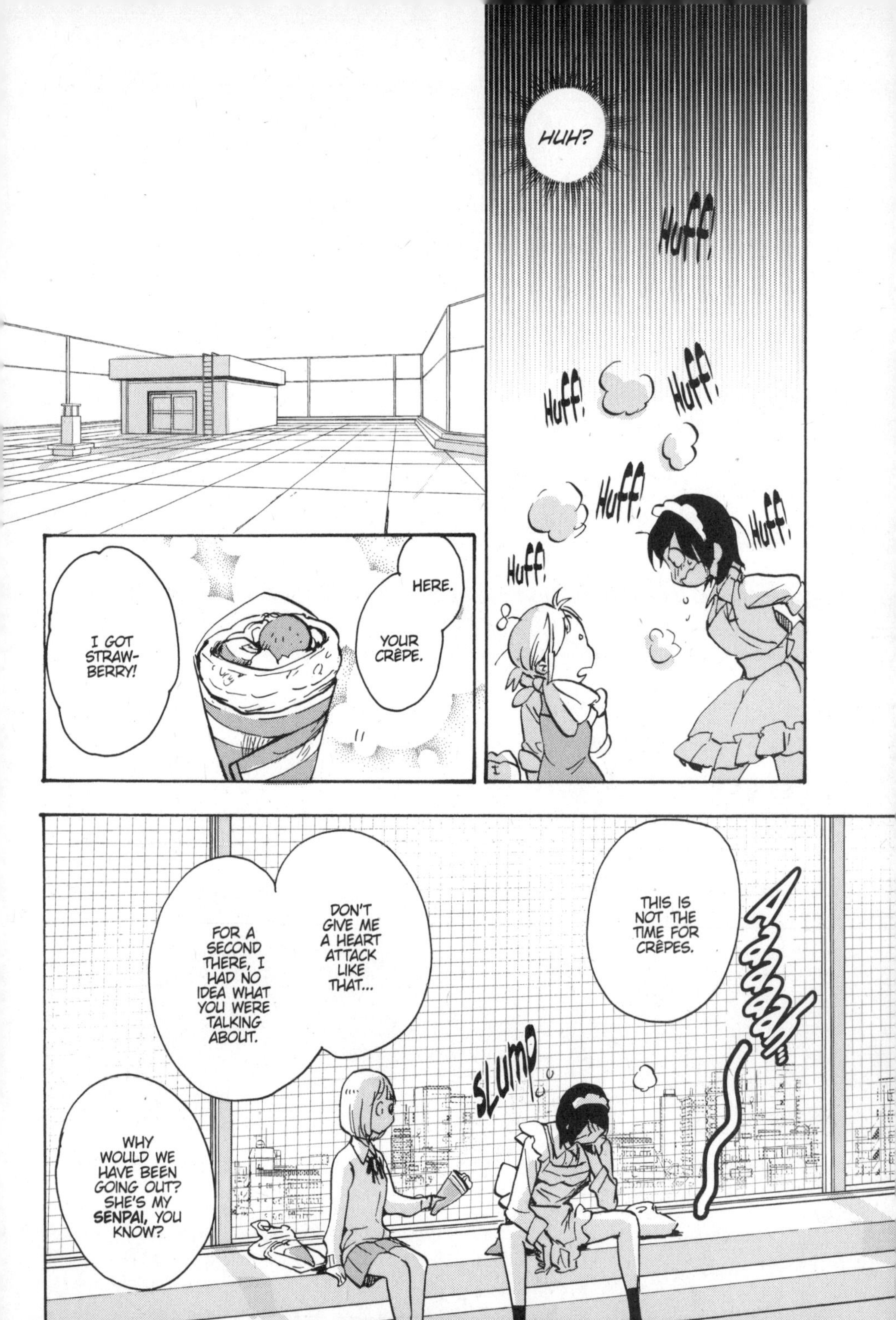
HUH?
HUFF!
HUFF!
HUFF!
HUFF!
HUFF!
HUFF!
HERE. YOUR CRÊPE.
I GOT STRAW-BERRY!
THIS IS NOT THE TIME FOR CRÊPES.
Aaaaah!
DON'T GIVE ME A HEART ATTACK LIKE THAT...
FOR A SECOND THERE, I HAD NO IDEA WHAT YOU WERE TALKING ABOUT.
SLUMP
WHY WOULD WE HAVE BEEN GOING OUT? SHE'S MY **SENPAI,** YOU KNOW?

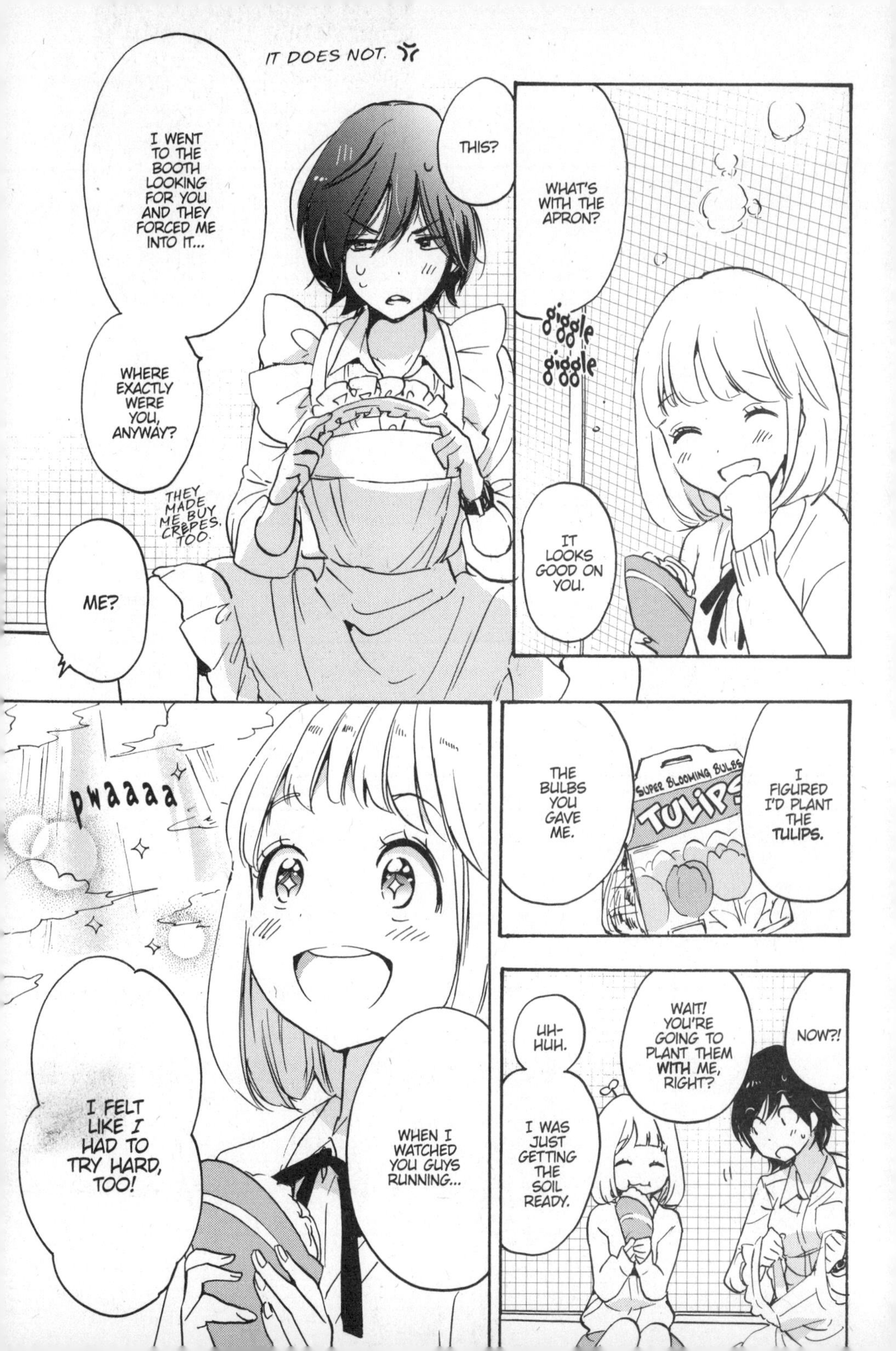
WHAT'S WITH THE APRON?
giggle giggle
IT LOOKS GOOD ON YOU.
IT DOES NOT.
THIS?
I WENT TO THE BOOTH LOOKING FOR YOU AND THEY FORCED ME INTO IT...
WHERE EXACTLY WERE YOU, ANYWAY?
THEY MADE ME BUY CREPES, TOO.
ME?
I FIGURED I'D PLANT THE **TULIPS.**
SUPER BLOOMING BULBS
TULIPS
THE BULBS YOU GAVE ME.
NOW?!
WAIT! YOU'RE GOING TO PLANT THEM **WITH ME,** RIGHT?
UH-HUH.
I WAS JUST GETTING THE SOIL READY.
pwaaaa
WHEN I WATCHED YOU GUYS RUNNING...
I FELT LIKE *I* HAD TO TRY HARD, TOO!

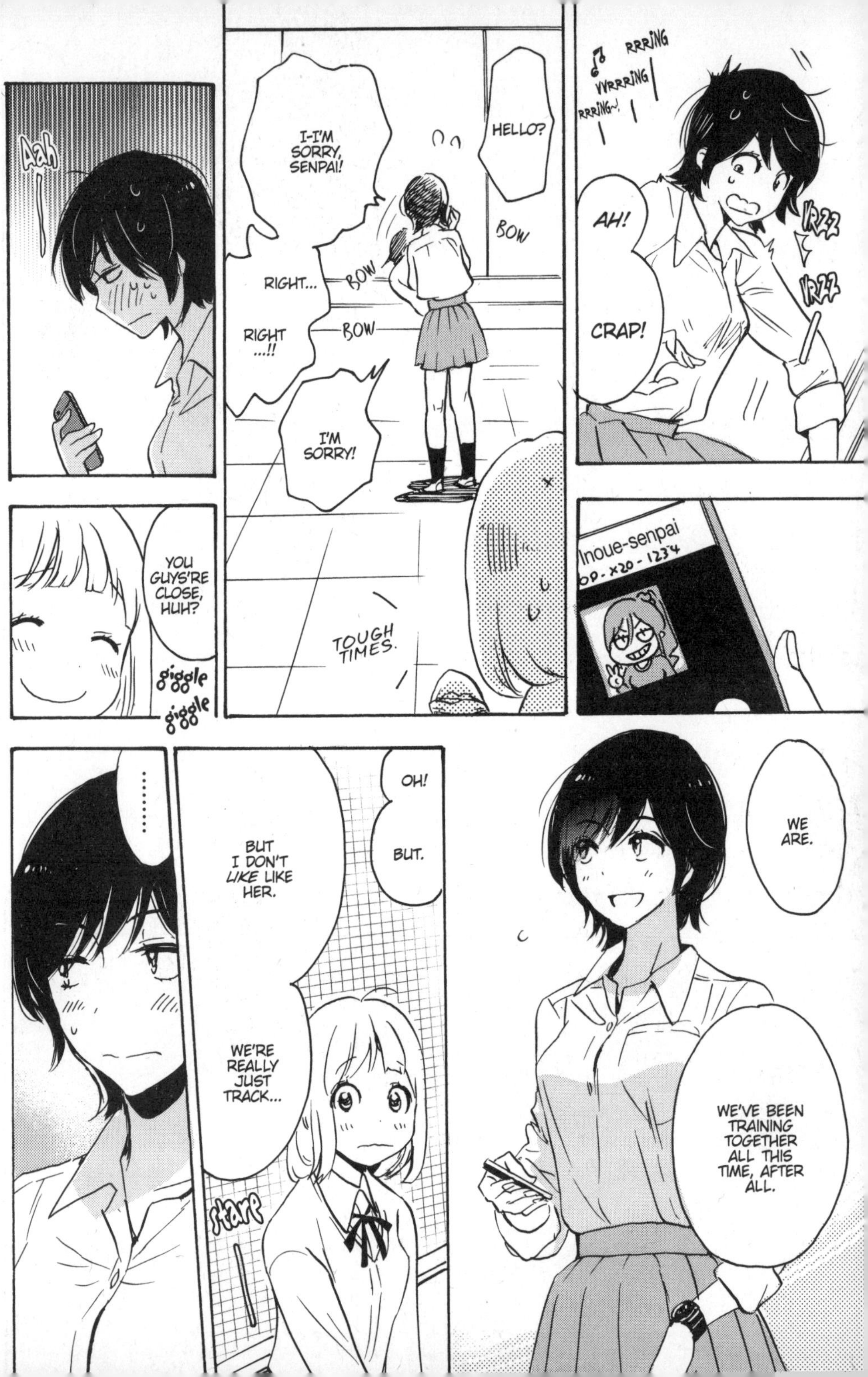
RRRING
VVRRRING
RRRING~!
AH!
CRAP!
VRZZ
VRZZ
Inoue-senpai
HELLO?
BOW
I-I'M SORRY, SENPAI!
RIGHT...
BOW
RIGHT ...!!
BOW
I'M SORRY!
TOUGH TIMES.
Aah
YOU GUYS'RE CLOSE, HUH?
giggle
giggle
WE ARE.
WE'VE BEEN TRAINING TOGETHER ALL THIS TIME, AFTER ALL.
OH!
BUT.
BUT I DON'T *LIKE* LIKE HER.
WE'RE REALLY JUST TRACK...
stare
......

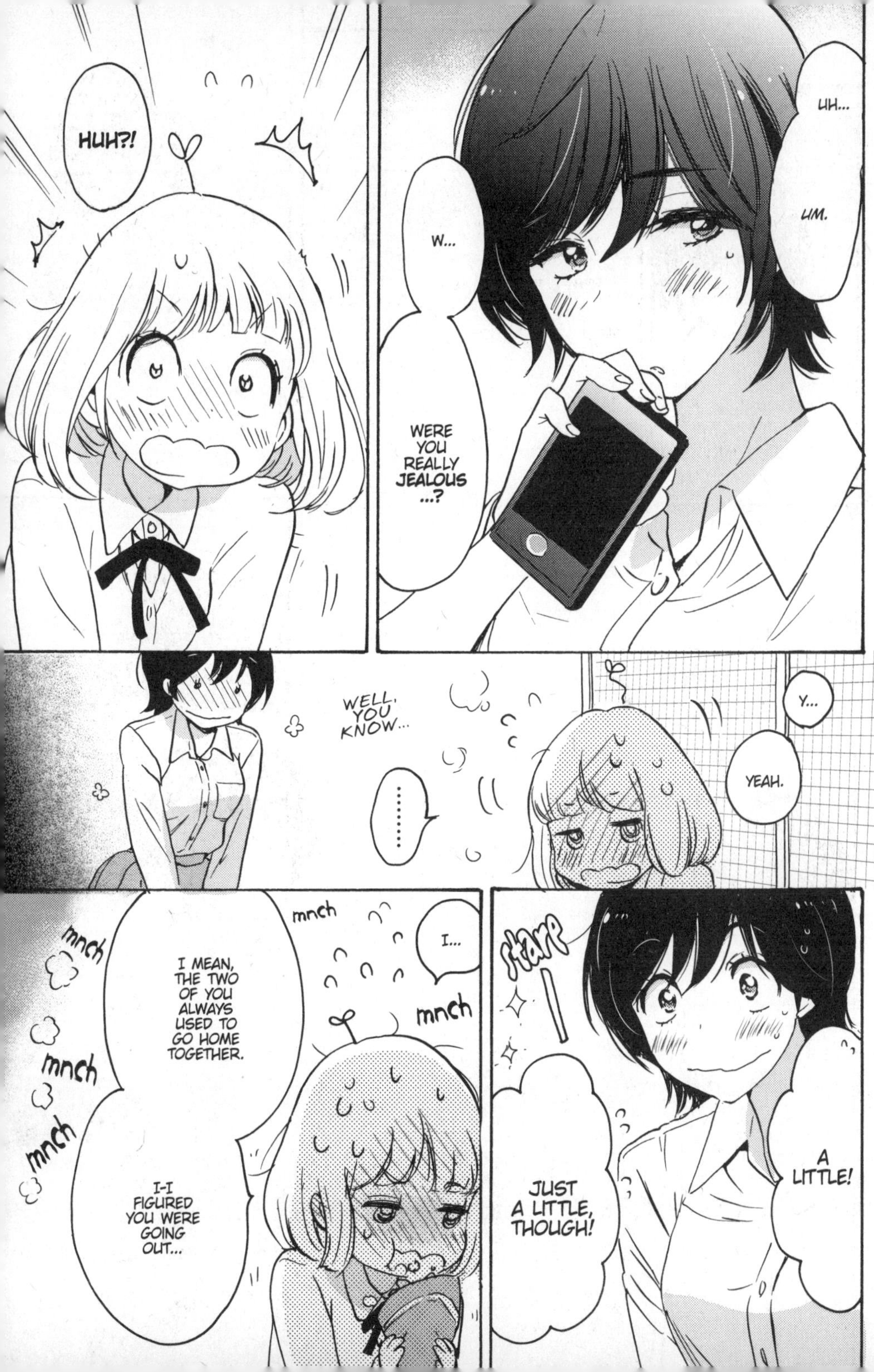

UH...
UM.
W...
WERE YOU REALLY JEALOUS ...?
HUH?!
Y...
YEAH.
......
WELL, YOU KNOW...
stare
A LITTLE!
JUST A LITTLE, THOUGH!
I...
mnch
mnch
I MEAN, THE TWO OF YOU ALWAYS USED TO GO HOME TOGETHER.
mnch
mnch
mnch
I-I FIGURED YOU WERE GOING OUT...

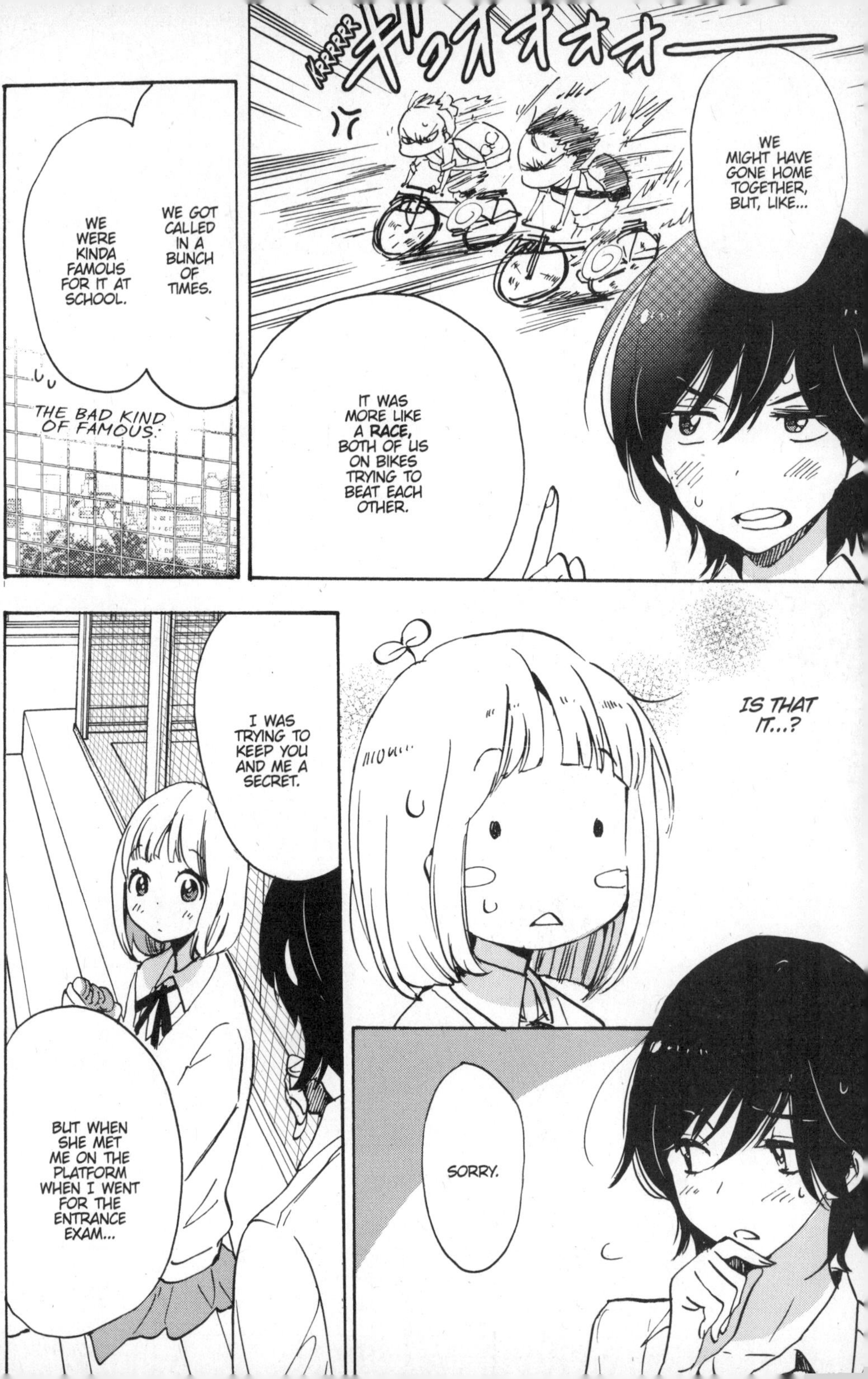
KRRRRR
WE MIGHT HAVE GONE HOME TOGETHER, BUT, LIKE...
IT WAS MORE LIKE A **RACE**, BOTH OF US ON BIKES TRYING TO BEAT EACH OTHER.
WE GOT CALLED IN A BUNCH OF TIMES.
WE WERE KINDA FAMOUS FOR IT AT SCHOOL.
THE BAD KIND OF FAMOUS.
IS THAT IT...?
SORRY.
I WAS TRYING TO KEEP YOU AND ME A SECRET.
BUT WHEN SHE MET ME ON THE PLATFORM WHEN I WENT FOR THE ENTRANCE EXAM...

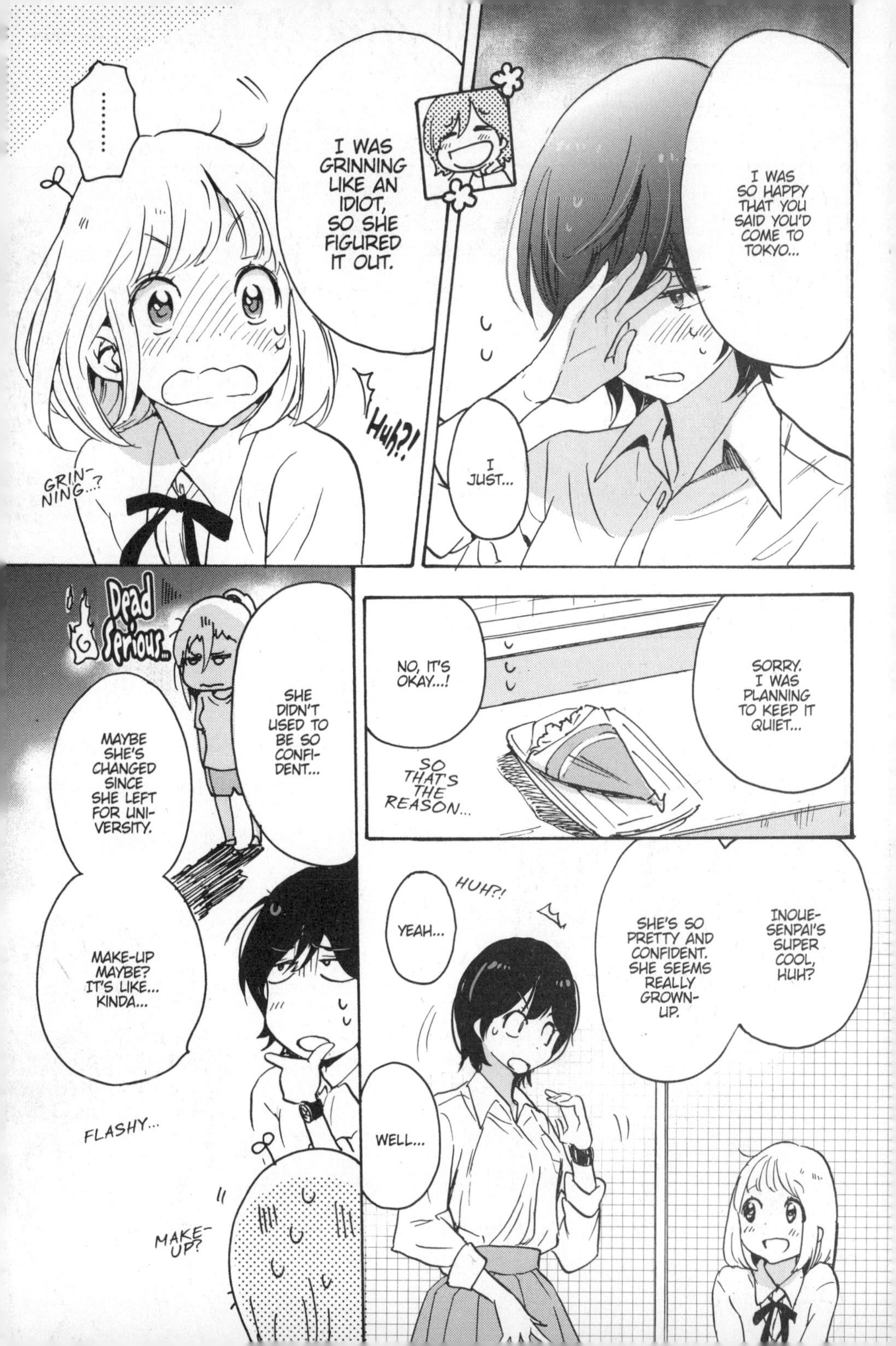
I WAS SO HAPPY THAT YOU SAID YOU'D COME TO TOKYO...
I JUST...
I WAS GRINNING LIKE AN IDIOT, SO SHE FIGURED IT OUT.
Huh?!
......
GRIN-NING...?
SORRY. I WAS PLANNING TO KEEP IT QUIET...
NO, IT'S OKAY...!
SO THAT'S THE REASON...
INOUE-SENPAI'S SUPER COOL, HUH?
SHE'S SO PRETTY AND CONFIDENT. SHE SEEMS REALLY GROWN-UP.
HUH?!
YEAH...
WELL...
SHE DIDN'T USED TO BE SO CONFI-DENT...
Dead Serious...
MAYBE SHE'S CHANGED SINCE SHE LEFT FOR UNI-VERSITY.
MAKE-UP MAYBE? IT'S LIKE... KINDA...
FLASHY...
MAKE-UP?

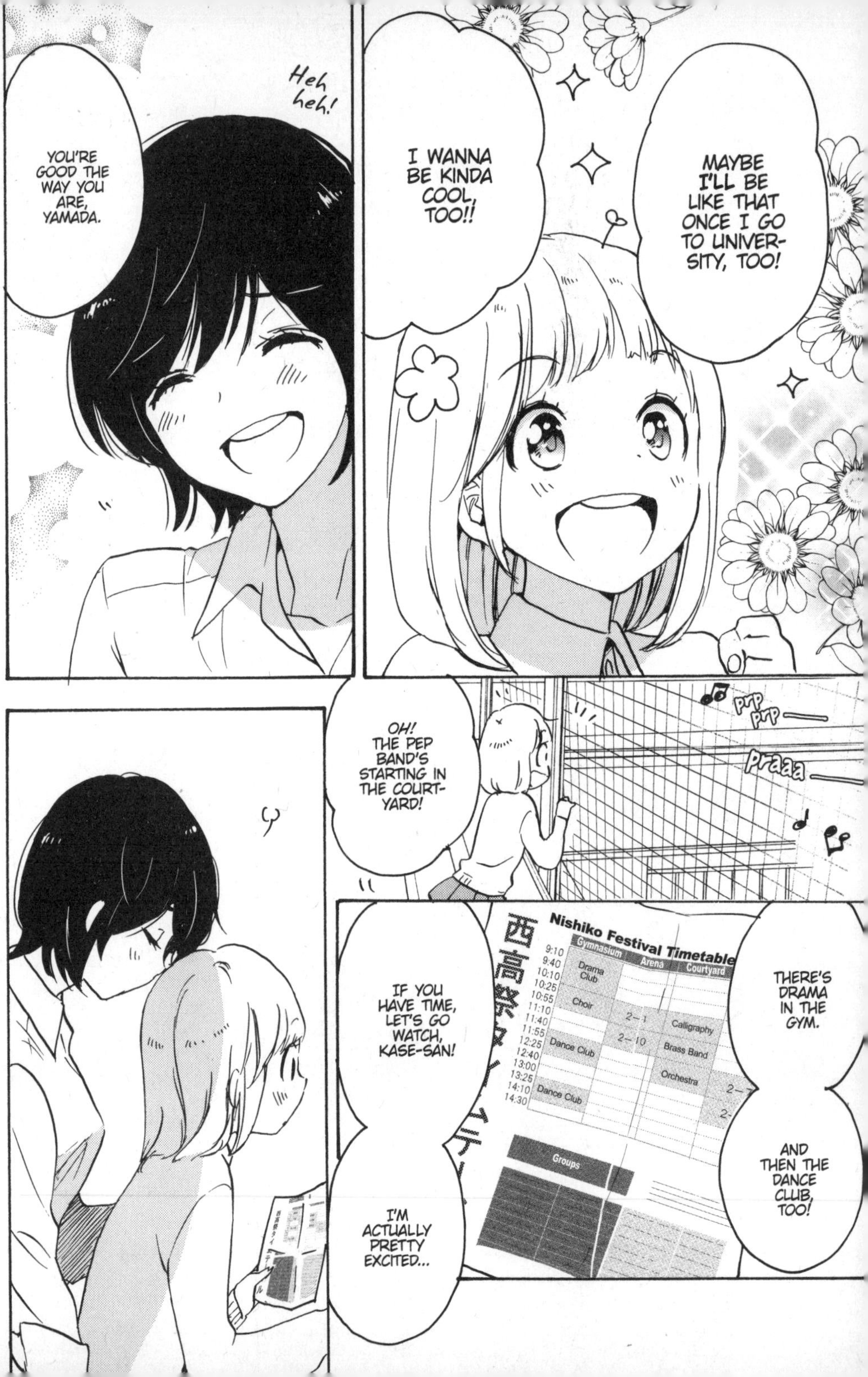
MAYBE I'LL BE LIKE THAT ONCE I GO TO UNIVERSITY, TOO!
I WANNA BE KINDA COOL, TOO!!
Heh heh!
YOU'RE GOOD THE WAY YOU ARE, YAMADA.
prp prp—
praaa—
OH! THE PEP BAND'S STARTING IN THE COURTYARD!
Nishiko Festival Timetable
Gymnasium
Arena
Courtyard
Groups
THERE'S DRAMA IN THE GYM.
AND THEN THE DANCE CLUB, TOO!
IF YOU HAVE TIME, LET'S GO WATCH, KASE-SAN!
I'M ACTUALLY PRETTY EXCITED...

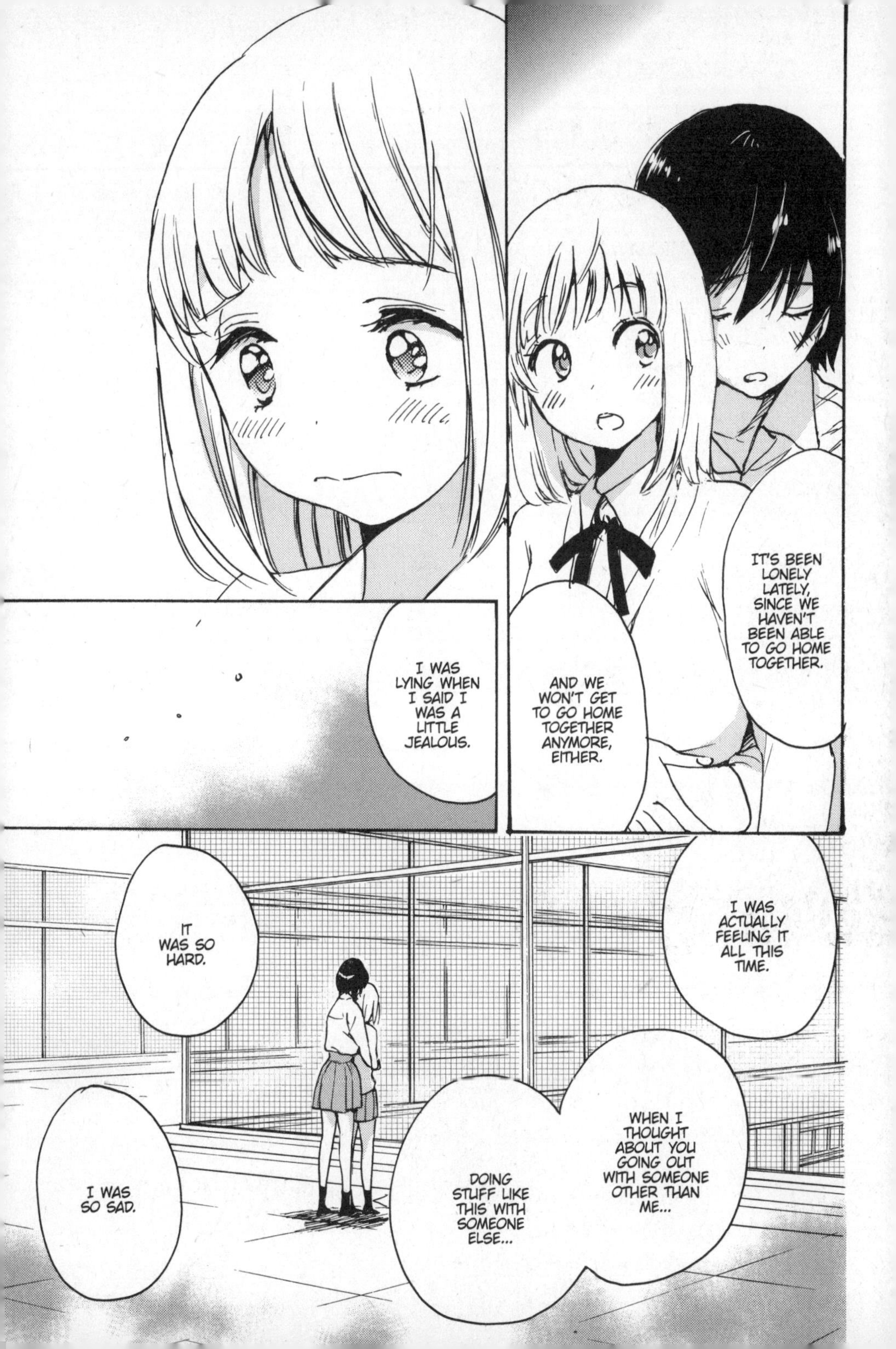
IT'S BEEN LONELY LATELY, SINCE WE HAVEN'T BEEN ABLE TO GO HOME TOGETHER.
AND WE WON'T GET TO GO HOME TOGETHER ANYMORE, EITHER.
I WAS LYING WHEN I SAID I WAS A LITTLE JEALOUS.
I WAS ACTUALLY FEELING IT ALL THIS TIME.
IT WAS SO HARD.
WHEN I THOUGHT ABOUT YOU GOING OUT WITH SOMEONE OTHER THAN ME...
DOING STUFF LIKE THIS WITH SOMEONE ELSE...
I WAS SO SAD.

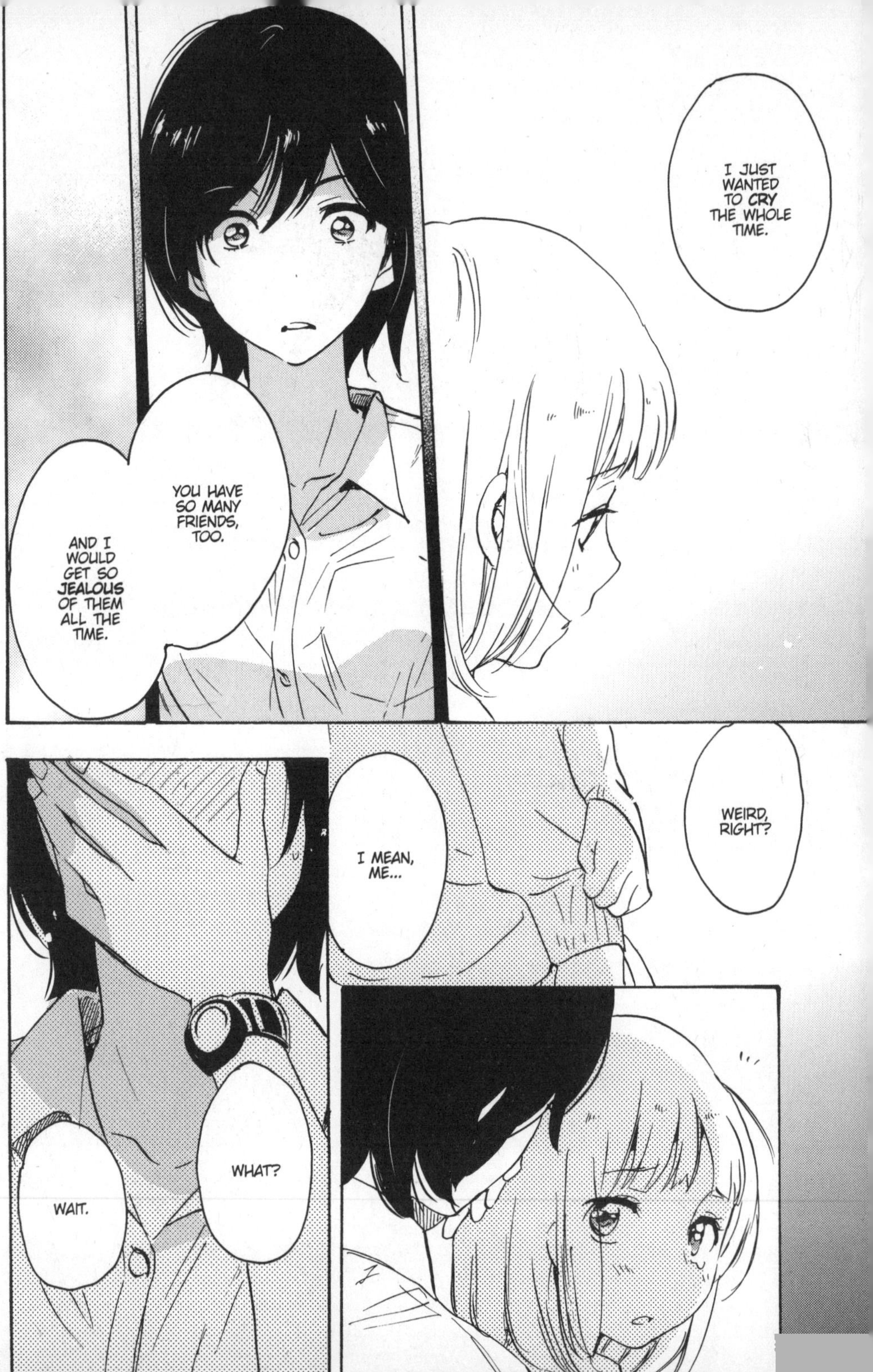
I JUST WANTED TO CRY THE WHOLE TIME.
YOU HAVE SO MANY FRIENDS, TOO.
AND I WOULD GET SO JEALOUS OF THEM ALL THE TIME.
WEIRD, RIGHT?
I MEAN, ME...
WHAT?
WAIT.

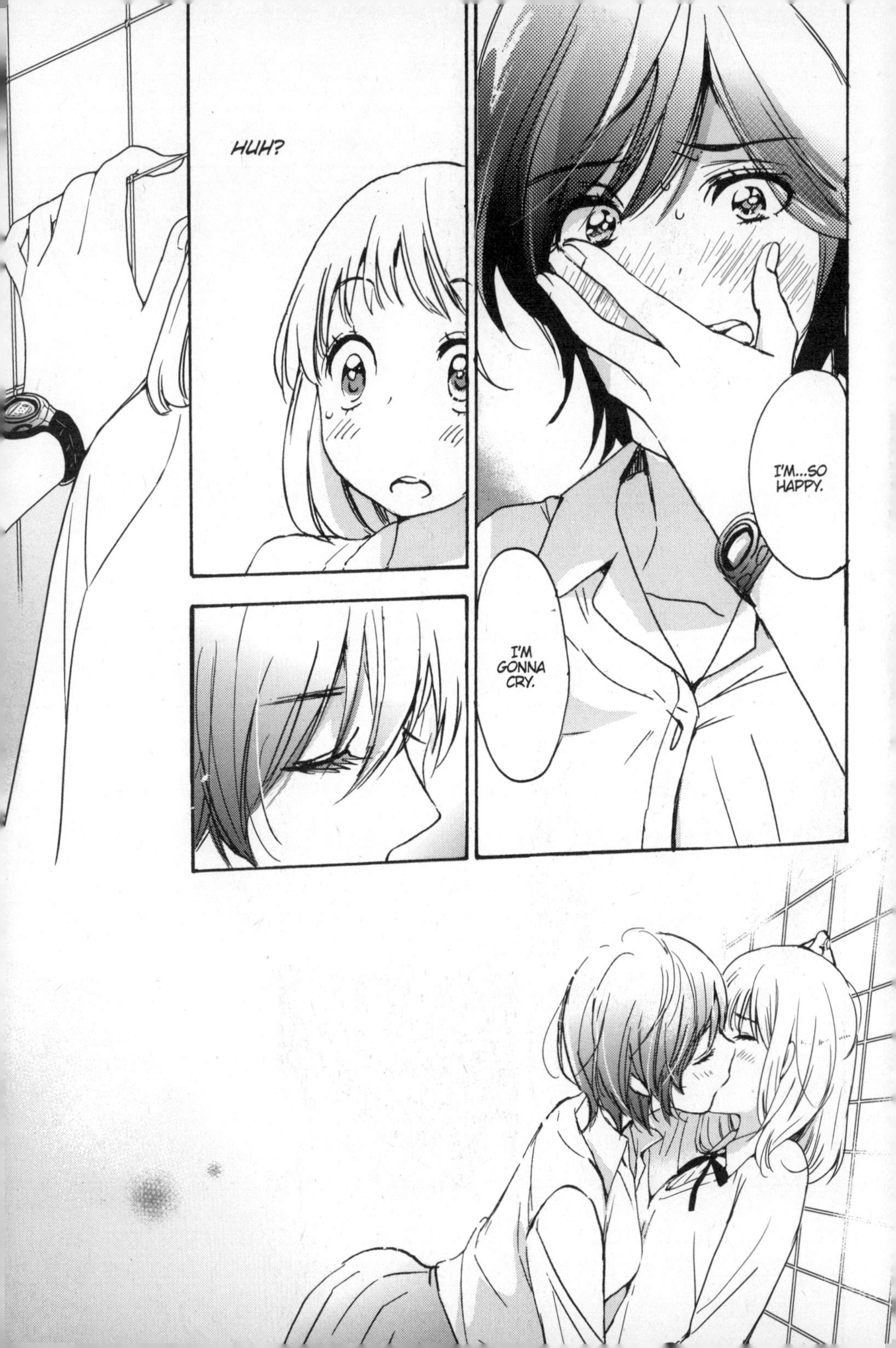
I'M...SO HAPPY.
I'M GONNA CRY.
HUH?

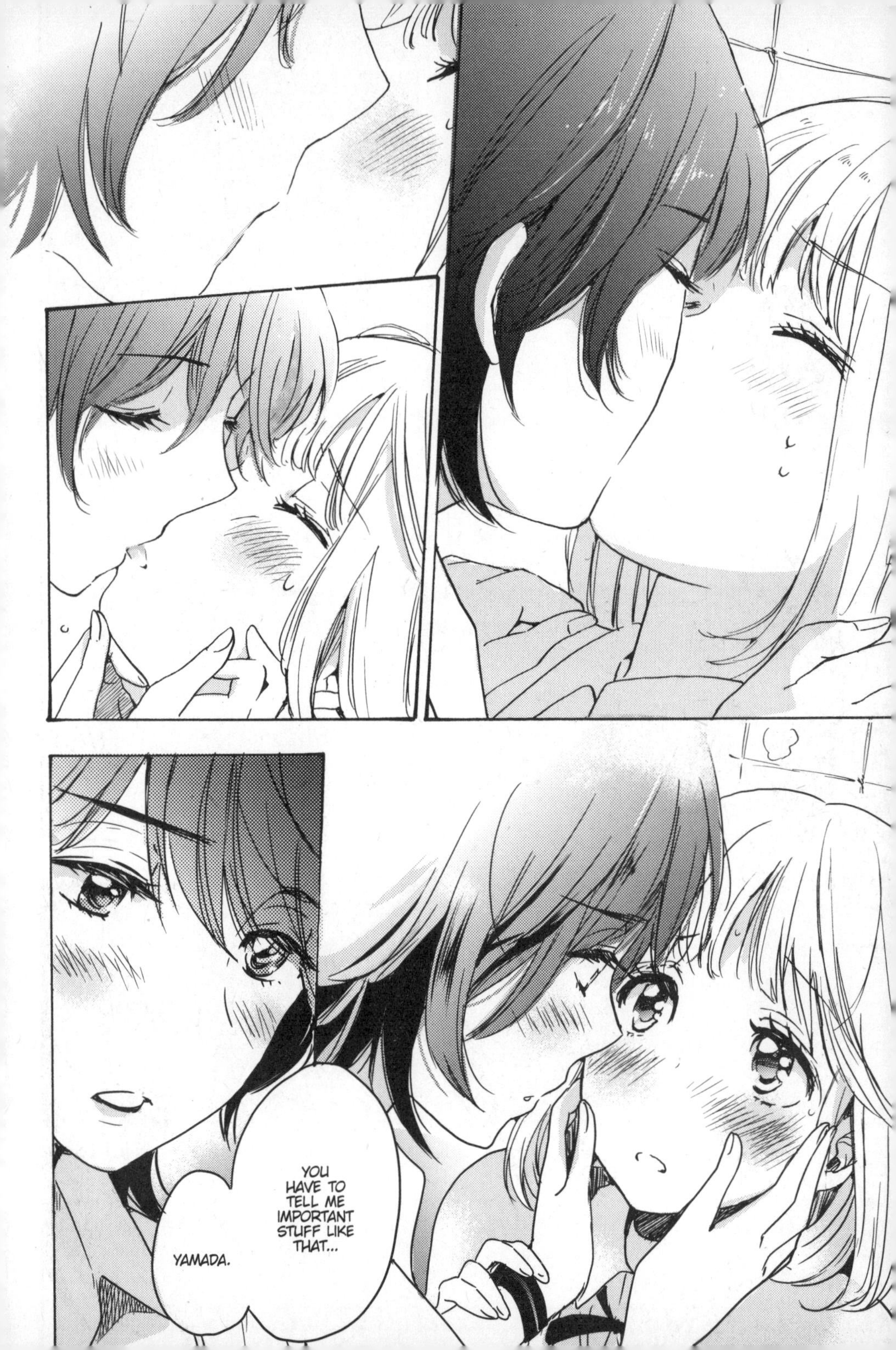
YOU HAVE TO TELL ME IMPORTANT STUFF LIKE THAT...
YAMADA.

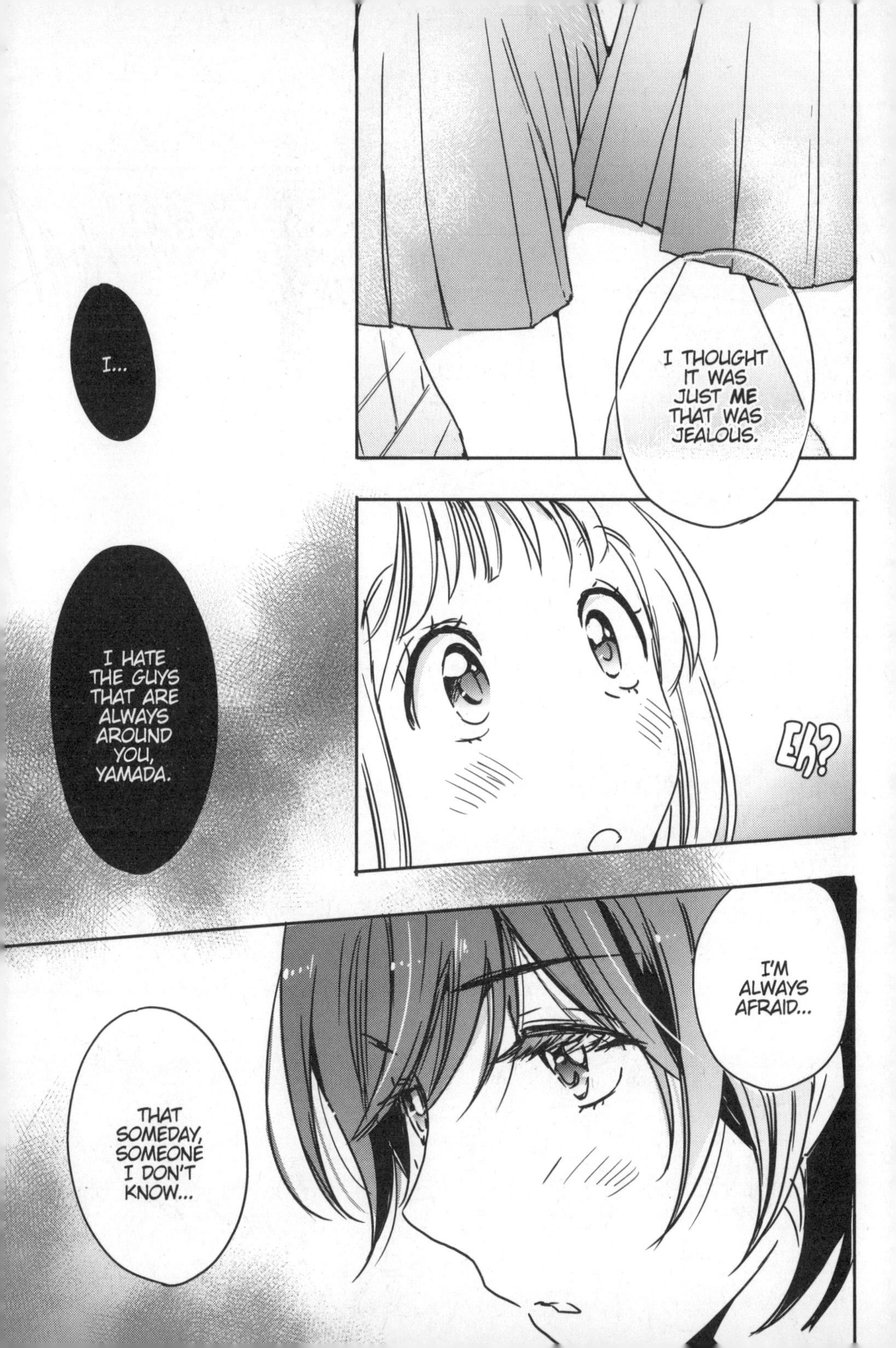
I THOUGHT IT WAS JUST ME THAT WAS JEALOUS.
Eh?
I...
I HATE THE GUYS THAT ARE ALWAYS AROUND YOU, YAMADA.
I'M ALWAYS AFRAID...
THAT SOMEDAY, SOMEONE I DON'T KNOW...

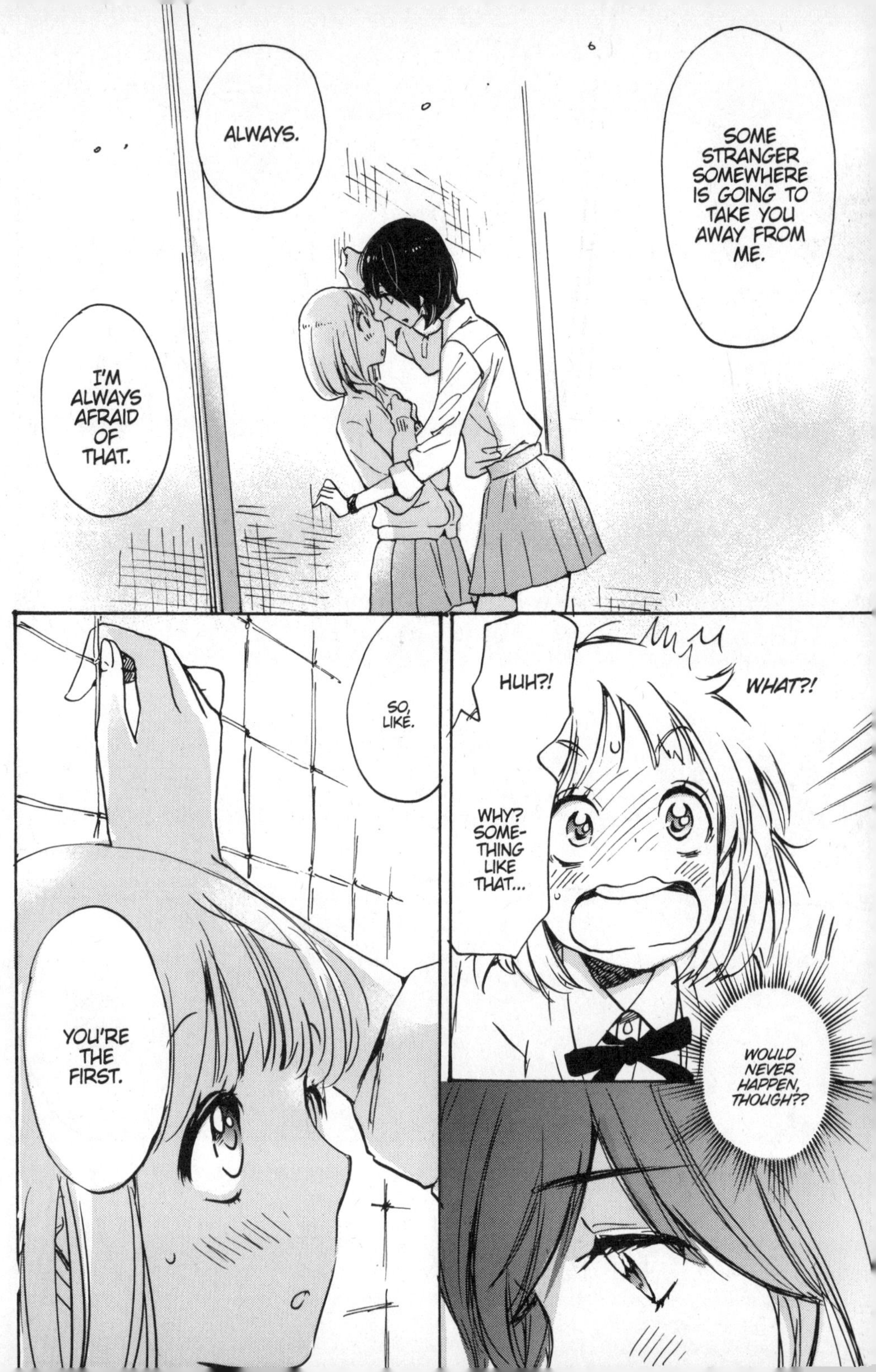
SOME STRANGER SOMEWHERE IS GOING TO TAKE YOU AWAY FROM ME.
ALWAYS.
I'M ALWAYS AFRAID OF THAT.
WHAT?!
HUH?!
WHY? SOME-THING LIKE THAT...
WOULD NEVER HAPPEN, THOUGH??
SO, LIKE.
YOU'RE THE FIRST.

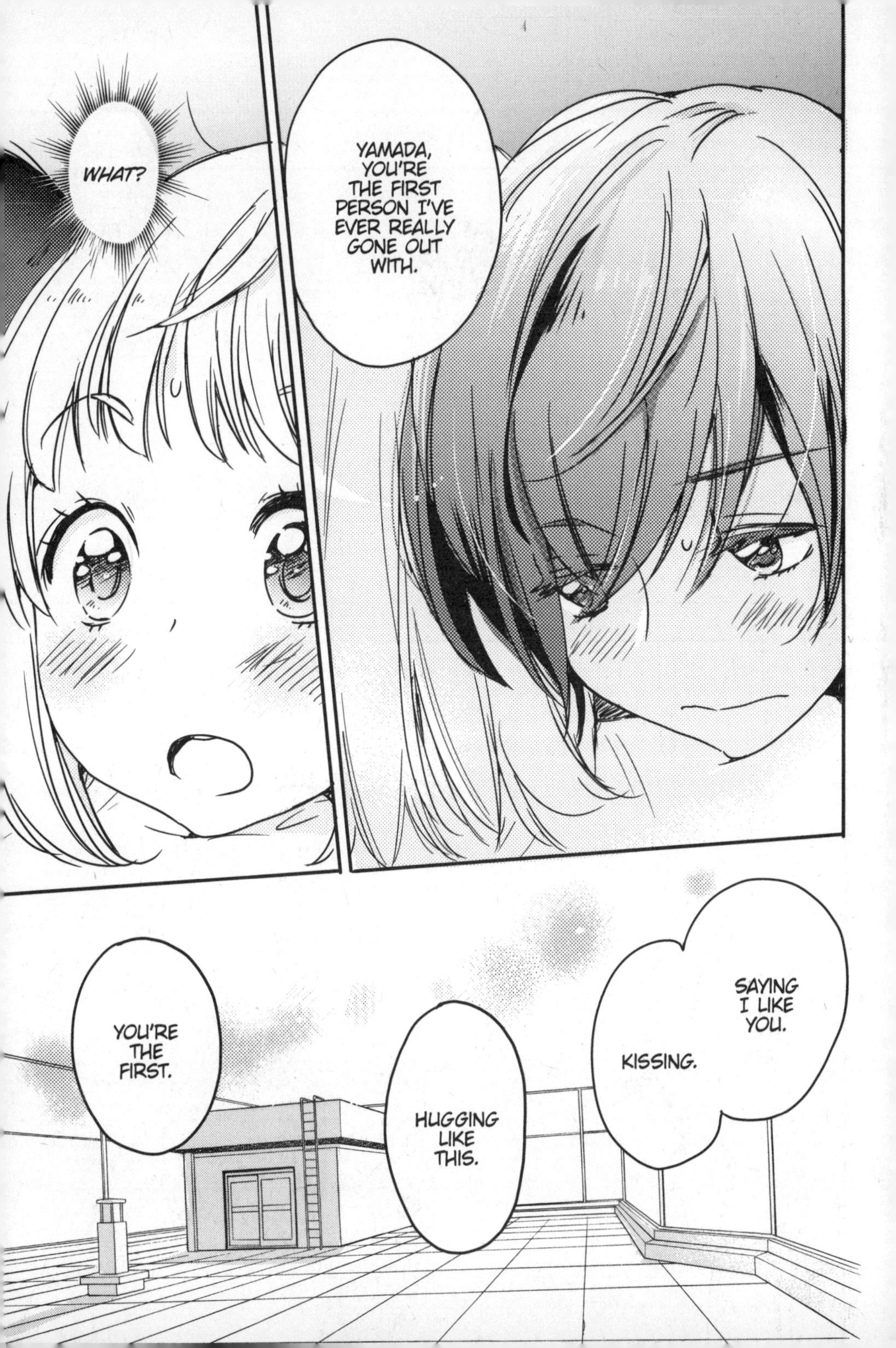
YAMADA, YOU'RE THE FIRST PERSON I'VE EVER REALLY GONE OUT WITH.
WHAT?
SAYING I LIKE YOU.
KISSING.
HUGGING LIKE THIS.
YOU'RE THE FIRST.

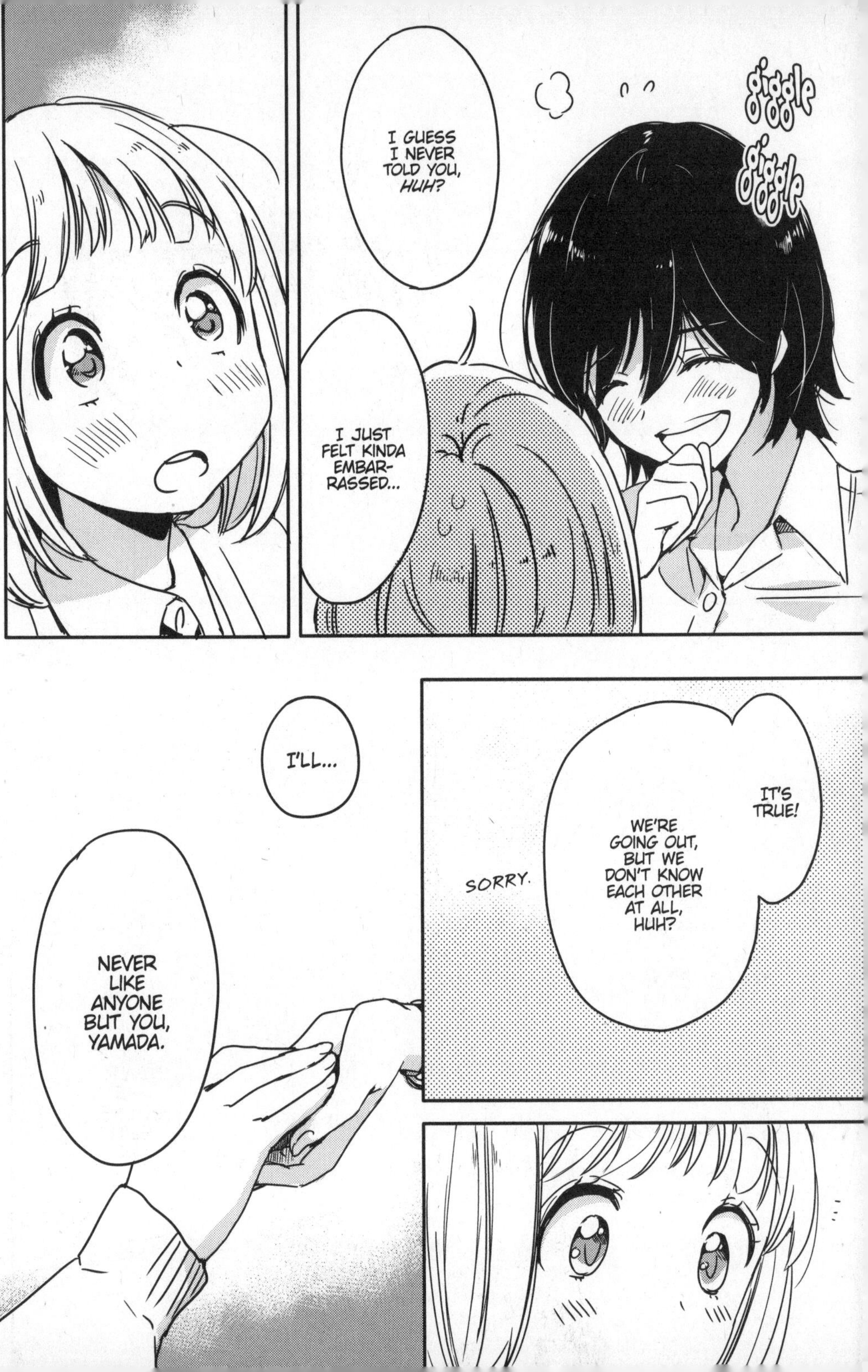
giggle giggle
I GUESS I NEVER TOLD YOU, HUH?
I JUST FELT KINDA EMBAR-RASSED...
IT'S TRUE!
WE'RE GOING OUT, BUT WE DON'T KNOW EACH OTHER AT ALL, HUH?
SORRY.
I'LL...
NEVER LIKE ANYONE BUT YOU, YAMADA.

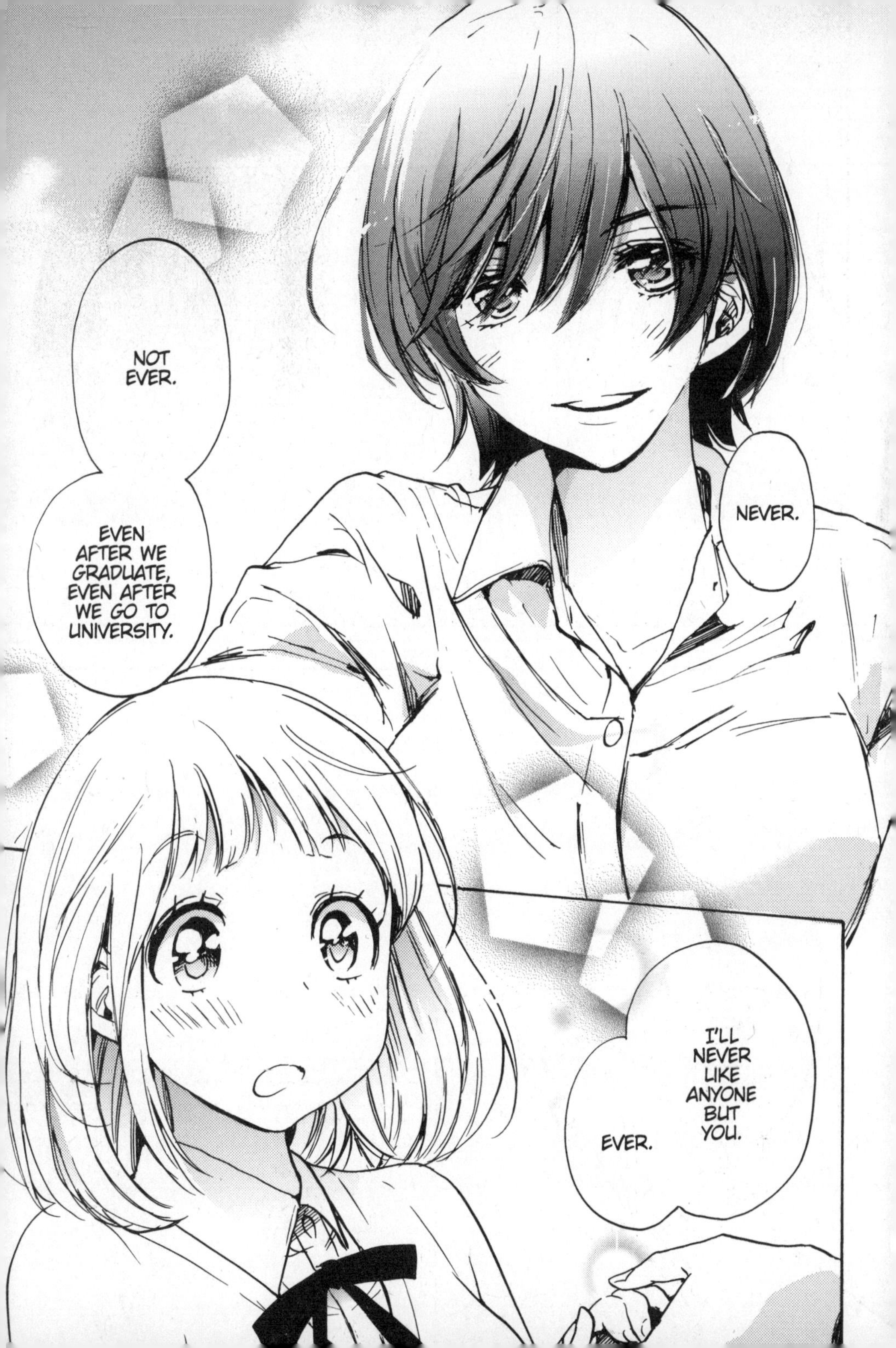
NEVER.
NOT EVER.
EVEN AFTER WE GRADUATE, EVEN AFTER WE GO TO UNIVERSITY.
I'LL NEVER LIKE ANYONE BUT YOU.
EVER.

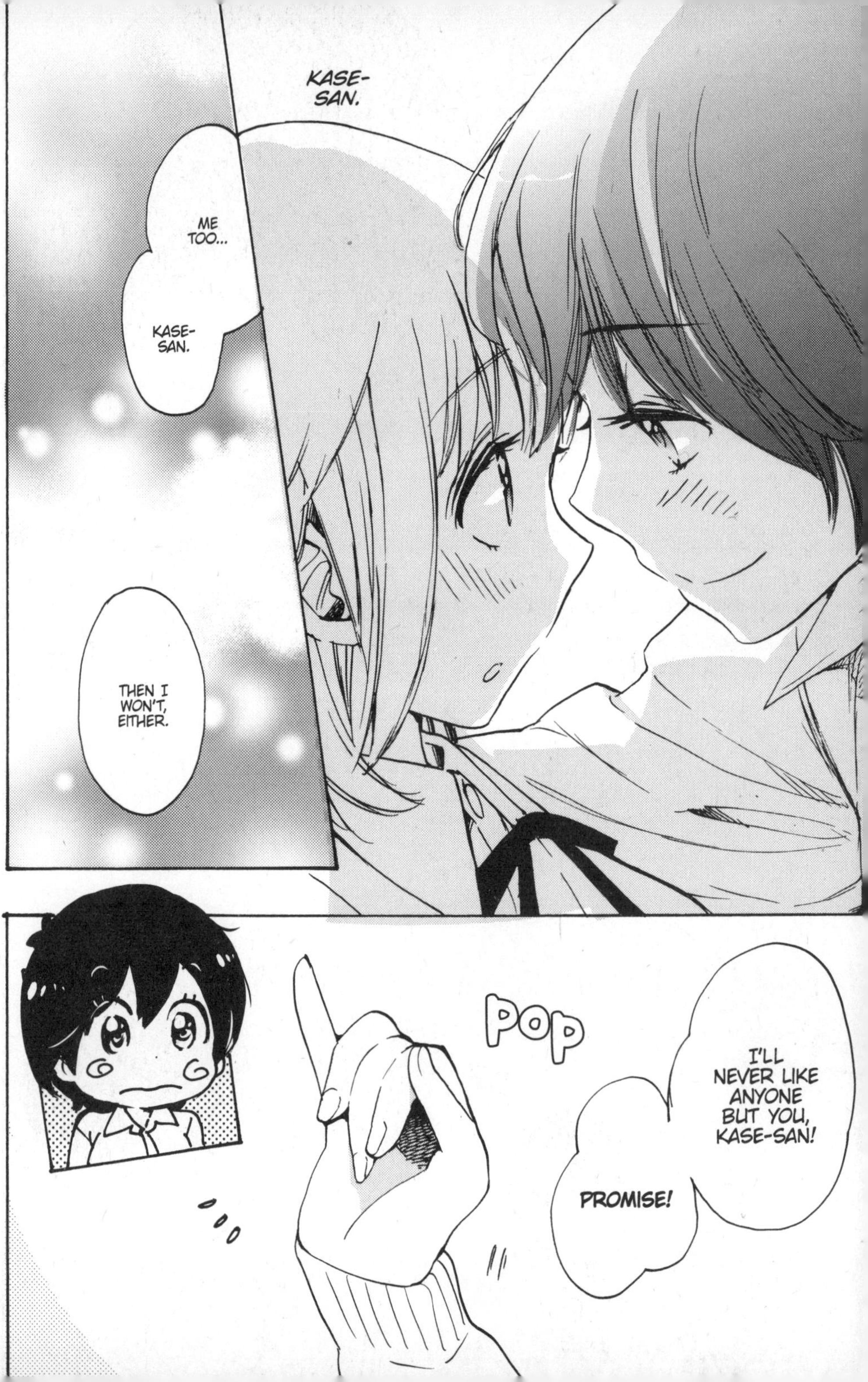
KASE-SAN.
ME TOO... KASE-SAN.
THEN I WON'T, EITHER.
I'LL NEVER LIKE ANYONE BUT YOU, KASE-SAN!
POP
PROMISE!

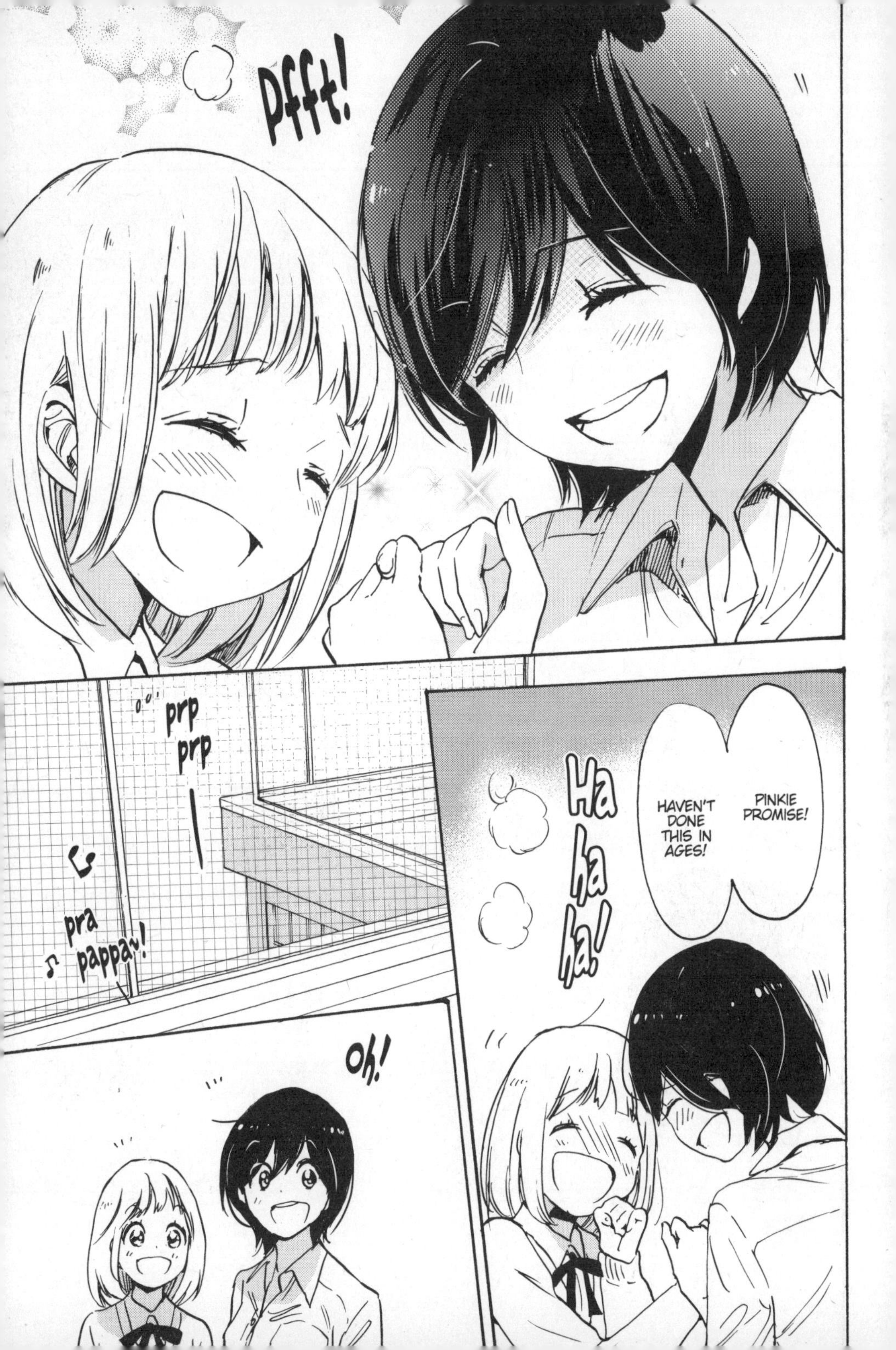
Pfft!
PINKIE PROMISE!
HAVEN'T DONE THIS IN AGES!
Ha ha ha!
prp prp
pra pappa~!
Oh!

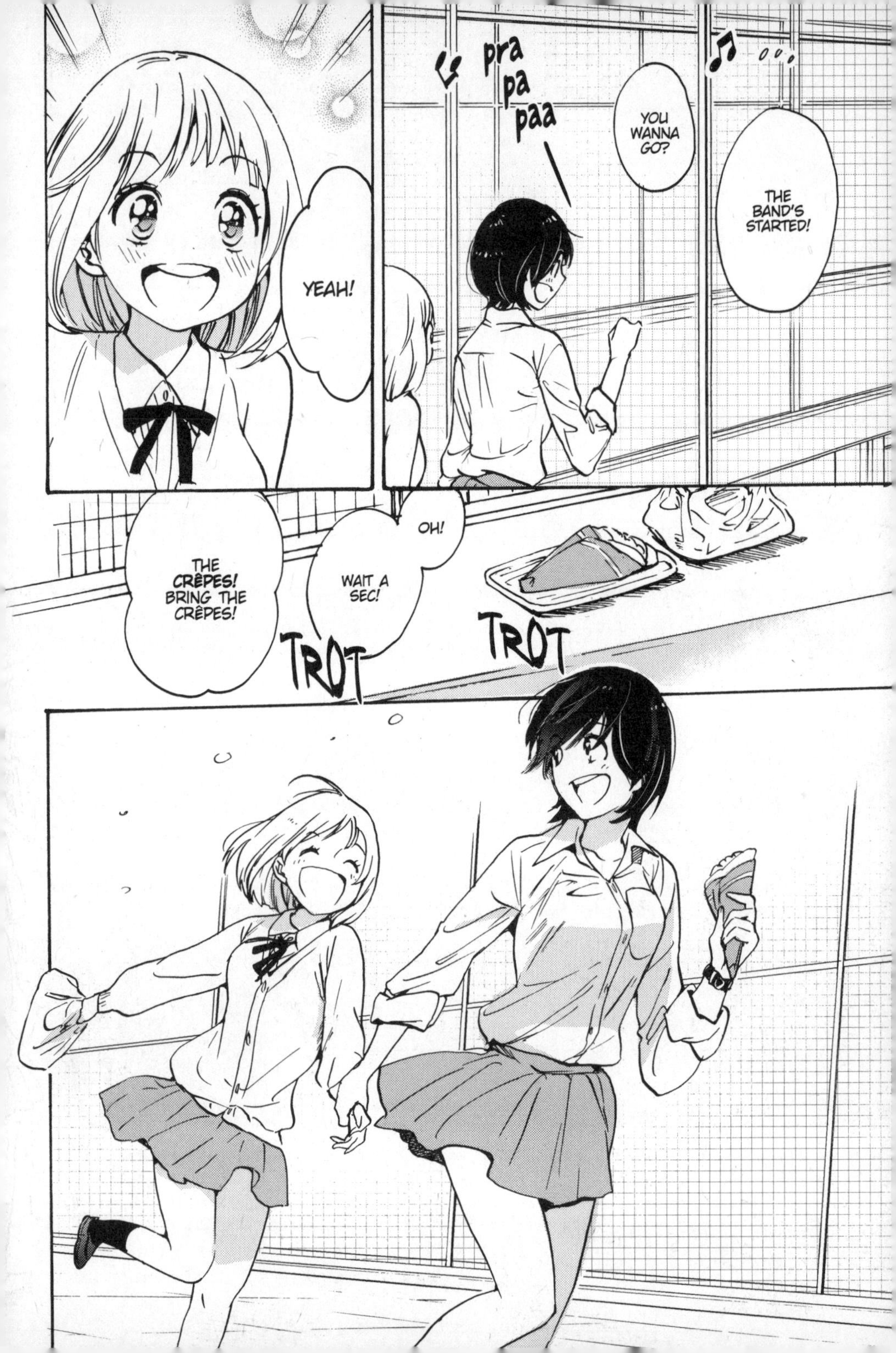
THE BAND'S STARTED!
YOU WANNA GO?
pra pa paa
YEAH!
OH!
WAIT A SEC!
THE CRÊPES! BRING THE CRÊPES!
TROT
TROT

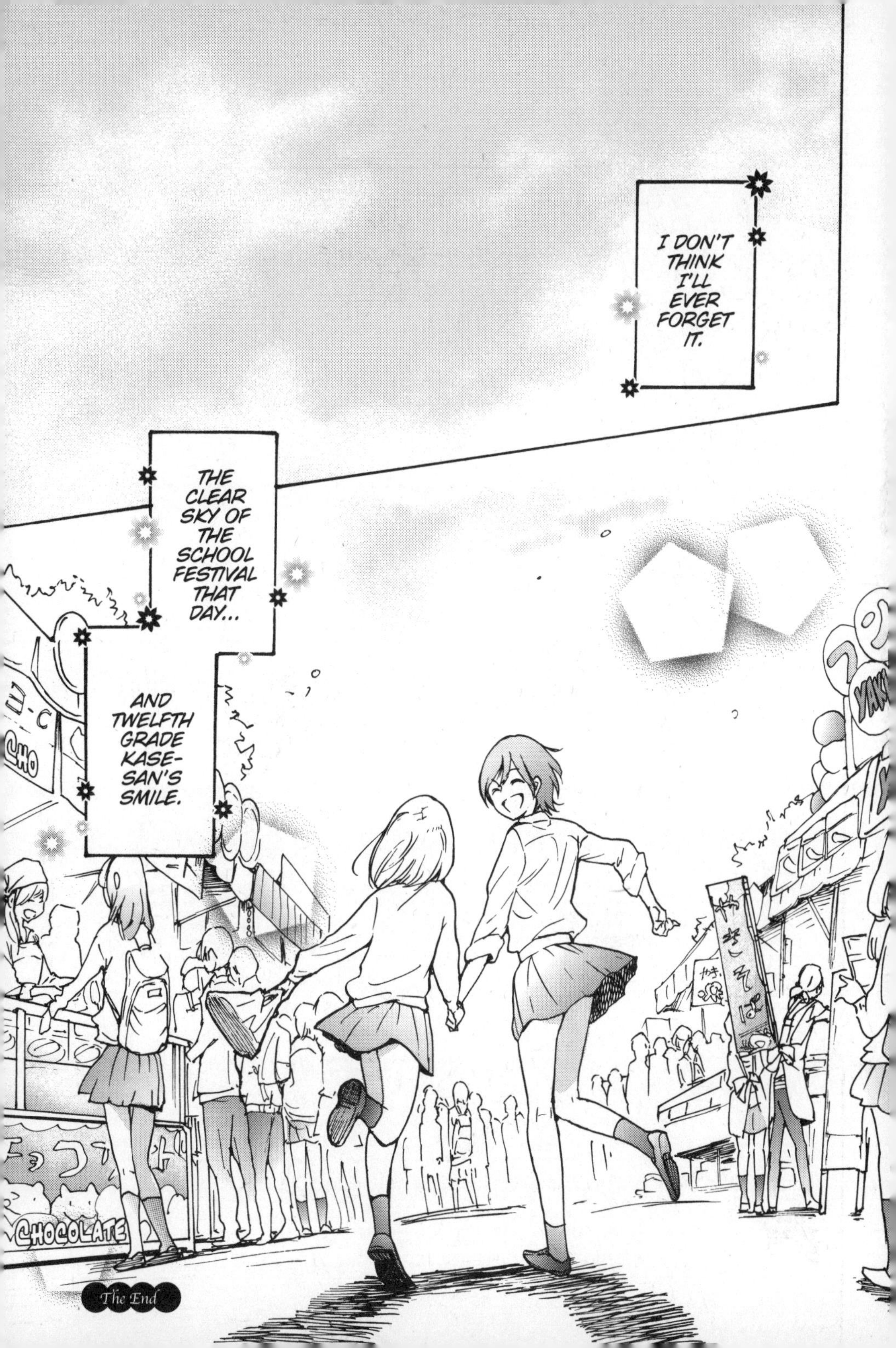
I DON'T THINK I'LL EVER FORGET IT.
THE CLEAR SKY OF THE SCHOOL FESTIVAL THAT DAY...
AND TWELFTH GRADE KASE-SAN'S SMILE.
CHO
CHOCOLATE
The End

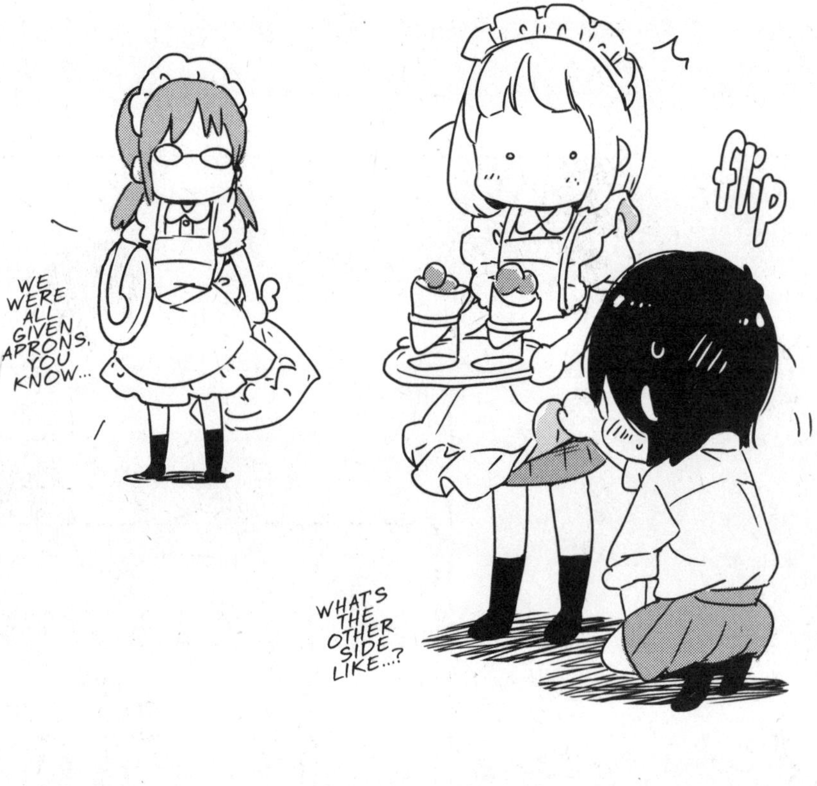
flip
WHAT'S THE OTHER SIDE LIKE...?
WE WERE ALL GIVEN APRONS, YOU KNOW...

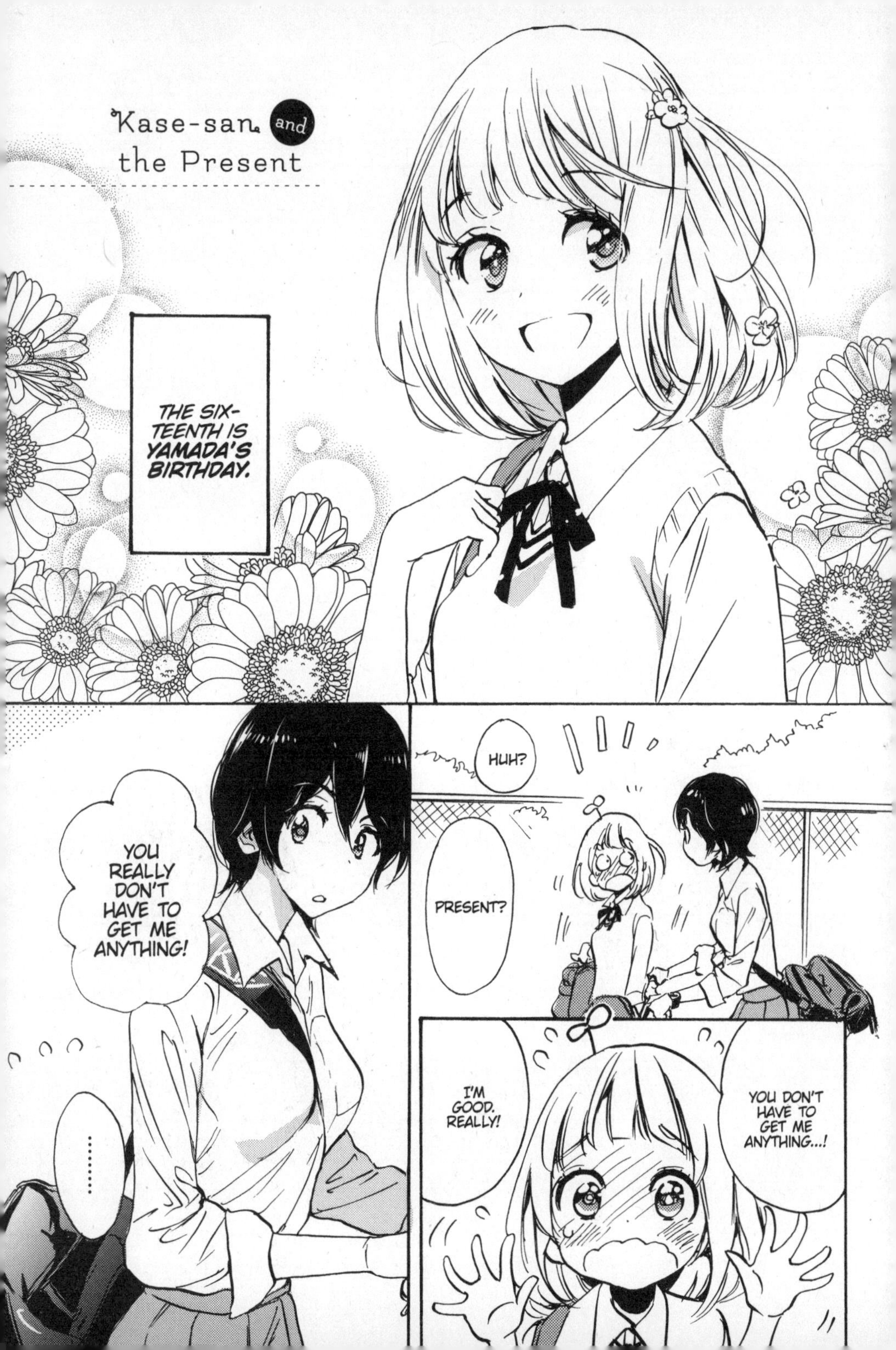
Kase-san and the Present
THE SIX-TEENTH IS YAMADA'S BIRTHDAY.
HUH?
PRESENT?
YOU DON'T HAVE TO GET ME ANYTHING...!
I'M GOOD. REALLY!
YOU REALLY DON'T HAVE TO GET ME ANYTHING!
......

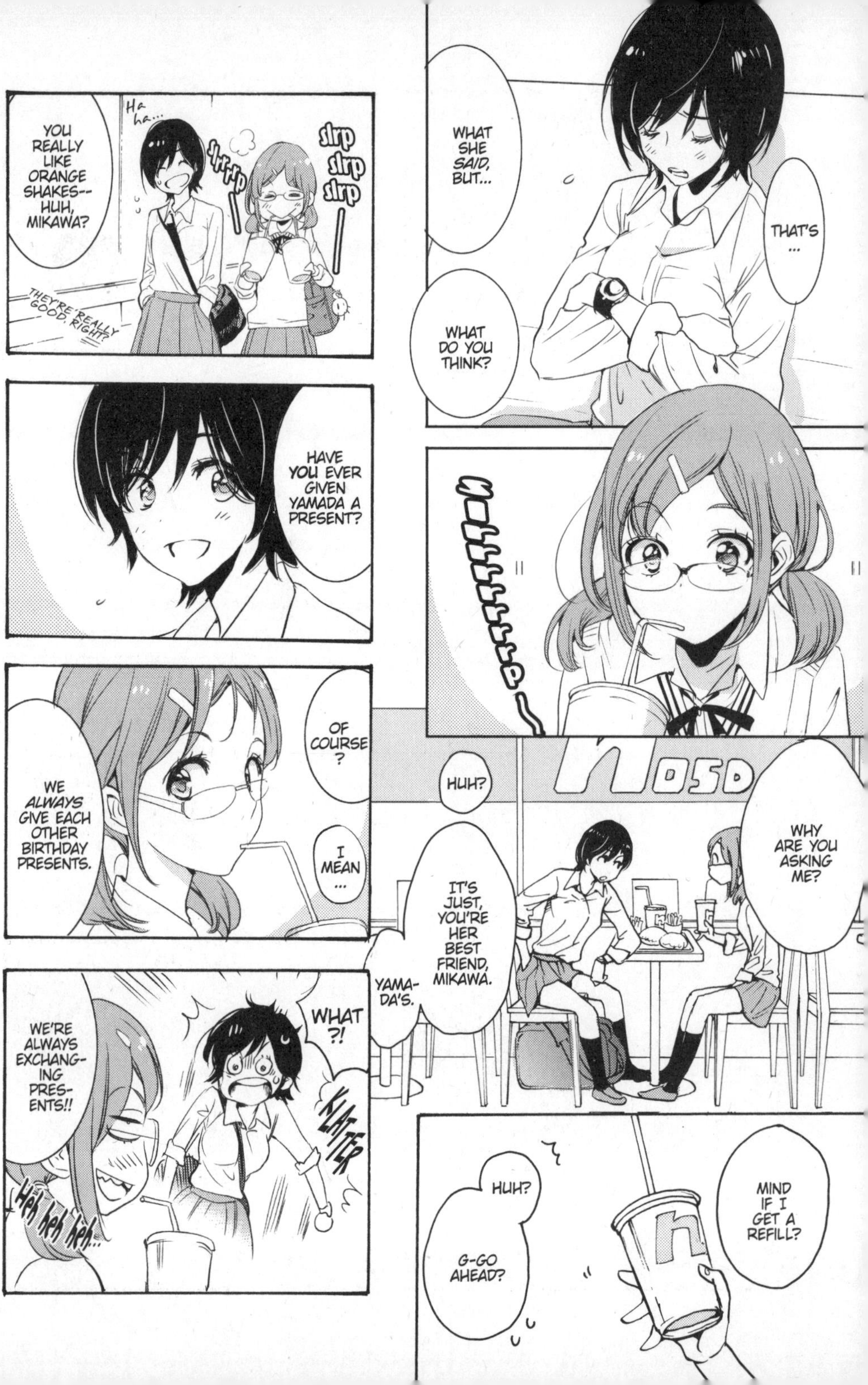
THAT'S...
WHAT SHE SAID, BUT...
WHAT DO YOU THINK?
WHY ARE YOU ASKING ME?
HUH?
IT'S JUST, YOU'RE HER BEST FRIEND, MIKAWA.
YAMA-DA'S.
MIND IF I GET A REFILL?
HUH?
G-GO AHEAD?
slrp slrp slrp
Ha ha...
YOU REALLY LIKE ORANGE SHAKES--HUH, MIKAWA?
THEY'RE REALLY GOOD, RIGHT?
HAVE YOU EVER GIVEN YAMADA A PRESENT?
OF COURSE?
I MEAN...
WE ALWAYS GIVE EACH OTHER BIRTHDAY PRESENTS.
WHAT?!
KLATTER
WE'RE ALWAYS EXCHANG-ING PRES-ENTS!!
Heh heh heh...

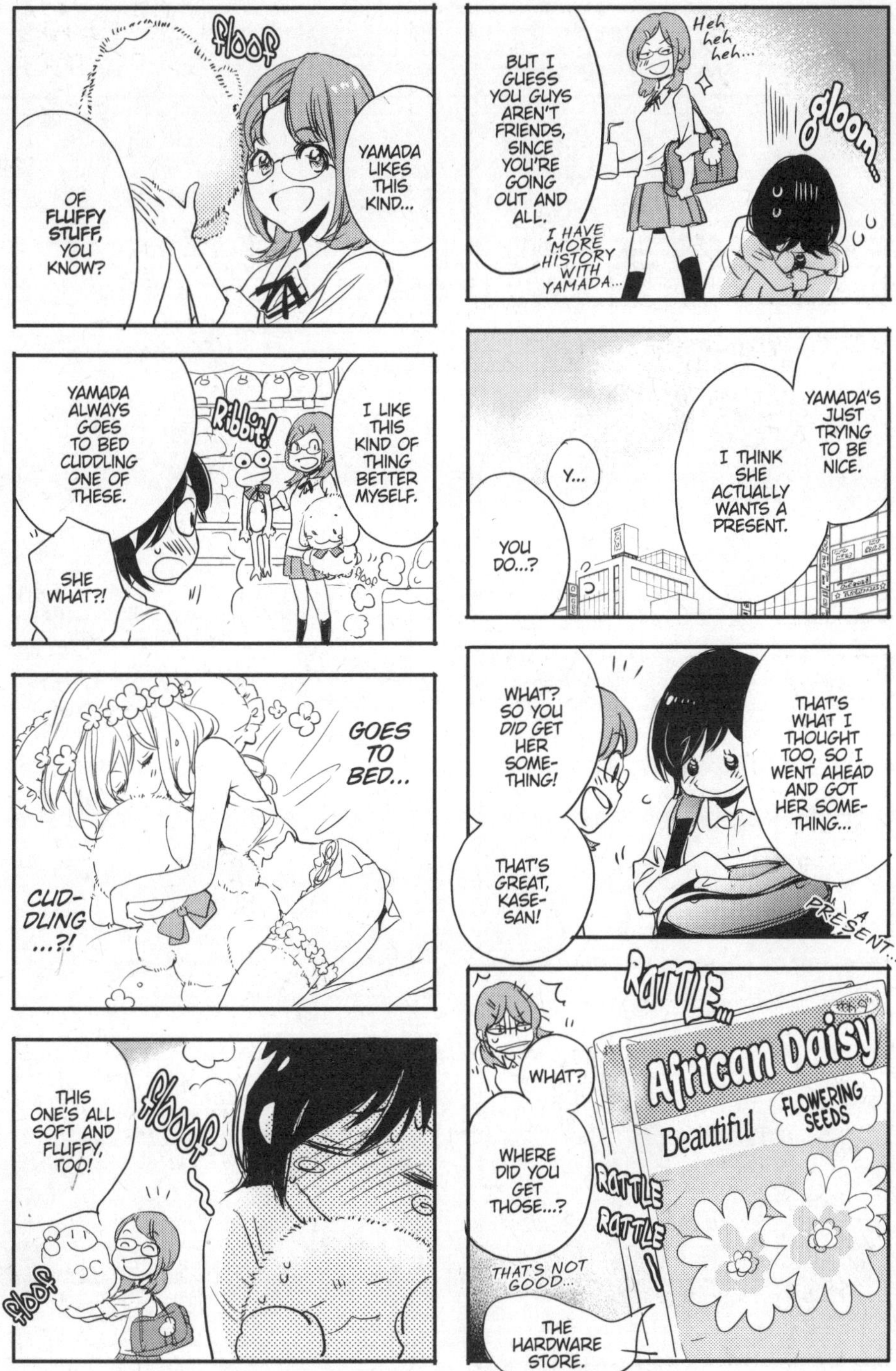
gloom...
Heh heh heh...
BUT I GUESS YOU GUYS AREN'T FRIENDS, SINCE YOU'RE GOING OUT AND ALL.
I HAVE MORE HISTORY WITH YAMADA...
YAMADA'S JUST TRYING TO BE NICE.
I THINK SHE ACTUALLY WANTS A PRESENT.
Y...
YOU DO...?
THAT'S WHAT I THOUGHT TOO, SO I WENT AHEAD AND GOT HER SOME-THING...
A PRESENT...
WHAT? SO YOU DID GET HER SOME-THING!
THAT'S GREAT, KASE-SAN!
RATTLE...
African Daisy
Beautiful
FLOWERING SEEDS
WHAT?
WHERE DID YOU GET THOSE...?
RATTLE RATTLE
THAT'S NOT GOOD...
THE HARDWARE STORE.
floof
YAMADA LIKES THIS KIND...
OF FLUFFY STUFF, YOU KNOW?
I LIKE THIS KIND OF THING BETTER MYSELF.
Ribbit!
YAMADA ALWAYS GOES TO BED CUDDLING ONE OF THESE.
SHE WHAT?!
GOES TO BED...
CUD-DLING...?!
floof
THIS ONE'S ALL SOFT AND FLUFFY, TOO!
floof

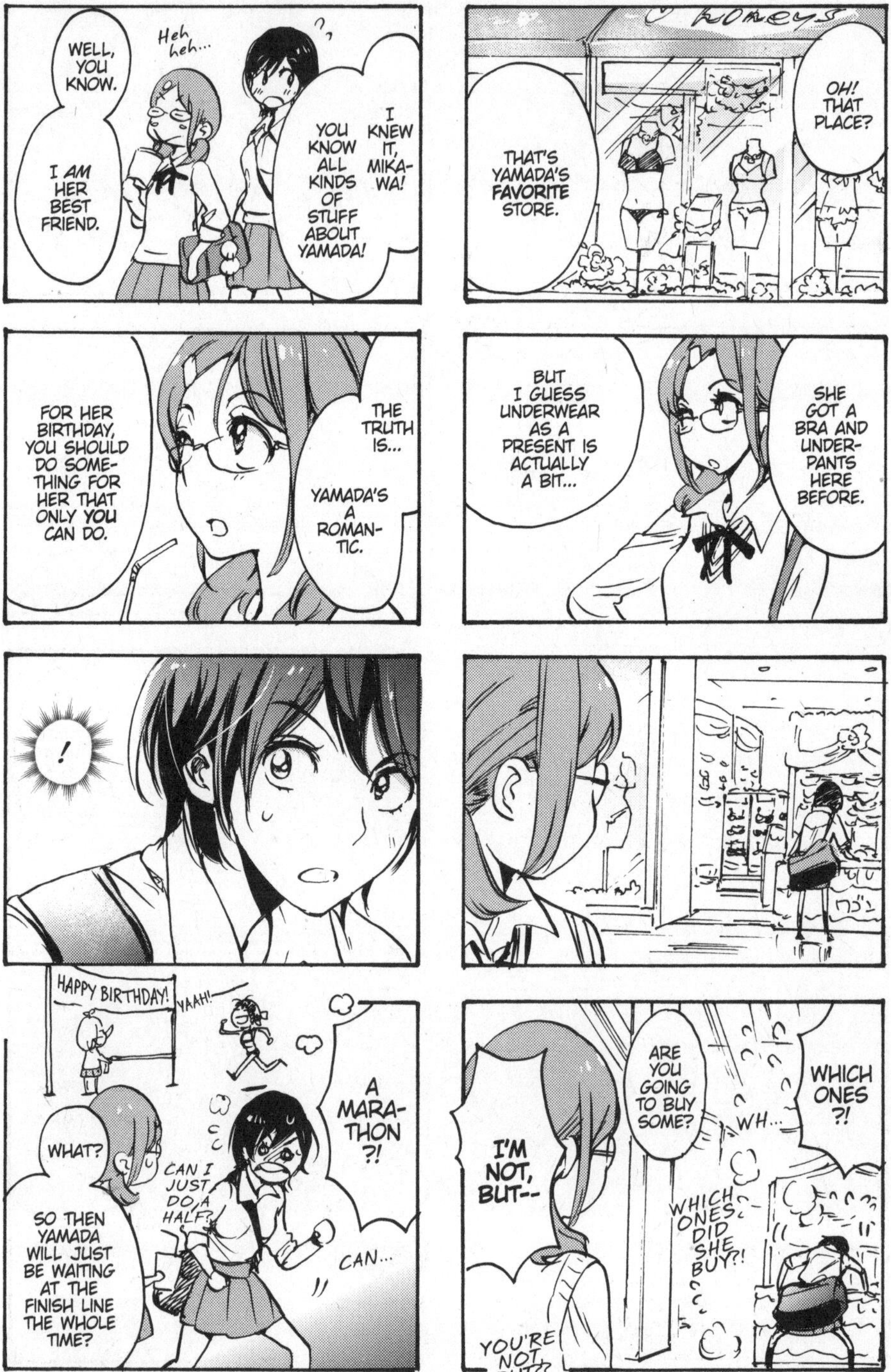
OH! THAT PLACE?
THAT'S YAMADA'S FAVORITE STORE.
I KNEW IT, MIKA-WA! YOU KNOW ALL KINDS OF STUFF ABOUT YAMADA!
Heh heh...
WELL, YOU KNOW.
I AM HER BEST FRIEND.
SHE GOT A BRA AND UNDER-PANTS HERE BEFORE.
BUT I GUESS UNDERWEAR AS A PRESENT IS ACTUALLY A BIT...
THE TRUTH IS...
YAMADA'S A ROMAN-TIC.
FOR HER BIRTHDAY, YOU SHOULD DO SOME-THING FOR HER THAT ONLY YOU CAN DO.
!
WHICH ONES ?!
WH...
ARE YOU GOING TO BUY SOME?
WHICH ONES DID SHE BUY?!
I'M NOT, BUT--
YOU'RE NOT, BUT??
A MARA-THON ?!
CAN...
CAN I JUST DO A HALF?
HAPPY BIRTHDAY!
YAAH!
WHAT?
SO THEN YAMADA WILL JUST BE WAITING AT THE FINISH LINE THE WHOLE TIME?

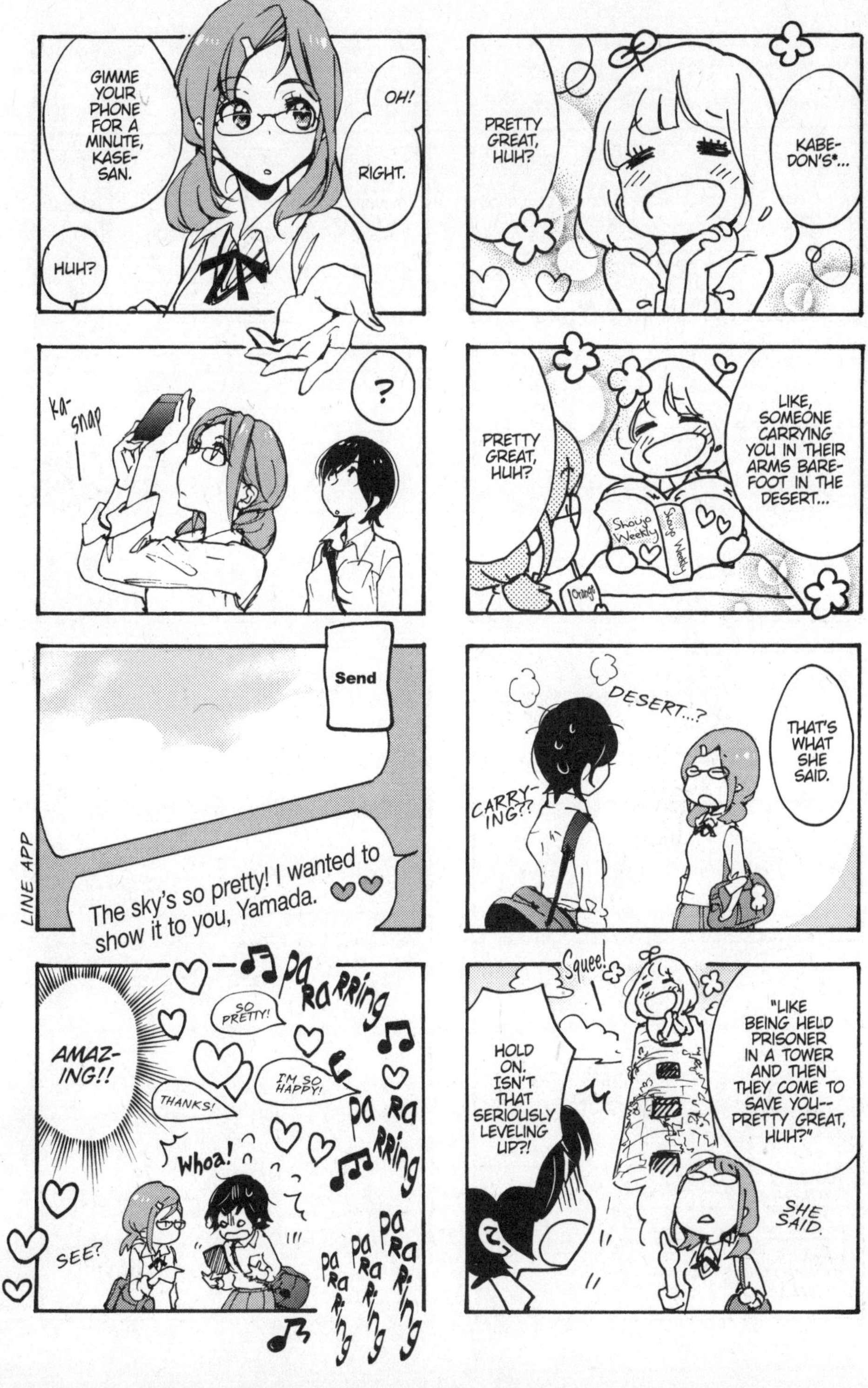
KABE-DON'S*...
PRETTY GREAT, HUH?
LIKE, SOMEONE CARRYING YOU IN THEIR ARMS BARE-FOOT IN THE DESERT...
PRETTY GREAT, HUH?
Shoujo Weekly
Shoujo Weekly
Orange
THAT'S WHAT SHE SAID.
DESERT...?
CARRY-ING??
"LIKE BEING HELD PRISONER IN A TOWER AND THEN THEY COME TO SAVE YOU--PRETTY GREAT, HUH?"
SHE SAID.
Squee!
HOLD ON. ISN'T THAT SERIOUSLY LEVELING UP?!
GIMME YOUR PHONE FOR A MINUTE, KASE-SAN.
OH!
RIGHT.
HUH?
?
ka-snap
Send
LINE APP
The sky's so pretty! I wanted to show it to you, Yamada.
AMAZ-ING!!
pa RA RRing
SO PRETTY!
I'M SO HAPPY!
THANKS!
pa RA RRing
Whoa!
SEE?
pa RA Ring pa RA Ring pa RA Ring

*Kabedon is when a person slams a hand down against the wall, pinning their love interest beneath them, a common trope in shoujo manga that is considered romantic.

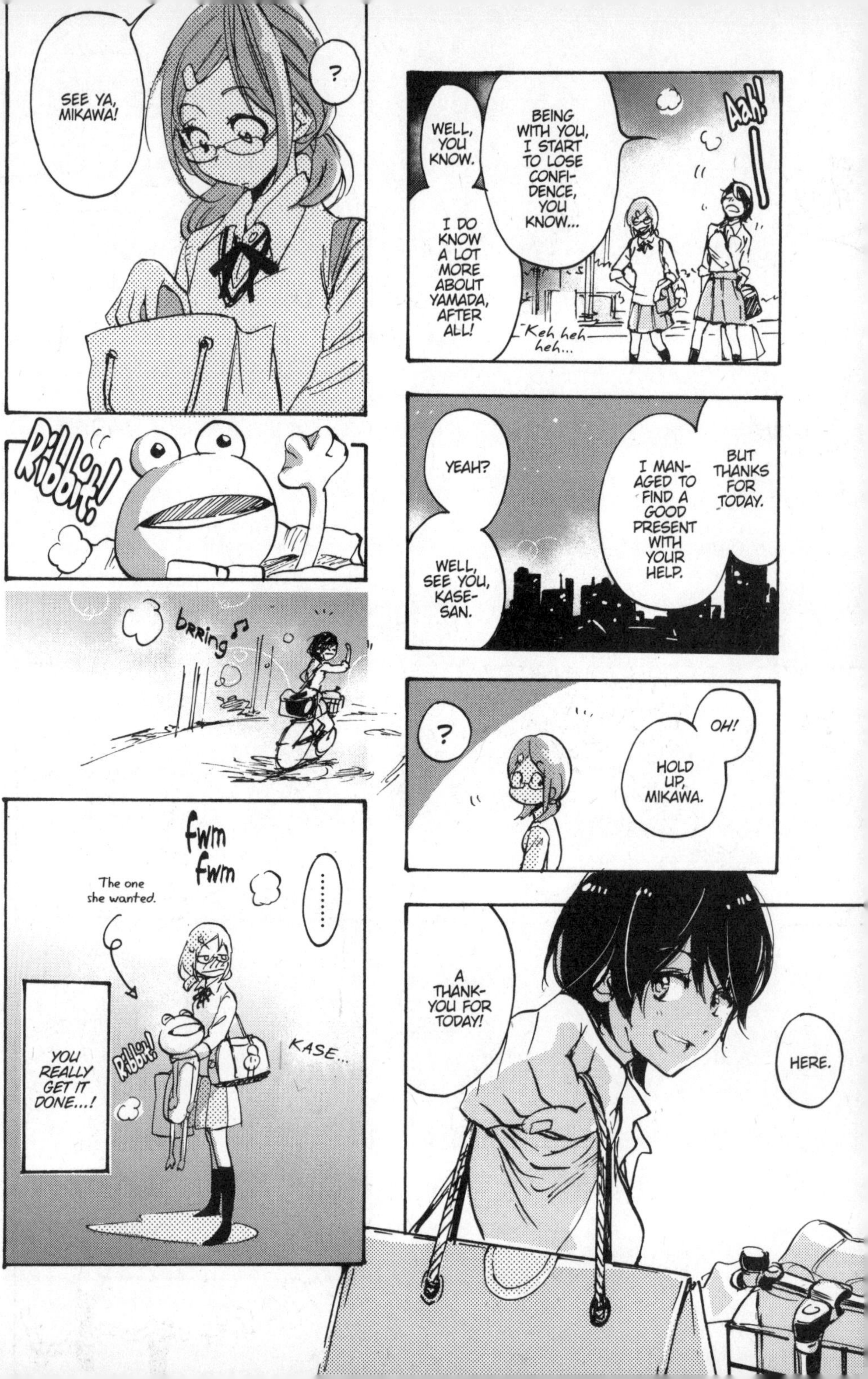
Aah!
WELL, YOU KNOW.
BEING WITH YOU, I START TO LOSE CONFI-DENCE, YOU KNOW...
I DO KNOW A LOT MORE ABOUT YAMADA, AFTER ALL!
Keh heh heh...
BUT THANKS FOR TODAY.
I MAN-AGED TO FIND A GOOD PRESENT WITH YOUR HELP.
YEAH?
WELL, SEE YOU, KASE-SAN.
OH!
HOLD UP, MIKAWA.
?
HERE.
A THANK-YOU FOR TODAY!
?
SEE YA, MIKAWA!
Ribbit!
brring
fwm fwm
....
The one she wanted.
KASE...
Ribbit!
YOU REALLY GET IT DONE...!

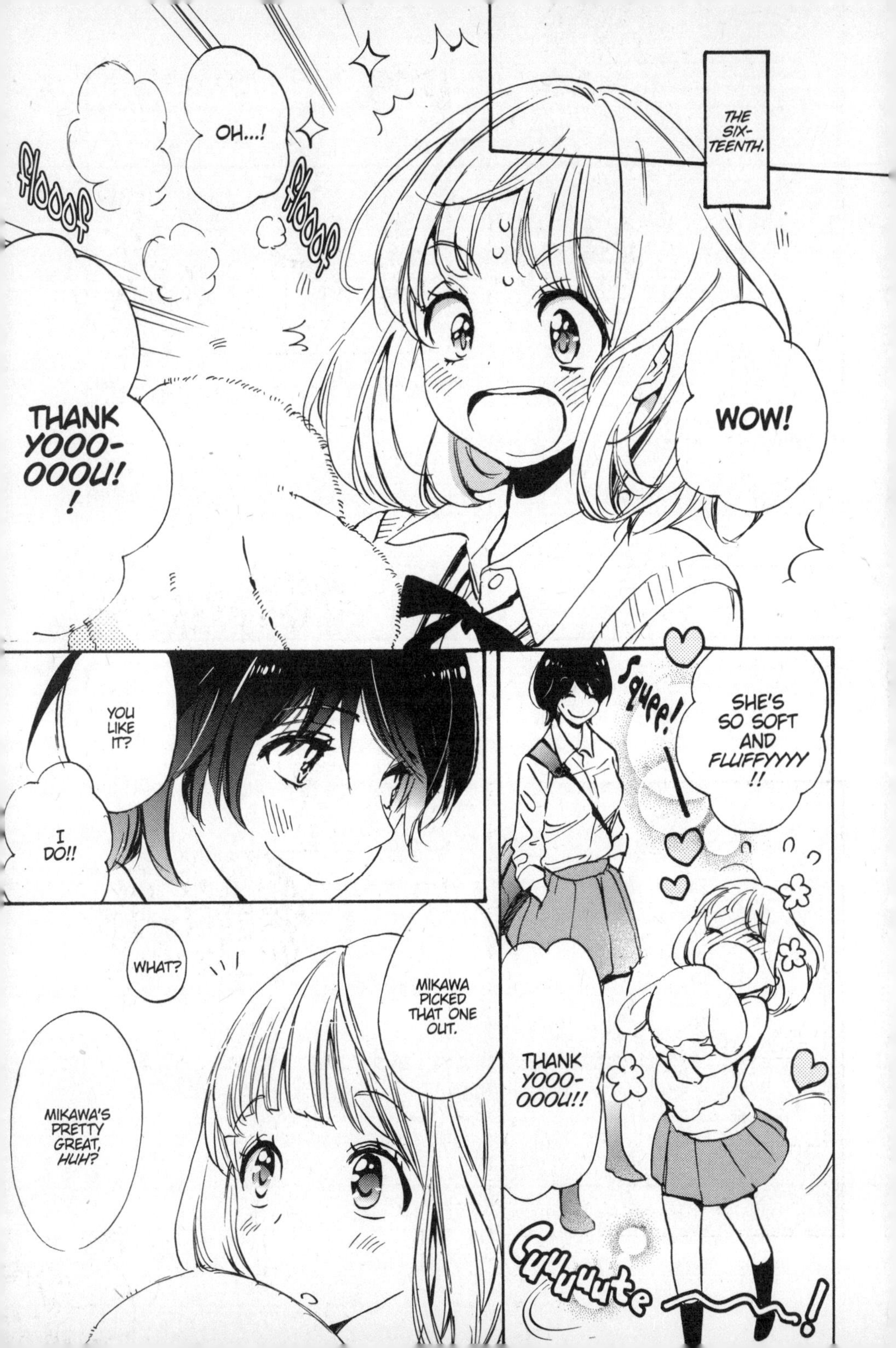
THE SIXTEENTH.
WOW!
OH...!
floof
floof
THANK YOOOOOOU!!
Squee!
SHE'S SO SOFT AND FLUFFYYYY!!
THANK YOOOOOOU!!
Cuuuute~!
YOU LIKE IT?
I DO!!
MIKAWA PICKED THAT ONE OUT.
WHAT?
MIKAWA'S PRETTY GREAT, HUH?

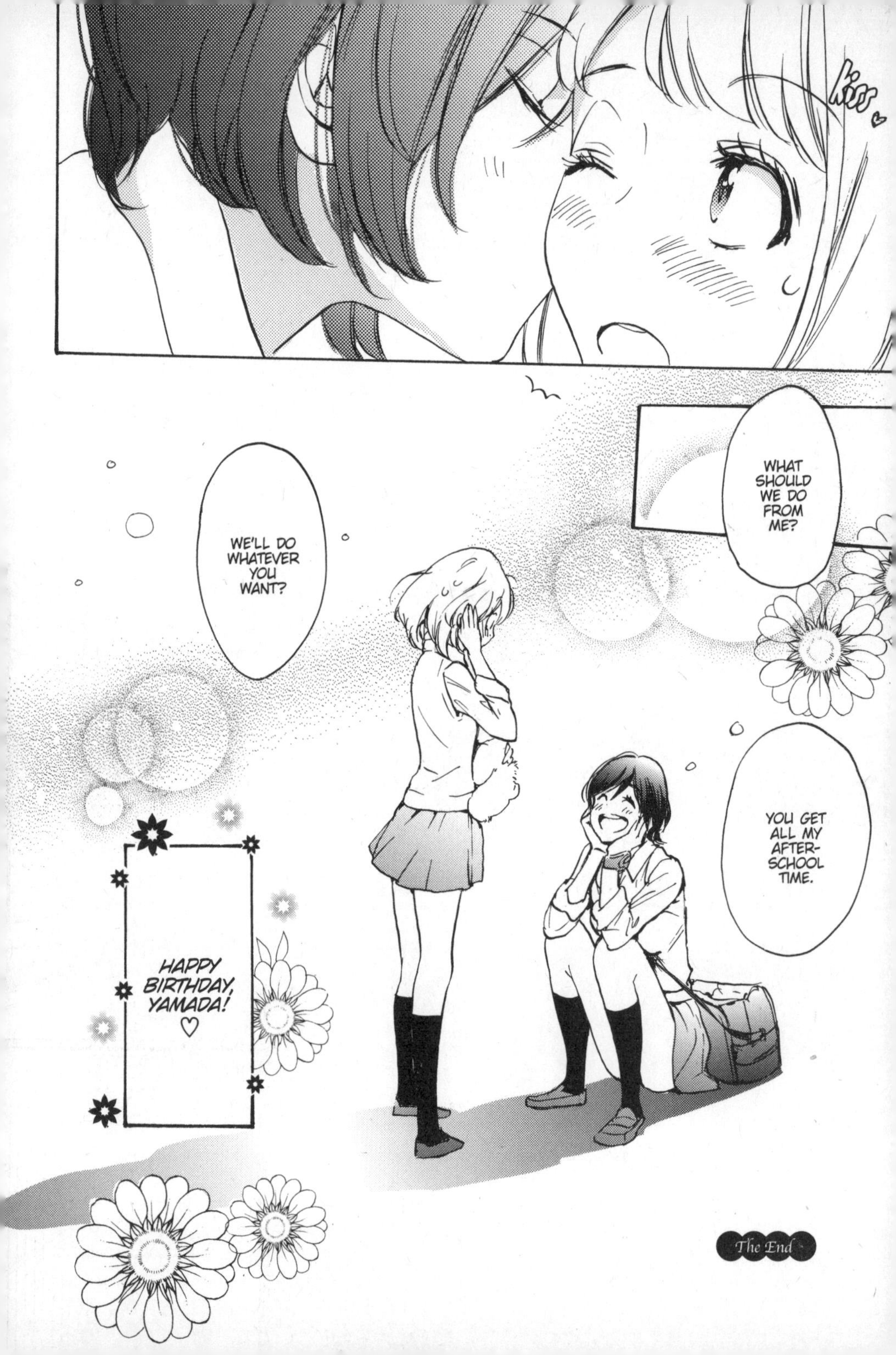
kiss
WHAT SHOULD WE DO FROM ME?
WE'LL DO WHATEVER YOU WANT?
YOU GET ALL MY AFTER-SCHOOL TIME.
HAPPY BIRTHDAY, YAMADA! ♡
The End

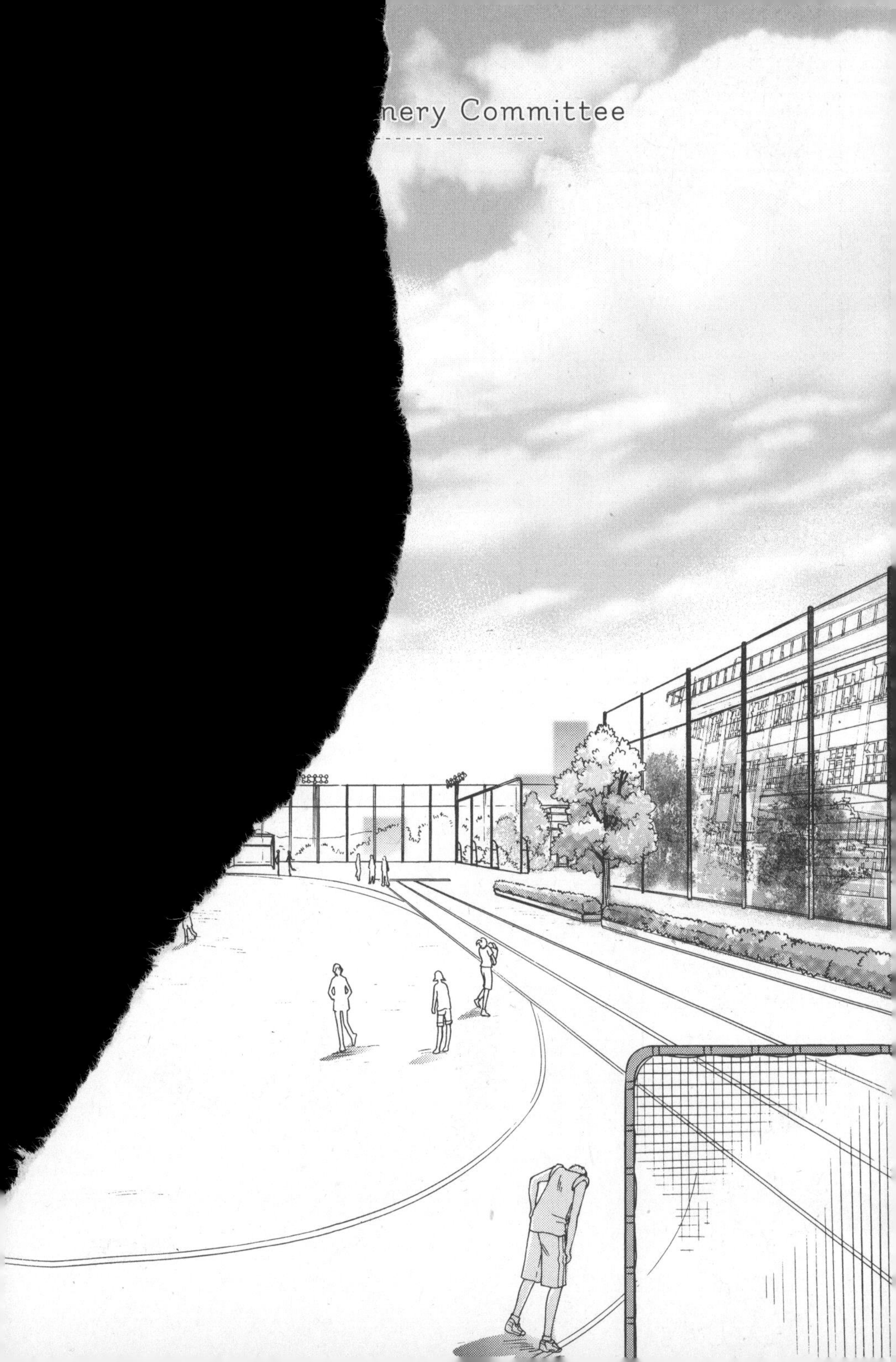
nery Committee

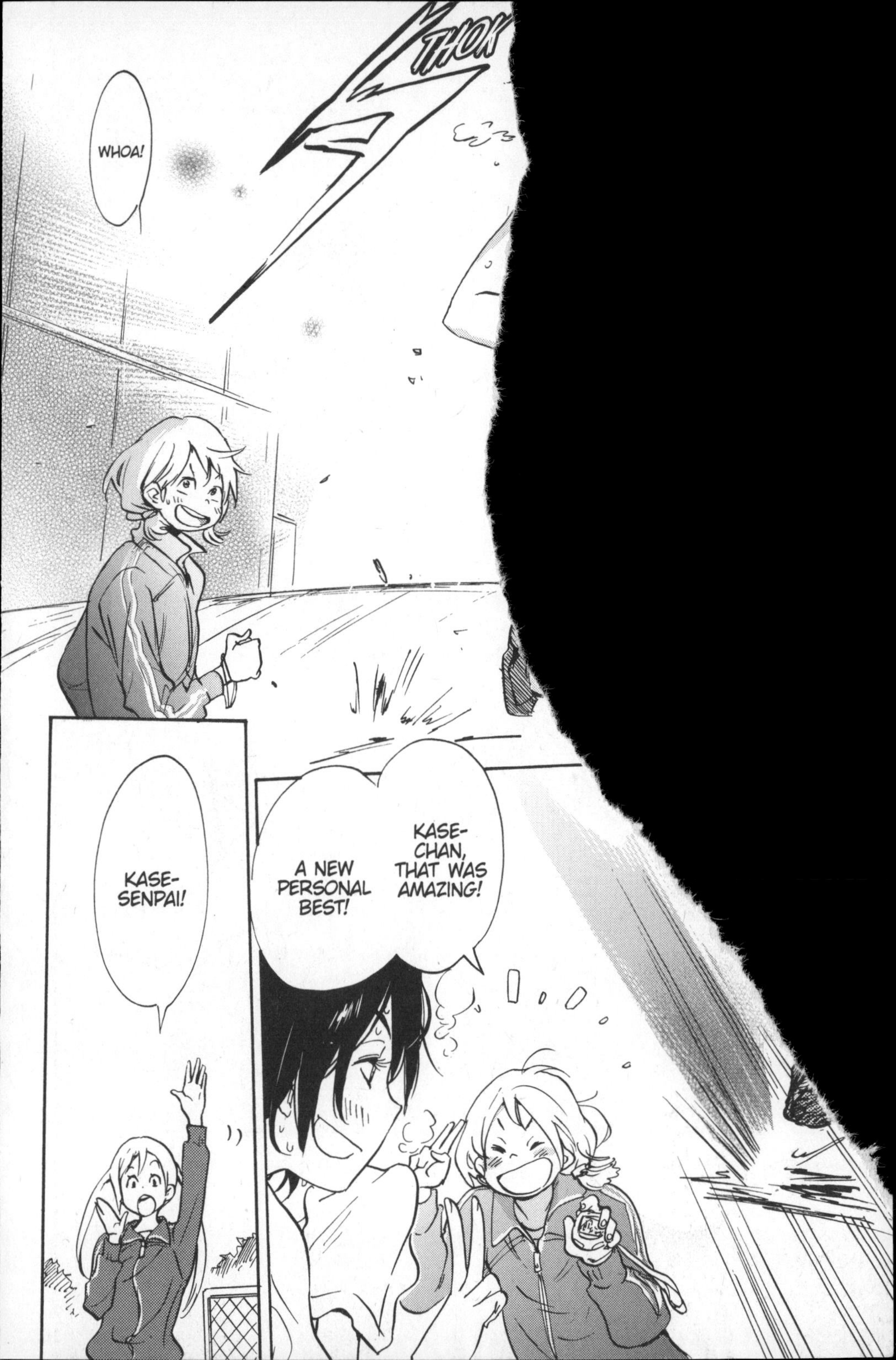
THOK
WHOA!
KASE-CHAN, THAT WAS AMAZING!
A NEW PERSONAL BEST!
KASE-SENPAI!

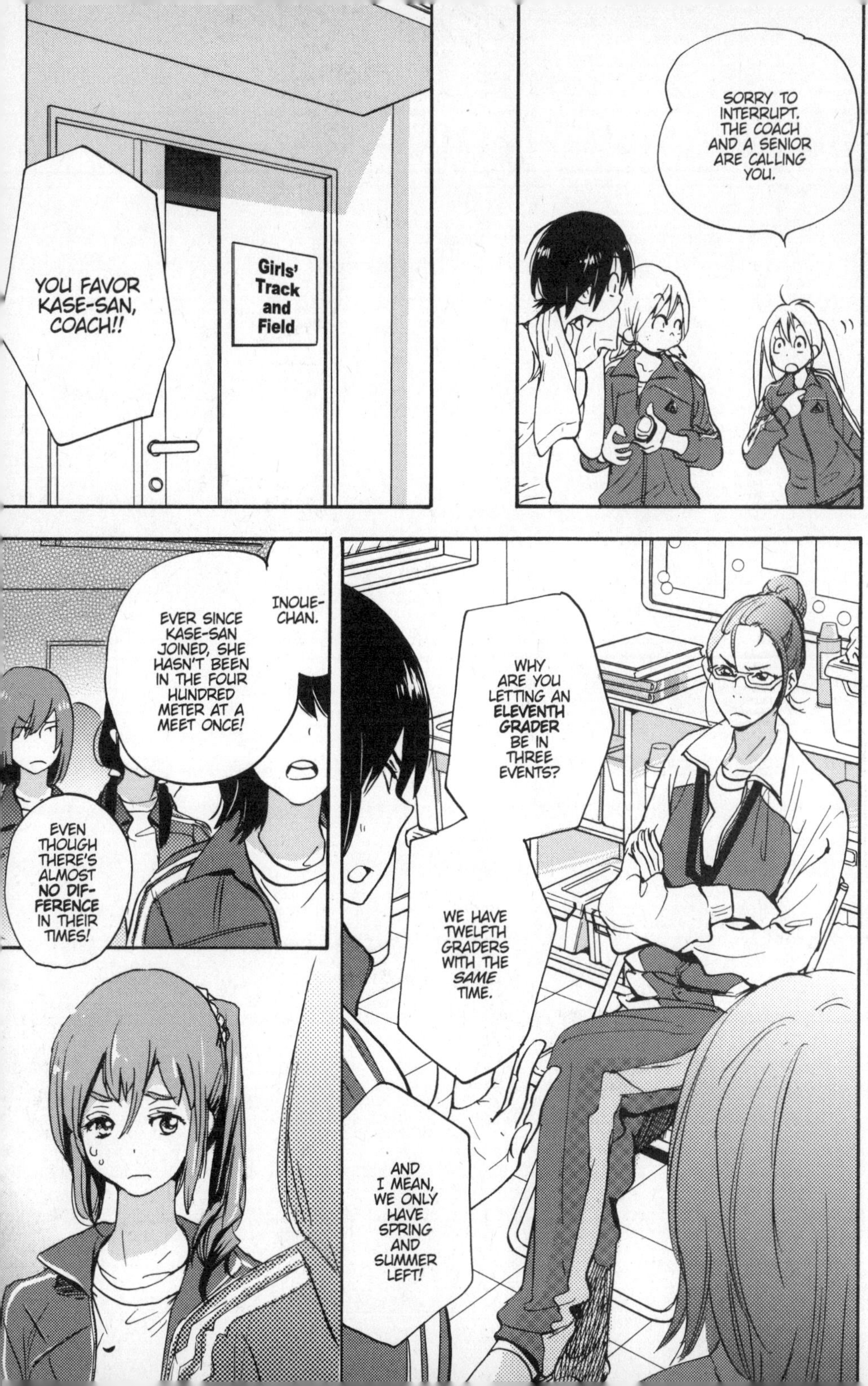
SORRY TO INTERRUPT. THE COACH AND A SENIOR ARE CALLING YOU.
Girls' Track and Field
YOU FAVOR KASE-SAN, COACH!!
WHY ARE YOU LETTING AN ELEVENTH GRADER BE IN THREE EVENTS?
WE HAVE TWELFTH GRADERS WITH THE SAME TIME.
AND I MEAN, WE ONLY HAVE SPRING AND SUMMER LEFT!
INOUE-CHAN.
EVER SINCE KASE-SAN JOINED, SHE HASN'T BEEN IN THE FOUR HUNDRED METER AT A MEET ONCE!
EVEN THOUGH THERE'S ALMOST NO DIFFERENCE IN THEIR TIMES!

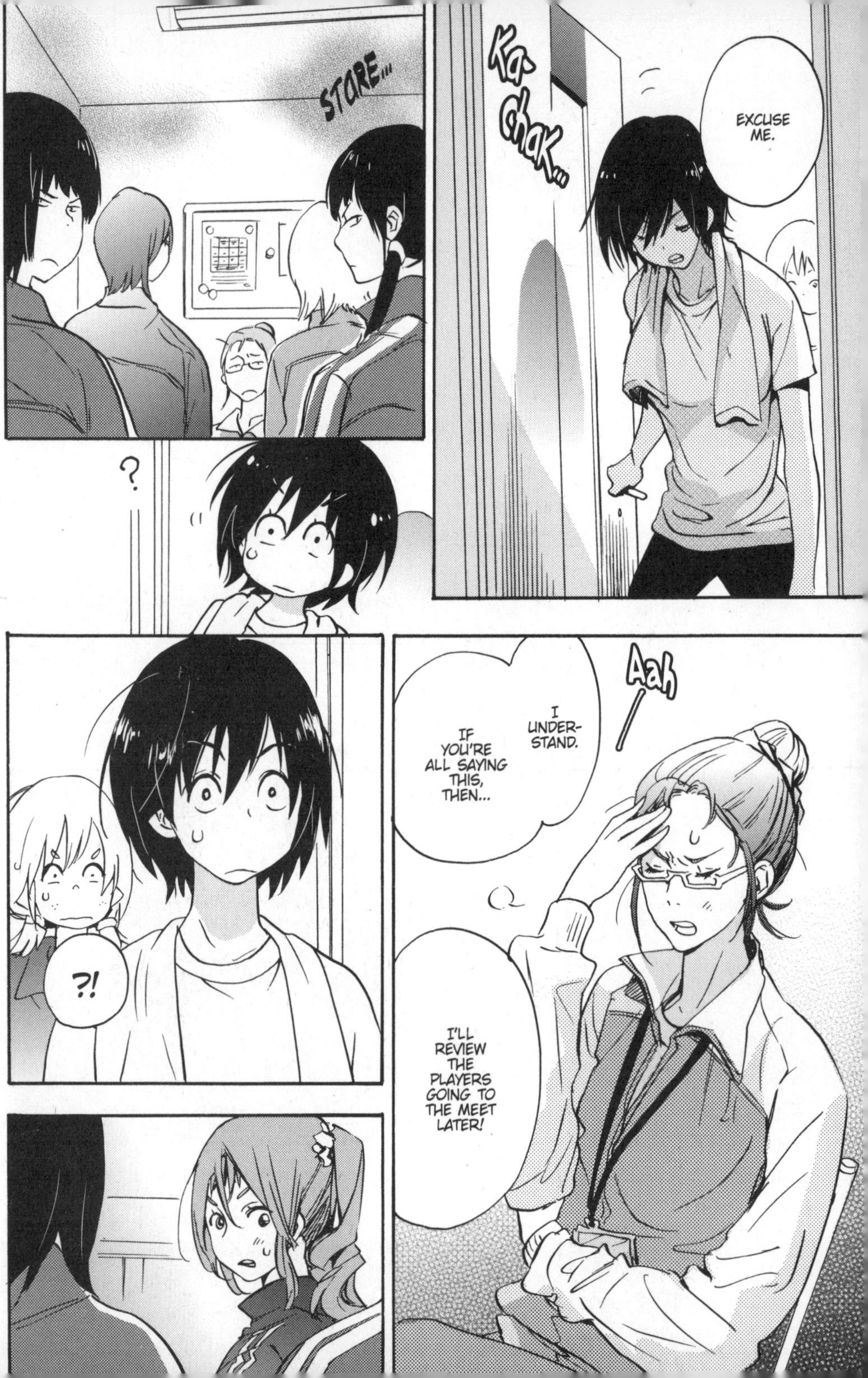
EXCUSE ME.
Ka-chak...
STARE...
?
Aah
I UNDER-STAND.
IF YOU'RE ALL SAYING THIS, THEN...
I'LL REVIEW THE PLAYERS GOING TO THE MEET LATER!
?!

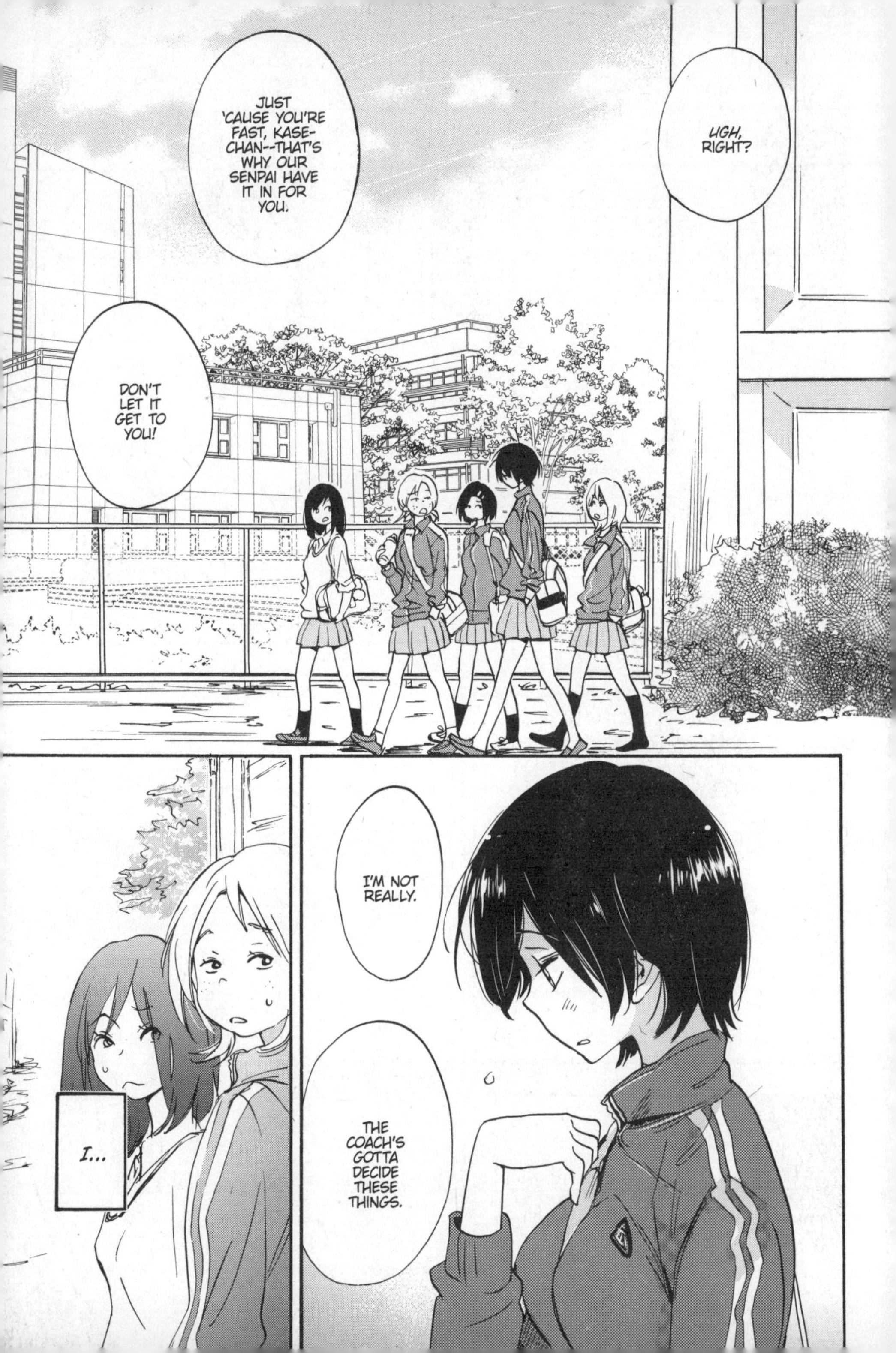
UGH, RIGHT?
JUST 'CAUSE YOU'RE FAST, KASE-CHAN--THAT'S WHY OUR SENPAI HAVE IT IN FOR YOU.
DON'T LET IT GET TO YOU!
I'M NOT REALLY.
THE COACH'S GOTTA DECIDE THESE THINGS.
I...

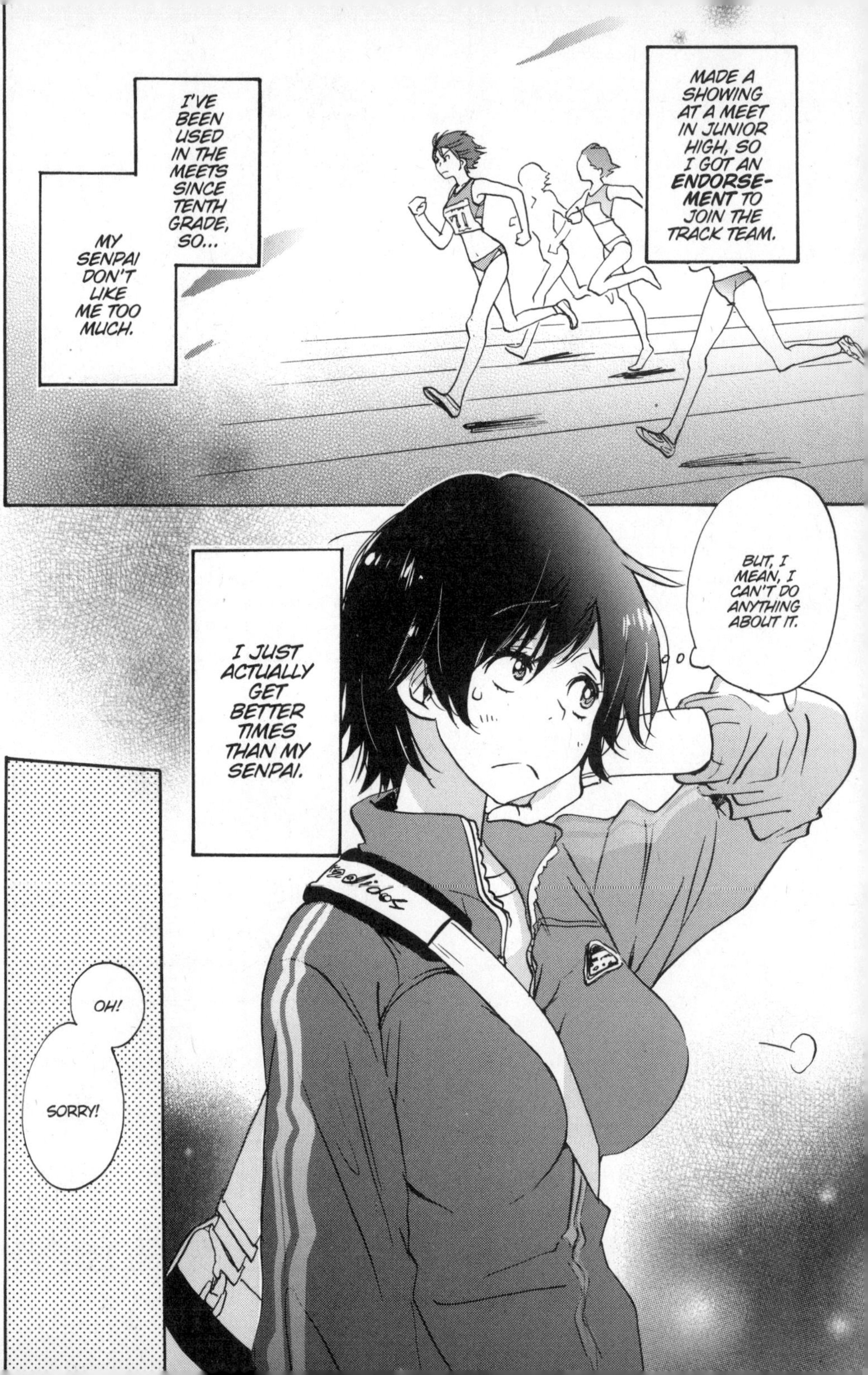
MADE A SHOWING AT A MEET IN JUNIOR HIGH, SO I GOT AN **ENDORSEMENT** TO JOIN THE TRACK TEAM.
I'VE BEEN USED IN THE MEETS SINCE TENTH GRADE, SO...
MY SENPAI DON'T LIKE ME TOO MUCH.
BUT, I MEAN, I CAN'T DO ANYTHING ABOUT IT.
I JUST ACTUALLY GET BETTER TIMES THAN MY SENPAI.
OH!
SORRY!

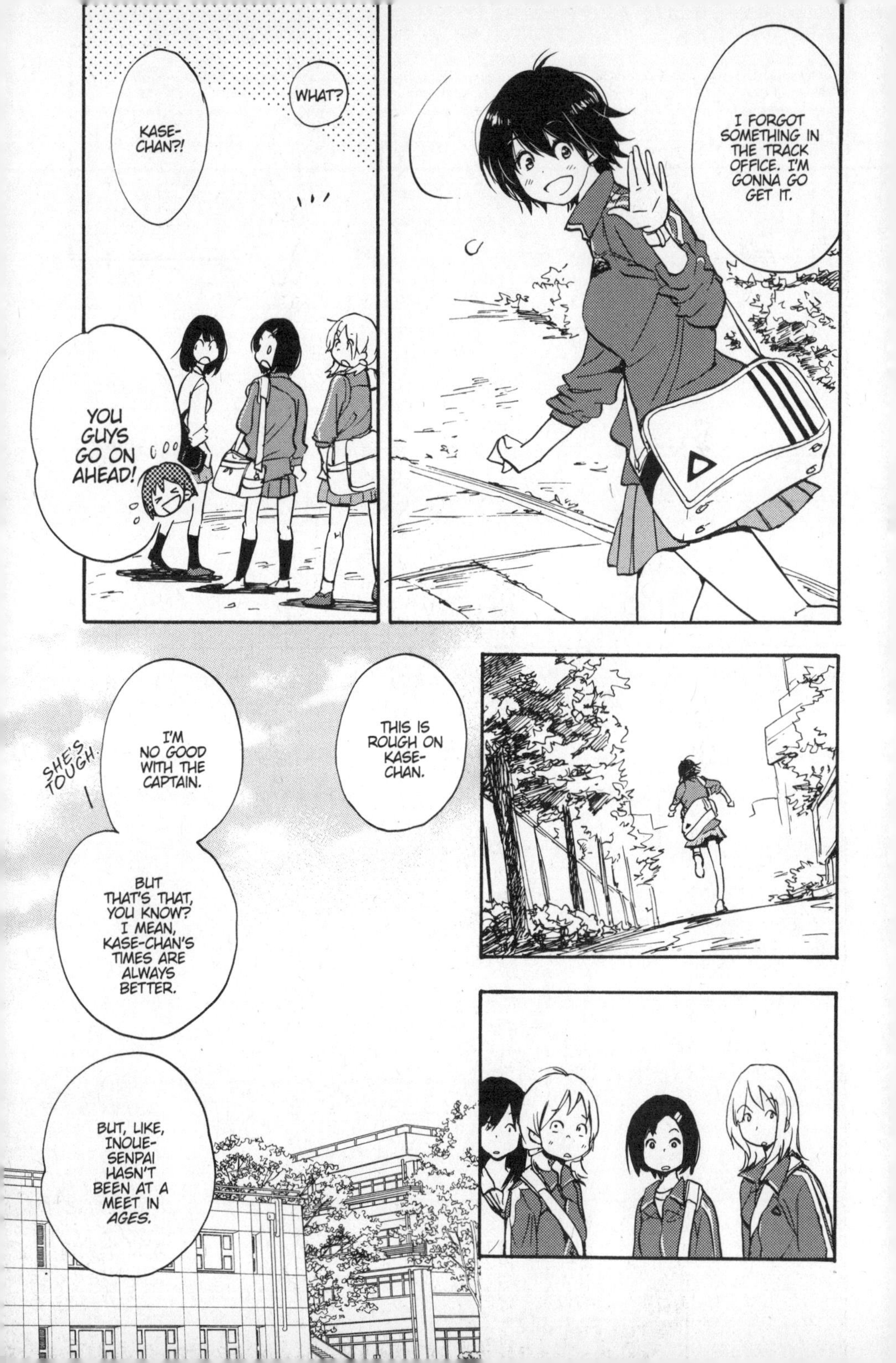
I FORGOT SOMETHING IN THE TRACK OFFICE. I'M GONNA GO GET IT.
WHAT?
KASE-CHAN?!
YOU GUYS GO ON AHEAD!
THIS IS ROUGH ON KASE-CHAN.
I'M NO GOOD WITH THE CAPTAIN.
SHE'S TOUGH.
BUT THAT'S THAT, YOU KNOW? I MEAN, KASE-CHAN'S TIMES ARE ALWAYS BETTER.
BUT, LIKE, INOUE-SENPAI HASN'T BEEN AT A MEET IN AGES.

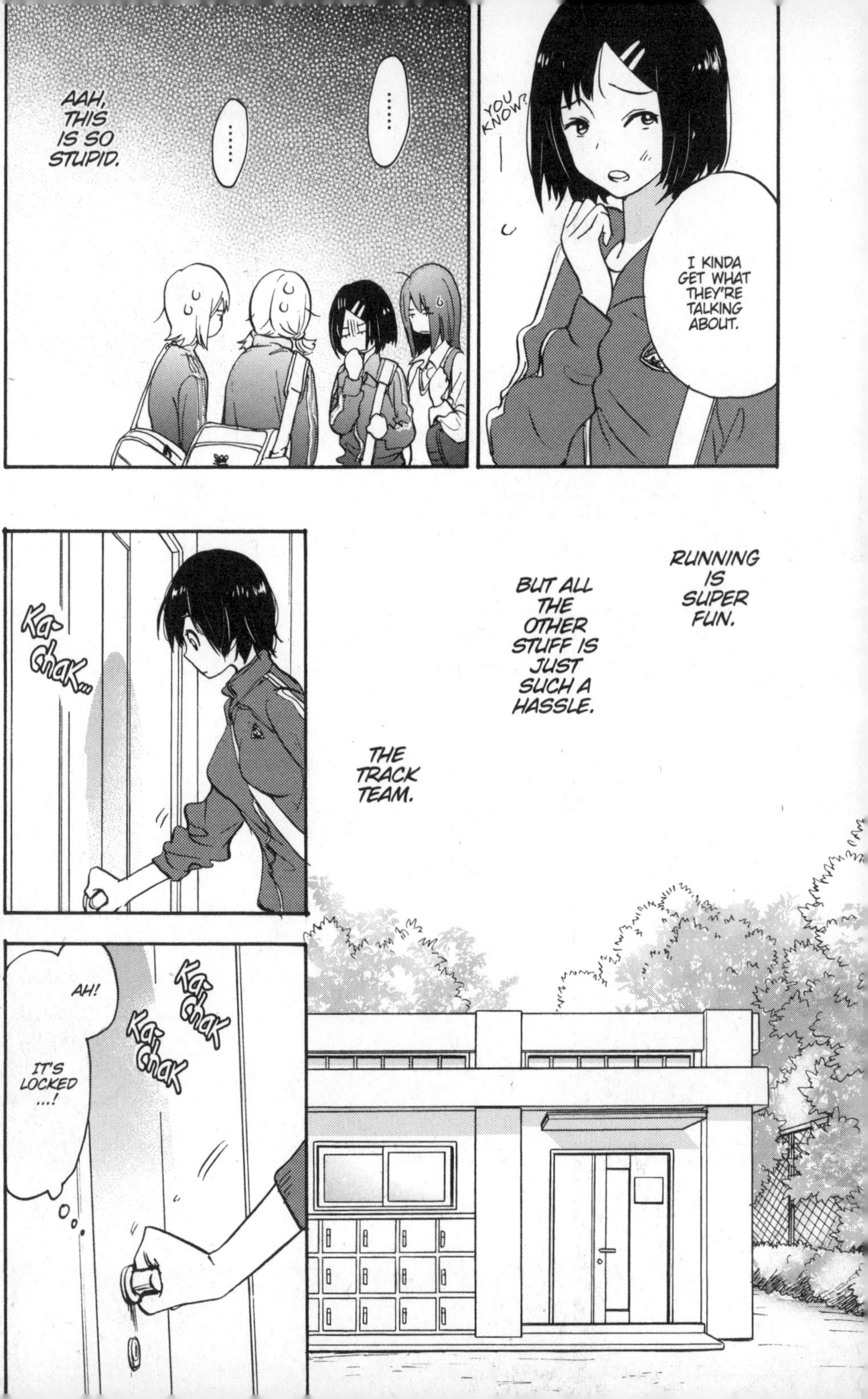
YOU KNOW?
I KINDA GET WHAT THEY'RE TALKING ABOUT.
......
......
AAH, THIS IS SO STUPID.
RUNNING IS SUPER FUN.
BUT ALL THE OTHER STUFF IS JUST SUCH A HASSLE.
THE TRACK TEAM.
Ka-chak...
Ka-chak
Ka-chak
AH!
IT'S LOCKED ...!

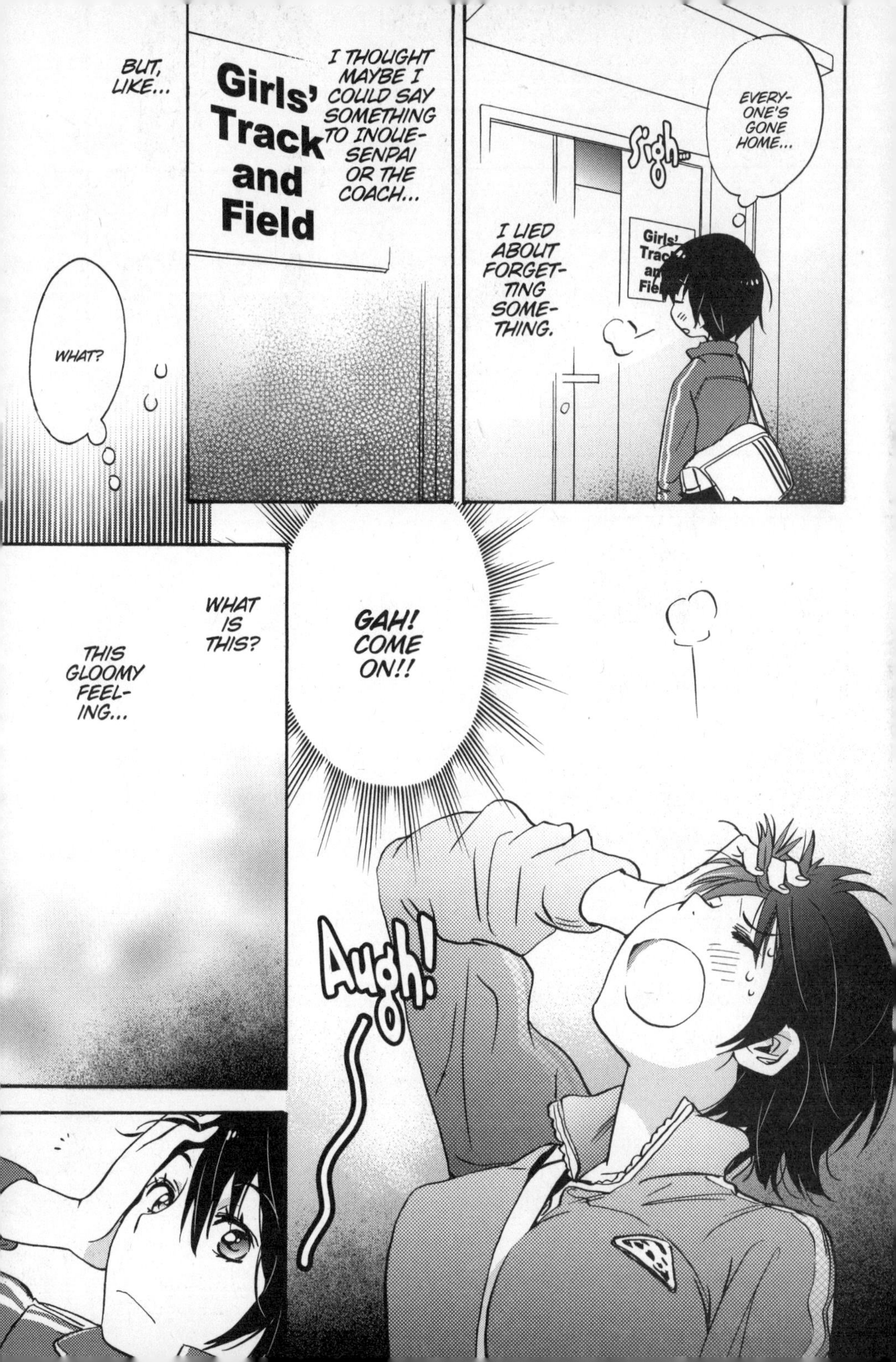
EVERYONE'S GONE HOME...
sigh...
I LIED ABOUT FORGETTING SOMETHING.
I THOUGHT MAYBE I COULD SAY SOMETHING TO INOUE-SENPAI OR THE COACH...
Girls' Track and Field
BUT, LIKE...
WHAT?
GAH! COME ON!!
Augh!
WHAT IS THIS?
THIS GLOOMY FEELING...

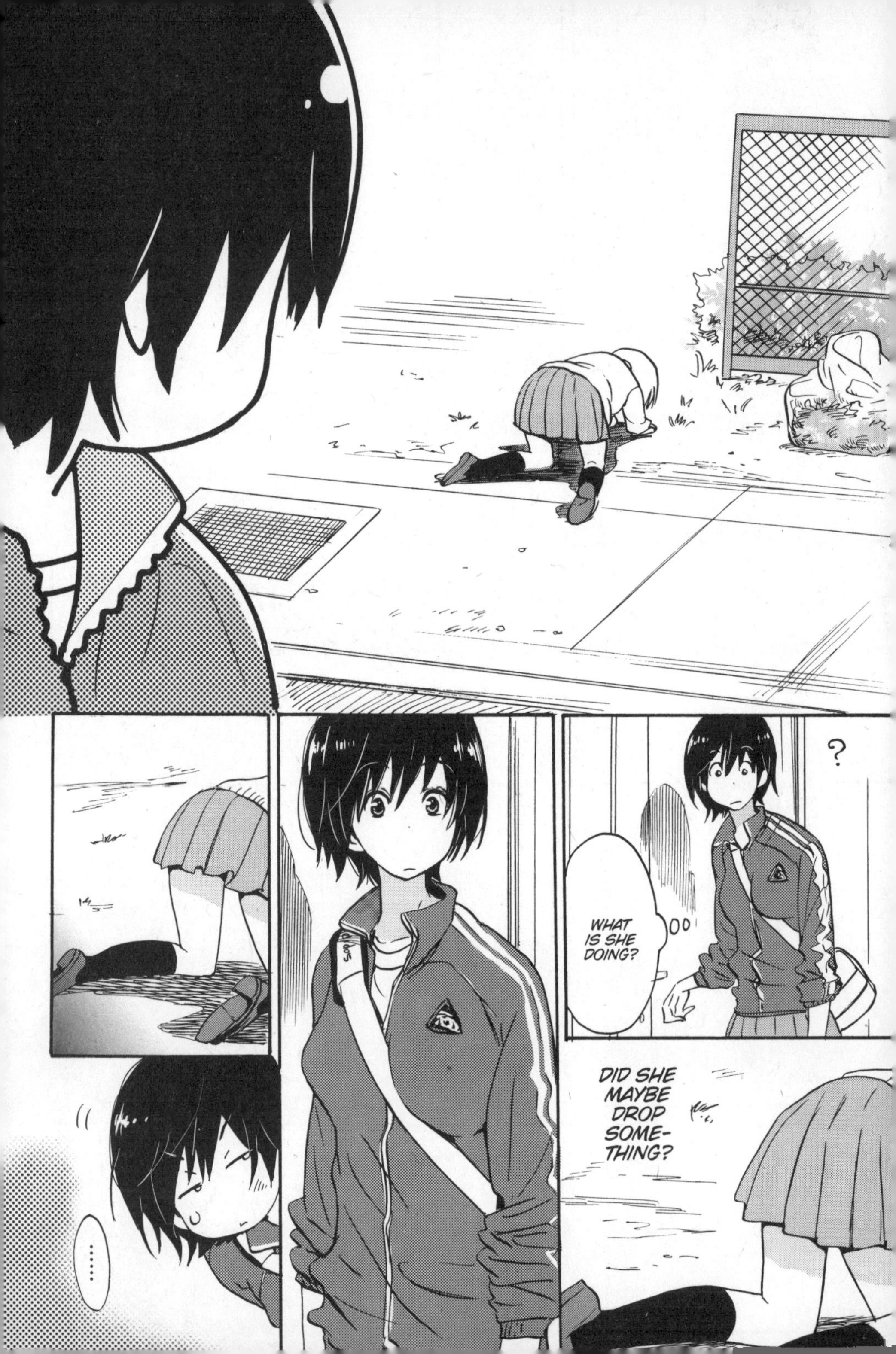
?
WHAT IS SHE DOING?
DID SHE MAYBE DROP SOMETHING?
......

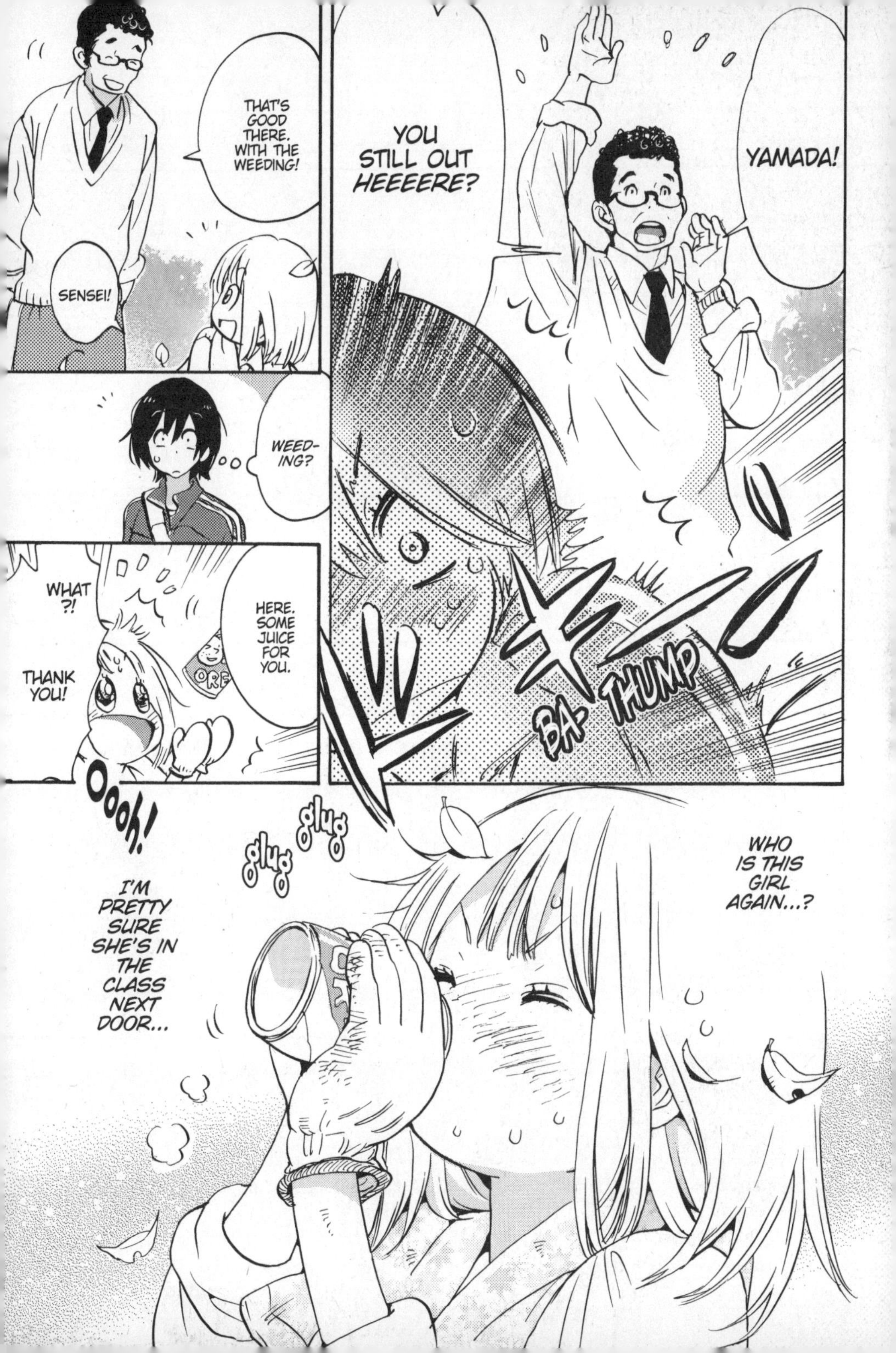
YAMADA!
YOU STILL OUT HEEEERE?
BA THUMP
THAT'S GOOD THERE. WITH THE WEEDING!
SENSEI!
WEEDING?
HERE. SOME JUICE FOR YOU.
WHAT?!
THANK YOU!
WHO IS THIS GIRL AGAIN...?
glug glug
Oooh!
I'M PRETTY SURE SHE'S IN THE CLASS NEXT DOOR...

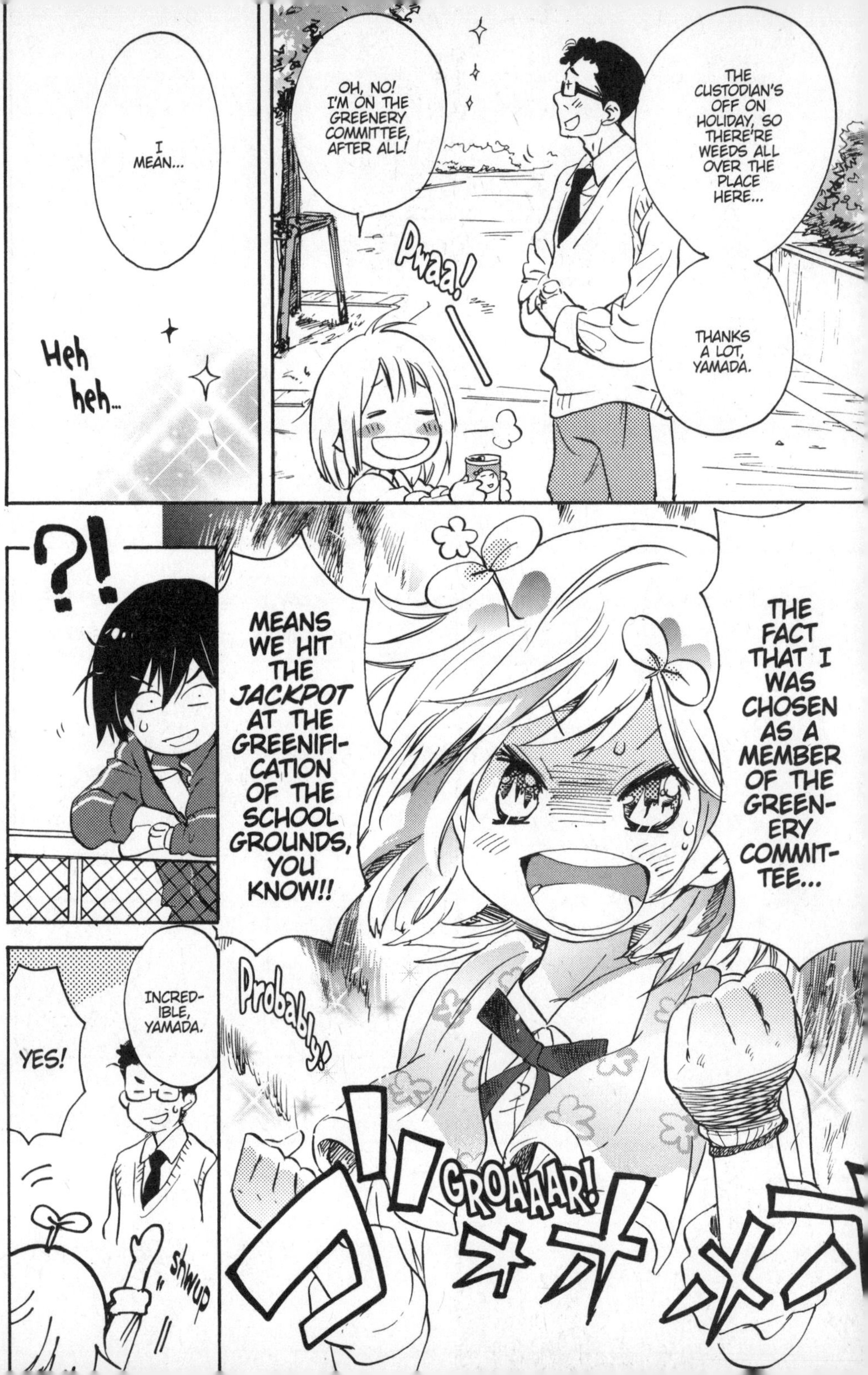
THE CUSTODIAN'S OFF ON HOLIDAY, SO THERE'RE WEEDS ALL OVER THE PLACE HERE...
THANKS A LOT, YAMADA.
OH, NO! I'M ON THE GREENERY COMMITTEE, AFTER ALL!
Pwaa!
I MEAN...
Heh heh...
THE FACT THAT I WAS CHOSEN AS A MEMBER OF THE GREENERY COMMITTEE...
MEANS WE HIT THE JACKPOT AT THE GREENIFICATION OF THE SCHOOL GROUNDS, YOU KNOW!!
GROAAAR!
Probably!
?!
INCREDIBLE, YAMADA.
YES!
shwup

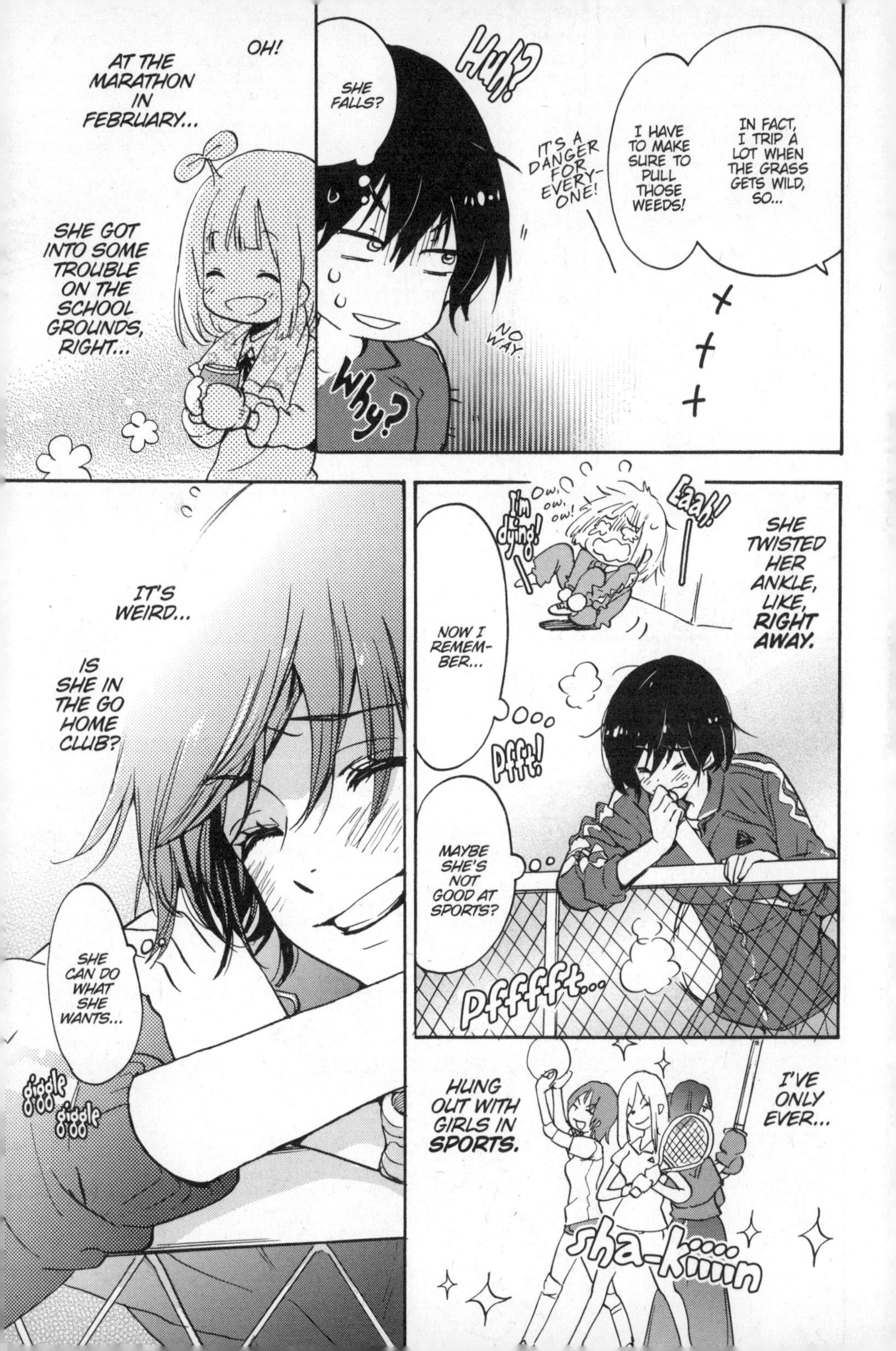
IN FACT, I TRIP A LOT WHEN THE GRASS GETS WILD, SO...
I HAVE TO MAKE SURE TO PULL THOSE WEEDS!
IT'S A DANGER FOR EVERY-ONE!
Huh?
SHE FALLS?
NO WAY
Why?
OH!
AT THE MARATHON IN FEBRUARY...
SHE GOT INTO SOME TROUBLE ON THE SCHOOL GROUNDS, RIGHT...
SHE TWISTED HER ANKLE, LIKE, RIGHT AWAY.
Eaah!
Ow, ow, ow!
I'm dying!
NOW I REMEM-BER...
Ooo
Pffft!
MAYBE SHE'S NOT GOOD AT SPORTS?
Pfffft...
I'VE ONLY EVER...
HUNG OUT WITH GIRLS IN SPORTS.
sha-kiiiin
IT'S WEIRD...
IS SHE IN THE GO HOME CLUB?
SHE CAN DO WHAT SHE WANTS...
giggle giggle

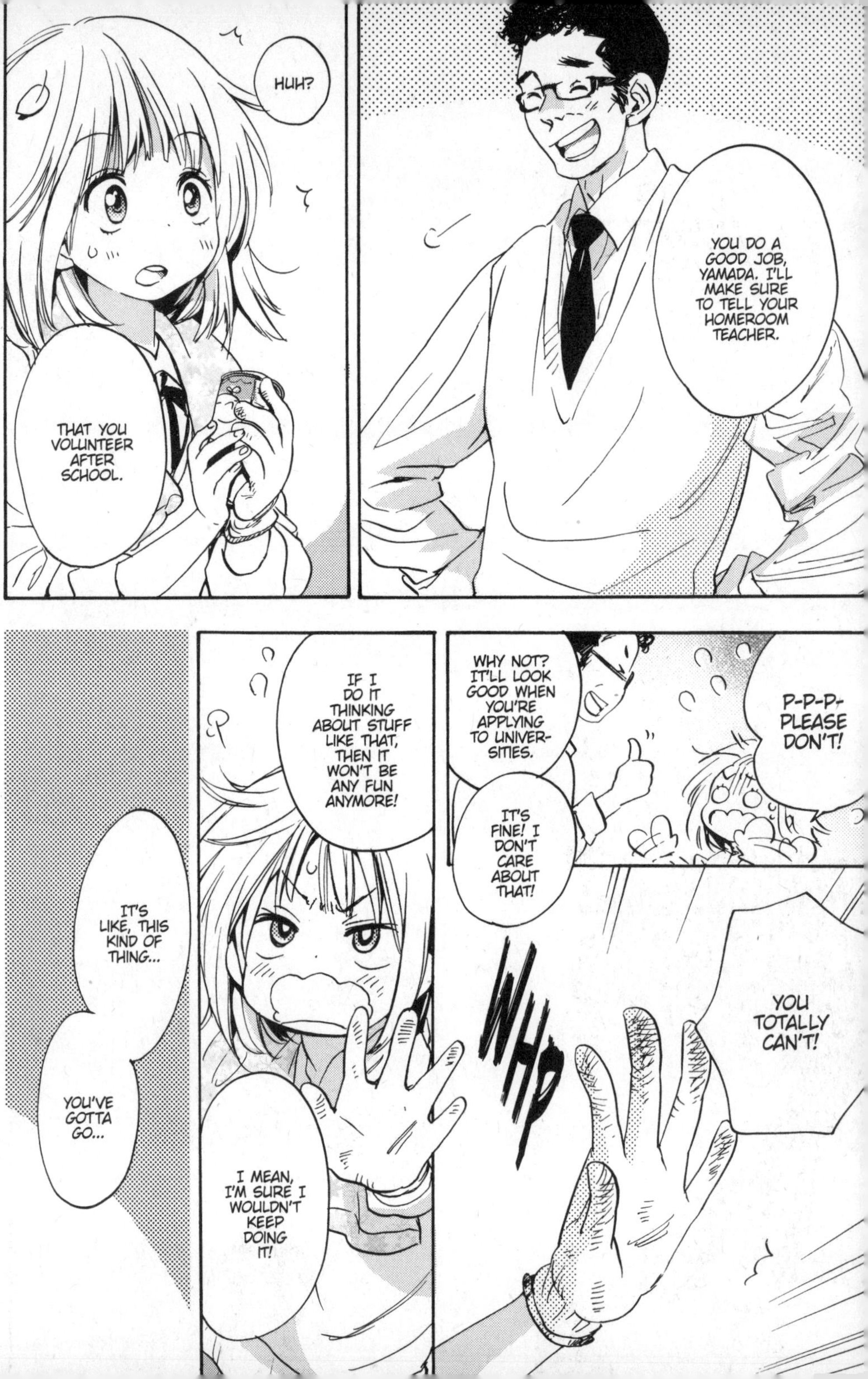
YOU DO A GOOD JOB, YAMADA. I'LL MAKE SURE TO TELL YOUR HOMEROOM TEACHER.
HUH?
THAT YOU VOLUNTEER AFTER SCHOOL.
P-P-P-PLEASE DON'T!
WHY NOT? IT'LL LOOK GOOD WHEN YOU'RE APPLYING TO UNIVERSITIES.
IT'S FINE! I DON'T CARE ABOUT THAT!
YOU TOTALLY CAN'T!
WHIP
IF I DO IT THINKING ABOUT STUFF LIKE THAT, THEN IT WON'T BE ANY FUN ANYMORE!
I MEAN, I'M SURE I WOULDN'T KEEP DOING IT!
IT'S LIKE, THIS KIND OF THING...
YOU'VE GOTTA GO...

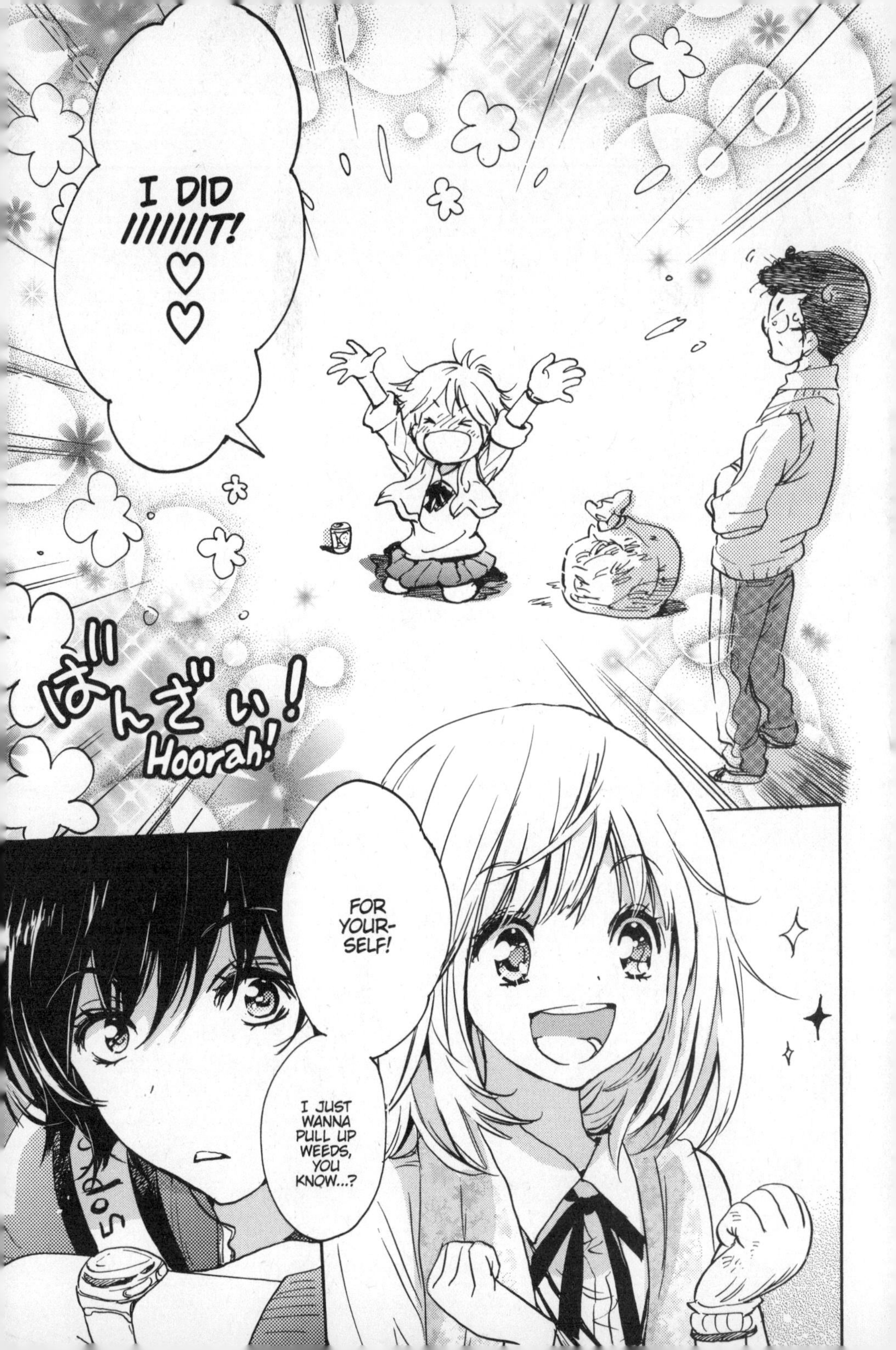

I DID IIIIIIIIT! ♡ ♡
ばんざい!
Hoorah!
FOR YOUR-SELF!
I JUST WANNA PULL UP WEEDS, YOU KNOW...?

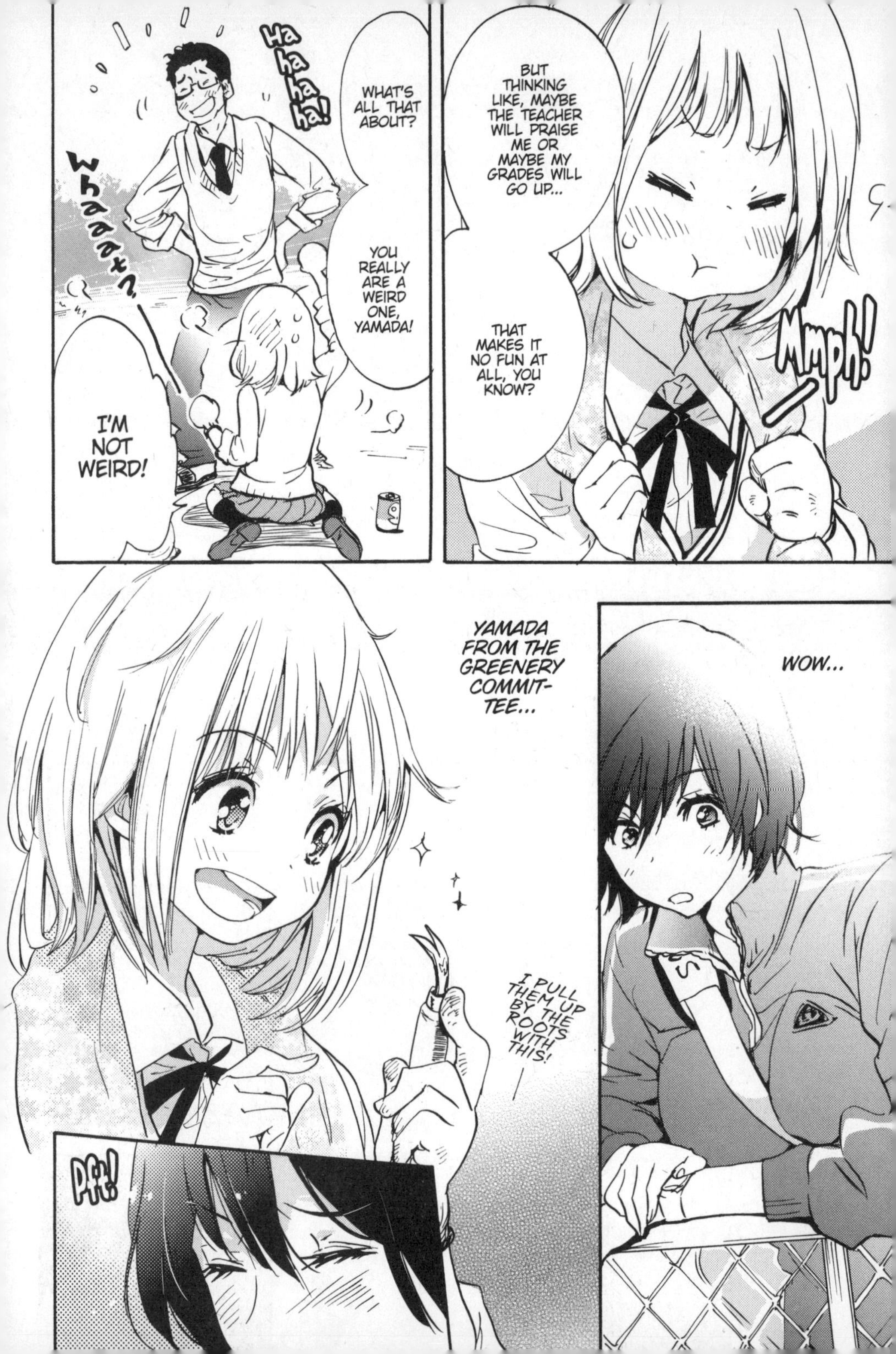
BUT THINKING LIKE, MAYBE THE TEACHER WILL PRAISE ME OR MAYBE MY GRADES WILL GO UP...
THAT MAKES IT NO FUN AT ALL, YOU KNOW?
Mmph!
Ha ha ha ha ha!
WHAT'S ALL THAT ABOUT?
YOU REALLY ARE A WEIRD ONE, YAMADA!
Whaaaat?
I'M NOT WEIRD!
WOW...
YAMADA FROM THE GREENERY COMMIT-TEE...
I PULL THEM UP BY THE ROOTS WITH THIS!
Pft!

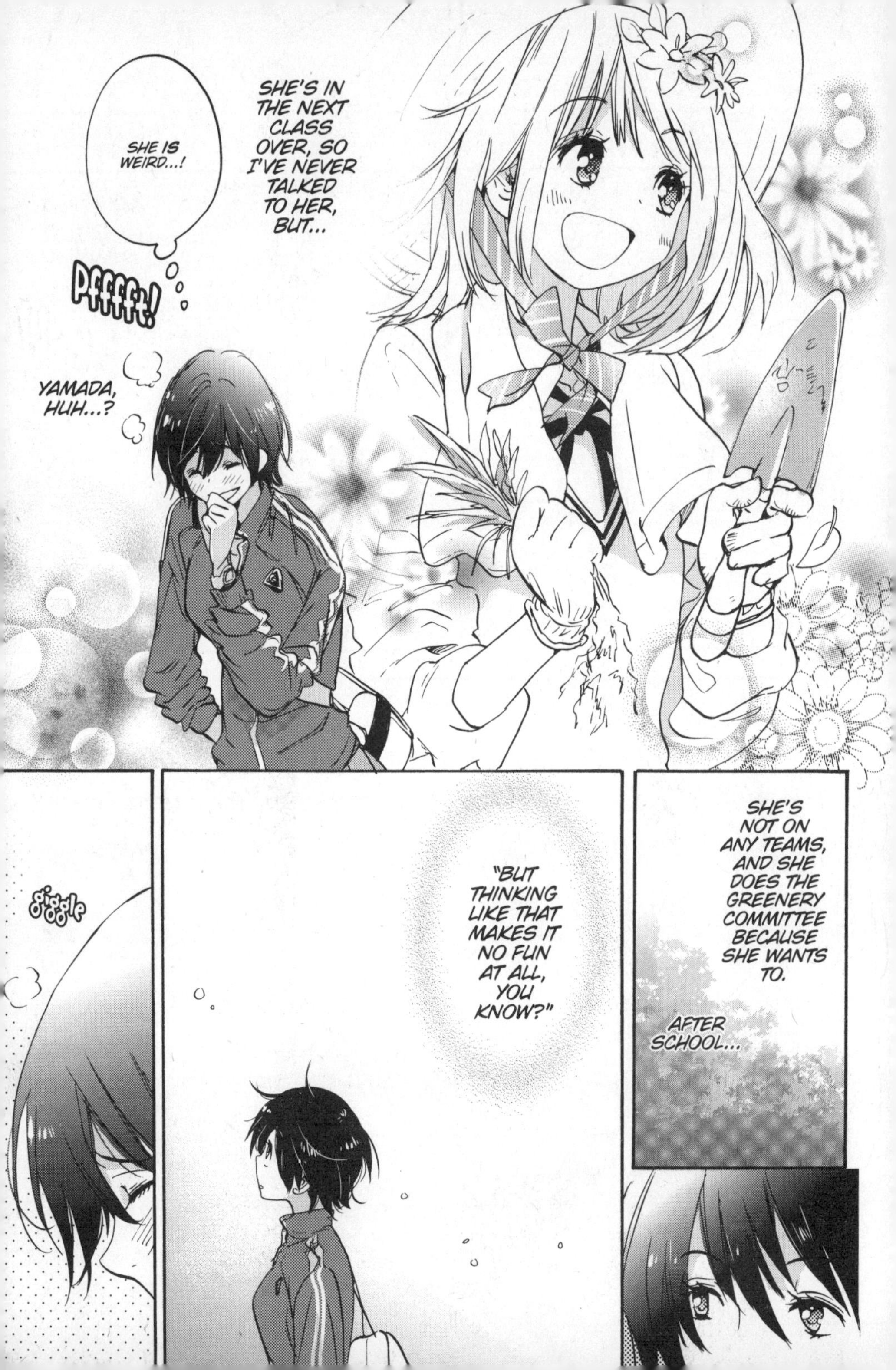
SHE'S IN THE NEXT CLASS OVER, SO I'VE NEVER TALKED TO HER, BUT...
SHE IS WEIRD...!
Pffffft!
YAMADA, HUH...?
SHE'S NOT ON ANY TEAMS, AND SHE DOES THE GREENERY COMMITTEE BECAUSE SHE WANTS TO.
AFTER SCHOOL...
"BUT THINKING LIKE THAT MAKES IT NO FUN AT ALL, YOU KNOW?"
giggle

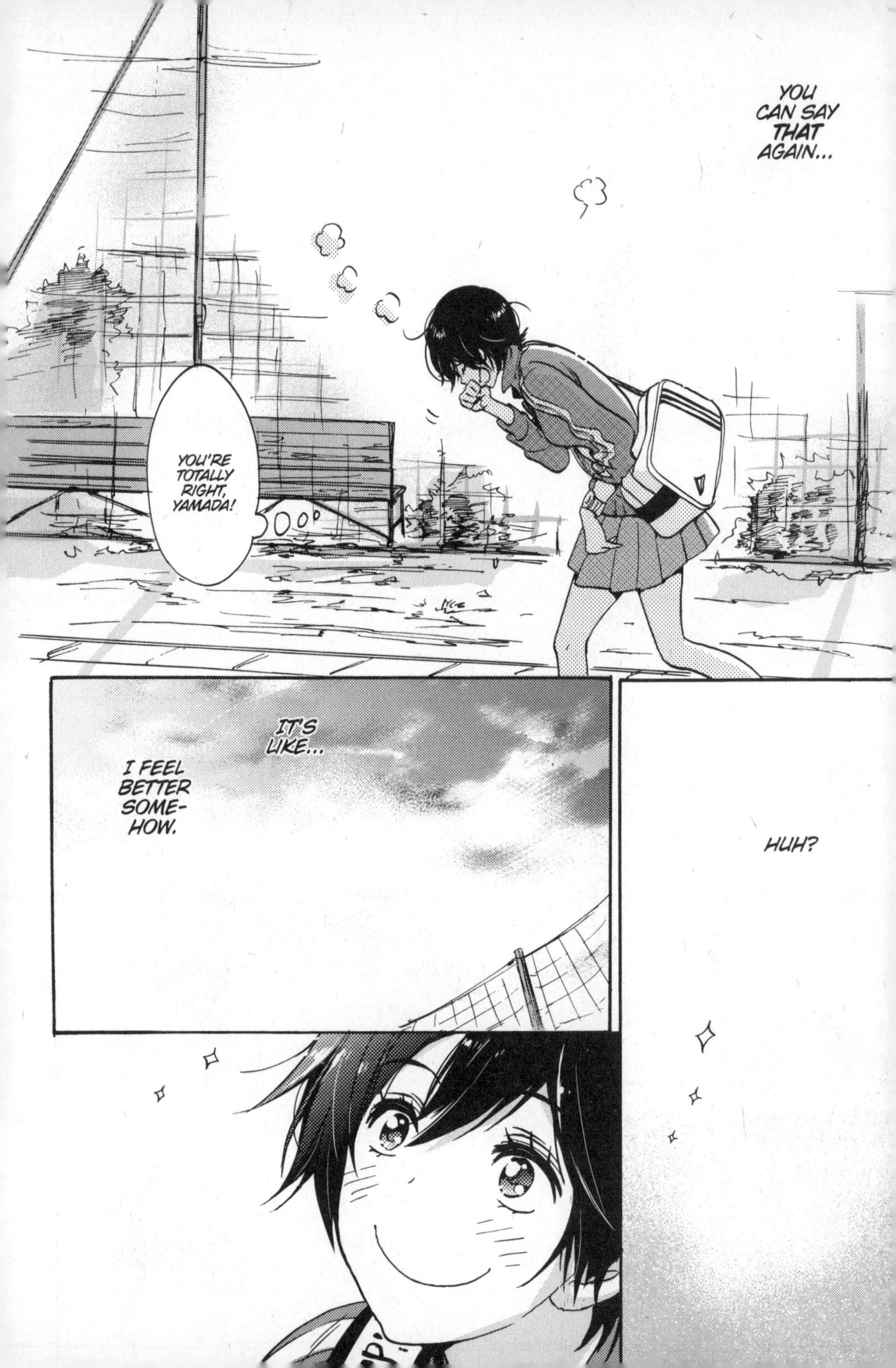
YOU CAN SAY THAT AGAIN...
YOU'RE TOTALLY RIGHT, YAMADA!
HUH?
IT'S LIKE...
I FEEL BETTER SOME-HOW.

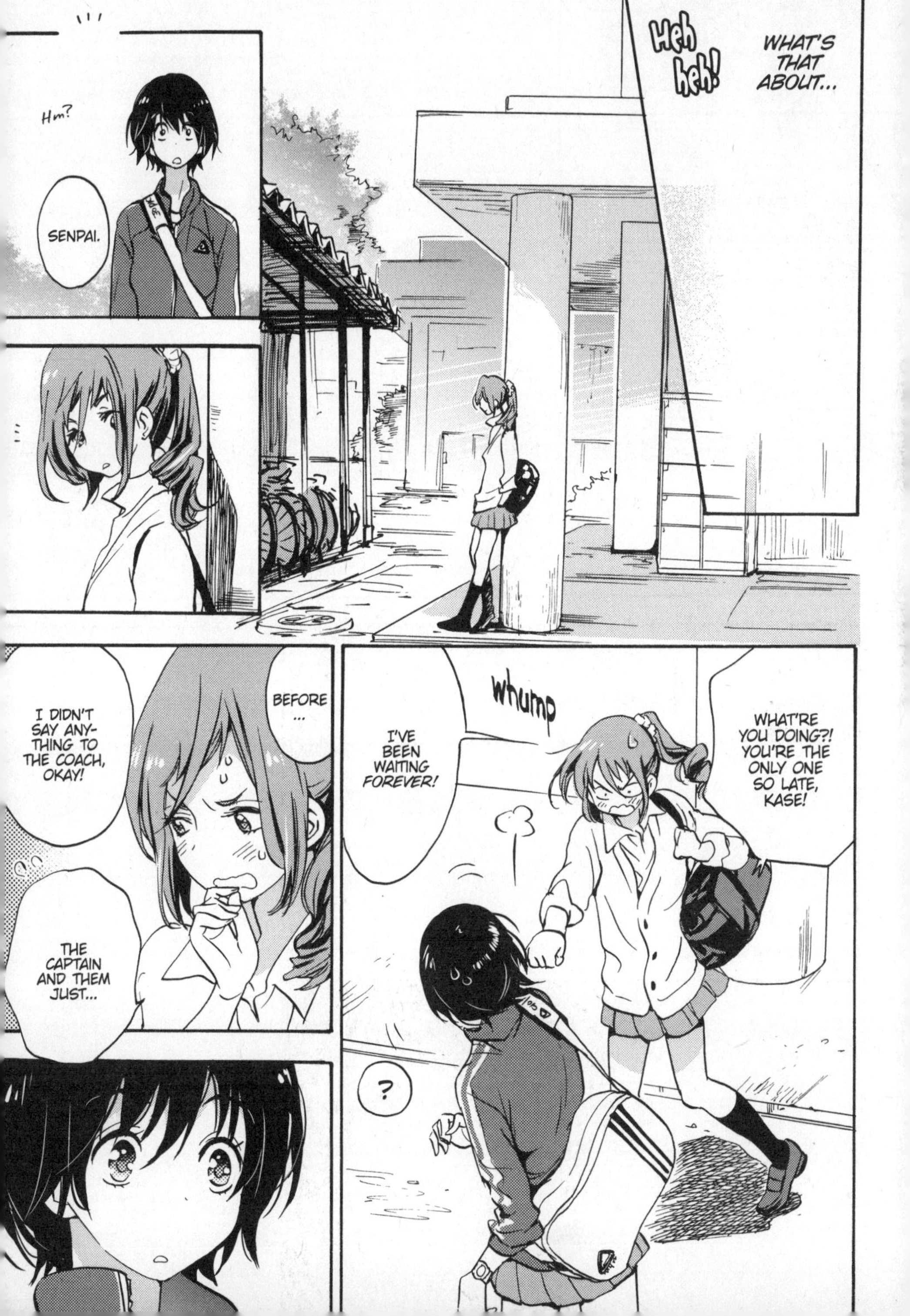
WHAT'S THAT ABOUT...
Heh heh!
Hm?
SENPAI.
WHAT'RE YOU DOING?! YOU'RE THE ONLY ONE SO LATE, KASE!
whump
I'VE BEEN WAITING FOREVER!
?
BEFORE...
I DIDN'T SAY ANY-THING TO THE COACH, OKAY!
THE CAPTAIN AND THEM JUST...

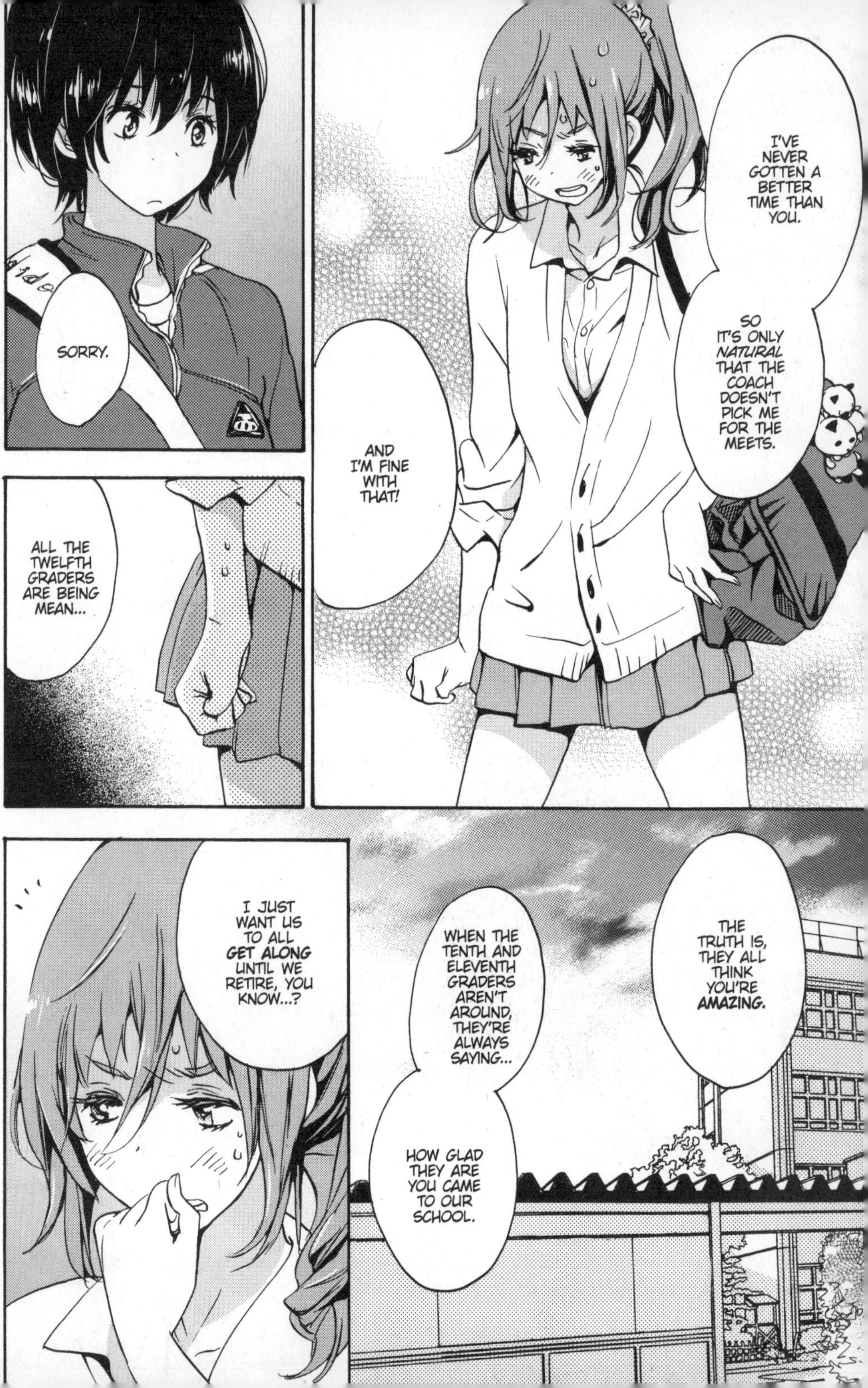
I'VE NEVER GOTTEN A BETTER TIME THAN YOU.
SO IT'S ONLY *NATURAL* THAT THE COACH DOESN'T PICK ME FOR THE MEETS.
AND I'M FINE WITH THAT!
SORRY.
ALL THE TWELFTH GRADERS ARE BEING MEAN...
THE TRUTH IS, THEY ALL THINK YOU'RE **AMAZING.**
WHEN THE TENTH AND ELEVENTH GRADERS AREN'T AROUND, THEY'RE ALWAYS SAYING...
HOW GLAD THEY ARE YOU CAME TO OUR SCHOOL.
I JUST WANT US TO ALL **GET ALONG** UNTIL WE RETIRE, YOU KNOW...?

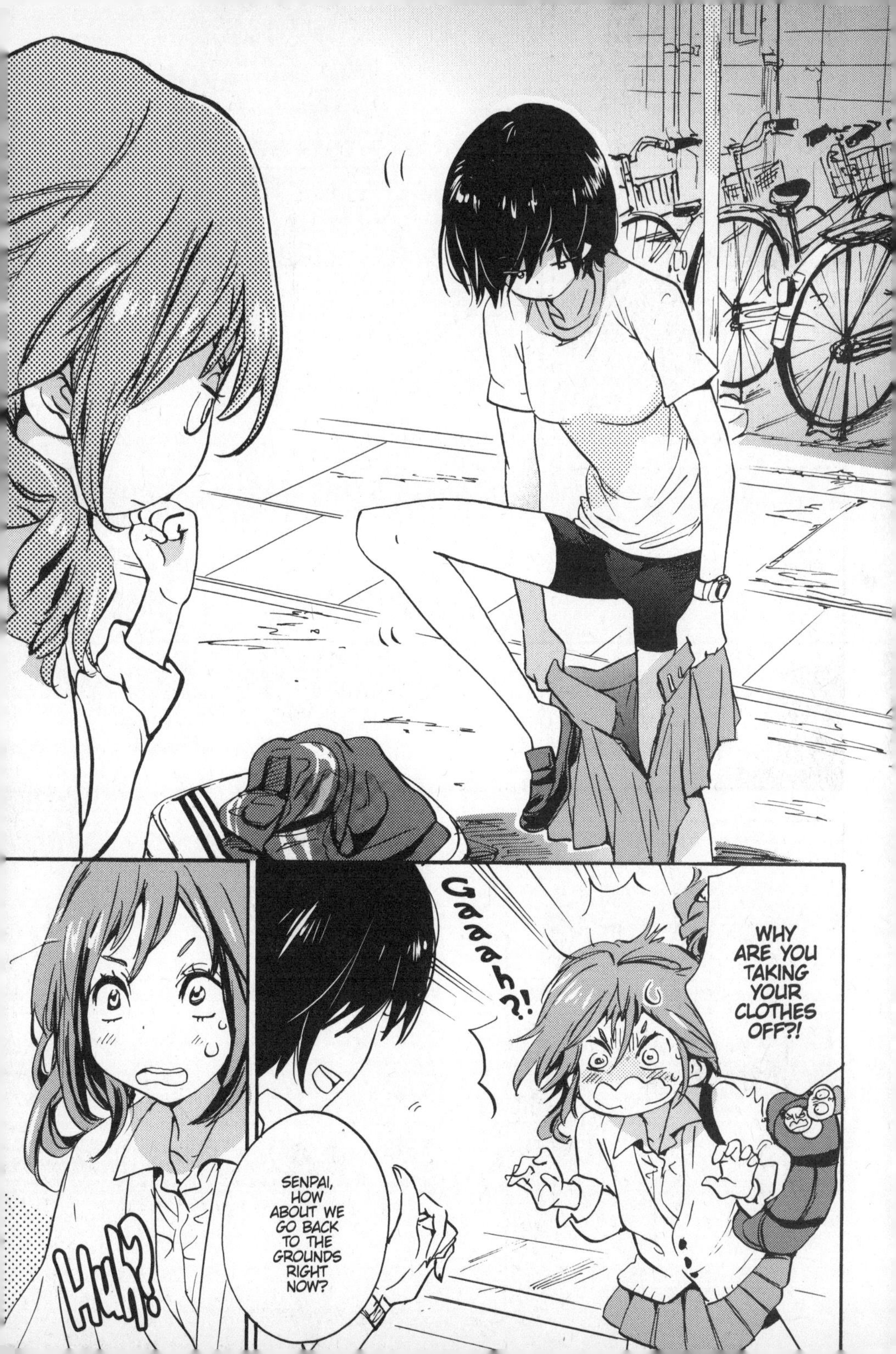
WHY ARE YOU TAKING YOUR CLOTHES OFF?!
Gaaaah?!
SENPAI, HOW ABOUT WE GO BACK TO THE GROUNDS RIGHT NOW?
Huh?

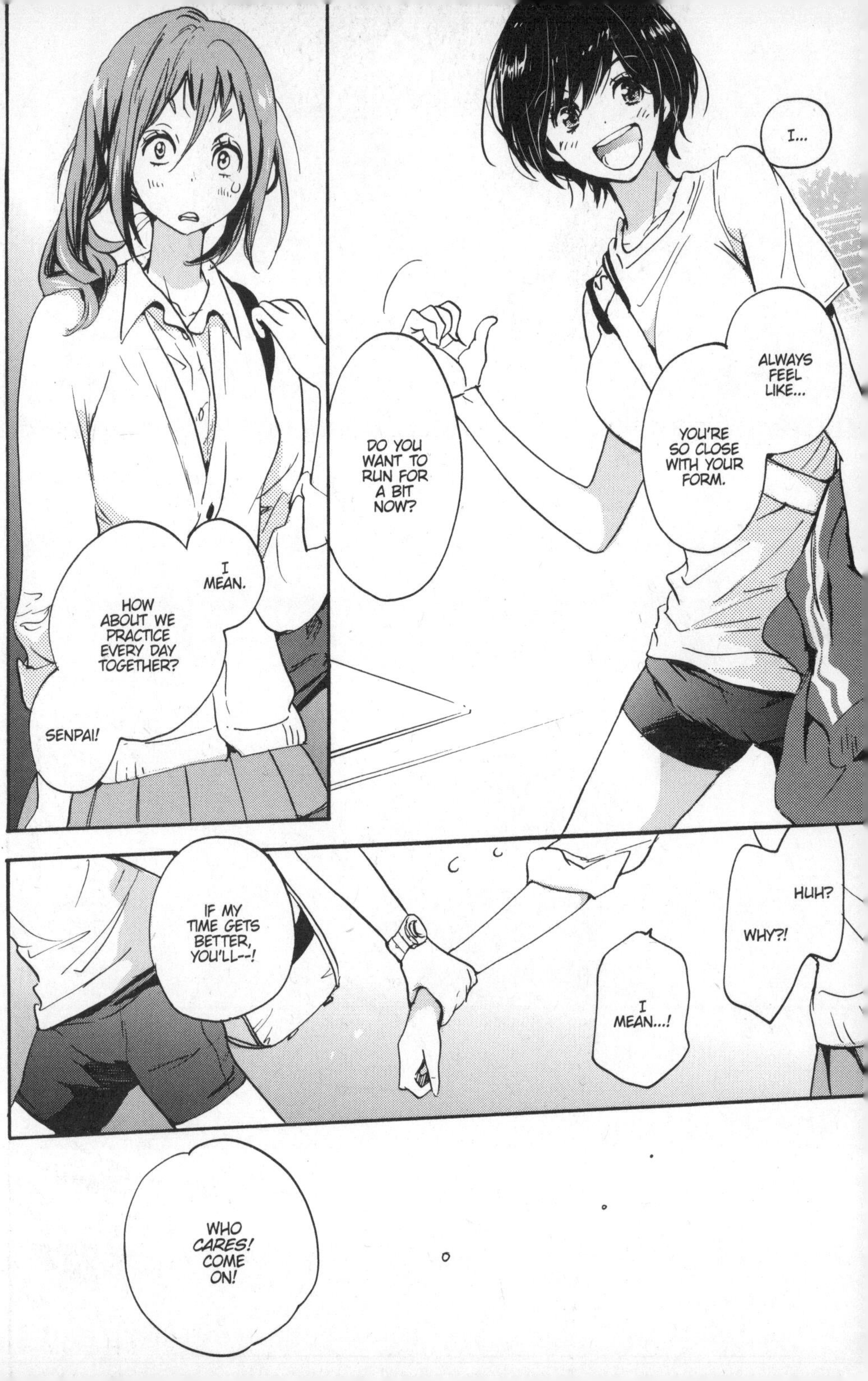
I...
ALWAYS FEEL LIKE...
YOU'RE SO CLOSE WITH YOUR FORM.
DO YOU WANT TO RUN FOR A BIT NOW?
I MEAN.
HOW ABOUT WE PRACTICE EVERY DAY TOGETHER?
SENPAI!
HUH?
WHY?!
I MEAN...!
IF MY TIME GETS BETTER, YOU'LL--!
WHO CARES! COME ON!

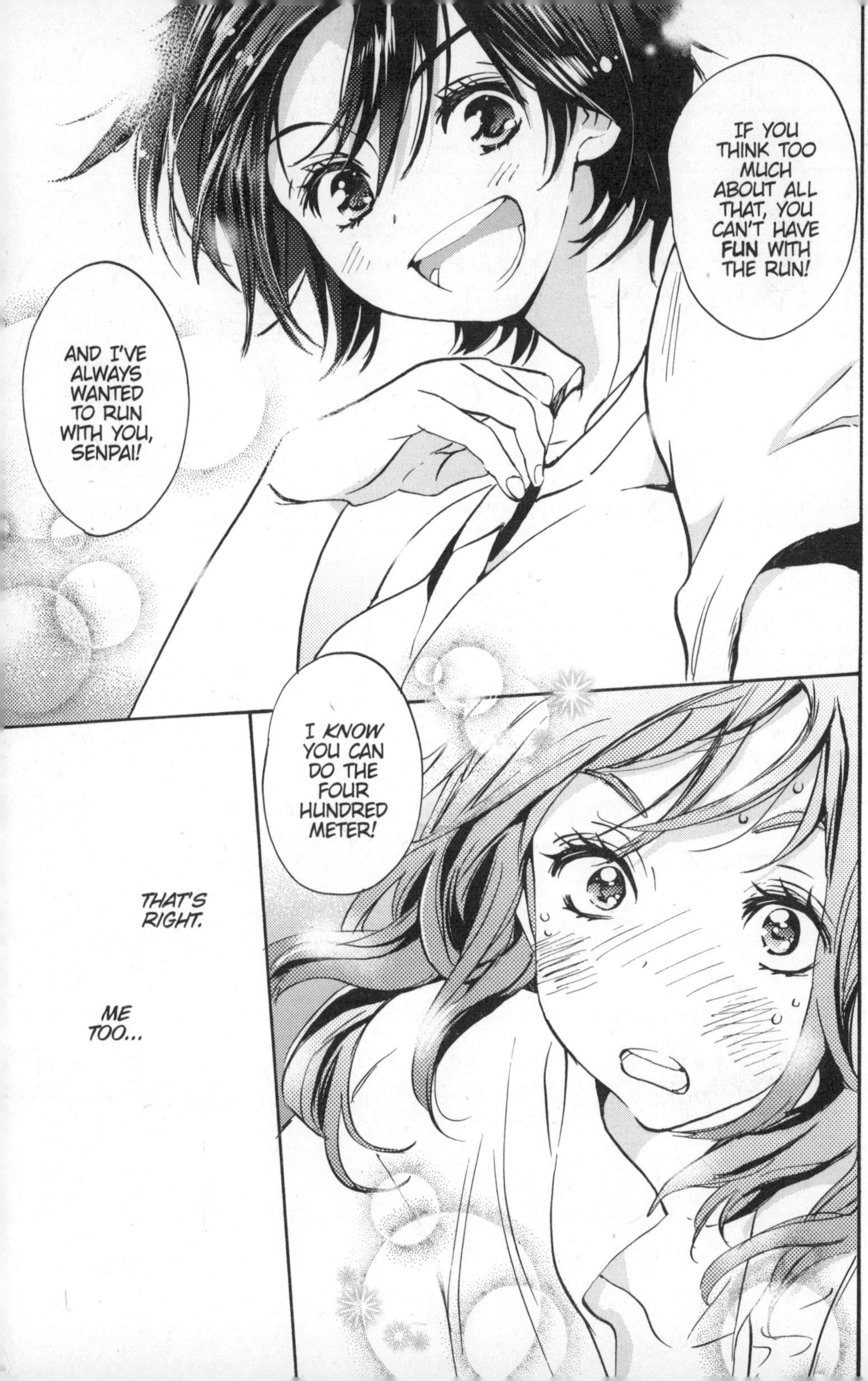
IF YOU THINK TOO MUCH ABOUT ALL THAT, YOU CAN'T HAVE FUN WITH THE RUN!
AND I'VE ALWAYS WANTED TO RUN WITH YOU, SENPAI!
I *KNOW* YOU CAN DO THE FOUR HUNDRED METER!
THAT'S RIGHT.
ME TOO...

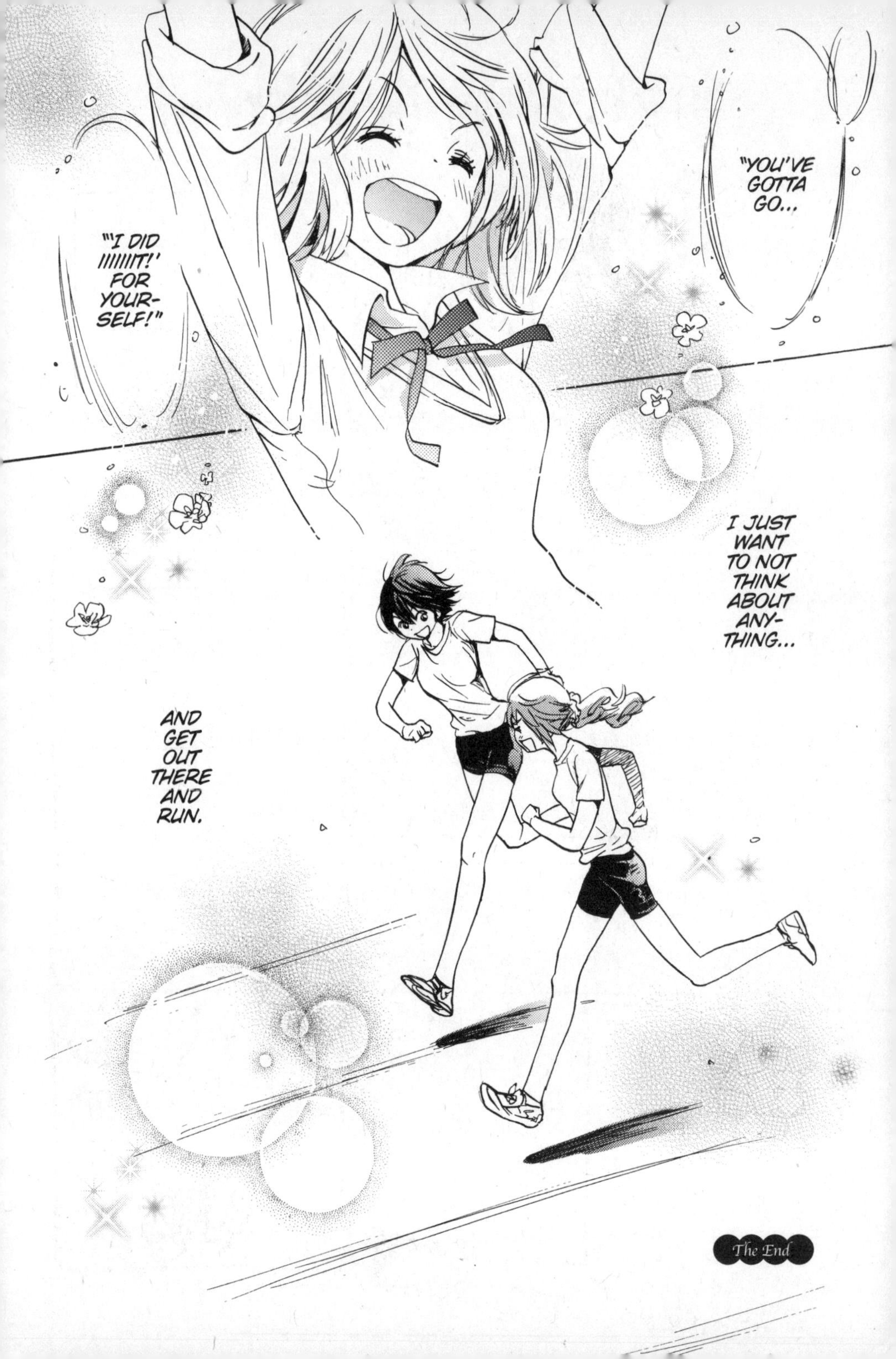
"YOU'VE GOTTA GO...
'I DID IIIIIIIT!' FOR YOURSELF!"
I JUST WANT TO NOT THINK ABOUT ANYTHING...
AND GET OUT THERE AND RUN.
The End

Kase-san and the Afterword

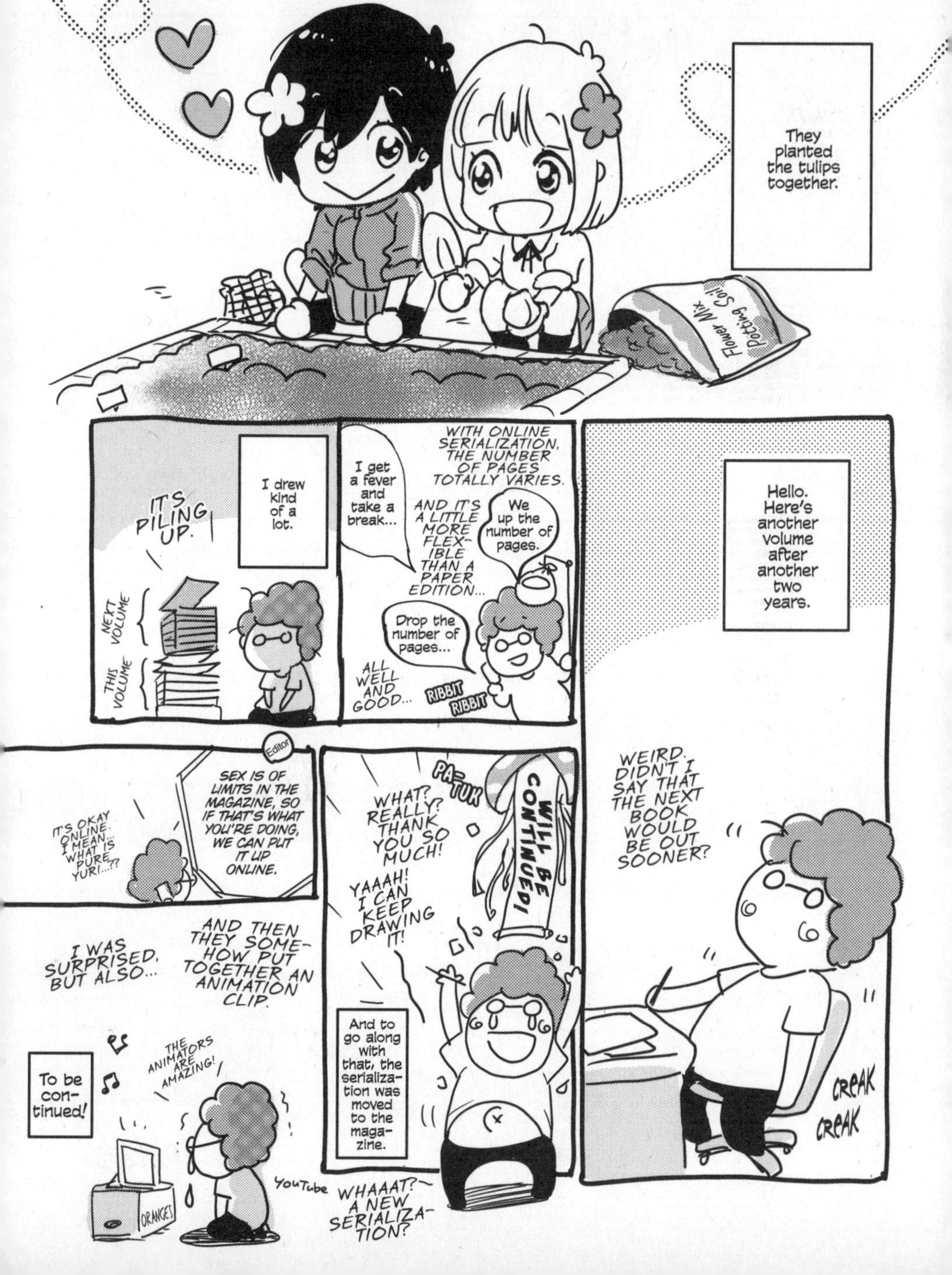
They planted the tulips together.
Flower Mix Potting Soil
Hello. Here's another volume after another two years.
WEIRD. DIDN'T I SAY THAT THE NEXT BOOK WOULD BE OUT SOONER?
CREAK CREAK
WITH ONLINE SERIALIZATION, THE NUMBER OF PAGES TOTALLY VARIES.
I get a fever and take a break...
AND IT'S A LITTLE MORE FLEX-IBLE THAN A PAPER EDITION...
We up the number of pages.
Drop the number of pages...
ALL WELL AND GOOD...
RIBBIT RIBBIT
I drew kind of a lot.
IT'S PILING UP.
NEXT VOLUME
THIS VOLUME
PA-TUK
WILL BE CONTINUED!
WHAT? REALLY? THANK YOU SO MUCH!
YAAAH! I CAN KEEP DRAWING IT!
And to go along with that, the serialization was moved to the magazine.
Editor
SEX IS OF LIMITS IN THE MAGAZINE, SO IF THAT'S WHAT YOU'RE DOING, WE CAN PUT IT UP ONLINE.
IT'S OKAY ONLINE. I MEAN... WHAT IS PURE YURI...??
AND THEN THEY SOME-HOW PUT TOGETHER AN ANIMATION CLIP.
I WAS SURPRISED, BUT ALSO...
THE ANIMATORS ARE AMAZING!
To be con-tinued!
YouTube
ORANGES
WHAAAT? A NEW SERIALIZA-TION?

SEVEN SEAS ENTERTAINMENT PRESENTS

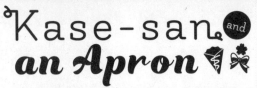

Kase-san and an Apron

story & art by HIROMI TAKASHIMA

TRANSLATION
Jocelyne Allen

ADAPTATION
Jenn Gruingen

LETTERING AND RETOUCH
CK Russell

LOGO DESIGN
KC Fabellon

COVER DESIGN
Nicky Lim

PROOFREADER
Shanti Whitesides

PRODUCTION MANAGER
Lissa Pattillo

EDITOR-IN-CHIEF
Adam Arnold

PUBLISHER
Jason DeAngelis

APRON TO KASE SAN

Originally published in Japan in 2017 by SHINSHOKAN CO., LTD., Tokyo.
English translation rights arranged with SHINSHOKAN CO., LTD., Tokyo, through TOHAN CORPORATION, Tokyo.

ISBN: 978-1-626927-43-8

Printed in Canada

First Printing: February 2018

10 9 8 7 6 5 4 3 2 1

FOLLOW US ONLINE: **www.sevenseasentertainment.com**

READING DIRECTIONS

This book reads from ***right to left***, Japanese style. If this is your first time reading manga, you start reading from the top right panel on each page and take it from there. If you get lost, just follow the numbered diagram here. It may seem backwards at first, but you'll get the hang of it! Have fun!!

1
2
3
4
5
6
7
8
9

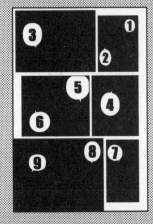